WALKING OUT
into the
SUNSHINE

Recollections and Reflections:
A Palestinian Personal Experience

WALKING OUT into the SUNSHINE

Recollections and Reflections:
A Palestinian Personal Experience

Windy City Publishers
2118 Plum Grove Rd., #349
Rolling Meadows, IL 60008

www.windycitypublishers.com

Published in the United States of America

Library of Congress Control Number:
2012949439

ISBN#:
978-1-935766-61-2

Windy City Publishers

CHICAGO

WALKING OUT
into the
SUNSHINE

Recollections and Reflections:
A Palestinian Personal Experience

by Ghazi Q. Hassoun, PhD

This book is dedicated in loving memory to my mother, Sa'da,
and my first wife, Virginia. No words can adequately tell the extent
of their influence on me, the degree to which they shaped my life,
and the great debt I feel due to them.

The work herein is conceived and intended as the best gift I can give,
with all the love I can fathom, to my Hassoun family,
to the Palestinian people, to the Arabs, to the Muslims,
and to my fellow men and women of the global village.
It is a special gift, because I know most about it and it is unique to me.
I present it to them to ponder, and to draw their own conclusions
about the human condition that I lived.
May it contribute to a better human condition for them to live in!

FOREWORD

The origins of this book go far back into my past. I have witnessed and experienced events that touched the deepest core of my being, which have shaped me in an essential way. I believe that they have made me far better than otherwise I would have been. I therefore feel it is incumbent upon me to record them for posterity lest they fade away with me. By 1996, I began to jot down miscellaneous notes towards that end. Late in 1997, I began somewhat systematically channeling and formalizing my effort. Here is what I wrote on December 27, 1997:

I am about to start the process of recalling how things in my past came to be. I hope in so doing to bring out some of the major events and challenges that came my way, and how they bear on who I am. How I dealt with them, sometimes successfully, other times not so successfully, might be of interest or help to somebody wrestling with potent events or challenges in their own life. Should this turn out to be the case, this narrative would not be in vain, and I would be eternally gratified.

PREFACE

As I embarked on this task, I have gradually and slowly become aware of some important hurdles. First, many names, particularly people's names, naturally come into the text. These names are often Arabic. They tend to intimidate the non-Arabic speaking reader. To minimize this, I have tried to use an English transliteration that is as easy to pronounce by the English reader as conceivably possible, while at the same time remaining close to the Arabic way of sounding that would be readily recognizable and identifiable by a native Arabic ear. It should be reassuring to the reader to be mindful that the transliteration of Arabic names to English is not unique and is apt to have a wide range of variation in the literature. The reader is therefore encouraged to read these names in as direct and straightforward a manner as the spelling in the text suggests. Second, the reader may be overwhelmed by the numerousness of these unfamiliar sounding words. To this, I advise patience and perseverance; in that things will become more familiar and less numerous as the reader presses on. As a further reassurance to the reader, I have tried to keep the numerousness at as low a level as possible without sacrificing the narrative. It is my sincere hope that at the end of the process readers will find that their efforts have not been in vain, but in fact quite worth it. Third, my narrative may project some of the individuals mentioned in an uncomplimentary image that could provoke their ire and condemnation or that of those closely related to them. As a result, I would like to state that this is far from my intent. All along, my motive has been solely to tell things the way I saw them at the time, to be faithful, and to sketch a comprehensive construction of the ingredients essential to an appreciation of the conditions that affected the course of events in the narrative. I have let the truth, as best as I could decipher it, take precedence over human sensitivities or political correctness; yet, hopefully, discretely, compassionately, courageously and in good taste.

The narration of events and interpersonal exchanges are my best effort at an accurate reconstruction. Most of the words employed, especially involving exchanges, could not be verbatim; for one thing, a great deal of these were in an Arabic setting and language, for another, a great deal of time has elapsed since then. Yet, if the actual words were vivid and in English, then naturally, I preserved them; otherwise, I sought out words that came as close as possible to preserve and convey the sense and spirit of these circumstances. All errors and misprints are my sole responsibility; I beg pardon in advance, and I welcome readers' feedback.

CONTENTS

PART I: PALESTINE AND LEBANON

PART II: USA

FAMILY TREE

Guide to Using the Family Tree Charts

There are five charts, two for each of my grandfathers, and, last but not least, one for my parents. Both of my grandfathers were married twice, out of which they had children. Both of my parents are offspring of their fathers' first marriage. The second marriages' charts of my grandfathers and their spouses are detailed only to the extent of showing (half) uncles and aunts that appear in the book. Offspring, wherever they appear on a chart, are in a descending order age-wise from left to right.

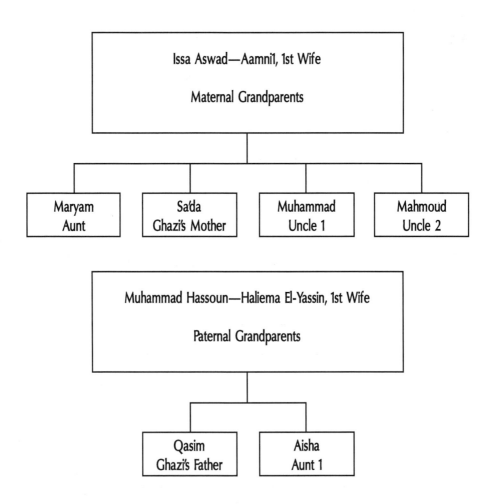

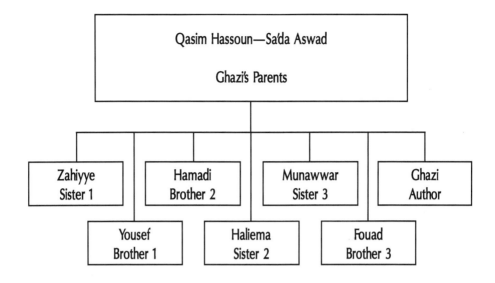

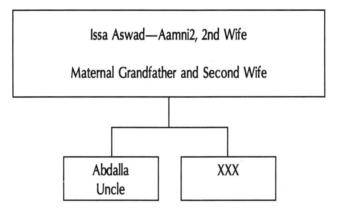

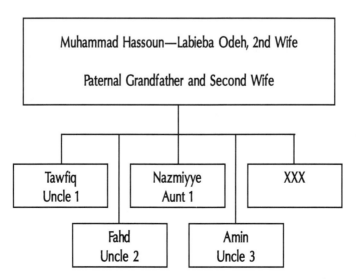

PART I: PALESTINE AND LEBANON

CHAPTER 1

SETTING THE STAGE

I am the youngest child from the union between Qasim Muhammad Hassoun and Sa'da Issa el-Aswad.[1] My parents were both born in Haifa, Palestine: my father in the year 1890 and my mother in the year 1895. Both were born into the Muslim (Sunni) religion. They were wed in the year 1909. It was a family arranged marriage. They had seven children that grew into adulthood: three girls, Zahiyye (b.1913, d.December 18, 2008), Haliema (b.March 17, 1924), and Munawwar (b.May 19, 1928); and four boys, Yousef (b.1915, d.February 24, 1998), Muhammad (b.December 17, 1921, d.July 12, 1989), affectionately known as Hamadi, Fouad (b.February 1, 1931), and me, Ghazi (b.June 21, 1935).

In addition to the above children, Mother had a few miscarriages and lost one child, Abdel-Karim, (b.~1926, d.~1928),[2] who lived to the crawling age. Mother did not seem to have ever gotten over her loss of him. The extent of my knowledge as to the cause of his death is that he succumbed to some kind of high fever resulting from a very brief illness. We, the children, were all born in the same room of the house that my mother and father had begun building shortly after they were married. They had bought a small piece of land just up the slope of Mount Carmel about a mile northeast of Wadi-Ennisnas[3], in an area called Hadar (Hebrew for splendor or beautiful). They built the house at # 7, Yona Street in stages over a period of about twenty years. The Hadar had been a developing, predominantly Jewish, neighborhood. My parents were born and grew up in Wadi-Ennisnas. Wadi-Ennisnas was, to the family, the root community and ethnic affiliation, where both of our grandparents owned homes and lived, as well as the bulk of our extended family: uncles, aunts, etc. They chose the Hadar to keep some healthy distance and independence from the immediate clan.

---

1   The definitive article 'Al', or its variation, 'El', precedes many Arabic names. The capitalization, when done, is usually to place emphasis on, dignify, or draw special attention to the name following it.

2   The tilde notation '~' is occassionally used in this text to mean about or approximately.

3   Wadi-Ennisnas was a major, well-known, section of Arab Haifa during my growing up years.

Mother and Father were quite young at the time of their marriage, particularly my mother. She related to us that, at the time of her marriage to my father, she had barely reached full puberty.[4] Mother's family, Aswad, was a fairly well-known family in Haifa. The word "Aswad" in Arabic means black. Her first name, Sa'da, means fortunate. Her middle name Issa (pronounced, Ee-sa; Arabic for Jesus) is her father's name. In the customary name usage of the Arab community of my time, one's middle name is the father's name, even for a woman. When signing her name, she always signed 'Sa'da Issa el-Aswad,' her *maiden* name. She never referred to herself as a 'Hassoun'. Educationally, my mother had four years of elementary schooling at the Haifa English School for girls, an Anglican missionary school. She spoke fondly and frequently of those years. She gratefully acknowledged the influence her teachers had on her, and how kind they were. She could easily read and write Arabic, and managed some basic English. When she spoke English, she had an unmistakable British accent that I occasionally coveted, but never learned. She also had rudimentary exposure to the piano; occasionally, she would sing Anglican Church hymns and conclude with "God Save the Queen!" When in a cheering mood or setting, she would say, "Hip hip hurray!"

Mother was the second daughter of her father from his first marriage. Her mother's name was Aamni. She had one sister, Maryam (Arabic for Mary or the Hebrew Miriam/Mirriam/Merriam). Maryam was two years older than Mother. She also had two younger brothers: Muhammad, about ten years younger, and Mahmoud, about twelve years younger. Grandmother Aamni died about 1912. I know virtually nothing about her or the circumstances of her death. My mother was heavily involved in the raising of her brothers, Muhammad and Mahmoud, after her mother's death, but particularly during the war years when Grandfather Issa was off to war, a draftee in the Ottoman

---

4   At about the age of eighteen, I heard from a family member, to my great surprise and by sheer accident, that Mother had been married once before her marriage to my father. When I asked Mother·if this was true, she said, "Yes." I then inquired about that marriage circumstances. She uncomfortably and briefly responded that it was to a much older man who passed away suddenly (possibly a heart attack) within a week or so of the marriage, and that the marriage was never consummated! As I had time to reflect on this further, I got the feeling that Grandfather Issa was quick to marry off his daughters; but this was not unique to him. Girls tended to be viewed as economic liability and potential cause of disgrace to the family should they, upon reaching puberty, get drawn clandestinely into relations with the opposite sex.

army. Several years later, after the end of World War I (1919), and upon his return to Haifa from the war, Grandfather Issa remarried a woman also named Aamni. He had four girls and one boy from the "second" Aamni. I got to know them fairly well, during my childhood in Haifa.

Mother was a very devout Muslim. She faithfully observed her religious duties; in particular, the five daily prayers and the fasting of the month of Ramadan.[5] She studied the Muslim holy book, the Quran, in her free time. She was in much demand as a chanter during Prophet Muhammad's birthday celebrations. It was not uncommon that I tagged along. I greatly enjoyed these chanting celebrations.

Mother was about 5'3" tall and about 110 pounds in weight. In her youth, she had black curly hair, braided in one or two braids. Typically, she had a serenely smiley countenance. She worked hard and played hard, though worked far more often than played. She appreciated good music, singing and folk dancing, especially the *dabke*. I have fond memories of seeing my mother dancing it at special festivities, notably weddings. She, not infrequently, would be the line leader with a fluttering handkerchief in her right hand. She enjoyed going to Arabic movies, mostly musical Egyptian ones. Ever since I could remember, we owned a phonograph with a manual crank and with records of some of the classic songs of top singers or icons. Among these, were Muhammad Abdel Wahab and Omm (also Umm or Emm: mother of; see fn 10) Kulthoum. Quranic recitations and Arabic music were generally all around us, daytimes and evenings.

Mother was above all, a homemaker. She was devoted to her family, both the inner most and the extended. She was an adequate seamstress. She owned a very old-fashioned Singer machine, which she cranked manually. She sewed most of our clothes. In this regard, she was impelled by economics. She sewed us underwear out of flour sackcloth. They were creamy white, heavy weight, and bulky. We kids wished we did not have to wear them, and tried to conceal them from our friends. But wear them, we did. We clamored to have factory made clothes. They looked more stylish to us. We got them for special occasions.

---

5   Ramadan is the Islamic fasting month in the lunar calendar. It is an especially holy month in that it is the month in which the first verses of the Quran were revealed to Muhammad, the prophet to be.

As a cook, however, Mother was superb. On festive occasions like weddings, she cooked on a large scale. She would cook, as well as supervise the cooking of others less experienced. Some of the classic dishes, which she elegantly prepared, were stuffed squash, stuffed eggplant, cabbage rolls, grape leaf rolls, *kibbe/kubbe* (a mixture of crushed, half-cooked, wheat (*burghul*, in Arabic), meat, and spices). Mother also preserved a variety of foods such as: white cheese (like the Greek Feta), yogurt balls in olive oil (*labni/labane*), olives, pickles and fruit jams from grapes, apricots, apples, etc.

She cared a lot and loved a lot; and that went all the way from the youngest to the oldest in the household. She spared no effort to see us clean and healthy. If anyone were to get sick, she would initially try to comfort them emotionally and physically. She would set up a corner for them in the house and keep watch. She would cook a nutritious meal and pray diligently to God for swift healing. Her mantra was always "God is our physician and healer, for me and the child." In extreme situations, she would pray well into the night out in the enclosed courtyard. In general, she did not readily or easily seek a physician's help; however, if the illness persisted, she would take him/her to a doctor while the prayer went on, unceasing.

Ever since I could remember, we had a family doctor, whom my mother knew well and treated as family. His name was Sa'd Mussallam.[6] Dr. Mussallam was highly regarded by all those who knew him in Haifa.

While mother was so very loving to us children, she was also very strict and tolerated no nonsense. When inquiring of me about some of my doings, comings and goings, as I grew a bit older, she would demand me to answer her questions with the unadulterated truth. She would sternly say, "Tell the truth even if it should lead to your beheading!"

My father's name, Qasim Muhammad Hassoun, is very Arabic and Islamic. His middle name, Muhammad, is the name of the prophet of Islam. The literal Arabic meaning of the word Muhammad is highly praised. In my father's case,

---

6   Dr. Sa'd Mussallam was a native of the southern Lebanese mountain town of Marjeyoun. He was a graduate of the American University of Beirut (AUB) Medical College. During World War II, his clinic received a direct hit from a German air raid intended to strike a British oil refinery just north of the city. Dr. Mussallam narrowly escaped injury as the building housing his clinic collapsed [Cf. Abdellatif Kanafani's book (AKB): 'Burj Street—#15-Haifa', in Arabic, Beisan Publishers, Beirut, 1996, fn on p.41 of the AKB text.]

by the cultural tradition cited earlier, it was also his father's name. Qasim means divider or distributor, which figuratively connotes giver or charitable. Prophet Muhammad's son's name was also Qasim. Hassoun is the emphasizing adjective of *hasan*. As an adjective, *hasan* literally means pretty or good; as a verb, it means to do well. Names in the Arabic culture are not just nice sounding labels; they often carry a rich cultural message and an expectation of certain qualities of character.

Ever since I was old enough to observe my father, he was a somewhat quiet and pensive person. He entrusted the family affairs almost completely to my mother. He was illiterate. When I would inquire why he never went to school, he would say, "The Ottoman rulers (Turks) were busy with conflicts inside and outside the country, which preoccupied them away from paying attention to basic social needs." They terribly neglected education, even at the most rudimentary and basic level. In fact, my sister Zahiyye and my mother's brother, Uncle Muhammad, met the same fate in that they never went to school. Uncle Mahmoud, mother's youngest brother, would have also been illiterate had it not been for his intense interest in Islam that impelled him to faithfully go to a religious school (*madrassa*), typically run by an Imam, and focused on the study of the Quran and the tenets of the religion. Mother's attending a private Anglican Christian missionary school was more the exception than the rule. It was probably a testimony to my Grandfather Issa's special sense of the importance of education, even at a Christian missionary school. I think it was also due to my mother's love for learning evidenced at a very tender age.

On top of the preoccupied Ottomans, my father had a preoccupied father, Muhammad. Grandfather Muhammad had virtually abandoned his first wife, Haliema, and his two children, my aunt Aisha and my father Qasim; the latter two at the tender age of about eight and six years respectively. His provision for the children was quite meager, if at all. I was told my Grandfather Muhammad married three additional women thereafter. I got to know only one of his other wives, namely, Labieba. She is also the only one, other than his first wife, Haliema, with whom he had children. In fact, he had four boys and five girls that grew into adulthood, who I came to know fairly well.[7]

---

7   Both of my grandfathers, Muhammad and Issa, sold daily fresh produce in their neighborhoods. Issa had a stand in front of his home. Muhammad, on the other hand, peddled the produce on a cart.

Although I know hardly anything about my father's childhood and adolescence before his marriage to my mother, it is fair to say that he had to go to work at a very young age to help support the family. He must have worked in construction because his acknowledged trade or craft in adulthood had been masonry and cement plastering. I further suspect that my Grandmother Haliema got some help from her side of the family (El-Yassin), probably brothers that dwelt in the village of Etteery (also Al-Tira), about 12 km (or ~7.5 miles) southeast of Haifa. My Grandmother Haliema lived with my parents upon their marriage. She became blind and passed away within a few years afterward. Father's only full sister, Aisha, a couple of years younger, must have been married off at a rather early age. She lived nearby with her husband, Mahmoud el-Weheb, in Wadi-Ennisnas. They were relatively prosperous (her husband was a successful gardener and a landlord) during my childhood. The couple did not have any children of their own.

Notwithstanding the passage of many years, at six or seven years old, I was aware that my father had a generally unhappy relationship with his father, and on reflection, it is understandable. In contrast, he had clear affection for his relatives on his mother's side in Etteery. One of my fond memories is of the time when my father walked to Etteery, several hours away, during the summer harvest season (~1942) to visit his mother's relatives, who were farmers. There, he spent a day with them, whereupon they loaned him a mule and loaded it with vegetables and fruits to bring home to us. The load had melons, grapes, figs, green beans, eggplants and the like. Upon arrival, he unloaded the "goodies" and stayed home overnight; the next day he returned the mule to the relatives in Etteery, and then walked back home. It was a three to four day project! I recall watching intently and with glee as my father unloaded the mule. It impressed me that he had such a strong bond with these relatives. My parents would from time to time mention these relatives in a complimentary way. Yet, I have no recollection of ever having visited them despite the fact that I have been to Etteery many times.

My mother's sister, Maryam, was married to a man from Etteery, Awad Zakariyya (also Zakaria). The two lived and farmed there. Aunt Maryam and

Uncle Awad had four boys and one girl. They were, to my way of thinking, the ultimate of the proverbial Arab hospitality. Maryam, being mother's only full sister, was very special to her. Our visit to Etteery invariably meant going to see Aunt Maryam. It was always a joyous occasion, that was felt by everybody, whether we visited Aunt Maryam, or vice versa. In contrast, our visits, though not infrequent, with Aunt Aisha were rather lukewarm.

Late in 1914 or early in 1915, at the onset of World War I, my father was drafted into the Ottoman army and eventually sent away to battle the British. The Ottomans were allied with the Germans.[8]

The draft was quite general in that it took a wide age-range of men, including Aunt Maryam's husband, Awad, and Grandfather Issa. Grandfather Muhammad Hassoun was spared because of his very poor sight. My mother said, "Hardly any men were left behind, only the unfit, the very young, and the very old." She also told me that early after my father was drafted and taken away, she lost track of his whereabouts, thanks to the deplorable means of communications availed by the Ottomans. It was six years later, past the end of World War I, before he returned home.

It is not hard to imagine that those years were very traumatic. Mother was pregnant at the time of father's draft, though my father did not know it. My brother Yousef was born while my father was off to war. Initially, mother named the newly born boy, Mufid, Arabic for useful. Baby Mufid was often sick in his first few months. Very concerned for his life, Mother sought the help of a man of God (Muslim Shaykh) to pray for her son's healing. The man of God saw in his prayer (a kind of clairvoyance) that the name Mufid did not suit the child, and that he should be given the name Yousef, after Prophet Yousef (Arabic for Joseph) who had endured many adversities and triumphed. Mother readily agreed. Henceforth, the child's name was changed to Yousef. Shortly thereafter, as told by Mother, brother Yousef's health began to mend. In my own experience with Yousef, I do not recall him ever being seriously ill. I have at times wondered why Mother initially picked the name Mufid for her first son. I am tempted to speculate

---

8   The 'Ottomans' refers to the Islamic rulers of the last Khalifate, who were primarily Turks. The Khalifate in Islam resembled the Papacy in the Holy Roman Empire; however, it crumbled at the end of World War I.

that she was feeling helpless and destitute at the time of his birth. As she was groping for a positive unfoldment, a sign of good news to alleviate her pain, she was led to the name Mufid. In addition to the sanctity of the name Yousef and the man of God's inspired advice, as I look back at brother Yousef's role in our family's life, it indeed has been triumphant, but also extremely useful.

The story of the Prophet Yousef is in the Quran as well as the Bible. In the Quran, it has a chapter of its own, Surat (Arabic, for quranic chapter) Yousef. As narrated in the Quran, it is one of the quite delightful stories. Everyone in our family, not least Yousef himself, associated this *surat* with our Yousef, who would listen intently to its recitation, and beam joyously at some of its verses, pointing to himself.

Not much is known about my father's life while at war except for a few basic facts. He was in the Ottoman cavalry. He fought the British forces of General Allenby in Southern Palestine and the Suez area (portrayed in the film *Lawrence of Arabia*). Father related that in his last engagement against the British, the soldiers all around him were being killed en masse and mercilessly, but somehow (providentially for my family) he was not even wounded. He was captured and taken as a prisoner of war into Egypt.

The Ottoman army was routed in Palestine. World War I came to an end with the British and their allies emerging victorious. One of the ironies of those times is that while many Arabs, in the Ottoman army, were fighting against the British, the Arab army of Sharif Hussein and his sons, Prince Abdallah and Prince Feisal (coordinating with Lawrence of Arabia), were fighting the Ottomans on the side of the British!

At the conclusion of World War I, the surviving soldiers generally came back home, including Grandfather Issa. However, Father was not among them for some time. He was presumed missing in action (MIA). It was about eighteen months later (~ late 1920) that he was released by the British and made it back home. When the war was over, and Father did not show up, my anxious mother did not lose hope. She sought the help of some Anglican missionary people that she came to know to use their influence with the British occupation force to somehow track him. It was only then that he was located as a prisoner of war in Egypt, and eventually released.

The Ottoman general draft, and ensuing World War I, found my mother with a two-year old daughter, Zahiyye, and a soon to be born Yousef, at her Hadar home (#7, Yona Street).[9] Additionally, she oversaw and attended to her two brothers, Muhammad and Mahmoud, living at their (quite humble) father's (Issa's) house in Wadi-Ennisnas with their grandfather, known to me only as Abu-Adla.[10] I surmise Grandfather Abu-Adla was my mother's grandfather on her mother's side. According to my mother, he was quite old, became very feeble, and passed away early on during the war years. My mother often told the story that when her Grandfather Abu-Adla passed away; she could not find anybody to help her with his burial. Consequently, she single-handedly washed his body and wrapped it in a clean white cloth, according to Muslim rites, and carried it with great difficulty either on her back or on a donkey's back to his final resting place.

Many years later, I often wondered if Uncle Muhammad and Uncle Mahmoud were around to witness the burial, or somehow had been sent away to stay with Aunt Maryam in Etteery, at least during the time when Grandfather Abu-Adla was nearing death. The sense in which I recall my mother telling the story suggests that she was really alone in his care at the time of his death; even her young brothers, somehow, were not around.

My mother managed the war years with a remarkable combination of a deep faith, domestic skills, absence of better options, and sheer hard work. Her skills as a cook found her part-time work in the kitchens of some of the wealthy ruling (Turkish) families in Haifa. While the work was of a significant help, it was inadequate and not steady enough to meet all the needs of the family. As the war worsened, even wealthy ruling families fell upon hard times. She supplemented it by chopping and gathering firewood from the slopes of Mount Carmel, and then selling the firewood. Firewood was the basic fuel for washing and cooking. Her firewood cutting and gathering usually started very early at predawn. She had no clock or watch,

---

9   The references 'Hadar home/ house' and '#7, Yona Street' are used interchangeably in this text and refer to the same place. The choice of a particular one is contextual.

10   The Arabic prefix, Abu, means father of. It is often used to refer to a man's name in terms of his oldest son, i.e., 'Abu Ramzi' means father of Ramzi, Ramzi being the oldest son.. My father's nickname would be thus: Abu Yousef. The female counterpart is Umm (or Omm, also Emm); hence my mothers' would be Umm Yousef, i.e., mother of Yousef.

so she timed her activity by the light level outside. She would bundle the chopped wood and carry it on her back or head and take it to the marketplace for early morning sale. I recall her telling the family that once she was so eager to start early, and the light level outside suggested dawn, that she arose, got dressed, and headed up the slopes. A near-full moon was up in the sky, and she became unsure about the time. Nevertheless, she pressed on, walked up to wood sites, chopped, gathered, bundled the wood, and carried it down to the marketplace. Upon arrival, nobody was there! She sat for a long while before any buyers showed up. She reasoned, thereafter, that she must have been wood chopping some hours before dawn!

Generally, there would be nobody to look after Yousef and Zahiyye while she left home for wood chopping, gathering, and marketing. So at bedtime, the evening before, she would rope them, while in their beds, to a bar in one of the windows in the room, with the length of the rope such that they would not get into any trouble while she was away. The beds were simply soft mattresses that were rolled-out on the floor for the night, and rolled-up off the floor in the morning.

Wartime, coupled with drought, resulted in food scarcity. Many people ate things such as orange peelings and melon rind to survive. For a time, the shortage of food was exacerbated by a wide locust infestation of the fields, with ruinous effect onto whatever crops there were. During that period in Haifa, a real state of famine set in, and it was not uncommon to see people dying of starvation in their homes and even in the streets.[11]

Sometime during the war, a Christian Arab neighbor of my mother, whom she called Muallem Boulous (Arabic for Teacher, Master (Reverend) Paul), offered my mother domestic work in his house. His full name was Muallem Boulous Duwani. He was an Anglican minister. His wife was ill with TB and, with two young sons, Fouad and Hanna (Arabic for John), they direly needed some help. Mother gladly rallied. This was the beginning of a long-lasting neighborly relationship between my family and Muallem Boulous' family.

---

11 Other causes had been offered that added to the state of famine, one was that the allies (British and French) had blockaded the seaports of the Levant countries and prevented food material from entering in; House of Stone, Intro. p.xvii, by Anthony Shadid, Houghton, Mifflin, Harcourt, 2012.

Muallem Boulous, through his contacts in the Anglican Church, played an important role in helping my mother locate the whereabouts of my father at the end of the war and getting him released. Mrs. Boulous' illness did not allow her to nurse Hanna, the younger son. Mother was nursing Yousef at the time, and she was asked if she would be willing to nurse Hanna as well. Here again, mother was glad to be of help. Mrs. Boulous passed away a short time later. Mother continued nursing Hanna for some time thereafter along with performing domestic work for Muallem Boulous. She, in effect, became a nanny to the children. As Yousef and Hanna grew up, and throughout many years thereafter, the two held a special affection for each other, referring to each other as "milk-brothers". Fouad eventually went to England and studied medicine. Within a few years after completing his studies (~1950?), he died there while practicing as a medical doctor. Muallem Boulous had died at least ten years earlier in Haifa, at a time beyond my recollection. Hanna studied pharmacy at the American University of Beirut, or AUB. He practiced as a pharmacist and operated a pharmacy in Haifa until the breakout of the Palestinian-Israeli hostilities in 1948. Hanna ended up a refugee in Beirut. He later on became an instructor in the AUB College of Pharmacy. When I became an AUB student, Hanna did not recognize me, as I was very young when he had last seen me, and I was too shy to introduce myself to him. Hanna, in 1955, married a senior coed by the name of Leila Sha'er. The event of his marriage to Leila made a special impression on me because earlier that year Leila and I had been members of a campus student study-group on Arab nationalism. Never did I think at that time that she even knew Hanna! In any case, I could not bring myself to walk up to him and say, "I am Yousef's brother, or Sa'da' son!" Both departed shortly thereafter for the USA, Hanna seeking to study for a PhD in Pharmacy.

CHAPTER 2

BETWEEN TWO WORLD WARS

My father was eventually released from the Egyptian war prison, toward the end of 1920. When my father was set free from the prison, nobody knew the precise time or place of his release. Hence, nobody was there to meet him. Therefore, he walked home. The place, where he was released, probably was some British military post in the countryside of Haifa. He had been transferred to it from a prison in Egypt. As he was walking back on a country trail to his home and wife, after six years of absence, two robbers attacked him seemingly out of the blue. They were bent on subduing him and stripping him of whatever they thought was on him. My father was appalled by the sudden turn of events after surviving the British guns that killed so many of his comrades in battle, and a year and a half of prison. Convinced that the robbers were about to kill him, he instinctively knocked one of them down to the ground and slammed him dead with a nearby rock. The other robber fled in panic after seeing what had happened to his companion.

Mother and the rest of the relatives, having waited so many years for his return and not knowing of his experience since his release, received him with great jubilation. When baby Yousef ran to meet his dad, my father did not know who this baby boy was! I do not know at what point in time he told my mother and the family of his encounter with the robbers; and how he managed the emotional quake of the encounter with the exultation of his reunion. However, in his narratives to me, the encounter with the robbers must have severely traumatized him for he frequently alluded to it. He often recalled the details of the encounter and pondered if he could have handled it any differently. Though the event was never investigated, nor was my father ever called to answer for it by any law enforcement body, it must have weighed heavily on him, even over twenty years after the fact, when I was old enough to listen to him. Only after I had become an adult myself did I begin to realize and appreciate how deeply troubled he must have been.

Within about a year from my father's return from World War I, my second brother was born (December 17, 1921). He was given the name Muhammad.

Traditionally, since my father was the oldest son of his father, Muhammad, he was expected to also name his first son Muhammad, after his father. This meant that brother Yousef should have been named Muhammad. As indicated earlier, Mother initially named him Mufid and then, upon the advice of the man of God, changed it to Yousef. Yousef was born while my father was away in the army, and the relationship between my father and his father, and by default or extension my mother, had already been quite strained. Nevertheless, when my father came back home and his second son was born, he must have softened toward his father, wanted to make a goodwill gesture, reconcile, and let the bygones be bygones. So, he named his newly-born second son, Muhammad, his father's namesake. Unfortunately, the gesture was lost by the subsequent revival of old hurts. When my father's half-brother (the first from his step-mother Labieba), Uncle Tawfiq, had his first son (around 1929), he gave him the name Muhammad, as if to tell my parents that the naming of their second son Muhammad did not count; or at least was not good enough![12]

The above notwithstanding, and to some extent in line with tradition, brother Muhammad/Hamadi married his cousin Khayriyye (in September 1942), Uncle Tawfiq's first daughter, and had three girls and six boys from her in a marriage that lasted until Hamadi's death in 1989. Hamadi's marriage was later followed by the marriage of brother Fouad to Uncle Tawfiq's second daughter, Fakhriyye (March 5, 1950). It is fair to say that the relationships of the next generation of Hassouns were much more cordial and familial. My generation did not carry, for the most part, the strains and hurts of the previous generation.

As a youngster, I have no recollections of seeing my father holding a regular steady line of work for any extended length of time. Stories abound that after the war, my father would get a job as a mason or cement plasterer for a short time, only to clash with the boss and quit, or get fired. My mother would listen to his grief patiently, and would try to help him find another job. Sometimes, she would recommend another line of work. He tried being a yard-goods peddler. It did not last more than a few months. He also got a job with Haifa's municipality in the street maintenance department. It was thought that this would be a 'low pressure' job. Again, it lasted only a few weeks.

---

12 There are times, however, when two sons may name their first son after their father without negative connotation.

Father was a mild mannered person and somewhat aloof, probably a result of his war years. He could not get enthused about most things. He did not seem to have ambition for much, and did not tolerate people faulting him for lack of ambition. While he continued to express a lot of love for his wife and children, he seemed disenchanted with humankind, and could not care less about "keeping up with the Joneses." Work-wise, he seemed content to carry out errands for his wife and children, like buying groceries, to help them meet everyday life needs; and later, in the context of the family laundry business. My mother accepted him lovingly for what he was, and we children emulated her.

In food, he was of simple taste. I often saw him make a meal out of a piece of flat bread, salt, raw onion, and olive oil. He would sit on the floor with the flat bread as his main utensil. He loved olive oil. According to my father, tomato salad, or any of its variations, would not be edible if it did not have olive oil. Additionally, when the family would be having the popular Palestinian dish *mujaddara* (made of lentils), he would expect tomato salad with it, and of course, olive oil. So, no olive oil meant no tomato salad, and no tomato salad meant no *mujaddara* could be had! This is the origin of our family practice of regularly having olive oil on hand, at any given time, in large volume, like several gallons!

In the fall, during the fresh olive oil season, father would go out looking for an olive oil peddler, often a farmer, who sold his own oil. The peddler typically would have a donkey laden with from two to four cans of olive oil. Each can had a capacity of about five gallons. My father would first strike a friendly general conversation with the peddler that had nothing to do with olive oil. Gradually, he would get to business. He would find out how fresh the oil was and the time of its extraction. Then, he would smell into one or more of the cans, and finally, he tasted a sample poured into the palm of his hand. After that was done, the price negotiations would begin until a mutually agreeable price was reached. More often than not, particularly when the family needed oil, the process ended happily with a transaction.

Father was not a particularly faithful observer of Islamic practices. The joke around the immediate family was that he observed prayers and the fasting of Ramadan only to the extent that kept Sa'da happy. My mother always treated my father, particularly when we children where around, in a very dignified manner and with a great deal of circumspection. I think they had their arguments but my mother was very careful not to have them in front of us, the children. Some of the memorable religious activities in which my father included me at a very young age, along with brother Fouad (and at times, nephew Qasim), were when I would don the traditional Arabic headdress and be whisked off, with full encouragement and blessing from my mother, to the big mosque in downtown Haifa for the Friday service, or for one of the Islamic *Eid* (Feast) services. Some of the traditional Eid chants that we chanted at the mosque back then ring occasionally and nostalgically in my ears to this day.

Father's aforementioned difficulties with his own father continued off and on again until Grandfather Muhammad passed away. At times, my father would threaten his father with publicly and legally dissolving (disowning) the father-son bond, an act that would have brought disgrace to the often excessively-proud Hassoun clan. He would further threaten with changing his family name from Hassoun to Shalah, after a well-to-do Christian family, an elderly couple with whom he had a close and warm friendship; a name change that would profoundly reflect negatively off the Hassoun family. After his return from the war, he was known to spend hours visiting with the Shalahs at their home. They lived in Wadi-Ennisnas. I never understood the nature of this friendship except for the fact that the chemistry was right.[13] My father's friendship with the Shalah family continued until our exodus out of Haifa, whereupon, alas, contact was lost.

Grandfather Muhammad passed away about September 1943. Mother, Munawwar, Fouad, Qasim, and I were visiting at Aunt Maryam's in Etteery when the news of Grandfather Muhammad's passing broke out. Upon receiving the news, we quickly packed up, and headed home for the funeral. I recall making it in time to see his body on the wash-platform (*maghsal*, in Islamic parlance) being prepared for burial, according to Islamic prescription. Islamic tradition urges speedy burial, usually within twenty-four hours from the time of death. A large number of persons of the Wadi-Ennisnas community and

---

13 Brother Fouad suggested that this family looked after him and even helped to raise him. I find it quite plausible.

beyond, especially from Etteery (roots of the Hassoun clan), came to bid him a last farewell.[14]

Father loved the fruits of Palestine; in particular, figs, melons and grapes. I recall fondly occasions when I would be with him and he would buy some of these fruits and find a peaceful shady tree away from the beaten track; the two of us would sit under it and enjoy them. Father was very good at quickly finding back roads to the countryside, well removed from the crowded city. It is on these outings that my father would tell me stories, his views on life, or feelings about different things. He would say to me: "When you grow up and have your own children, you will then have things to do and share with them, just like what I am doing with you now." This used to evoke a sense of sadness in me; as if he was saying, "I am with you today, I will be gone tomorrow." He saw the human scene as a mirage or vanity. He was a loner except for a few very special people. He was very skeptical of friends and friendship. Two of his life refrains, though neither he nor I adhered strictly to them, were: "If you loan money to a friend, you loose the money and the friend," and a kind of old folk song that he would hum almost faintly to himself (liberally adapted from Arabic):

Oh loneliness, oh loneliness!
So much heartache is of fellows and friends!
Where fellowship is betrayed and friendship ends.

On this earth, if walk you must,
But with those, yet guardedly,
Who to God's way might guide thee!

Father's work problems, after his return from the war, meant that my mother had to continue to fend for the family herself. She continued her housework with Muallem Boulous and the firewood business for several years afterward.

---

14 One of the few things I remember about Grandfather Muhammad was his effusive pride for being of the Hassoun clan. He occasionally would say, as if to remind others, that one of his ancestors, the father of the Hassoun clan, Shaykh Hassoun, was the Mukhtar (Mayor) of Etteery; and that he was held in high esteem and reverence by the majority of its townspeople to the extent that his camel had free reign over their pastures!

My father teamed up with her in the latter work. In the meantime, the children kept coming.[15] After Hamadi, came along Haliema, followed by Abdel Karim. With the family size growing steadily and the income still meager, Mother found it necessary to take Yousef out of school and put him to work at the young age of eleven. Before that time, Yousef attended the French missionary school, the Frères, for four years. Zahiyye was not sent to school, but put to help with the housework, partly because of her being a female, and partly because of the time at which she was coming into school age. When Zahiyye was six-years old, Father had not yet come back from the war and Mother had not begun to emerge out of the depth of her family challenges. Furthermore, the country was still reeling from the effects of the war. Yousef had a variety of jobs, mostly peddling things. Two oft mentioned at family reminiscences were peddling *booza* (ice-milk) and *turmos* (lupine yellow beans that were soaked in water overnight, salted and eaten like peanuts). Mother also kept a dairy cow at home. Part of its milk went for the children, while the surplus milk was sold out in the neighborhood for supplementary income. None of Yousef's peddling jobs were all that rewarding or satisfactory. As a result, the family was continually looking for something better for him to do. By the time he turned fifteen, he landed a job in a Jewish family-run laundry business. The owners and their family were refugees from Russia. We referred to them as Adon (Hebrew for Mr. or Lord) Lehrman's family.

The laundry shop, on Herzel's Street in the Hadar, was about a kilometer north of our house. The laundry's clothes were washed and pressed at the Lehrmans' apartment. Their home was probably another kilometer west, downhill, from the laundry shop. The Lehrmans had grown-up children. While I did not learn the particulars of their family make-up, I did know that there were at least two children, a boy and a girl. The girl was married and lived in Haifa, whereas the boy had emigrated to the United States and had served in the U.S. Navy during World War II. Yousef started out as an errand boy with the Lehrmans. He went around to Adon Lehrman's clients and picked up the dirty laundry. When the clothes were washed and pressed, he would carry

---

15 My mother evinced to me years later, her view that it was ungodly for a wife to deny a husband's advances or vice versa except for health or hygienic reasons; presumably when made in good faith and the proper setting.

them back to the clients. Mr. Lehrman initially did quite a bit of the pressing, but hired a rural Arab woman that went by the name of Umm Hussein to do the washing. Mrs. Lehrman typically served as a receptionist and handled the paper side of the business. At times, when needed, she also helped with dry-cleaning and washing. The Lehrmans' laundry clientele were mostly Jewish, but not exclusively. The white clothes were washed mostly by hand. Other things, like wool suits and such, were sorted out and washed either by hand or dry-cleaned, depending on the level of their "soiledness." The Lehrmans had a rather small dry-cleaning machine that handled a few suits at a time.

Yousef carried out his errands very diligently and faithfully. He quickly won the approval, trust, and affection of Mr. and Mrs. Lehrman. The Lehrmans slowly began to assign more responsibilities to him, including pressing. His salary proportionately improved. He also began to pick up the Hebrew language, which he reinforced by studying it formally at a nearby night school. It was not long before he became quite fluent in Hebrew. I have often heard it said that Yousef's Hebrew was like that of a native. The Jewish clientele liked Yousef. Yousef had a very affable nature. Yousef took very well to the laundry business. It was a quantum leap upward from his *booza* and *turmos* peddling. In a matter of a few years, he became recognized throughout Haifa as a master presser, especially of delicate women's dresses. He was sought out for special tasks, like pressing women's party or wedding dresses. He eventually learned the washing, dry-cleaning, and dyeing sides of the business as well. As he was approaching twenty years of age, my mother, in the best of early Arab tradition, was thinking of marriage for him.

Parents or guardians, in general, arranged for the marriage of their prospective groom and bride. Mother had quite an old-fashioned view of marriage, which she voiced openly, freely, and repeatedly to us, her children. When a son reaches adulthood and he is enjoying a steady, stable income that can support a wife and a home, modest though it might be, then he ought to get married. This way, it would be unlikely that he would seek illegal and unclean sex, nor would he likely come under the influence, or into the company of bad men. As for a daughter, once she is of marriageable age (roughly 16 years), the tendency is to marry her off to the first suitor unless there is a clear incompatibility of one sort or another, especially age. The rationale is that she will be settled in a home with a guardian and will have a family of her own, and will not get into a premarital illicit relationship with a man and be a threat to her family's honor.

Legally and technically according to Islamic law, the bride and groom have the right to approve or disapprove their mate choice. In practice, however, the groom tends to have a lot more say than the bride. The bride is often passive and goes along with her parents' or guardians' choice.

Against such cultural setting, Zahiyye was married off before her seventeenth birthday to Nayef Aswad, a first cousin of my mother (note same family name). Nayef was about twenty-one years of age. He was illiterate but ambitious. He took an early interest in cars, particularly trucks. He was one of the first people I knew who could operate a truck. He was also involved in the quarry business and building construction and he set up a trucking business to transport large stones from quarries to construction sites. Nayef at one time boasted a fleet of several trucks to his business. The business went through cycles of boom and bust, as Nayef seemed to lack managerial skills. Within a few years, the business went broke. He never rebuilt, and spent most of the rest of his active life, until the exodus in 1948, as a truck driver, working for others. This failure, no doubt, had done its harm on his psyche. However, people in those days rarely bothered to pay attention to such subtleties. Zahiyye's marriage to Nayef at times was marred by clear tension and discord; she would grudgingly carry out her domestic work. As I grew older and queried my mother about it, I learned that Nayef, on their wedding night, might have been impatient in his physical approach to Zahiyye. I further asked my mother if Zahiyye had not cooperated or perhaps rejected his advances. My mother said Zahiyye was quite unprepared for marriage, and did not know about the natural intimacies that are engaged in by a couple on their wedding night. As a result, Zahiyye became mentally disturbed and estranged. She was psychiatrically treated for a time before she was rehabilitated back to the marriage. In due course, they managed to smooth over many of the rough spots and had three boys and seven girls that grew into adulthood, my very cherished nephews and nieces. In my interactions with Nayef, I found him to possess a high level of native intelligence, friendly, and of a generous spirit. Whenever I visited him and sister Zahiyye, he would very hospitably receive me with fruits and beverages, even when I was a kid. Throughout, I definitely held brotherly affection for him. Zahiyye and Nayef, it seems to me like many of us, have been victims of the culture and conditions of the time! Nayef passed away in Tyre, Lebanon, on November 13, 1987, at an age of about seventy-eight years.

Yousef had no female cousins about his age for potential brides. Traditionally, these cousins would have precedence over his marrying somebody outside the clan. As it happened, the washwoman at Lehrmans' Laundry, Umm Hussein, had a daughter younger than Yousef. The daughter's name, of all names, was Haliema![16] Haliema, by any standard, was a very pretty young woman. Umm Hussein was a widow with two sons and this one daughter. Haliema fell, age-wise, between the oldest son, Hussein, and the younger son, Muhammad. I would estimate she was three years younger than Yousef, very likely illiterate. Umm Hussein had hailed from the much smaller Palestinian town of Jenin. Haifa had much greater opportunities for work, and to support her family. As the story goes, Umm Hussein liked Yousef very much and let him know that she would be happy to have him for a son-in-law. My parents were brought into the process. My parents, already thinking marriage for Yousef, liked what they saw when they met the young Haliema, and gave their seal of approval. The Lehrmans also blessed the impending union. Yousef married Haliema Ennaatour a little over a month after I was born. This point of reference stems from a rather important occurrence early in my life at Yousef's wedding. My mother preoccupied with the festivities at our Hadar home, and with welcoming guests, laid me down in some corner of the house. Thereafter, as some of the guests took off their extra clothing and laid them down at that same corner, unaware that there was a one-month-old baby lying there, I got pretty much covered up and nearly suffocated. Somehow, providentially, I was discovered and rescued in the nick of time! It was one of those rare occasions, I am told, when my father was very furious with my mother, and scolded her by exclaiming, "Do you want to marry one and bury one!"

---

16 What is in a name? A lot! Haliema was my father's mother name, my second sister's name, after grandmother; also the name of the Prophet Muhammad's nurse! It is interesting to mention that though my mother was the backbone of our family, there was no effort to name any of the children after any of her side of the family; father, mother or brothers, etc. We were Hassouns, not Aswads! That is the tribal way!

My parents, well in advance of Yousef's marriage, decided to add two bedrooms for the anticipated growth of their family. The added bedrooms were above the main floor of our home. Yousef and his new bride, Haliema, moved into one of these bedrooms.

Yousef and Haliema had their first son, Qasim, on December 14, 1936. A Jewish midwife delivered Qasim. She was called into our house from the Haifa Hadassa Hospital nearby. In contrast, eighteen months earlier, an Arab midwife delivered me at home. Her name was Fatima Essabha, from Wadi-Ennisnas; she could neither write nor read. Shortly thereafter, Haliema was found to be ill with TB. After considerable effort and expense treating her, including sending her to a famous sanitarium in the town of Bheness in Lebanon, she succumbed to the illness in May 1937. It seemed natural, given the setting, that Mother would assume, at least for a time, the matter of caring for baby Qasim. Mother weaned me and began breast-feeding Qasim. Umm Hussein, Qasim's other grandmother, used to periodically come to our house to spend time with her grandson. At other times, Yousef would take Qasim over to Umm Hussein's home to spend time with her. Sometimes, I accompanied Qasim on his grandmother's visits. All contact with Umm Hussein was lost after our Haifa exodus.

The years 1936 and 1937 saw significant rise in tension between the Palestinians and the British, and the Palestinians and the Jews. The Palestinians wanted a stop, or at least slow down, of Jewish immigration. They clamored for the end of the British mandate over Palestine, and aspired to independence. For well over a millennium, Palestine's population had been overwhelmingly Arabic in character, largely Islamic, but including minority Christian and Jewish communities. The British and (Zionist) Jews had other plans. While not always in concert, they were setting the stage for the establishment of a Jewish state. The Palestinians, led by Hajj[17] Amin Al-Husseini, Grand Mufti (Interpreter of Muslim Law) of Jerusalem, resorted initially to a variety of civil disobedience practices, most notably lack of cooperation with the occupation in the form of strikes, to make it unbearable

---

17 The word *Hajj* is a title bestowed on a male-person who has performed the pilgrimage to Mecca; it carries with it a certain spiritual and moral status; Hajji is, in general, the title bestowed upon a female pilgrim.

for the British to hang on. It is fair to say that I was literally weaned on cries against the occupation, and chants of "Palestine is Arab."

With the coming of 1936, Palestinians had become quite alarmed at the level and extent of Jewish influx into the country. In the spring of 1936 the leadership called for a general and indefinite strike to send a message of protest, and to demand that the British to put a stop to their policies of admitting large numbers of (mostly European and some Russian) Jews into the country. The strike, which lasted about six months, was terminated only after "appeals by the kings of Saudi Arabia and Iraq and the Emir of Transjordan."[18] A month following the end of the strike, November 1936, the British government set up a commission, chaired by Lord Peel, known as the Peel Commission, to go to Palestine, to study and assess conditions on the ground, and report back with recommendations. In July 1937, the Peel Commission put out a report "recommending partition of Palestine into a Jewish state, a Palestinian state to be incorporated by Transjordan, and enclaves reserved for the Mandatory."[19] Also it further stated, "that they [the Palestinian Arabs] be forcibly transferred if necessary, out of the Jewish state."[20] The Palestinians received Peel's recommendations with disbelief and utter outrage. An armed rebellion ensued in the latter half of 1937 with the aim of pushing the British out through armed struggle. The rebels, employing small firearms and old rifles, the World War I type, attacked British presence and infrastructure. These attacks were for the most part of the hit-and-run kind. The rebels often sought hideouts, including caves, in the most mountainous, rugged, and inaccessible parts of the country. It was to make it as difficult as possible for the British army, with their far superior organization and war machinery, to chase after them. Armed militant Zionist groups tended to join the British army in action against the Palestinians. Attacks often resulted in counter-attacks. They brought to the fore the profoundly conflicting goals and aspirations of Palestinian Arabs and Zionist Jews, and only served to exacerbate the situation.

---

18 Walid Khalidi's (WK), 'Before Their Diaspora', Chronology, p.193, Institute For Palestinian Studies, Washington, DC, 1984.

19 ibid, p.189

20 ibid, p.190

My parents, with their home in a predominantly Jewish neighborhood, became quite apprehensive of becoming a target of militant Zionist violence. They had to weigh Yousef's work at the Lehrmans' against their safety. Although their relationship with the Lehrmans' continued to be quite amicable, the surrounding environs became threatening. Toward the end of 1937, my family rented a home in Wadi-Ennisnas and locked up the home at #7, Yona Street.

In order to provide for our family, despite the turmoil all around, at the start of 1938, my mother launched a laundry business in partnership with Yousef in Wadi-Ennisnas. Father had a secondary supporting role. Our contacts with the Lehrmans came to a complete halt; it would have been quite misguided and dangerous to nurture them in any form, lest they be interpreted as collaboration. Nothing was known, for two years, as to how the Lehrmans were getting along with their business, nor did the Lehrmans know how we were getting along either.

The newly launched laundry business got off to a good start. My brother Hamadi, near completing the 9th grade at the nearby government school, gradually got into the business. The 9th grade was the highest and last grade available at the school anyhow. The Hassoun Brothers Laundry, as it came to be known, met a real need and conscientiously served the Arab community in Wadi-Ennisnas and surrounding areas, that is the Abbas area. The word Abbas is the Arabic name given to the world center of the Baha'i faith, a highly revered and holy place. The center encloses the tomb of the leader of the faith, Abbas Baha'ullah, and the area around the shrine is referred to for brevity as "Abbas."

The year 1938, and the beginning of 1939, saw quite a bit of guerrilla warfare waged by the Palestinian Arab rebels against the British. The British were not inclined to accommodate Palestinian demands and cracked down hard against the rebels. They declared that anybody caught committing acts of violence against the authorities, or even found in possession of firearms or the wherewithal of revolutionary paraphernalia, would face military courts that could result in the death penalty (usually by hanging rather than a firing squad).

While the Palestinian revolution was in full swing, my mother, true to her marriage philosophy, determined that Yousef should not stay a widower for a long time. She put out feelers for a new bride. In a short span of weeks, she found a seventeen-year-old girl named Nadiema Abu Hawwash to be his new bride. Nadiema came from a well-known Haifa Muslim family that had kinship connections with the Aswad clan. In particular, Nadiema was a first cousin of Nayef, Zahiyye's husband, on his mother's side. Nadiema was illiterate. Yousef and Nadiema were wed in the spring of 1938. Because my mother did not want to burden the newly-wed couple with the responsibility of caring for Qasim, she assumed the task of raising him. It is also fair to say that Nadiema's parents did not wish to see their daughter assume that responsibility either, particularly in view of her youth and the fact that it was her first marriage.

For most intents and purposes, Qasim was raised as a younger brother. Yousef contributed monetarily to his son's maintenance, but only in a very informal and sporadic fashion. Qasim had in some sense, a hybrid upbringing. He was Yousef's son, and my mother's adopted baby. When Yousef got married, he, with the new wife, continued to live in the same dwelling (physical structure) with my parents and family. He and his wife merely had separate quarters within that dwelling. In that separate quarter, they had independence with respect to food and other personal affairs. This is in contrast to when Zahiyye got married. In her case, being a woman, she actually physically moved out from her parents dwelling to a new physical dwelling provided by her husband. This pattern was not uncommon in those days in the Palestinian community. In the case of Zahiyye, her in-laws had already passed away at the time of her marriage to Nayef, so there were no in-laws to move in with. As far as my mother raising Qasim, it is noteworthy that I have no recollection of ever entertaining any sense of resentment or jealousy towards him. To this very day, I have the greatest affection for him. I attribute this in a large measure to my mother; she made sure that I was never wanting for love or attention from her.

The British conducted a fierce and ruthless campaign to disarm the Palestinians. Whenever and wherever an act of violence erupted, they would surround the whole neighborhood and conduct a brutal search, home by home, for the perpetrator, for firearms, or for any sign of collaboration with any one perpetrator.

I recall one time when the British soldiers, with automatic guns in their hands ready to fire, barged into our rented home in Wadi-Ennisnas, and started turning the place upside down, so-to-speak; dumping rice supplies out of bags onto the floor, followed by dumping out flour, beans, lentils, and whatever food supplies my parents had stored for our survival, looking for firearms. They did not respect the privacy not only of the men, but also the women and children. A grave human violation let alone a Muslim violation. When they left, our home was in the biggest mess you would ever want to imagine. No firearms were found.

On another occasion, they surrounded Wadi-Ennisnas and ordered all its inhabitants out of their homes. They herded the inhabitants like sheep to an open ground nearby, referred to by the community as the "Land of Saliem El-Khoury" after its owner, a Palestinian landlord, Mr. Saliem El-Khoury. With the homes empty and open, they rampaged through them looking for weapons. The day was quite warm, but no matter. They spared no one: young, old, man, woman, in good health or in bad health. At the time, my sister Munawwar was ten-years old and in bed, sick with typhoid; yet, she had to quickly get up, get dressed, and move out with everybody else. Again, they found nothing.

Many of the Palestinian leaders during this period were imprisoned, exiled, hung, or they escaped the country. The rebellion nevertheless continued. Palestinian opposition to British occupation was unqualified and virtually complete. Hence, a deep distrust of the British, and their collusion with the Zionists.

As an illustration of the prevalent sense and mood of the times, I recall some personal events. My ingrained disapproval of the British surfaced several years later, circa 1944, rather spontaneously one day, when I happened to walk by a couple of their soldiers in Wadi-Ennisnas. I instinctively ran towards them to within a few yards and shouted in Arabic: "*Engliezi, ilhas tiezi!*" which is literally translated, "English, lick my ass!" In Arabic, it rhymes! I surprised myself with such unseemly behavior.[21] It was further compounded by embarrassment in that at the very moment I was uttering those words, one

---

21 The phrase, per se, was in common circulation in the Palestinian community of those days; but I did not expect myself to confront two soldiers with it in the manner I did.

of my very admired schoolteachers, who was also new to the school, walked by. He unmistakably heard what I had just shouted and gave me a scolding and disapproving look. I was mortified. Heretofore, I had presented myself in a different light to him and our relationship was on a high plane. For weeks afterwards, I was distressed by the different image I displayed, and wondered if I would ever be able to change what I presumed to be his resulting negative image of me. Yet, my encounters with the British soldiers were not always hostile.

As a contrasting example, one very rainy day, in 1942, a British soldier sought refuge in our Hadar house, for he was dripping wet. My mother welcomed him in, gave him dry clothes to temporarily wear as he took off his wet uniform and gave it to my mother to dry. Yousef then pressed them. He was with us for at least a couple of hours before he bade us farewell.

In the early months of 1939, the British, on the verge of World War II, decided to use carrot diplomacy, in addition to the stick; harsh military crackdown on the ground, to end the revolution. Consequently, in May of that year, Malcolm MacDonald, Colonial Secretary of State in the British Government, issued the so-called "White Paper" of 1939. It presented an outline of a solution to the Palestine conflict. In particular, it included a "conditional independence" for a "unitary" Palestinian state to be set up at the end of a ten-year period, the annual admission of 15,000 Jewish immigrants into Palestine over a five-year period, "and protection of Palestinian land rights against Zionist acquisition."[22] The House of Commons approved the "White Paper" within days of its issuance. It was a clear discredit and revocation of Peel's recommendations, which were at the root of the Palestinian revolution. It was received as a step in the right direction by the Palestinians, albeit with reservations, and quite unfavorably by the Zionists. In October 1939, immediately after the outbreak of World War II, the extremist militant Zionist group, Stern Gang, decrying the White Paper, called upon Jews to wage war (siding with Germany's Axis!) against the British.

In spite of such unrest, the British government succeeded to a large extent to keep the lid on the simmering Palestinian pot. It brought a semblance of

22 WK, p.195

civil calm as World War II broke out. The British had even the audacity to call for volunteers, Arabs and Jews, to aid in the war effort against the Axis powers; recruiting offices were opened all over Palestine. Remarkably, many responded, albeit in smaller numbers among Arabs than Jews. The upshot was that a manageable order returned to the country.

CHAPTER 3

WORLD WAR II

With the British lid pressed down on the Palestinian simmering pot, the outbreak of World War II, its progress and implications for the future, took center stage in the minds of most people, Arabs and Jews alike. The communal tension began to recede into the background. About mid-1940, my parents deemed it safe to return to our home at #7, Yona Street. Contact with the Lehrmans was reestablished. They were glad to see Yousef again. At the time, Yousef was remarried and a full partner in the family laundry business in Wadi-Ennisnas. Nevertheless, Yousef was willing, and agreed to work for the Lehrmans on a part-time basis. With Hamadi full-time in the family business, Yousef managed for a while to split his time between the Hassoun's and Lehrman's laundries. However, a few months later, Yousef and Hamadi worked out a relationship with the Lehrmans whereby their laundry work would be subcontracted to the Hassoun Laundry and carried out at the Hadar house; the finished product was delivered back to the Lehrmans' main outlet on Hertzel's Street. To keep up with the news of the war, the family purchased a German-made (Roentgen) short-wave radio.[23] We gathered every evening around it to hear the news from Cairo, London, Paris, or Berlin.

In the fall of 1941, Hamadi began to feel restless: partly because of his age (hardly twenty years old), differences of opinion with Yousef as to how to run the business, and partly because he was not ready to settle down and make a long-term commitment to the laundry business. He wanted to try his wings on his own and away from home. Hamadi's personality was quite different from Yousef's. He was an idea person.[24] In his teens, he

---

23 The cost of the radio came to about forty pounds sterling! Since the entire family's monthly income of those days was about sixty pounds sterling, the purchase was a major investment.

24 Hamadi, while growing up, was treated with kid gloves, especially by my father, to the extent of spoiling him; so the story goes. My father indulged in doing things for him and showering him with gifts. Yet (and perhaps alas), Hamadi, as an adolescent, was the most intolerant of my father's inability to hold jobs, and for being a rather poor provider. It

was fascinated by prime numbers. He would spend hours trying to identify a recursion relation or a generating formula for them![25] He did not enjoy physical work. One day, without notifying anyone, he packed up some of his belongings and stealthily left home. My parents were beside themselves when they became aware of his disappearance. They frantically searched for him through all the channels they could think of. Before too long, he was located in a British military training camp for Arab recruits in the outskirts of Haifa. He had enlisted to serve the British!

My parents diligently worked hard to persuade him to change his mind, swallow his pride, and request release. Hamadi relented. To the relief of the family as a whole, his request was made during the time period a recruit is allowed to change his mind. It was a close call, for it was a mere day or so before the end of the grace period after which, he would have been shipped out of Haifa.

Back home, my parents initially lectured him sternly. How could he behave with such a great folly and cause so much unhappiness to the family? After that, my parents tried to understand why he had done it and how to turn things around for him. While I was too young to appreciate all that was talked about, my parents ultimately offered him more say in the running and managing of the business, and less hands-on physical labor. This was followed in short order by making him equal partner with Yousef and Mother. He seemed agreeable to give it a try. His managerial talents gradually received more recognition and he rapidly assumed the role of manager of the Hassoun Brothers Laundry. Not too long thereafter, my parents further prevailed on him to think of marriage and settling down. As was noted earlier, Hamadi married his cousin Khayriyye. She was five years younger and had fourth grade education. The couple moved into the second room of the second floor addition to the house at #7, Yona Street. They were across the hallway from Yousef's and Nadiema's quarters.

---

seemed to have made him feel lesser than some of his friends and classmates who often came from the upper crust of Haifa's Arab society. Such emotions, family members speculated, contributed to his oft-manifest ill health.

25   As yet an unsolved problem!

For the next four years, the laundry business continued to flourish. The Lehrmans further entrusted their laundry work to the Hassoun laundry. Two pressers and a wash-man were hired. Yousef assumed the role of a master presser in charge of delicate clothes that demanded special skills. Mother was in charge of washing. Father carried out supporting errands and bought groceries for all three family units at the #7, Yona Street house. Hamadi became the undisputed manager, led public relations and promoted the business to a larger circle of clienteles. Two additional laundries in the Hadar subcontracted the Hassoun laundry for specialized tasks, such as white linen, shirts and underwear. My brother Fouad would also be called upon to help, after school hours, as an errand boy and a junior presser. The two rooms on the ground level at the Hadar house, directly below Hamadi's and Yousef's quarters, were set aside and converted into washing and pressing rooms to keep up with the increased business. All the washing was done in the newly-converted room. Pressing, however, was done both at the Hadar house and in Wadi-Ennisnas. Typically, the subcontracted work from the Hadar laundries was all done at the Hadar house, while the laundry received at the Wadi-Ennisnas was washed at the Hadar, but pressed in Wadi-Ennisnas, and delivered out from there. My parents, and the remaining dependent children, continued to live in the (original) main family room of the house, set in the back by a raised-up, walled-in courtyard, and about halfway between the ground level and the second floor (kind of a split level design, with a water cistern underneath) of the house.

Between the years 1938 to 1941, my mother often entrusted me to my sister Haliema's care. She usually found ways to play with me and keep me out of trouble. Stories abound about my incessant wanting to go outside to enjoy the outdoors and the sunshine. "Walk me out into the sunshine," I would plead with her;[26] sometimes, I would even throw up a tantrum. I would further ask her to take me to Grandfather Issa's house, a short walk away. I was very fond of him.

---

26 I have always disliked being confined indoors, especially if it is dark and gloomy. For years, I did not appreciate darkly-lit places, even for ambience! Mother had a commanding expression that I have always relished, "Wide open the windows, so we may see the face of our Lord!"

Grandfather Issa had a fresh produce stand outside his house, and was well regarded for his honest business practices. He was a faithful observer of Islamic duties, chiefly praying and fasting. He belonged to a group of men that got together periodically at individual homes to study the Quran and the Sunna (Way) of the Prophet. In the holy month of Ramadan, they met more frequently and prayed the *tarawieh* prayer well into the night.[27] Uncle Mahmoud was often a member of the group. Uncle Mahmoud's knowledge of the Quran, in my eyes as a child, looked very impressive. He had a good chanting voice for Quranic recitals, and he knew many Islamic-related stories (parables, anecdotes, etc.) that illustrated a point or explained an ethical value. When he would visit us at home, the family looked forward to hearing some of these stories. My brother Yousef, from time to time, would challenge the standard interpretations and would offer his own usually twisted, but funny, interpretation. Yousef had a knack at seeing the comical side of things, even in the most serious of circumstances. For example: Whenever he would be asked, "Where is your birthplace?" he would answer with a stern face, "My mother's womb!" (The Arabic version is considerably funnier, but somewhat vulgar!) It was an answer that infuriated bureaucrats and government officials. Also, when his newly-born baby boy passed away, Yousef explained it this way, "The baby looked over the family he had been born into and his surroundings. He did not like what he saw, so, he left!"

Upon one of my visits to Grandfather Issa's house, I recall (in about 1939) being behind sister Haliema when she crossed the street to the other side. I decided to follow suit when a speeding bicyclist hit me hard and knocked me down on the pavement. My head was cut and bleeding profusely when Haliema carried me back home in a hurry. My mother ran with me down to Dr. Musallam's clinic, where the cut was cleaned, stitched, and my head was banded like a turban!

As Haliema reminisces over these days, of my frequent demands to walk into the sunshine and going to Grandpa Issa's, she tends to say, "When an idea got into Ghazi's head, it was very difficult to distract him away from it. He was a very persistent and stubborn boy!"

---

27 This additional Ramadan prayer is to further one's cleansing and purification from the mundane and to lift one up to the spiritual. The sight of Grandfather Issa and Uncle Mahmoud gathered with their friends to study the Quran and pray instilled in me a deep and lasting affection for Islam and its way.

Sister Haliema was married, by arrangement, to Fadhel Saleh Arafi in April 1943. Fadhel's mother, named Ammouni (nickname for Aamni) was Nadiema's aunt on her father's side. Haliema had four years of schooling. She attended the Siba'i girls school (a private Islamic school). Fadhel had sixth grade education and worked as a mail delivery postman. Fadhel turned out to have a very weak personality that clashed sharply with Haliema's, which was quite assertive. The marriage ended in divorce one year and eight months later. A baby girl was born (Ibtihaj) in the first year of their marriage. Haliema and her newly-born baby came back to live with us in December 1944.

An interesting side note to the time when Haliema was married to Fadhel is that she moved to live within his mother's household. The mother, Ammouni, was twice widowed by then. Two of her elder and unwed sons were living in the same household. On my visits to Haliema at the time, I would occasionally run into the brothers-in-law. They were both quite friendly and interesting chaps. One of them, Hasan El-Buhairi, half brother of Fadhel from his mother's first marriage, was a recognized Haifa poet and writer. Hasan had a private room of his own where he did his literary work. I recall times when I would see Hasan in the company of the Haifa *oudist* (a lutist or guitarist), Ahmad Shukri, working on the music of a new song. With considerable intrigue, I would watch the two and listen as they rehearsed a line or a note here and there!

Haliema was remarried in August 1945, eight months after her divorce, to Khalil Esh-Shatta. Khalil hailed from Damascus, Syria. He was about fifteen years her senior. He was illiterate but talented with his hands. He could fix plumbing, pumps, sewing machines, *primuses* (type of gasoline stoves), etc. Over several years, Khalil had done many repairs around our house, and my mother was quite impressed by him. On occasion, during those years, after a repair job, my mother would invite him to stay for a meal, and we would chitchat with him. He lived by himself, and had no relatives in all of Palestine. Khalil did not seem to have been married before. My mother had compassion for him, as did the whole family.

Mother did not want sister Haliema, a divorcee at age twenty with a child, in our household to support and watch over. For one thing, she would be an economic liability. But even far more importantly, there might be temptations for Haliema to get involved in relations with male strangers. That would be utterly disastrous for family honor and reputation. Consequently, one might say that she encouraged Khalil to think in terms of becoming a member of the family, taking Haliema for a wife, and acquiring a sense of belonging. Khalil was comfortable in his association with us and liked us as a family. He felt we could provide him with a home away from home, and thus normalize his life. Mother's way seemed to have fallen on a receptive heart. In due course, Khalil asked for Haliema's hand. He also agreed to accept responsibility for the raising of her child, Ibtihaj, as well. The wedding took place at the Hadar house.

At the wedding party, Khalil, in cahoots with Uncle Abdalla,[28] Mother's half brother, managed to smuggle some wine to serve literally, under the table, to some of their cohorts. My mother was kept in the dark, as it was a foregone conclusion that she would not allow it. Wine or any form of liquor is expressly forbidden in Islam. I somehow caught onto what was happening. I pressed Uncle Abdalla to include me in the drinking. I was very curious about liquor, and how it affects people. For whatever reason, he not only agreed, he served it generously, perhaps to shut me up. As the party came to end, my mother discovered, to her shock, that she had an intoxicated ten-year-old son on her hands.

Haliema and Ibtihaj moved out to live with Khalil in his little apartment, just outside the southwestern edge of Wadi-Ennisnas.

Late in 1945, just before our move to our new home at Carmel's Station, Munawwar's hand was asked for in marriage. The prospective suitor was a young machinist, Muhammad Sha'abiya. It was done through the customary family arranged channels. He worked for the British army in one of their machine and army vehicles body shops, south of the city. Muhammad lived with his parents on the northern end of Haifa in the area called Shaykh Abdalla's (also known as Halleesa). He was the oldest of seven children. The Sha'abiya family was not known to us before, but on further investigation, they were found to be a hard working and honorable family. Munawwar was married to Muhammad in August 1946. The wedding party was held in our Carmel's Station home (see page 48). Munawwar went to live with Muhammad within his parents' household immediately following the marriage party.

---

28 Abdalla was the only son Grandfather Issa had from his second wife, Aamni, see Chapter 1. He was only eight years older than me.

The war years, particularly 1940 through 1945, pulled together the Arab and Jewish communities of Palestine into a relatively harmonious cooperation and existence. The British could not afford otherwise; a tribute in part to their savviness, though Palestinian leaders such as Hajj Amin Al-Husseini had sought refuge in Nazi Germany, while others were executed, thrown in jail, or hiding at large. I recall many a time when I would be taken by brother Yousef, along with brother Fouad and nephew Qasim, during those years to the famous Azaziyye Beach, south of Haifa, for an afternoon swim and fun in the sun. There, we would find a mix of humanity, Arabs, Jews, and British, associating freely with each other, absent politics, and having "a jolly good time." Lively Arabic, Hebrew, and English sounds filled the air. Aunt Maryam's oldest son, Ahmad Zakariyya, owned a small coffee shop, with snacks and beverages, right on the beach. It served all guests equally with no regard to creed, color, language, or national origin. It was our favorite spot to go to. Cousin Ahmad was always filled with smiles at seeing us, and served us cold pop "on the house" promptly!

Brother Yousef enjoyed the beaches. He also liked to go to another beach in southern Haifa, named Bayt-Galiem; Hebrew for "House of Waves." It was private, predominantly Jewish, with an admission charge. Occasionally, he would take me along with Qasim, and sometimes, Fouad. There was a children's pool where Qasim and I could swim. Yousef, being very comfortable with both Arabic and Hebrew, socialized merrily with many people there. He may also have enjoyed watching the preponderant young Jewish women in their swimsuits. I do not recall, back then, seeing Arab women in swimsuits at the beach.

Beaches were not the only settings were Arabs and Jews mixed and had positive, amicable interactions. Far from it!

One time, during those early forties, a young Jewish woman came to our Hadar home, ostensibly with clothing for the Hassoun laundry to do. After some chatting with Yousef, the two decided that they would spend the rest of the day at Bayt-Galiem. Yousef quickly dropped off his laundry work, put together his swim gear, rolled it up in a towel, and headed off with her to the Bayt-Galiem bus stop, which was about hundred or so meters away. Nadiema, Yousef's wife, was in her room on the second level unaware of what was going on below. Within minutes, however, the word got out to my mother who was in a different room, but on the same level of the house. My mother, shocked by the news, wasted no time. She threw a scarf on her head, slipped her feet into a pair of slippers, and dashed to the bus stop after Yousef. I tagged behind. She found Yousef and his woman companion standing in line waiting for the bus. She lovingly explained to the companion, mostly using gestures, the marital status of Yousef, spoke of his children, and talked Yousef into coming home. Yousef, rather unhappy, did not argue; he parted with the young woman as politely as he could under the circumstance, and sheepishly accompanied Mother and me home.

During that era, Uncle Fahd, Uncle Tawfiq's next younger brother, despite being married and his wife also being his cousin, went out habitually with Shushanna (Hebrew for Susan/Susanna/Suzanna), a Jewish woman refugee from Europe. The relationship lasted for a time until politics and family pressure caused them to break up. I recall him coming to our house shortly after the break-up, somewhat intoxicated, in tears over the separation, and repeatedly muttering, "Oh Shushanna, *habibati* (my darling)!"

Benny, a Jewish yard-goods peddler, lived nearby, about a hundred yards away.[29] He loved to come to our house to show, and eventually sell to the ladies (Mother, Nadiema, and Khayriyya) of the house his most recent procurements, which he carried over his shoulder. He would be well received, for the ladies enjoyed the time with him and being kept abreast of the latest merchandise. He was very mildly mannered and patient. In fact, I used to be amazed by the tremendous patience Benny had with the ladies. He would unfold one roll of yard goods after the other for their inspection and admiration. If he were to run out of rolls, and none yet attracted or commanded serious interest, he would excuse himself for a few minutes to go home to get more rolls while leaving the other rolls behind! With Benny's few Arabic words and the ladies few Hebrew words, they communicated jovially and amazingly quite well for long times. If some fabric got the serious interest of any one of the ladies, it led then into the quality of it, which he invariably vouched to be high. Then, a lot of friendly back and forth bargaining would usually follow before settling

---

29 The peddler's actual name, Benny, may very well be incorrectly recollected. It is fundamentally immaterial to the story.

on a price, which typically made the ladies feel they were getting a good deal, and at the same time, allowed Benny some profit. Should a question or doubt arise as to the veracity of any of Benny's assertions, he would hasten to swear by the "ten words" (as he literally put it in Arabic, *ashar kalemat,* or the Decalogue or Ten Commandments) that it was true. From time to time, the process of visiting, displaying the yard goods and bargaining would spill over into Saturday, the Jewish Sabbath. He did not seem to mind continuing it and closing a deal on Saturdays; however, he would not accept getting paid (cash) until after Saturday. He would explain that religious law did not allow him to touch any money on the Sabbath! Therefore, he would return on another day for payment.

There was also the case of Younes (Arabic for Jonas, Yona in Hebrew) and Rachel. Before converting the front roadside room of our Hadar house to a laundry facility, it was rented to Younes/Rachel, the Muslim Arab chicken peddler and the Jewish nurse, Rachel. When seeing these two, you could not help but sense that they were deeply in love. They helped each other most affectionately in all aspects of day-to-day living. In hindsight, it was inspirational for a young boy like me to see. They may have encountered societal disapproval and pressure for being politically incorrect. Yet, as far as I could follow their life course, they kept going on undaunted and happily teaming together, not allowing external forces to come between them.

There were, at that time, many more examples of genuine human Arab-Jewish interactions that transcended the political chasm; I cited the few that I witnessed and still vivid in my memory.

CHAPTER 4

HAIFA SCHOOL YEARS

In the summer of 1941, I fell ill with typhoid. It was like following in the footsteps of my sister, Munawwar, a few years before. Initially, the family kept close and prayerful watch over me. As the gravity of my illness increased, my mother excused herself from washing duties and took me to her trusted doctor, Sa'd Mussallam, besides being lovingly cared for in the customary way. My father, from time to time, would take me out for a walk in the fresh air. I slowly began to mend. One time, to my great surprise, he came home with a pretty red tricycle in his arms. It was a present for me! That really made me feel special, for I was not aware of any of my brothers or sisters getting anything like this before. I recall struggling as I tried to ride it, for it was a bit too big for my size. My brother Fouad did not have any trouble riding it. For days, Fouad was having a heyday with my tricycle. Within a week or so, while Fouad was having fun riding it, it broke down. My father took the broken tricycle back and had it replaced by a better built and somewhat smaller tricycle. I rode that tricycle and enjoyed it for a long time thereafter.

As the summer of 1941 was coming to an end, preparing to enroll me into first grade at Haifa's government school was in earnest. It was the same school Hamadi had attended and Fouad was attending. Before the government school, I had been to two kindergartens (in 1940). The first was in Wadi-Ennisnas. I recall having a problem counting, knowing whether three came before four, or was it the other way around! That kindergarten somehow closed down and shortly thereafter I was sent to the second kindergarten located just outside Wadi-Ennisnas by Abbass. The second kindergarten concentrated on (Islamic) religious education. We were taught about honesty, obedience to parents, and cleanliness, among other fundamentals, according to Islam. Both kindergartens had short hours of attendance, typically from 9:00 am to 12:00 noon.

Both kindergartens were gender mixed; however, in the government schools, soon to follow, the boys and girls were separated. The government school for girls was located in another section of Haifa. It terminated with the seventh grade whereas the boys' school terminated with the ninth grade.[30]

The government school had three basic time blocks: (1) early-morning, 8:00 am to 10:15 am, (2) mid-morning, 10:30 am to 12:00 pm and (3) afternoon, 1:30 pm to 3:00 pm. The blocks were divided into class periods. A class period was 45 minutes in duration; there were a total of seven classes a day. The subjects of the lessons were: Arabic, arithmetic, history, geography, art, and religion. English and woodwork shop were added into the curriculum beginning with the fourth grade. Music was never considered to belong in the curriculum. While the formal class day was over at 3:00 pm, there were a variety of activities after classes. These activities were primarily sports related; most common and popular was soccer. However, there were important other sports like track, long jump, high jump, the potato sack race, the relay race, the three-legged race. Schools in a given district competed in these sports. Haifa's school was in the Nazareth district. The boys' schools annually competed in a major two-day meet, held in Nazareth, the district seat, with a lot of fanfare, ceremonies, and prize awarding. Fouad participated in a big way in these meets at least three years in a row. I accompanied him once, as a spectator.

I started first grade in the fall of 1941; my parents had prevailed on the principal to admit me though I was below the minimum age (of about seven years). I was still recuperating from typhoid and was initially too weak to walk the distance from home to school, roughly one mile. Therefore, for the first few weeks, my father would carry me on his back in the morning, meet me at noon for the lunch break, take me home on his back if needed, bring me back at 1:30 pm for the afternoon block, then meet me at 3:00 pm to take me home on his back.

My early days at the government school were characterized by apprehension and anxiety. I did not know anybody in my classes and did not know what to do during recesses. Initially, I sought the company of my brother Fouad, who was in the fifth grade, and I would trail him. This, however, did not bring me

---

30 For all of Arab Haifa, a city of about one hundred thirty thousand at the time, there was only one government (public) girls' school and one single government (public) boys' school. The boys' school was the larger; yet, it did not exceed three hundred fifty students in enrollment.

relief; Fouad had friends of his own. He did a variety of things with them; I did not fit in with these friends and activities. My trailing would also annoy Fouad. Eventually, he would shoo me away saying, "Go find your own friends and play with them." In a matter of a few weeks, this was precisely what I did.

The government school building was a lovely two-story building with red roof tiles. It was located at the top of an east-west sloping road, Tal'it el-Jabal (literally, the mount up-slope) just beneath the Baha'i Shrine, in between Abbas and Wadi-Ennisnas. It looked over the Mediterranean Sea to the west with Mount Carmel to its back.

To me, as a first grader, the teachers had impressive personalities and seemed quite knowledgeable.[31] They commanded a great deal of respect mixed with awe. I particularly loved my Arabic and religion classes. Mr. Hasan Kitmitto was our teacher. He taught religion across the first six grades. He was a friendly and smiley teacher, and hard not to like. However, if you were to misbehave or cross him for any reason, you better watch out. He would be stern in his corporeal punishment; either by ruler strikes on the palms of your hands or spanked on your rear.

Corporeal punishment was permitted. Usually, the school principal and senior faculty administered it. Another form of punishment was detention from play recess, lunch break, or at going-home time, at the end of the day. The detention time varied depending on the nature of the offense, typically from fifteen minutes to an hour. Detention was often coupled by having to kneel in humility on a bare floor against a corner in some room. I have heard of, but not experienced nor witnessed, a kneeling on sharp gravel as a form of accented punishment. Early on, I developed distaste for and fear of getting punished. I carefully strove not to cause it. Punishment was administered for a clear misbehavior; at times, it was also administered for not doing assigned schoolwork. For the latter, the punishment was more in the form of tongue-lashings than corporal or open humiliation. I recall when I was in fifth grade my English teacher, Mr. Arafat Dweik, called upon me to read and explain some paragraphs from our English reading book. His call came to me as a surprise. When I tripped over some of the words or fumbled through sentences, he

---

31 Typically they had a high school education followed by a couple of years of "Teacher Training" in some kind of a "Teachers' College."

"scoldingly" told me, for all classmates to hear, that I was not fit to be a student, rather, I ought to be carrying a (large) basket on my back as a (street) porter![32]

In the religion classes, one thing never sat well with me. Namely, at the beginning of the class, a handful of students, typically between one and three in a class of fifty, would be excused to leave unattended, with no substitute activity or alternative religion class. Those were the Christian students. There were no Jewish students. The religion class taught Islam, the religion of the majority. The class period focused more on reciting and memorizing short *suras*, or chapters, of the Quran, mostly parroting them without appreciable comprehension, and less on tenets of the faith or the duties of the Muslim. I have often wondered how it would feel to be one of those that were excused.

The Christian student population in the government school was quite small, about six percent; which was significantly less than the percentage of the Arab Christian population in Haifa at the time. A majority of Christian students attended private Christian schools, Salesian, Frères', Anglican-English, Saint Luke's, Orthodox, etc. The English School for girls and Saint Luke's School for boys were the most prestigious. There were also two major private Islamic schools, one for boys and the other for girls; the boys' school had a full high school while the girls' school ended after the seventh grade. The private Christian schools, it is fair to say, seemed more preponderant and typically had a missionary Western Christian affiliation, that is Italian, French, English, or American. Muslim students did attend Christian schools, although in smaller numbers, and often children of the wealthy. Christian students rarely attended Muslim schools. I was never aware of Jewish students attending the Arab Haifa schools, be they public, private Muslim, or Christian. The Jewish communities, generally, congregated separately, and had their own private schools with Hebrew as the primary language of instruction.

My first friend at the government school was Illyas Al-Jisr. I was particularly attracted to Illyas (variation of the Biblical name Elias) by his outgoing and cheerful personality. He was courageous and did not take nonsense from

---

32 I have, since, oft reflected on these remarks for the appalling lack of sensitivity for the student's feelings by the teacher; unfortunately, this sort of sarcasm and insult was not uncommon. What further baffled me was that Mr. Dweik was educated in England, with a BA in English (rather unusual in those days), and was a well-known and regarded teacher.

anybody. We both played soccer aggressively. Illyas was the youngest child in his Christian family of five; his parents and three children; an older brother, As'ad, and a sister, Blanche, who was the oldest of the three. As'ad was also attending the same school, but was five grades ahead of us. Illyas' father worked as a mail sorter for the main post office in downtown Haifa. My friendship with Illyas grew steadily; at times, we would play together even after school. I would play at his home more often than he would play at my home. His family lived in an apartment in a fairly modern good size building that was about halfway between the Hassoun laundry in Wadi-Ennisnas and my home at #7, Yona Street. His home was in a distinctly Arab section. His family was quite small compared to my extended household; thus, it was easier for his family to have me at his home than my family to have Illyas at my home. I was always welcomed at his home. His mother (homemaker) and sister showed interest in me and would occasionally engage me in some friendly chats. His sister went to a private girls school, I surmised, where French and English were emphasized in the curriculum, for she was fluent in both, in addition to Arabic. At times, they would have me eat with Illyas at their kitchen table. One food that was often present in their kitchen was ham, an item that was never in my family's kitchen. Yet, they were quite careful that I did not eat it, lest it offend my parents.[33]

As time went by, and I advanced through the grades, my circle of friends grew. Another classmate that early on also became a special friend was Mas'oud El-Hasan. Mas'oud was a bit older than me, and physically, significantly bigger. He was a good soccer player, dogged in his chase of the ball, good-natured, and of a loving heart. He and I milled around the schoolyard a lot together. However, we did things together only at school. His home was quite a distance from the school and from my home. Mas'oud came from a rather large family of very limited means. He had three brothers and an unknown (to me) number of sisters. I recall being very surprised when I found that his father was blind. I could not visualize how a blind man could have so many children and support them! Their home, I was told, was a refurbished dwelling in one of some existing caves in the hills south of Haifa, near a major shrine that Christians referred to as Saint George's (presumably of the Dragon

---

33 In Islam, ham, or pork meat, is unlawful food.

Legend, buried in Lydda).[34] Muslims referred to it as Sayyidna (Arabic for Our Lord) El-Khader.[35] Both Muslims and Christians revered the saint. It was the prevalent view that very poor people, who could not afford normal homes in the city, sought temporary shelter in these caves.

Mother occasionally took the family to the shrine for an afternoon of offerings and blessings. More specifically, mother used to pray to Sayyidna El-Khader, especially when she would be facing a major problem; typically, a grave illness of a family member. She would promise an offering to God that becomes an obligation, should her prayer be answered. The most common offering used to be a slaughtered lamb whose meat would be distributed to the poor. My mother prayed diligently and passionately. On a few occasions, I have seen my mother get up past midnight, go out into our courtyard, bare her breast, look up to the clear star-studded sky, and fervently, audibly, and humbly, ask God for help, calling upon Sayyidna El-Khader to intercede for her with God to plead her case.

On our visits to Sayyidna El-Khader's shrine, I would see an altar inside one of the caves with candles, some lit and some not, and Christians, with candles in their hands walking to the altar to light other candles and place their candles on the altar.[36] One time, and from a distance, I was shown that Mas'oud El-Hasan's family lived in one of the caves; this, the very same family whose boys were our schoolmates. I glimpsed Mas'oud's father in the distance and he wore the attire of a Muslim Shaykh (a spiritual teacher).

Mas'oud's oldest brother was Khaled. He was about seven years older than us. He had distinguished himself by going on further in school, beyond the terminal ninth grade of the government school, at the private Haifa Islamic High School, and had graduated from it. Completing high school in those days was regarded as a major accomplishment, particularly when achieved by a member of a humble family. Although I saw very little of Khaled during my friendship years with Mas'oud, nevertheless when I did, I was met with an acknowledging and warm smile. Many years later, Khaled became the second

---

34 http://en.wikipedia.org/wiki/Saint_George.

35 It is assumed that Saint George and Sayyidna El-Khader are one and the same.

36 Muslims traditionally have not used candles in their rituals and ceremonies, the suggestion being it is a form of idolatry.

man, next only to Yasser Arafat, in command of the Palestine Liberation Organization (PLO). Mas'oud's second brother, about three or four years older than us, was Ali. Ali was a classmate and a friend of my brother Fouad. Fouad was, however, more into sports than Ali, especially soccer. In fact, Fouad, from grade six to grade nine, was one of the stars of the government soccer team. Ali was more into religious and social studies. After the school's closure in November 1947, we heard no further news of Ali.

Mas'oud's third and youngest brother, two years Mas'oud's junior, was Hani. Hani was two grades behind us. He was a classmate of my nephew Qasim, and a good friend of his as well. They hung out together quite a bit when at the government school. After hearing nothing about him for many years, I was elated one day to read, while news browsing, his name as member of the Executive Committee of the PLO, and that he was heavily involved in peace negotiations with the Israelis long before the so-called Madrid Peace Conference of October 1991.

Khaled parted ways with Arafat at the onset of the Oslo negotiations (1992), retiring for good from politics to live in Morocco.

Other friends come to mind as well, especially those I had in the third, fourth, fifth, and sixth grades. Among them, these stand out: Uthman Abu Ghayda, Mustapha Shukri, and Salah Al-Ouri. Recalling them evokes a deep sense of camaraderie, love, and joy mixed with yearning to know what became of each one of them. Uthman's father was a successful businessman in Haifa. The family lived in the prestigious Abbas section. Mustapha came from a very cultured family; they were involved in music and the arts. I never knew what his father did—possibly a landlord. Mustapha was the brother of the Haifa *oudist* and composer, Ahmad. The Shukris lived in the exclusive German Quarter, near Abbas. I surmise they were of the clan of the last Arab Mayor of Haifa, Hasan Shukri. Salah came from a learned Muslim family with a couple of older brothers and some sisters. His father was a Muslim judge. They lived a short walk from Wadi-Ennisnas on Stanton's Street.

One time, a classmate in the fourth grade, named Jamil, was standing in the middle of the schoolyard daring anyone to come and fight him. Somehow, I accepted his challenge. Right at the outset of the fight, I seem to have punched him in a sensitive spot beneath his heart. He fell down to the ground and fainted. Upon seeing him having fainted on the ground, I panicked, thinking the guy was dead, ran home, and did not return to school the rest of the day. It was a great relief when I learned that Jamil had recovered shortly afterwards and was fine. In my future encounters with him, he would look sheepishly friendly. I never saw him bully others again. I was amazed at the change in him which, at the time, I never expected.

While I enjoyed school and thought very highly of my teachers, most of my energy in the first two grades was channeled into playing (goofing off!) much like my brother Fouad. Fouad was found deficient in two subjects (History and English) in his fifth grade, upon which, he was made to repeat the grade notwithstanding his excellence in mathematics. In the first term of my second grade, to my unpleasant surprise, I was ranked sixty-second out of sixty-three students in the class, behind my nephew-classmate, Rashid, Zahiyye's oldest son. As his uncle, I found it hard to swallow. His rank was about fiftieth. This made an impression on me. Further, some of my classmate-friends, like Illyas, had ranked in the top ten. It felt awkward to be his friend and so far behind him in rank. Also, I did not want to have to repeat the second grade and fall behind my friends. It caused me to pay a little more attention to schoolwork. My rank improved considerably in the latter two terms (ranked in the thirties), and I managed to pass successfully onto the third grade. In the third grade, my rank improved further to being around twenty-fifth. It was kind of average; I was more comfortable with that. Noting that brother Fouad had a reputation as being his class math "wiz" (notwithstanding his repeating the fifth grade), I wanted to be good in mathematics also. My mathematics teacher, having been Fouad's teacher before, expected me to be good in mathematics as well. I strove diligently not to disappoint him nor blemish Fouad's image. I was only partially successful in my third and latter grades at the government school.

I also tried to emulate Fouad in sports. As noted earlier, Fouad had participated at least three years in succession in the annual Nazareth meets. In addition to his soccer activity, he was in the 100m, 200m dashes, the school relay race, the potato sack race, and the three-legged race. To my recollection, Fouad would come second or third in some of these meets and would bring home prizes. I had hoped, perhaps yearned, that he would, for once, win a first prize at least in one of these sports. As far as I can recall now, he never did. This made me more respectful of the Nazareth competitions, for I felt Fouad was very good. I never qualified to be on the Haifa school team to participate in the Nazareth meets. I only managed to convince Fouad and my parents to go with him to *one* of these meets *just to watch*. I think it was at the end of my fifth grade. We stayed at the home of one of his soccer buddies, Hasan Abu As'ad. Hasan's family in Nazareth was well-to-do and afforded us great hospitality. Hasan was a very good-looking boy who played soccer with impressive grace. For some unknown reason to me, he chose to attend the Haifa Government School and commute back and forth to Haifa from his family home in Nazareth. Perhaps because of an older cousin of his, Omar, who taught vocational crafts at the Haifa Government School, and commuted likewise, or perhaps the Arab Nazareth School was not as good?

Fouad's soccer playing, over and above his other sports activities, somehow was a significant theme in our daily school routine. In the morning, we typically walked together to school. During our morning walks to school, I often asked Fouad questions about what was in store for the day, or why something was done this way and not that way. Sometimes, I would ask him other more fundamental questions about life, social values, and even religion. I expected my older brother to know all the answers. I recall him tiring of my constant questioning; he would turn to me with an annoyed look trying to stop me, to shut me up. There were times I would get upset with him to the point of challenging him for a fight; I was mean with my kicks. Invariably, Fouad would not retaliate when he easily could have done so; he would only gently restrain me in self-defense. This endeared him to me. At the end of the school day, no matter whatever else had happened, we walked back home together, unless something was scheduled after classes. More often than not, there was some activity after classes. When there would be soccer practice, I would either go watch it or walk alone back home. If I went to watch the practice, I was custodian of Fouad's books and his other clothes. If I went home, I had to carry the same home with me. I usually did not relish these tasks but carried them out anyhow. To entice me into doing them, he would set up what amounted to a credit-points account for me. The credit-points would translate into rental payment for using (borrowing) one or more of his trinkets for a time period. Fouad loved watches and cameras. For several years, he would have on hand a couple of watches and at least one camera. I had neither, and I particularly liked to wear his watches. Therefore, he would rent one to me for a defined period of time.

Both Fouad and I had weekly allowances. My allowance was considerably smaller than his; partly because I was much younger, and partly because he performed errands at the laundry that I was too young to perform. Consequently, aside from the trinkets, he often had more cash on hand than I. When there were actual games, then it was a foregone conclusion that I would watch the games. As I look back on those days, I got to meet some very impressive, wonderful fellows like Mahmoud Abu Ghayda (Uthman's cousin), Walid Mnaymni, and Na'im Uwayda. All three were fine athletes, friendly and kind.[37]

By the time I reached age ten, I was eager to prove my worth at the laundry. I had already performed occasional errands there like carrying clothes back and forth between the laundry and clients. While I was initially reluctant to accept tips from customers for delivering their laundered clothes to their homes, as I felt it was demeaning, I was told by my brothers, Yousef and Hamadi, that it was okay to accept tips, and it was a way of augmenting my weekly allowance. I was also free to do as I pleased with the tips. The laundry business was going strong both in Wadi-Ennisnas and the Hadar. Hamadi welcomed my enthusiasm. Fouad had already been helping with pressing on weekends and school holidays. The pressure on Fouad was to get more involved in the business. He would press in the pressing room, which had earlier been converted from a rental room, at our home, #7, Yona Street. An ironing board was thus set up for me. It was a rather standard type of an ironing board for those days, too high for my size, and not the adjustable kind. I was hardly tall enough to reach the far side of the ironing board. I was given the task of pressing the inside seams of men's trousers, the pockets and linings, then turning the trousers right side out and handing them over to Fouad to finish. Typically, these trousers had been water-washed and were quite wrinkled; many were wool. This speeded Fouad's pressing and increased the laundry's output. My performance was well

---

37 Mahmoud became a lawyer and worked in Kuwait as a legal consultant for the Kuwaiti Airlines for many years. Walid became a noted Medical Doctor at AUB, and later, settled and practiced medicine in Miami, Florida. While I lost track of Na'im, he inspired me to persevere as I watched him run, with great determination, the one-mile race, and set a record at the Haifa Government School.

received by the family. I was very careful to do a good job, as I wanted to be recognized and given more responsibility. In a short time, I was given the task of pressing the exterior waist of the trousers as well, before turning them over to Fouad to finish. Fouad and I became salaried employees of the laundry. Unofficially, I also became Fouad's partner, albeit his junior partner! I got paid less than he did and rightly so; he supervised me and was responsible for the final product before the big brothers. On a good day, we would press over fifty trousers, a major contribution to the Hassoun Brothers Laundry's business. Our pay was relative to our output. The bulk of my salary was turned over happily to my mother, perhaps to save for a rainy day?

CHAPTER 5

THE ROAD TO THE NAKBA[38]

Shortly after the end of World War II, the old problems between Palestinian Arabs and Jews came back to center stage. The Jewish community was quite euphoric at the end of World War II, with the collapse of Germany (on May 8, 1945). I recall when the news came out that Hitler was indeed dead, there was dancing in the streets of Hadar and free handing out of presents to kids. I was among the recipients.

As 1946 rolled on, the social climate began to look more ominous, however. The Jews were clamoring for more immigration of Jewish refugees to Palestine. They coupled this with a series of terrorist acts directed against the British to pressure them to allow more inflow. From time to time, the Arabs would get drawn in, one way or another. The numbers of incoming Jewish refugees were at times in the tens of thousands; often these refugees came on ships into the Haifa harbor, legally or illegally. The Arab population would voice loud outcries of protestation without tangible evidence from the British to curb the influx. In fact, if anything, there appeared to be British acquiescence. Arabs and Jews were at loggerheads and on a collision course.

My parents, particularly my father, and brothers Yousef and Hamadi, could see violent confrontations were barely beneath the surface. They thought in earnest of moving the family from the Hadar home to an Arab part of Haifa, at least as a precaution. They started prospecting for a suitable house. They were not thinking of becoming refugees or displacing out of Palestine, but rather in terms of Arabs and Jews living in separated communities within the cities and the country until things cooled off. It did not take long before a house and a seller were found. The house had four bedrooms, two spacious halls, a good size kitchen, a front yard, and a very pleasant backyard with several flower beds and an almond tree. The house was in a section of Haifa called Carmel Station by the south coast of town, quite away from any Jewish neighborhood—so it seemed. Carmel Station

---

38 Connotes "debilitating catastrophe" in Arabic; this word is increasingly being incorporated into the English lexicon of recent Palestinian history.

was a few miles away from school, and not an easy walk, as the Hadar and Wadi-Ennisnas locations had been. Nevertheless, the family moved early in 1946, with an immediate sense of relief. For over a year thereafter, the Hadar laundry business continued functioning and serving the Hadar laundry subcontractors. However, the logistics of us working there changed significantly. My mother and the two brothers, especially, had to commute between Carmel Station, Wadi-Ennisnas, and the Hadar. For Fouad, Qasim, and me, we had to ride the bus or walk briskly about half an hour to get to school. A Jewish company operated the bus line. The passengers were predominantly Jewish. Additionally, Fouad and I could no longer spend the kind of time helping out pressing at the Hadar as before. Within several months after our move, Khalil and Haliema started complaining about the inadequacy of their little apartment, and its vulnerable location, being in a fairly open part of Haifa, not within an exclusively Arab neighborhood. Munawwar had just gotten married and moved out. Ultimately, my parents, against Hamadi's protests, agreed to Khalil, Haliema and the child moving into the new house with the rest of the family.

The two rooms formerly lived in by Hamadi and Yousef, along with their growing families, in the Hadar house, were rented out to two small Jewish refugee families. We rented out the intermediate level family room, our primary dwelling, to a single Jewish man, Moshe Rahmani. (The lower level, two rooms, was retained for the laundry business.) Moshe had been a tenant in the house that we had just purchased in Carmel Station and he would not vacate his space there to us unless we found him an adequate substitute dwelling, as there was a severe housing shortage in Haifa. He was very happy with the exchange.

Moshe was an immigrant from Eastern Europe, but he had been in Palestine for some time when we first met him; he was in his early thirties. As far as we knew, he had worked at the Haifa harbor. He was friendly and would visit Fouad and me, from time to time, in the pressing room. We also were friendly to him. He would sit in one of the corners across from our ironing boards and chat with us on a variety of topics; very often the conversation would turn to Palestine and the Arab-Jewish conflict. Even though his Arabic was quite broken and with a heavy European accent, we were often surprised at how much Arabic he understood, even slang expressions. Much of what we talked about is now a very distant and faded memory; both Fouad and I were just kids

(15 and 11 years of age respectively). Nevertheless, a few matters come clearly to mind. Whenever we would suggest that Arabs would have to resort to force to stop the Jewish influx, he would respond by saying that the Jews would counter back with a greater force. While we chatted in a friendly and even jesting way, I recall feeling quite disturbed and threatened by his responses. His mere questioning of our legitimacy within Palestine was very unsettling. *Where would such a Jewish minority garner a greater force?* I used to ask myself. After all, he is a mere refugee-tenant in our house. To me, it seemed self-evident that Palestine was our country; we have been the natives over the centuries and are the overwhelming majority. How dare he dispute the obvious? I further argued to myself that were it not for the British, the Jews would not have been able to immigrate at the level they did. Moreover, I reasoned, *When the British mandate ends and they evacuate, this immigration will come to an end, for there will be no British to facilitate it, and the Palestinians will naturally assume control of their country and destiny.* Any other scenario was inconceivable to me. Yet Moshe had other scenarios, laughed at our precepts, and seemed sure of himself and the strength of the Jewish community. As time passed by, I was in for many rude awakenings.

The shuttle service of clothes between the Hadar house and Lehrman's shop on Herzel's Street tended to initially be in smaller, frequent loads. Gradually, the loads got bigger and less frequent. In the early forties, when the Arab and Jewish communities were relatively harmonious, the shuttle was routine. However, by the mid-forties, the shuttle consolidated to one trip daily, at the end of the day. As the second half of the forties rolled in, it was accompanied by communal polarization, and charged with potential hostility. Until that time, Yousef and Adon Lehrman handled the shuttle.

Perhaps, as a result of my ambition to contribute to the workings of the laundry business, and my successful assistance with the pressing alongside Fouad, brother Hamadi decided to assign the shuttle to Fouad and me. The hired help must have somehow quit or disappeared. Both Fouad and I never really wanted this job and resisted taking it on. Hamadi, however, decided that we could do it, and that we should do it. Aside from it being quite physically demanding—having to carry a significant amount of clothes over a kilometer one way—it was to be done in an Arab-Jewish atmosphere of rising tension.

Out of a sense of duty to the family and respect for the elders, we carried on with it. We were, however, rewarded by getting paid an additional special wage, which was somewhat generous, ten piasters for both of us (the equivalence of 30 cents back then). A full-time daily wage for a Hassoun hired presser was fifty piasters. On top of this, and it dovetailed with the job, was the task of bringing the dirty laundry, stuffed compactly in a large bag of heavy fabric (weighing 20 to 30 pounds) with us on the way back. Initially, Fouad and I carried the bag either jointly or alternately over our back. A cart, on which to load the laundry, was soon procured. With the cart we were able to move through Herzel's Street considerably faster. Additionally, with the carriage/cart, we had the ability to go to the Lehrmans' home to pick up certain other laundry that needed special preparation or care; another trip of a kilometer, one way. The shuttle service continued into the middle of 1947. However, as we got further into 1947, Herzel's Street became almost exclusively Jewish, and we stood out like a sore thumb, two Arab boys pushing a laundry cart in the heart of the Jewish community. Overt hostility became increasingly likely. It started out with young Jewish boys pointing at us and saying, "*Zay Araviim*" which means, "These (are) Arabs." We, nevertheless, continued with our work. In time, it evolved into interference by what seemed to be gangster boys. Both Fouad and I would walk around them quickly. We instinctively felt that the thing to do was to avoid confrontation. We would not make eye contact nor engage in word exchange. We knew that trying to react or fight back would be a no-win response. We began to dread the coming of the time to do the job, and would heave a big sigh of relief when we got back home unscathed. Ultimately, the gangsters were not satisfied with verbal harassment. They began to raise fists at us, and once, with brass knuckles. We ran away. It was after this incident that we told the family, "Thus far and no further." We felt pretty sure that it was a matter of time before we would get beaten up or worse. In a relatively short time thereafter, mid 1947, our work with the Lehrmans' came to an end. The Lehrmans understood. The family locked up the two laundry-consigned rooms at the Hadar home.

The Hassoun Brothers Laundry business, however, continued in Wadi-Ennisnas, with the washing being carried at our newly purchased home in

Carmel Station, a far less convenient place than the Hadar home. My mother continued to go to the Hadar home on occasions to check things out and to collect the rent, but even that became unsafe by October of 1947. Earlier in 1947, a washer helper at the Hadar dropped out. The two hired pressers in Wadi-Ennisnas began to fail to show up for work. They both lived quite a way from Wadi-Ennisnas; their ability to commute back and forth became severely hampered. Fouad's services became more needed. He was in the ninth grade. About halfway through the school year 1946-1947, Fouad dropped out of school. It was argued that since he was eventually headed to join the other two brothers in the business, and the ninth grade was the terminal grade at the school anyhow, the last half-year would not make a difference. Toward the end of 1947, the hired pressers simply quit. One had worked for the laundry for well over five years, and was considered like family.

The Hassoun Brothers Laundry business prospered very well during the war years. At times, it had as many as four hired helpers. In hiring, the family hired based on merit, and with no regard to religion or national origin. In particular, one of the more illustrious workers was a fellow by the name of George. He was a Christian from Syria (Latakya area) who had left home seeking a work opportunity in Haifa. He was virtually homeless at the time he approached us for work. Right away, my mother felt compassion for him, had him clean up, gave him temporary living quarters in a loft within our household, and a job. Within a few years, he learned the business so well that he was able to leave the Hassoun laundry to start his own laundry business in another section of town. He continued to visit us from time to time until it was no longer safe to do so.

The Hassoun Brothers Laundry, in Wadi-Ennisnas, was located in a collection of shops that might be termed a local market place. While many of the proprietors were related to each other, not all were. In fact the proprietors were religion-wise mixed, Christians and Muslims. There were a couple of barbershops, a butcher's shop, a few grocery stores, and a *fool-hummos* (fava-garbanzo beans, respectively) breakfast shop.[39]

Of particular relevance to this narrative is the grocery of Ahmad El-Akhal, which was immediately next to the Hassoun Brothers Laundry, to the west. The

---

39 Two common and popular Middle Eastern breakfast bean dishes.

Hassoun Brothers Laundry and Ahmad's Grocery were housed in Mustapha El-Akhal's building. This building also abutted Hasan Shublaq's building to the east. Hasan's building had a couple of shops on the ground floor, one of which was a lively barbershop owned by Mahmoud Hajeer. The second was a minor general home supplies shop.[40] The two buildings of El-Akhal and Shublaq formed an informal hub of Wadi-Ennisnas' market place. Mustapha El-Akhal lived with his family in the floor above the laundry and the grocery store. He was also the son-in-law of Ahmad, the grocery proprietor. Ahmad was also a cousin of my mother. Hasan, likewise, lived on the second floor of his building above Hajeer's barbershop and the home supplies shop. A complex network of intermarriages related the Akhals, the Shublaqs, the Aswads, the Hassouns, and the Hajeers to each other. This was in fact typical of many of the older and larger families in Haifa, and throughout Palestine.

Hasan Shublaq was a highly patriotic man held in high esteem in Wadi-Ennisnas and probably in all of Haifa. While men in Wadi-Ennisnas wore a variety of headdresses, including no headdress at all, Hasan consistently wore the traditional Arab headdress, namely, the *kafiya* (*hatta*, in Arabic) and the head ropes (*iqal*, in Arabic). There was a special air of purposefulness about him. He usually spoke slowly and deliberately, and commanded the attention of those around him. Even I, as a kid, behaved very properly in his presence. He was by trade a construction subcontractor. His education was quite rudimentary, not exceeding the elementary level. He was the only one in the neighborhood who owned a private car, which he personally chauffeured. He changed cars quite frequently, primarily because they were second (or third!) hand and generally did not run very well. They were of the early thirties, the Ford T Type models. Many a morning, I saw him in front of the Hassoun laundry cranking like crazy to get his car started. It was not uncommon that the car would not start by cranking, and that several of the adults around would rally to push the car while in neutral to high speed, and then try to start it by shifting it into gear. My brother Yousef loved to tell jokes about Hasan's cars; of course, he would not dare tell them to Hasan's face. A frequent joke went like this, "Hasan's cars ran very well… (big pause)… downhill!"

---

40 I do not recall the proprietor's name. I had very little interaction with him.

The Wadi-Ennisnas shops formed a major service complex for most of its inhabitants and some of Abbas' inhabitants as well. They also became a major social and political setting for the neighborhood. The neighborhood was closely knit like one extended family. It was quite common for shoppers and proprietors to socialize with each other as they transacted business. This happened most often on the front sidewalk of the Hassoun-Akhal shops. There would even be a few chairs to sit on and the coffee peddler, making music by rattling his demitasse cups, was usually not very far away. The socializing covered all topics under the sun, from the price of beans and meat, to who had the best soccer team in Haifa or Palestine, to where the next boxing match was going to be held and the price of the admission tickets, to what was the latest Egyptian movie or song—especially for Muhammad Abdel Wahab and Umm Kulthoum, etc. Interspersed in all of these would be discussions of what the British and the Zionists were up to, and what our top leaders were doing or trying to do, most notably Hajj Amin Al-Husseini. In some sense, it was a microcosm of Arab Palestine.

Over the years, ever since the Hassoun Brothers Laundry was launched, most everybody that lived in Wadi-Ennisnas and Abbas, and sometimes beyond (e.g., the German quarter), would at some time or another stop by the local market place, especially at the Shublaq-Akhal compound, for business and socialization. Some of these notable people are: Raji Sahyoun (last name is Arabic for Zion!), Emile Habiby, Younes Ennaffaa, and Rashid Jarbou.

Raji Sahyoun had taught at the Haifa Government School in the late thirties and became a friend of brother Hamadi. His educational attainment, until much later in life, was a high school diploma and a teacher-training course. Raji, after a short stint in teaching, became a national radio broadcaster for the Palestine Broadcasting Station. He became a household name when he broadcast the progress of the battle of Al-Qastal, in which the (highly revered) Palestinian hero, Abdel-Qadir Al-Husseini, was killed. In the fall of 1995, Raji wrote his memoirs in a book in Arabic, titled, *Lest We Forget.*[41]

---

41 Raji's path and mine crossed again, over a period of a couple of years in the mid-fifties, in Beirut, at his UNESCO (United Nations Educational, Scientific, and Cultural Organization) office and on the AUB Campus. My last encounter with him, accompanied with brother Fouad, took place at an AAUG (Arab-American University Graduates) Convention (in the fall of 1993, Washington, D.C.), when he told us of his upcoming memoir.

Emile Habiby, also a friend of Hamadi, became a celebrated Haifa journalist and the author of the highly acclaimed book, *The Secret Life of Saeed: The Ill-Fated Pessoptimist.* Emile managed to continue to live in Haifa, notwithstanding the 1948 exodus, until his passing in 1996.[42]

Younes Ennaffaa was the highest Arab officer in the Haifa municipality at the end of World War II. He was also the president of the Islamic Sport Club, one of the top two sport clubs in the city. The other was the Shabab El-Arab Club, literally, The Youth of the Arabs Club. The soccer teams of these two clubs were often fierce competitors for first place. There was a third prominent club, the Terra Santa. However, the Terra Santa generally was of lesser standing than the other two.[43] Younes was also the head of the Haifa Boy Scouts (*Annajjada*). Younes was, as well, a friend and relative of Ahmad El-Akhal, the next-door grocery proprietor. Younes loved to walk to me by the laundry and pet me on the head; at times, seat me on his lap. Brother Fouad had joined the Islamic Sport Club sometime in 1946, and already brought a lot of attention to himself as a rising soccer star on the second (junior) team. Younes used to encourage Fouad musingly to build himself up for the first team so he could, at some point in the future, play against Shabab El-Arab. The Islamic Club was always vying for a soccer star or stars to counter the Shabab's many stars; most notable among them was Jabra Ezzarqa. Jabra was Palestine's Pelé.

Rashied Jarbou was one more among those elite few young men who succeeded in completing high school, followed by a teacher-training course, and becoming a teacher. His parents had hailed from Etteery, but had moved to live in Wadi-Ennisnas, a few hundred meters up the hill east of Hassoun's laundry, where Rashied grew up. He exuded intelligence and patriotism. He would bring some of his laundry to us to wash and press. At the same time, he enjoyed chatting with the Hassoun older brothers, Yousef and Hamadi. In the background of his visits and chats was a special sense of kinship with the

---

42 My last encounter with Emile took place at the same aforementioned AAUG Convention in the fall of 1993, again with Fouad. He was manifestly happy to see both of us and encouraged us to visit him in Haifa!

43 Shabab El-Arab Club invariably attracted the Christian players, but had a large constituency of supporters: Christians and Muslims. The Terra Santa attracted the youth who tended to identify with the town of Etteery as their root town, hence the image of being, "Sons' of Etteery."

Hassouns in view of the common Etteery roots. Often the conversation would be about the British occupation and the Zionist threat. He expressed himself with unusual articulation and eloquence. I recall not wanting him to leave, as I relished listening to him presenting an idea or making a point. He resigned his teaching career at the end of the 1945 school year and enrolled in the Syrian Military College in Damascus. He continued to stop and visit the laundry when he would be on leave from the College. He participated in the 1948 Arab-Israeli War. In the early 1950s, the last time I heard about his military career, he had become an upper level officer in the Syrian Army, stationed on the Golan Heights.

The polarization of the Jewish and Arab communities progressively intensified during the years 1946 and 1947. The Zionists lobbied worldwide, and especially with the British, for partitioning Palestine into Jewish and Arab states. To the Arabs, the word partition had the ring of death, for Palestine was simply an Arab country; such partition would be only over their dead bodies. They therefore countered with a worldwide diplomatic campaign to prevent partition. At the same time, they felt an urgent need to build themselves up militarily for the eventuality of armed conflict. Regarding the Jewish community, the fact of the matter was that Jewish settlements early on, ever since the onset of the British mandate over Palestine, began to prepare their youth for possible, perhaps inevitable, military confrontation with the Arabs. As events began to lead toward World War II, a Jewish brigade was set up within the British army. One of its primary motives was to create a cadre of Jewish individuals experienced in the affairs of warfare that would become a leadership nucleus in the likely armed conflict with the Arabs. One of these individuals was Moshe Dayan. He eventually became Chief of Staff of the Military, and then followed it by becoming Minister of Defense of the nascent state of Israel. Keen Palestinian observers became quite aware of the disparity in the military preparedness between the two sides.

It so happened that our home at #7, Yona Street was adjacent to a Jewish school. In fact, the northern boundary of our house abutted the southern boundary of the schoolyard. Consequently, we could readily see across to the schoolyard students, mixed-gender, playing at times and at other times exercising in physical education type of activity. My father, with his Ottoman military background, would remark at every opportune moment to us at home, and to his select friends in Wadi-Ennisnas, that the exercises were no mere physical fitness athletic exercises, but in fact, were military training exercises.

By the turn of the year 1947, it was becoming abundantly clear to the Palestinian leadership throughout the country that they must organize and must act to defend themselves. Because of the British crackdown on Arabs' possession of firearms, the organizational effort had to have a civilian semblance. The Boy Scouts and Sport Clubs were two natural civic institutions in which the process of preparation began to take place. Behind the scenes, decisions were made to set up a grassroots communal National Guard from within, and a Palestine/Arab Liberation Army, which would have to be from without, as long as the British were still in power. There is no doubt in my mind that the British repressive measures toward the Palestinians, as the Palestinians endeavored to arm themselves, delayed the initiation of the process and inhibited greatly its evolution on a massive scale and to full fruition. On the outside, the failure of the Arab League countries to appreciate the depth and utmost urgency of the threat, and to coordinate with local Palestinian leaderships' plans of defense, was another important factor. Younes Ennaffaa was a prominent member in the Haifa National Guard Command, entrusted with the defense of the city. I recall Younes' visits to Ahmad El-Akhal and Hasan Shublaq, and their exchanges on matters that must have been of major gravity, which had to be very subdued, constrained, and clandestine. Hasan's travels all over Palestine and out into Syria increased quite a bit, car troubles notwithstanding. There was implicit assumption that Hasan was active in prospecting for arms sources for the National Guard, and in facilitating channels for procuring them and moving them around without British or Zionist knowledge and interception. If true, it must have been a very dangerous undertaking. The prevailing mood was: Don't discuss questions; mum is the answer.

The British continued its repressive policies against the Palestinians well into 1947. One time, perhaps in September of 1947, the British surrounded Wadi-Ennisnas and had their military search it for arms. In almost a flash, a few soldiers set up positions across the street from the laundry, one of them lying flat on his stomach and manning a machine-gun aimed at the entrance of the laundry with his finger on the trigger. I recall the event vividly as I happened to be standing by the laundry entrance, first in the firing line!

Unable or unwilling to reconcile Palestinian claims and Zionist counterclaims, the British, in October of 1947, resigned to turn the matter to the United Nations. It was also in anticipation of terminating the mandate, which the British had announced in early 1948, would occur on May 14, 1948. Shortly after the British turned the Palestine conflict over to the UN, Palestinians began to feel an ease-up of the British crackdown on arming themselves. Signs of the National Guard surfaced, and youth training activities began to be conducted. A blue-eyed blonde Bosnian/Turkish officer suddenly appeared in Wadi-Ennisnas. He wore civilian clothes and a red fez. He was a very smiley, friendly and dynamic person. His mission was to conduct in-a-hurry military training for the youth of the neighborhood and help in the setting up of the defense of Wadi-Ennisnas. The training was very modest; I managed, despite my young age of about twelve years, to sneak into some of the sessions. Typically, the attendees did not exceed two dozen. Within a month, on November 29, 1947, the General Assembly of the United Nations passed a resolution recommending the partition of Palestine. While the Jewish communities rejoiced, the Palestinians, in particular, and the Arabs, in general, went into a state of frenzied shock, denial, and rejection.

A few weeks before the UN resolution, Grandfather Issa was about his usual business getting up very early in the morning to go to Haifa's downtown fresh produce wholesale market. While loading his purchase of the day to bring back to his home stand, he was hit by a car and was badly bruised. He was placed in bed at his home and given simple medical inspection and family care. Within a week of the accident, he went into a coma and died several hours later. He passed away about midday in the large living room of his home, where I had spent many happy hours visiting and playing. I was fortunate to be by his bedside during his last couple of hours, as he slipped away.

With the UN vote for partition, all hell broke loose. The government school suspended classes indefinitely. All entrances to Wadi-Ennisnas were barricaded and manned by armed National Guard. Similar things were happening in other areas of Haifa, perhaps not as speedily, since Wadi-Ennisnas was downhill from the Jewish Hadar. Even though I lived at our Carmel Station home at the time, I did not get assimilated into the culture of that section of town, but continued to feel a strong sense of belonging to the Hadar/ Wadi-Ennisnas area.

My family's comings and goings between our home at Carmel Station and the laundry in Wadi-Ennisnas were no longer safe; brother Hamadi contracted a private car to provide family members with shuttle service between home and the laundry.

Younes Ennaffaa oversaw the provision of arms for the National Guard. The arms were basically World War II type rifles with munitions and hand grenades. Very rarely, I would see a mortar canon. Civilians were urged to arm up to defend themselves and their homes. Families had to purchase their own armament. Arm peddlers began to show up, but arms were sold at exorbitant prices. The family agonized over the question of buying any firearms. My mother loathed the mere idea. Finally, and with coaxing from the son-in-law, Khalil, the family bought a French type of pistol that had a fairly long muzzle with several rounds of bullets. Each round had nine bullets. The money for the purchase was about one months' income of our entire household. Since none of us boys (Yousef, Hamadi, Fouad and me) had any experience with firearms, and since my father was too old for the task, it fell to Khalil to be in charge of the gun, and therefore, the defense of the family. He did not seem to mind.

Across the street from the Hassoun laundry, there resided what seemed to me at the time to be an elderly couple with their three children; Hajj Yousef El-Yacoub (Arabic for Jacob) and his wife Zaynab, Mustapha (oldest), As'ad (middle), and Khayriyye (youngest). Hajj Yousef was highly regarded for his piety and charitableness. He was a member of the Quranic study group that included Grandfather Issa and Uncle Mahmoud. He and his wife were very education minded and paid considerable attention to their children's upbringing. His son Mustapha had graduated from the prestigious private Saint Luke's High School in Haifa. He then attended the Gerard's American Institute in Sidon, Lebanon, where he completed a program in business administration and commerce in 1943. He went on to manage his father's business thereafter. As'ad also graduated from Saint Luke's High School in 1945 and was enrolled at the American University of Beirut in the civil engineering program. Khayriyye received elementary education through the seventh grade in the private Siba'i girls' school. She continued briefly with a home economics institute nearby, before she settled at home to help her mother with domestic work.

Hajj Yousef was a very prosperous landlord and a grain merchant. His land was in Sarafand, near Etteery, where he had originally hailed from. His grain business was in a store on Kings' Street, in the downtown of Haifa. The Palestine National Bus Company was located nearby. Across the sidewalk from his store, buses lined up to load passengers to different towns within the country, and some out into Lebanon and Syria as well. On December 5, 1947, sometime in mid-afternoon, Mustapha, while inside the grain store, heard a big commotion by the bus stop. He walked towards the door of the store to check out what seemed to be the matter. At that very moment, a big explosion was heard. The explosion was caused by a bomb in the guise of an oil can—perhaps olive oil can—that was placed hurriedly by a fellow who entered the middle bus (in a string of three buses) from the back and exited it from the front. The bus was loading passengers to Sidon, Lebanon. One of the passengers became suspicious of the can of oil and hollered at the other passengers to evacuate the bus, which led to a big commotion that just preceded the explosion. Mustapha and many others near the buses lay injured and bleeding on the ground with varying wounds. Mustapha, with the other casualties, was rushed to the Haifa Government Hospital. Within a couple of hours, Mustapha was dead, his body delivered to his parents' home at about eight o'clock in the evening. As'ad, in his junior year at the American University of Beirut, was called that same day and told to drop everything and come home right away for his father was quite ill. He was not told of the truth as to what actually had happened. At the time of the call, he was in fact preparing for an upcoming examination. The next morning the whole neighborhood of Wadi-Ennisnas was in a state of shock and trying to do whatever could be done to comfort and rally around the family. I instinctively went into the living room of the house, among others, where the body was laid. The body was wrapped in a white cloth that was heavily stained with blood. The scene I saw then has lingered in my mind and will probably continue to do so till my dying day. The burial was held back until As'ad arrived in the afternoon for a farewell look. As previously noted, burial is to be carried out on the same day of death, if possible. The normal Islamic ritual of washing the body before burial does not apply in the case of violent death as Mustapha's.

Several others perished in that explosion and many were injured; yet, others, amazingly, survived unscathed as well.[44]

Further into December, military encounters and engagements with the nearby Jewish communities occurred with increasing frequency. Particularly at night, it became common to exchange fire with the Jewish armed groups around the perimeter. Arab and Jewish armed men would exchange fire by a variety of means and launch so-called commando raids.[45] Small arms possessed by civilians were no longer associated with great fear from the British; particularly well within the barricaded areas. I recall one time around this period that I was inside Ahmad's grocery store when the store was attended by his grandson. Ahmad was briefly away. It was his practice to entrust the store to this capable grandson. The grandson and I were friendly schoolmates. Occasionally, I would carry out an errand for him were the need to arise. As we chatted while he organized things in the store, he inadvertently opened a drawer, out of the many around. In that drawer lay a revolver, presumably loaded. We exchanged quick glances, and without words, decided to leave the gun alone and close the drawer.

On another occasion, some of the armed men that watched the perimeter of Wadi-Ennisnas had abducted, at the point of a gun, an unarmed Jewish man, wearing a seemingly British army uniform, just outside the west side of Wadi-Ennisnas. They brought him over to Ahmad El-Akhal, at the grocery store, to determine what should be done with him. The abductors alleged that the abducted was checking out the defenses of the area. The fellow was at least about thirty-five-years old and looked terrified; one gun was pointed to his head. Ahmad looked him over and tried to ask him questions. The fellow showed no signs of understanding Arabic or the questions. Some hotheads argued for his execution on the spot. Fortunately, the cool heads,

---

44 I am very grateful to Khayriyye, sister of Mustapha, who generously shared details of the tragedy with me while I was preparing the above narrative (in the spring of 1999). Khayriyye became my aunt, when she and Uncle Amin got married in Lebanon in March 1955. Uncle Amin is my father's youngest half brother (from Labieba and Grandfather Muhammad), and full brother of Tawfiq and Fahd, cited earlier in the text. Aunt Khayrriyye died in July 2003; Uncle Amin preceded her by five years.

45 For more details Cf. WK ibid. Chronology, p.315ff.

with Ahmad in the lead, decided that he should be blindfolded, taken out of Wadi-Ennisnas towards the Hadar, and be let go![46]

Younes Ennaffaa, now in the top Command of Haifa's National Guard, continually visited Wadi-Ennisnas to check on how things were getting along. Hasan Shublaq also kept a heavy schedule of activities crisscrossing the country in his ancient Ford T Type model car. The southeastern side of Wadi-Ennisnas had a key inlet on a high ground that led downhill into the heart of the neighborhood. It was heavily barricaded. Because of its strategic importance, Younes assigned his nephew, Khalil, in charge of its defense. After about two weeks in charge of the defense of this inlet, Khalil was killed defending it against a late night Jewish incursion. Younes had no children of his own. Khalil was very close to, and especially beloved by, Uncle Younes. Khalil had been a goalkeeper of the Islamic soccer club's junior team. On occasions, he would, as he very much aspired to, play as goalkeeper on the first class team. I, too, had developed affection for Khalil as I watched him guard the goal of his soccer team, game after game, bravely and gracefully.

Late into 1947, the Bosnian/Turkish officer, with two of his newly-trained young men, embarked on a commando raid of some Jewish installations in the Bayt-Galiem area. The mission was to clandestinely plant some timed explosives in a key position to blow up some installations. Having placed the explosives as planned, and having returned to their escape car, the driver, in the excitement of the moment, flooded the carburetor and the car stalled; thereupon, they were discovered and came under heavy fire, wherein they all met their death. The "blow up" did not take place; the mission ended in disaster.

As January of 1948 came around, many families began to think in terms of leaving the country for safer ground, typically to the nearby Arab neighboring countries of Egypt, Trans-Jordan, Lebanon and Syria. Some, in fact, did begin to move, at least partially. These early movers tended to be those who had family connections abroad, or were particularly mobile size-wise and able economically. My father's level of concern was rapidly rising and he began to press my mother and the brothers Hamadi and Yousef to plan for a speedy and

---

46 Whenever I recall this episode, I take a very deep sigh of relief and thank God that this man's life was spared, and I was not a witness to what would have been a very terrible and traumatic act.

orderly exit. My mother and brothers Yousef and Hamadi were hearing out my father but only slowly moving towards any action. For people who have lived all their life in one place and whose roots in it go back generations, and who have rarely been more than fifty miles away from home, which was indeed the case for my mother and the rest of the family, the notion of packing up and leaving into the unknown is not easy to swallow and very hard to act on. As days went by and things got more threatening, I rode less often to Wadi-Ennisnas and pretty much stayed at home in Carmel Station. One time, when I was some fifty meters from our home at Carmel Station, at about two in the afternoon, I saw a man in his forties walking hurriedly into the neighborhood with one arm bleeding, and with the other pointing to where the shot had come from. A sniper had shot him some hundred meters further away, in an open ground. I quickly realized Carmel Station was not that far from Zionist guns after all! To my amazement, I learned much later (fall of 1998) that Khalil Kanafani, brother of Abdellatif Kanafani, was killed during that same period by a similar sniper bullet on the edge of Carmel Station.[47]

The armed clashes between Arabs and Jews kept up unabated. These clashes were particularly thick at night. It happened one night that the sounds of fire exchanges got louder and louder. The word got out that the Jews were attacking Carmel Station. Everybody in our house got out of bed and huddled in the large inner hall of the house away from any windows. We also kept the light to a minimum. Khalil pulled out a military helmet from a cupboard in his room and donned it on his head. It was the first time I had seen or known that he had such a helmet. He further reached for our only gun in the house, carried it in his hand, with rounds of munitions in his coat pocket, and went out of the house to scout what was behind all these firing sounds. As he walked out of the house, my mother cried out to him with a deep worried voice to, "Please be careful!" After about forty-five minutes, the firing sounds began to subside. Shortly thereafter, Khalil came back and we were all happy and relieved to see him. As he was putting his helmet, munitions, and gun away, my mother pleaded with him to be sure to empty the gun of all bullets before he put it away. My mother had been very fearful of loaded guns all through her life.

---

47 AKB, op. cit. p.140

As he was doing this, and as if to assure her that he has indeed taken all the bullets out, he turned the gun away from us towards the floor and pressed the trigger. To the startled family, with the press of the trigger, a big flash and an almost deafening bang ensued. My mother nearly fainted. The bullet made a hole in the tiled floor! The rest of that night passed quietly but with little sleep by most.

A few days following that eventful night, in the latter part of January, the family woke up to the news that armed Jewish bands had attacked the little village of Sa'sa, adjacent to Balad E-Shaykh, just north of Haifa. It was further reported that the attackers had inflicted atrocities on women and children, and that the bodies of the victims had been placed in the morgue of the Haifa Government Hospital for relatives' identification. Uncle Muhammad, my mother's brother, lived with his family (wife and over half a dozen children) in the Sa'sa area. The Government Hospital was nearby. In a fit of panic, my mother put on her clothes and headed to the morgue to check out the bodies. My father followed behind her. Everybody else stayed home. When they came back, it was a relief that none of the victims were of my uncle's family; nevertheless, a frightened look, testament to the horror of having seen mangled and mutilated bodies, covered their faces. My father would never be the same. Immediately after the visit to the morgue, my father began to have nightmares whereat he would jump out of bed and would speak loudly in panic, "The Jews are at the house coming to slaughter my family." I recall one night when he got up out of bed vigorously, walked to the bedroom door, and as if seeing somebody at the door, shouted, "Jew get out!" He then spat as if at the face of where that person was. The family, particularly my mother, tried to calm him down saying, "No, no, Abu Yousef, there is nobody at the door!"

With my father's nightmares, there was no more debating the question, "To leave (Haifa) or not to leave?" As it happened in the first week of February, Uncle Fahd, had already been traveling to Lebanon to prepare for his own family's escape. Uncle Fahd's wife had family ties in Tyre, Lebanon. By the second week of February, Uncle Fahd had already rented a place for his family in Tyre and moved them out there. It was decided that my parents, along with brother Fouad, would go to Tyre and have Uncle Fahd help them locate a place for our entire household. This meant a place for Yousef, his wife and children; Hamadi, his wife and children; my parents; Fouad, Qasim, and me; a total of fifteen persons. My brother-in-law Khalil indicated that he, Haliema, and their two children (a baby girl, Samira, had been born to the couple a few months earlier) would stay only temporarily in Tyre. Should it turn out that their stay was going to be of a longer term, he would move with his family to Damascus, Syria, his original hometown and birthplace. Fouad and my parents left for Tyre on February16, 1948. There they linked up with Uncle Fahd. Within a few days, they rented a place. With a few very basic items, Fouad and my father moved into the newly-rented place. Mother came back to Haifa to aid in the process of moving the entire family and in the smooth closing of the laundry business. My mother, Yousef and Hamadi decided that the rest of the family would be sent right away to Tyre and that they would stay behind in Haifa till the closing down of the laundry business. It was further decided that a truckload of furniture would accompany the family to Tyre. On about February 23, brother-in-law Nayef (Zahiyye's husband) came in the morning with a truck to the house at Carmel Station. The truck box was about twice as large as the box of a typical pick-up size truck. The truck was loaded with basic furniture only, such as rollaway mattresses, blankets, clothes, pots and pans. Heavy and big pieces of furniture, like cabinets, bed frames, springs, and large tables were not loaded. Secondary things such as books, toys, the phonograph and records, and the precious short-wave radio were also left behind. My school-books and my life savings of a half Palestinian Ginayh, enfolded as a paper note in my World Atlas, were also left behind. A Ginayh, a hundred piasters, was equal in value at the time to about one British pound sterling. Yousef's wife, Nadiema, and her three children; Hamadi's wife, Khayriyye, and her three children; nephew Qasim, and me were all packed (ten of us plus the hired driver) in a six-passenger car (Hudson/Studebaker 1947 model) and rode off to Tyre. Tyre is located about eighty kilometers up the coast north of Haifa, but the ride took well over two hours on a narrow two lane road with two stops at the border crossings. Khalil, Haliema and their two children decided to stay behind a little longer. The general sense about the move was that we would stay in Tyre until things cooled off in a matter of weeks, or at most, a few months.

Brother Fouad and my father met us in Tyre. Nayef and the truck arrived the same day, somewhat later. Till nightfall, we all participated in unloading the truck and settling down into the new dwelling! Nayef stayed with us for a couple of days in order to find a place to soon move his family to as well.

CHAPTER 6

FROM MAGNANIMOUS PEOPLE TO REFUGEES

The rented place occupied two-thirds of a villa slightly off the main street leading into Tyre from the east. It was less than a hundred meters from the beach. The owner of the villa was trying to build a two-story place for his family. The second story was barely started when he ran out of money. He therefore partitioned the main floor between his family and us. Our portion had three bedrooms, a sizable hallway and a front verandah facing the sea. His family's portion had two bedrooms with a hallway facing citrus orchards belonging to a well-to-do landlord neighbor. There was a small kitchen and a bathroom attached to each portion. From a distance, the place looked very pleasant, even luxurious. However, when you got inside of it, you realized that it had some serious problems. For one thing, it had no plumbing, running water, or electricity. Furthermore, as you looked at the windows, you realized that the wooden shutters were in place but the glass windows were not installed. When inquired about, we were told that the installation had been delayed because of lack of funds, but as soon as money became available, the glass windows would be first to be installed. When would that actually happen? Nobody even ventured to guess. As to the water, there was a well adjacent to the west side of the house where water could be drawn. Nobody knew or cared to inquire about the quality of this well water. It happened that the well was in the proximity (a mere few meters away) of the bathroom where human waste went down a hole that had no outlet, no septic tank. The collected waste was supposed to biodegrade naturally. In fact, it did not, because the inflow was considerable whereas the natural biodegradation was quite slow. There was no practice or effort of any kind at emptying, treating or flushing out the sewage. The soil was quite sandy, and the possibility of wastewater seepage to the well was very real.

Our first night was quite an experience. We rolled out the mattresses on the floors of the three bedrooms and covered ourselves as best as we could. The howling wind through the wooden shutters kept us awake a good deal of the night. For the next two weeks, howling wind and at times, heavy rain, came into the house via the shutters. Brother Fouad, barely seventeen-years-old, was in charge of the household, a total of twelve persons. He was the sole money dispenser; most importantly, he went daily to the market place, bought groceries and carried them home to the new abode for Nadiema and Khayriyye to prepare. The food was pretty much what we had in Haifa, at least early on, with some restraint on the amounts, a mild form of rationing.[48] The meals were served on a cloth-sheet on the floor. Often, we ate collectively from a central dish or pan. Flat bread and spoons were the only utensils. For the most part, I did not venture far out of the house, since the town was still new to me. My father increasingly seemed not himself and worried about the safe arrival of my mother and my other two brothers. Finally, my mother, Hamadi, and Yousef made it safely to Tyre in the first week of March. When questioned how things went for them as they planned their exit, Hamadi told unhappily of the few items of clothing that were never picked up by their proprietors. These items had to be left hanging on clothes bars in the laundry shop; their owners may have been killed or somehow disappeared. Within a few days of their arrival, sister Haliema and her husband, Khalil, showed up at our new doorstep with the two daughters. With the new arrivals, all nineteen of us packed into the new place. When night came, the rolled out mattresses that we slept on covered a large portion of the entire house floor. In the morning, the mattresses were rolled up and stacked away in different corners of the dwelling. Before too long, like a week or so, Khalil saw that it was time to move on to Damascus with his family.

On the eastern outskirts of Tyre, there was an abandoned refugee camp called el-Buss, about a square kilometer in area. It was originally set up of concrete single-room dwellings (roughly 12 ft. x 12 ft.) to house World War I Armenian refugees. After the end of World War I, the Armenians managed to move out. The camp had fallen into great disrepair. The city of Tyre, feeling the pressure on its houses from Palestinian escapees, and out of a sense of

---

48 As our refugee existence lingered on, the rationing became more stringent and the food gravitated towards more bread, rice and potatoes with some vegetable stews and/or hot dishes. Fortunately, Lebanon like Palestine is blessed with abundance of vegetables. Hot dishes tended to have lamb meat, but in small portions. Chicken was scarcely eaten, typically only on special, festive occasions, when a live chicken would be purchased.

kinship with Palestinians needing refuge, availed the camp to Palestinians to move into at no cost. The city availed these dwellings on a first-come first-served basis, provided the new occupants assumed full responsibility for all needed cleanup and repairs; and there was a lot to be done. Virtually all the units had neither windows nor doors. There were only holes in the walls, one window hole and a door hole to a unit. Each unit had a nearby outhouse that had not been used for over twenty years; here again a great deal of effort was needed to reclaim it. The camp had neither plumbing nor electricity. Water had to be procured from one of a few wells within the camp. Over the years, the campground had also accumulated a lot of garbage and junk.

People whose means would allow it, steered away from the el-Buss Camp. The reality was, however, that many did not have the means; it got worse in time. My brother-in-law, Nayef, settled on a unit at the camp and moved his family (sister Zahiyye with three girls and three boys at the time) in within days following his unloading our luggage into Tyre. Nayef himself worked hard at fixing up the place. He also hired a carpenter to put up a door and a glass window with outside wooden shutters.

The el-Buss Camp was only a few hundred meters from our newly-rented home. Visiting sister Zahiyye and her family at the camp became a great pastime for me. I would meet many people there and hear their circumstances of escape and travail. The spectrum of people was great—from farmers, to teachers, to various healthcare workers from nurses to medical doctors.

Conversely, on their way to downtown Tyre, Zahiyye or Nayef, and/or their children, would stop by to visit. Usually, the visiting would be in the verandah facing the sea. Lemonade, tea or coffee would be readily served and we would talk ad infinitum about the Nakba and the new predicaments.

Mother and brothers Yousef and Hamadi, in particular, had assumed that the move from Haifa to Tyre would completely remove the basis of my father's fear of bloodshed and violent death. Alas, my father's nightmares persisted and his fear of being massacred with his family became a central challenge. All of us tried to reason with my father that we were now in Lebanon, that there were no Jews in the Tyre area, and that by leaving Haifa all these threats were left behind, but to no avail; my father was mentally no longer in control. The problem got more troublesome when we became unable to contain it within the confines of our house. My father began to approach strangers on the street to try to tell them what the Jews were out to do. By the end of March, it was no longer possible to leave my father unattended. There were no mental health facilities of any kind in all of southern Lebanon. However, on the eastern hills outside of Beirut (some 50 miles from Tyre), there was a major, national hospital for the mentally ill, called Assfouriyya. The family was able to get him admitted with the expenses assumed by the International Red Cross. His admission to Assfouriyya, accompanied by Mother, Yousef, and Hamadi, was on about the second of April 1948. Within a few days thereafter, my mother, with brother Yousef, went to further check up on how he was doing. They found him lying in bed unable to get up or move around, breathing heavily and with bodily bruises, particularly to his chest. When they inquired as to what had happened, they learned that one of the attendants, while trying to force my father to be restrained in bed overnight, had met with strong resistance from my father and that, in the process of trying to subdue him, the attendant resorted to raw force. When my mother and Yousef came back home, my mother was extremely distraught. She kept murmuring that Abu Yousef's condition did not look hopeful, and that he was breathing with a great deal of difficulty. My mother mentioned sometime later that he confided to her on that day that he may not last very long because of the pain he was experiencing in his chest. Within a day or two from their visit, word came to us in Tyre that Father had passed away during the night, and that family members should come to get his body. He died April 8, 1948.[49]

My mother, accompanied by brothers Yousef and Fouad and her brother, Uncle Mahmoud, rented a "taxi-service" car that drove them to the Assfouriyya, whereupon they loaded the body and headed back to Tyre, the same day. The body was kept cold with bags of ice. Brother Fouad and Uncle Mahmoud could not return with the body as the car was too crowded for that. Instead, the two returned to Tyre by bus. Mother, Yousef, and Father's body were met at home by a large number of mourners, relatives and friends. The body-party arrived too late for burial the same day, per Islamic law. Islamic rites were

---

49 I have no recollection of anybody saying what the cause of death was. As I reflected on the events of the time, years later, I had come to the view that it was most likely a punctured lung.

administered the next day, followed by the burial. I watched my father's body being washed and wrapped in white linen in preparation for burial. I walked in his funeral to the main Sunni Mosque of Tyre, a distance of about a mile, where the prayer of the dead was performed for him, and saw his body lowered into the ground of the mosque's yard cemetery. He was about fifty-eight years old. The question of holding the attendant responsible and the hospital to court was never raised or entertained. The family was too preoccupied with major survival issues of the living, and probably did not believe any meaningful redress would be forthcoming.

By the time of my father's death, several members of the extended family on both sides of my parents (Hassouns, Aswads) had already moved out of Haifa to Tyre. For example, Uncle Mahmoud had just moved his family into one unit of el-Buss Camp, a few units away from where sister Zahiyye's family had moved. Uncle Tawfiq rented an apartment for his family a short walk from our place. As a result, many of our relatives were in attendance at the funeral and provided considerable comfort to the household. Uncle Tawfiq and his wife, Aunt Ramziyye, visited the family almost daily for years thereafter.

The news from Palestine was a major daily preoccupation of the Palestinian community in Tyre. We sought it out from travelers, newspapers, and radios. With electricity absent in most of our new homes, radio news had to be sought out in public places, typically coffee houses with electric power. The news would then be passed from mouth to mouth, and house to house, across the community. It was not uncommon to see a sizable gathering of people around a radio, in a coffeehouse, when a newscast was on. While we yearned for good news, of successful military feats, the news was generally not very encouraging. This was the case despite the fact that Arab news sources tried hard to put a positive spin on their reports. On the day of my father's burial, the news was particularly distressing when we learned of the death of Abdel-Qadir Al-Husseini in the battle of Al-Qastal (briefly cited earlier). Al-Qastal was a Palestinian Arab village, strategically located about five miles west of Jerusalem controlling a supply road, the Jaffa-Jerusalem road, to the Jewish community in Jerusalem. The Jewish Haganah (later to become the Israeli army) initially captured the village. It was regained by a counter Palestinian attack led by Abdel-Qadir, during which he was killed. His death sent shock waves through the rank and file of the fighting force resulting in reduced battle coherence and alertness, which very likely contributed to the subsequent loss of the village to the Haganah. I recall hearing a vivid and very moving description of the battle broadcast by our friend, Raji Sahyoun, on Radio Palestine. About the same time followed the news of atrocities committed by the Irgun and the Stern Gang against the Palestinian population of the village of Deir Yassin, on the western outskirts of Jerusalem, nearby to Al-Qastal.

The situation in Palestine continued to deteriorate and more families from Haifa showed up in Tyre looking for places to stay. Others moved on farther north to Sidon and Beirut. Hardly anybody knew how long this was going to last.

On April 21, the Haganah forces launched a general attack on all of Arab-Haifa. According to eyewitnesses traveling through Tyre, the British seemed to step aside or even facilitate the way for the Haganah. The Haganah outnumbered and outgunned the Palestinian National Guard. Attempts at sending reinforcements and fighters to assist the city, for example, the National Guard from nearby towns, particularly Etteery, were blocked by the British. The Palestinian National Guard was overwhelmed and Haifa fell on April 22, 1948. With the fall of Haifa, the bulk of the remaining civilian Arab population, numbering in the tens of thousands, fled in panic and despair to safer areas. Eyewitnesses recounted how the British motioned the fleeing civilians to the main coastal highway north, toward the Lebanese border, as well as to the Haifa harbor, where they could embark on boats and primarily head up north, mainly to the Tyre harbor; some sailed further north, to Sidon.[50]

The influx of Palestinians into Tyre by land and by sea was far more than the city, with its very limited means, could manage. The Tyre community, ordinary Lebanese and the recently arrived Palestinians, nevertheless, rallied to deal with this influx as best as they could. Schools, mosques, and churches mobilized to provide for the refugees. Uppermost was the need to provide a place for them to sleep after which, it was to provide subsistence food. I found myself in the midst of those meeting them at the Tyre harbor to help with

---

50 More detailed accounts of some of the specifics of the above three paragraphs may be found in WK, op. cit. p.305ff. See also the "Battle of Haifa (1948)" http://en.wikipedia.org/wiki/Battle_of_Haifa_(1948).

whatever belongings they had and to find their way to the Jaffariyya College, a private Shi'a high school, grade one through twelve. The college dining hall was converted into a dormitory. To provide a semblance of privacy, curtains and bedspreads were used to compartmentalize it. As individual families arrived at the hall, they were assigned a quarter each, typically ten-feet by ten-feet. The floor of the dining hall was tiled and cold; thus, before anybody could sleep, appropriate covering had to be found. Once settled, food was distributed, mostly bread, cheese, olives and preserves. The effort was designed to give the refugees a breathing space for a few days as they pondered their next move. As I was shuttling refugee families from the harbor to the college, I glanced in the distance through the crowds and saw Younes Enneffaa disembarking. Right away any doubts I may have had about the severity of the situation in Haifa disappeared. I could not bring myself to run to greet him. I instinctively knew it was not the time. It was a most grievous moment. He was hurriedly whisked off and driven north to Sidon. That was the last time I saw him.

It was not uncommon both in Palestine and Lebanon to refer to a high school as "college," people understood the connotation. The only other school to Jaffariyya in Tyre was the public government school. It had a total of six grades. The Jaffariyya College was the only full high school in the entire south of Lebanon, south of Sidon, a population of at least half a million. It had a boarding facility for out of town students. The boarding students were about a third of the total student population. The total student population was about four hundred. Tyre's total population was about fifteen thousand. Typically, the lucky few and rather privileged students enrolled at the Jaffariyya College, particularly for education beyond the sixth grade. The college was founded and managed by the Sharafeddine family, a family deeply rooted in Tyre. The family claimed lineage to the family of the Prophet Muhammad, was very socially conscious, and worked very hard to promote the welfare of the "South" in many fields, particularly education. Many of the family members were highly steeped in the theology of Shiism. They had strong ties with people and institutions in the cities of Najaf and Karbala, in southern Iraq; two major centers of World Shiism. The family head at the time, also the head of the college, was Imam Hussein Sharafeddine. When the Imam would happen to walk a street of Tyre, persons of all walks of life and ages would rush to kiss his hand and receive his blessing. While Shiites were very small in number in Haifa and Palestine, they were the overwhelming majority in South Lebanon.

Amid the influx of refugees into Tyre showing up at the doorsteps of our new abode, was sister Munawwar with her husband, Muhammad, a few months old child, and the entire household of her in-laws: parents, brothers, and sisters of Muhammad; nine in number. In addition to my sister, her husband, and the child, we took in four more. The other five found a place elsewhere in downtown Tyre, at an uncle of Muhammad, who managed to have come to Tyre with his family two weeks earlier. At sleeping time, for the few nights they stayed with us, the covering of the house floor by sleeping bodies was so complete that it spilled over even to the outside verandah.

The fall of Haifa was followed in a matter of days by the fall of other neighboring towns and communities. Among these were Etteery and Balad-e-Shaykh. Aunt Maryam, her husband, Awad, and their entire household of one unmarried younger son, three married sons and a married daughter, their spouses, and their children, totaling about fifteen, turned up in Tyre. Uncle Muhammad Aswad (mother's brother) with his household, about ten, turned up as well. Tents were set up from the edge of Tyre south of el-Buss along the coast to what became known later as the Rashidiyye Camp. Some refugees set up tents in the nearby hills east of town. Lebanon asked for help from the Red Cross and the Syrian Government. The Red Cross began to send immediate relief in terms of tents, blankets, and basic staples, such as flour, sugar, Crisco oil, beans; and the like. Syria opened its doors and activated a formerly dormant train shuttle, on an already existing track, to move refugees from the Tyre area to various places in Syria, most notably Aleppo and Damascus, its two largest cities. Most of the refugees got on the train and ended up in Syria; among these were sister Munawwar, her husband and child, and her in-laws, and Uncle Muhammad (Aswad) and his household. Aunt Maryam and her household stuck it out in Tyre. The very close bond between Aunt Maryam and my mother, and our family's presence in Tyre, had a great deal to do with their decision to stay.

As the dust of the exodus began to settle, my sister-in-law Nadiema learned from an eyewitness that her oldest brother, Fadhel Abu Hawwash, had been killed in the battle of Haifa; he was about twenty years old at the time. The family never got the body. Nobody knew what became of it. His mother mourned his loss for as long as I knew her.

More refugees kept coming from south of the border, as more towns fell to the Zionist onslaught, including the city of Acre, halfway along the coast between Haifa and Tyre. Acre fell about the middle of May, the official date for the end of the British mandate over Palestine. About this time, I happened to be in Tyre's Sunni Mosque cemetery yard visiting my father's grave when a great commotion was taking place at the entrance to the yard. As I walked over to find out what was happening, I saw several open, wooden coffin-like boxes with badly mangled bodies of young men, children, and women. From their attire, they appeared to be rural Palestinians. I was told they had been killed on the road between Acre and the Lebanese border, as they were escaping the fighting. Graves were hurriedly dug up and the bodies unceremoniously buried.

CHAPTER 7

COPING WITH THE NEW STATUS

As our refugee status began to take deeper and stronger roots and the prospects for returning to our homes in the near future got dimmer, Mother and my brothers began to contemplate in earnest what might be the next move. We were rapidly spending the family's savings. The savings were not much because the bulk of it had already been spent on purchasing our second home at Carmel Station, two years earlier. The newly-instituted Red Cross ration for refugees hardly provided basic subsistence. While it included flour, sugar, beans, and Crisco oil, it provided for no clothes, meat, rent, transportation, etc. Brother Hamadi was first to see that we had to have, beside the ration, some means of earning money to meet our other expenses. Mother supported his initiative for a new laundry business. At first, sometime in June, he rented a small shop, only eight by ten feet, to launch a mini-laundry business. Two people could barely fit inside the space at the same time. It was adjacent to a major, rather rowdy, coffeehouse in the main square of downtown. The location discouraged normal laundry customers from frequenting it; nevertheless, some business activity did take place that brought in some income. The little laundering it brought in, washing and pressing, was readily done by Mother and Yousef.

A couple of months after the mini-laundry launch, it became abundantly clear that it was inadequate, both in size and location. Hamadi began to look in earnest for an alternative. Luckily, he found an already existing laundry business for sale. It was located on a regular downtown business street. He readily negotiated an affordable price with the seller. It quickly became to us the "Tyre Hassoun Brothers Laundry." The shop housing it was still very modest, about twelve by fifteen feet, and its location was definitely no Wadi-Ennisnas! But as refugees, we all knew that we could not be too choosy. We felt that it was fine for the time being, until the situation in Palestine somehow cleared up! The entire pressing was done in the shop, while the washing was done back at the rented house. Actually, the washing was done on the side of the house beneath an external stairway that led up to the unfinished second floor of the rented house. The landlord did not seem to object. Fouad became a presser in the shop; Yousef and my mother were in charge of washing and Hamadi was the manager and public relations man. Yousef often was done with washing by noon, so he would go to the shop in the afternoon to help Fouad with the pressing, or to allow Fouad time off for his athletic pursuits. There were also times, when business would be slow, and Yousef would go to a downtown coffeehouse to socialize and play cards with acquaintances and friends; this was a pastime that he had started earlier, shortly after the move to Tyre but which steadily grew on him with time, to the displeasure of Hamadi and Mother. Occasionally, nephew Qasim and I would sit beside Yousef and watch his card game. Invariably, Yousef would buy each of us a cold soft drink. Yousef had been, ever since I can recall, very generous to a fault with whomever he came in contact. The family teasingly would say in reference to him, "That which was in his pocket was not his, but his friends." Yousef often cited a familiar Arabic idiom in defense; freely translated, it means, "Spend that which is in your pocket. It will come back to you in a bucket!" There is a hidden connotation in this to the effect that if you are generously good to others, God will recompense you amply.

From the time we moved into Tyre until midsummer, Fouad and I had a lot of time to make friends and play. Fouad's skills as a soccer player were noticed fairly early. There were two major soccer clubs in Tyre that competed fiercely for being number one. They were of far lesser caliber than the Haifa teams, so much so that Fouad stood out as he practiced with either of the two major teams, whereas, in Haifa, he did not qualify for first rank teams although he was considered to have the right stuff to qualify in due course. Both clubs vied for him to be on their team. He joined one of them, the Cyclone (Zowba'a, in Arabic) Club. The other club's name was the Solidarity (Tadhamun, in Arabic) Club. When the Cyclone and the Solidarity teams were to have a match, half the town went out to see the game. Fouad's soccer playing gave the family a lot of visibility.

Among those who found refuge in Tyre was the Palestinian soccer hero, Jabra Ezzarqa. Jabra, the greatest right forward Haifa and Palestine's soccer had known, seemed to eschew the crowds and keep a very low profile. Like most Palestinians, I think, he was in a daze as to what had just befallen his people. He showed no interest in interacting with any of the soccer clubs in town. I saw him by the beach one time with a group of fishermen, wearing the typical rudimentary fishing clothes, drawing on a large fishing net for the catch of the day. Net fishing was done as of old, where fishermen would go out to sea before dawn, cast out their wide net, and then slowly draw it back out onto the beach. It was very clear to me that he was not doing it for sport, but to eke subsistence like so many of his compatriots. Months later, he moved north to Beirut, then to Amman, Jordan, where he briefly played on first rank teams before he wound up on the Syrian Army's Police team.[51]

Fouad's enthusiastic soccer involvement enabled us to meet and befriend the most educated and prosperous youth of Tyre. When he joined the Cyclone Club, I simply tagged along. Everybody in the club assumed me to be a junior member. In fact, the Cyclone Club did have a junior soccer team (class two), on which I did play. The Cyclone Club, we discovered after the fact, was an off-shoot of the Syrian Social Nationalist Party (SSNP), a political party that fervently championed the geographic, economic, and cultural oneness of the peoples of Syria, Lebanon, Palestine, Jordan, and maybe Iraq, which constituted the Syrian Nation, over what is termed Greater Syria. The Solidarity Club did not seem to have a formal political affiliation although many of its members developed, years later, Arab nationalistic leanings. The "cyclone," in the shape of a swirling eye of a storm, was the SSNP's emblem. It signified the party's spirit to bring about a rapid and radical change of the prevalent medieval stagnation hanging over Greater Syria.

The head of the SSNP was Antun Sa'adeh. He was a native of the Lebanese mountain town of Dhur Eshshweir. Antun Sa'adeh was a well-traveled prolific writer and social philosopher. He had spent many years of his life as a political journalist in South America, particularly Brazil. The party demanded rigorous discipline of its members and had laid out a detailed program and agenda for action. Simply put, it aimed at building a modern dynamic Greater Syria, which would enable its people to take their rightful and dignified place among the other peoples of the world.

Fouad and I were handed party literature. Fouad's focus, however, was primarily soccer. We learned the fundamentals of party teachings and goals but

---

51 AKB, op. cit. p.111

did not participate in political activities, nor were we pressured to participate in any. Fouad was well liked by party members and admired for his performance on the soccer field. While I resonated a great deal with the goals of the party and its teachings, and liked the individual members, my inner sense desired to see more invocation of Arabism in their teachings, and a program of inclusion vis-à-vis Egypt, the Arabian Peninsula, and Arab North Africa. In hindsight, I seem to have had, at a very early age, more Arab nationalistic tendencies. Be this as it may, I associated well with the Syrian Nationalists. Perhaps instinctively and simplistically, I felt that the two points of view were at least reconcilable, if not compatible, in the sense that the Syrian Nationalists might be viewed as a subgroup of the larger Arab Nationalists' group. I never felt the differences were grounds for not cooperating or not socializing with them.

One weekend, the party was having a major meeting of its southern flank in Tyre. Antun Sa'aadeh was to make an appearance. There was a lot of anticipation and excitement. Activist members encouraged Fouad and me to come to the meeting and to be sure to greet Ezza'im Antun (as he was referred to by his fervent followers; Ezza'im, in Arabic, signifies leader or boss). We did just that. Mr. Sa'adeh, in his mid-forties, looked very classy and impressive. He was handsomely dressed in a white linen suit. He had a very warm and loving demeanor. Fouad got to shake his hand![52]

The Cyclone Club's soccer team played occasionally against soccer teams in other towns of Lebanon, usually Syrian party teams in those towns. When a match was to take place out of town, the Tyre Club would charter a bus to transport the team and its fans to where the match was to be held. On the bus, we chanted party songs in praise of the Syrian Nation and of Ezza'im Antun. Almost always, we got back home the same day. Everybody brought along his individual gear, including food. My mother was very generous in making sure that Fouad and I were well supplied food-wise. The transportation cost was modest enough as not to be a hardship, prohibiting our participation. As in Haifa, I carried and looked after a good deal of Fouad's gear as well as my own,

---

52 A short year later, July 1949, Antun Sa'adeh met his death before a firing squad in Beirut, charged by the Lebanese Government of Prime Minister Riad Essolh of plotting to overthrow the Government. The SSNP went underground vowing to avenge their leader's death. Two years later, in the summer of 1951, Prime Minister Essolh paid the price with his life; he was assassinated at the Airport of Amman, Jordan.

especially at match time. We got to see many towns of Lebanon, especially the mountain ones, and meet a broad cross section of the Lebanese people.

The club had a housing center near the harbor, downtown. Members of the Cyclone Club had a variety of social activities as well. We played games at the center; cards, dominoes, backgammon, Ping-Pong, etc. Many of the members were also avid swimmers. The members also organized outings in and around the Tyre area. A popular place was about eight miles south of town, called Ras el-Ain, a stone's throw south of the Palestinian Rashidiyye camp-to-be, which was not yet set up at the time. There was a natural spring of fresh water giving rise to a pond, which was conducive to swimming and outdoor playing, and frequented by sightseers. Because of the abundance of water, the land around it was lush green most of the year and very fruitful. On one occasion, mid-summer, a group of us, about half a dozen, including brother Fouad, were having an outdoor picnic lunch near a watermelon field at its prime. We had swum and played all morning and ate with great appetite. As we neared the end of the meal, some were eyeing the melons, and almost in jest, wondering who was going to go pick a melon to finish the meal with? There was a big silence for a brief moment while we all eyed each other. I was surprised by the silence and the absence of volunteers. Impetuously, I got up, said, "I'll do it," and dashed into the field. Fouad hollered, "Ghazi, don't!" It was too late! Within a flash, I was back with a big melon, almost too big for me to carry. I was barely thirteen-years-old and probably the youngest in the bunch. The group members were mostly Fouad's friends. Fouad shook his head, others laughed. The melon was very red, juicy, and sweet. We all helped ourselves. One thought crossed my mind as I was coming back with the melon, "I hope the landlord or the field attendant does not see me and shoot me!" Luckily, nobody did!

Sometime during that summer of 1948, about the same time Hamadi was launching the modest laundry business, it was evident that I had too much idle time. I was not heavily into soccer, and the family finances were rapidly dwindling. Consequently, a thought emerged in the family that perhaps I could be channeled into some useful work. I met the thought with eagerness. It was felt by all concerned, including myself, that the work would keep me out of trouble. I might learn some line of work that could earn me, long-term, an acceptable livelihood. Meanwhile, it would provide me with some pocket money. Thus, with assistance from Fouad, I began to look around for work. Before long, through a Cyclone Club member and a soccer pal of Fouad, Muhsin,[53] I found out that Muhsin's father, Hajj Salman, owned a major grain and other food staples store on Tyre's main street and would have all kinds of things for me to do at his store. Muhsin, a lad about twenty-years-old, was also working for his father at the store. He thought that I could start whenever I was ready, and indicated a wage of half a Lebanese pound (roughly equivalent to 20 cents) a day. He was pretty sure that his father would agree; as indeed the father did. By then, Fouad and I had known Muhsin for a few months and interacted with him in several events, in and outside of Tyre. He was very athletic and of a friendly, obliging disposition. Fouad and I both liked him quite well so we took the offer back to my mother and my two other brothers. The family essentially said, "Why not?" which gave me the go ahead. The wage was modest, but then maybe in a short time thereafter, I told myself, *it would be raised to three quarters of a pound!*

The new job required that I be at the store by sunrise. Typically, at predawn, farmers from towns around Tyre would, at harvest time, load their camels and donkeys with crops and ride into town by the break of the day to sell them to the downtown merchants. Hajj Salman had his own circle of farmers that brought the goods to his store. He bought goods from these farmers, and then, usually after consolidation, sold them either to local individual consumers, or, wholesale, to merchants in Beirut. The wholesale transactions involved middlemen who showed up at the store with trucks ready to buy the goods, load them, and ship them off to Beirut. Muhsin and I would be first to receive the farmers. We would help unload the goods, weigh them, grade their quality, and enter the information or data into a record book under the name of that particular farmer; usually a pre-existing account. I did a lot of the weighing. I enjoyed it; it made me feel important. Hajj Salman, with records at his desk, negotiated prices and closed deals. He also handled all money exchanges. He further negotiated with prospective buyers who usually showed up a little later. Some of the buyers would negotiate future deals. The crops that I dealt with

---

53   The names in this section are pseudonyms to protect their identity.

most were wheat and barley, however, there were occasional loads of lentils and dried beans. Hajj Salman also dealt with figs and apricots. For the latter, if they were not sold fresh that same day, he would have people come to take them away for drying and packing.

The business was most brisk in the first few hours of the morning. Most of the buying from the farmers would be over by 10:30 am. The attention was then directed at selling the goods to the host of shoppers that had gathered around, most of whom had come from Beirut. Hajj Salman, Muhsin, and I each, brought our own separate lunch bags with us to work. Lunch would be had, usually, on the run. Hajj Salman, from time to time, while all of us were eating, would pass fruits that happened to be around. There was no shortage of dried figs and apricots. Hajj Salman faithfully took time out before lunch to perform the noon prayer. In the early afternoon, our effort focused, for the most part, on weighing and loading the sold merchandise onto buyers' trucks to ship off to the big city. By mid-afternoon, things slackened off and became leisurely. Occasionally, with Hajj Salman's permission, Muhsin and I would be excused to take off for the rest of the day. Typically, we would go, separately or together, to the home of the Cyclone Club socializing and playing games. On days when there was soccer practice or a game, we went to the soccer field. When the weather was right and no soccer was scheduled, we would go swimming instead. For soccer or swimming, we first went home to change clothes. Tyre had several beautiful swimming spots. Muhsin was a very good swimmer. I loved the water, although I was not particularly good at swimming. Muhsin offered to teach me and I, of course, welcomed it. One day, after being at the job a couple of months, the weather seemed ideal for swimming; no soccer was planned that afternoon. As soon as we were done with the work at the store, we went, each to his home, got the swimming gear, and met at a favorite spot where we had swum before. As we were swimming and playing around in the water, with Muhsin occasionally showing me this stroke or that, he came from behind, put his arms around me, pressed his body against mine, and asked in a whisper if I was having fun. After a brief pause, I broke loose from him. I swam to the beach; he offered no resistance, but trailed behind. We both got dressed, as we had done times before behind our individual towels, but this time, in complete silence. With the words, "See you in the morning," each of us walked away to his respective home.[54]

The next morning we were both on the job; outwardly, business as usual. In actuality, however, we both became guarded and distant but quite polite with each other. I kept the matter to myself; I could not bring myself to tell anybody, not even brother Fouad. I did not see any good coming out of telling anybody.[55] While I was contemplating my next step, a natural occasion, within a week or so from the event, presented an opportunity for me to make a move. While I was at the store waiting on a farmer with several sacks of barley, weighing and sampling for quality grading, I felt a great itch all over my body. Shortly thereafter, my body, including my face, started breaking out all over. I was terrified and in pain. Hajj Salman and Muhsin saw what was happening. They murmured that it is some kind of allergy, a concept quite new and foreign to me at that time. They told me to go home, wash, and take the rest of the day off. My mother hugged me as I arrived home. She calmed my fears by concurring that it was an allergy, that others have had similar experiences, and that it would go away. After bathing several times that same day, my body slowly began to normalize. The next day I went to work, but this time with a lot of trepidation. I lost my joy for the work and became apprehensive every time I saw a sack of barley.[56] In a matter of days thereafter, I informed Hajj Salman and Muhsin, after securing mother's approval, that I was no longer able to work at the store. They, understandingly, accepted my decision and wished me well.

By the time I quit my job at the grain store in the fall of 1948, Hamadi had already gotten the Hassoun laundry going in downtown Tyre. It was thus natural for me to frequent the laundry as I had done back in Haifa. I performed errands for Hamadi and Fouad. I generally stayed away from the ironing board, even though I had done considerable pressing in Haifa. There were two main reasons for that: first, the workload did not warrant it; and second, pressing

---

54   At that age, I actually did not fathom what Muhsin was up to. I just instinctively knew what he was doing was very wrong and improper.

55   Years later, I did, in passing, mention it to Fouad, who simply dismissed it.

56   I have not had any breakout experience such as that ever since. It was suggested to me, by people around at the time, that the barley I was in contact with at the breakout must have had some sort of a tiny invisible germ or bug that caused the breakout.

at the Tyre laundry was out in the public eye, quite open to the passers-by. In Haifa, in contrast, I pressed in a semi-private room at the Hadar house. It was felt that customers shouldn't see their clothes being pressed by a thirteen-year-old kid—hardly a "confidence builder"!

Downtown Tyre was a maze of very narrow streets, typically less than fifteen feet wide, with small shops on the street level. The shops lined both sides of the street and residential apartments were built above them, on the second level. There were rarely third levels, and the buildings tightly abutted each other. The center of the streets had an open rain drain-sewer. The street maze was so extensive that it was at least several months before I felt comfortable finding my way around the town as I carried out laundry errands. The laundry's street had quite a mix of shops. Next to our laundry to the south, was a tailor's shop, further down was a barber, across from us, a couple of shoe shops—one for new shoes and some leather goods; the other, more of a shoe repair shop. Next to the laundry to the north was a metal plating shop. It mostly tin-plated copper cooking pots and pans to protect food from copper oxide's poisoning. Next to the plating shop further north was a small repair shop of sundry machines, most often kerosene *primuses*, stoves and lamps, but occasionally, motorcycles. Further north were more shoe shops, yard goods, and a fool-hummus breakfast restaurants. The tailor shop next to us to the south was quite compatible with the laundry business, however, the plating shop north of us tended to generate quite a bit of heat (especially felt in the summer), some unpleasant chemical odors, and at times, smoke and some soot. As such, it left something to be desired. Everybody around, however, seemed to tolerate it. We were the first and only Palestinians to "set up shop" on that street. The majority of the business owners on that street were Shiite Muslims. We were, however, readily accepted in their midst, and quickly developed a healthy camaraderie with them. The prevailing attitude on the street seemed to be "live and let live," even among those whose businesses were the same. If any competition existed, it was quite mild, and overshadowed by a strong fraternal feeling. Many of the shops had, on the sidewalk in front of them, short wooden chairs with straw-woven seats for the business owners, their relatives, guests, or customers, to sit on. When business was slow, people socialized over a cup of coffee or tea, or a bottle of pop. They shared stories, anecdotes, and jokes with each other, interspersed with smiles and laughter. The town's beat was remarkably stable; the concept of change, advancement, or growth was not in their vocabulary. While the tailor next door, Ibrahim (Abraham), had a brisk business and often had his nose to the sewing machine, the barber, Tawfiq, next to him, was not as busy. So, it was not uncommon for him to stop at the laundry for a chat. We found out that he had a very sentimental crooning voice, and he loved to sing. Consequently, when customers were not around, we would coax him to sing, particularly if Hamadi was also not around. Hamadi, at times when things were not going well, would be intolerant and snap and say, "This is a place of business and earning a livelihood and not an entertainment club." Tawfiq and Yousef, however, became good friends. Over time, we enjoyed listening to his crooning on many occasions. In fact, all of us, Yousef, Hamadi, Fouad, and I became his loyal customers for several years. With our haircuts, we got free singing. While the regular fare for the haircut was half a Lebanese pound (same as was my daily wage at Hajj Salman's store, equivalent to about twenty cents), he would only accept a quarter of a pound from me because he would say, "You're just a kid." In return, I would go to his shop and perform some chores, e.g., sweep the hair off the floor of his shop, fill his pitcher with water from a nearby fountain at the camels' inn (*khan*): yes, I really do mean camels! On warm days, I manually operated a fan contraption that hung over the barber's chair to cool off the customer while under the scissors. Occasionally, I got a tip from the customer but it never was much nor a compelling motive. I just had fun doing it. Also, my brothers pressed his shirts and pants for a nominal fare; he was single. There were moments when I aspired to become a barber like him; his life seemed to be carefree, but then I knew it did not provide well for the family.

Hussein, the owner of the repair shop next to and north of the plating shop, became friendly with us also. He was no singer but a real wiz when it came to fixing machines, kind of like brother- in-law, Khalil. He also had a passion for history. He came from an influential family in town but seemed to scoff at that. He owned a motorcycle and rode it all over town and the suburbs. He was single, about thirty-years-old, and a free spirit. Outwardly at least, he expressed disinterest in marriage as an institution. Inwardly he felt, I think, that he could not afford to get married and give children a good quality of life. I often marveled at seeing him driving his motorcycle with both hands off the steering bar. While his business kept him fairly busy, he nevertheless found time to come to our shop to visit. He wanted to know all that went on in Palestine that led to our great debacle. Of course, Fouad and I were only too eager to tell him. Hamadi, if around, would also join in. In fact, gradually Hamadi and Hussein became pals. Hussein, at hearing our stories, would get very upset and would swear at the British and the Americans, and then he would turn his wrath at the Arab regimes, denouncing their backwardness, selfishness, disunity, and their servitude to the West. Both Hamadi and Hussein would argue that western capitalism and materialism in collusion with Zionism are ultimately the enemies that must be fought off and expelled out of the Middle East. In order for us to be able to do that, they further argued, the Arab society will have to be radically cleansed at its very roots, and that we Arabs would have to befriend and learn from the Russians and the communists. They, that is the Russians and communists, were for the downtrodden and the working class. It was the same brother Hamadi that seven years ago ran away from home to volunteer for the British military service, saying this. Both Hussein and Hamadi read, at times avidly, communist literature, but never seriously considered becoming party members or activists. All these discussions were sidewalk venting of emotions and cussing parties. Both Hussein and Hamadi were too eager to eke out a meager living. Hamadi, in particular, was very mindful, by that time, of his responsibility to his wife, children, and the extended household.

In addition to Fouad's soccer friends during this period, two Palestinian friends, Mahmoud Essouri and Mahmoud Shublaq, became frequent visitors to the Hassoun laundry. (Because confusion will likely arise in this narrative, I shall refer to them by their last names.) Essouri was a classmate of Fouad at the Haifa Government School. Sometime during the last year in Haifa, both Essouri and Fouad dropped out of school and did not see each other very much. Essouri's family lived quite far away from ours. In Tyre, however, they found much in common, and their friendship grew close. Mahmoud Shublaq was the nephew of our former Wadi-Ennisnas much-esteemed neighbor and patriot, Hasan Shublaq. He was also from Wadi-Ennisnas, and of the same age as Fouad and the other Mahmoud (Essouri). While, before our diaspora, we used to see Mahmoud Shublaq around in Wadi-Ennisnas, we did not interact much with him back then. His home was a little way up the eastern slope from the laundry; he also, back then, was busy working for his father in some aspect of business. All the preceding aside, Mahmoud Shublaq was also a distant cousin. He had a very smiley, fun-loving, happy-go-lucky personality. Thus, it was quite easy to take him into the fold. There was a third friend, Ibrahim el-Aswad, Fouad's age, and first cousin of my mother. But Ibrahim was not as frequent or regular a visitor as the two Mahmouds. None of these three fellows worked at the time. So, they developed a routine of stopping in the morning at the laundry to socialize. While Fouad pressed clothes, they talked about whatever came to mind. Most of the chat centered on the Palestinian predicament and how to deal with it. There was a very deep yearning to fathom what had happened, why it happened, what was happening or being done about it at that moment, and what was going to become of us, Palestinians.

The regular get-together at the laundry gradually evolved into daily morning sessions to survey the Palestinian human condition, particularly around Tyre. Mahmoud Shublaq assumed the role of the news gatherer. He closely followed, both by reading daily newspapers and listening to radio broadcasts, Palestinian-related events at the UN in New York, the Arab League in Cairo, and other Arab capitals. In his daily reports, he loved to mimic the Secretary General of the Arab League at the time, Mahmoud Azzaam Pasha. He would put on a mocking act, making similar pronouncements and declarations as the Secretary General; the point being there were too many pronouncements, but no results. He did it to such an extent that we all saw it fitting to nickname him Azzaam Pasha,[57] often called for brevity, Azzaam. He relished the nickname. Our discussions did digress from time to time and delve into lighter matters such as: Who were the good-looking young women in town? What were the prospects that any one of us would ever get a chance to meet any one of them, or even exchange a word or two? The Muslim women of Tyre overwhelmingly walked in public covered up from head to toe. Therefore, it was quite hard to assess accurately, through their veils, the various claims of beauty, flirtiness, etc., and substantiate them. We often had to resort to body language or the crystal ball. So much so that those women who regularly passed by the laundry

---

57 "Pasha" is a Turkish title in the Ottoman era given to a person of high social or government standing, like "Excellency."

were so classified, and even given nicknames. The laundry was on a fairly major route in the old city. When one of these young women walked by, the conversation, whatever the subject matter might have been, usually came to a sudden halt and silence overshadowed the moment.

For a time during this period, Fouad, seemingly out of the blue, started getting romantic letters from Muhsin's sister (also Hajj Salman's daughter), a young woman of about Fouad's age. All of us at the laundry, including Fouad, had seen her only veiled, and from a distance, as she would walk by. To say the least, this was most intriguing. The letters, delivered cleverly by young kids, were followed further by gifts of sweets and fruits. Tremendous excitement was evoked by these actions and generated a great deal of teasing from friends that at times rendered Fouad very red in the face. The news eventually got to my mother. The family agreed, after deliberation, to firmly but very discreetly discourage these overtures. For one thing, if these actions became common knowledge, it could disgrace the girl's family. For another, it was not the right time for Fouad to get involved in such a relationship. He had his cousin, Fakhriyye, committed to him, as willed by my father, and approved by Fakhriyye's father, Uncle Tawfiq. With no response from Fouad's side, the young woman, in due course, slowly but surely got the disinterest message and gave up.

One morning, in the fall of 1948, the friends; Essouri, Azzaam Pasha, Ibrahim el-Aswad, Fouad at the ironing board, and me gathered for our morning session. While in a quite a playful mood, an idea somehow sprang up that we do something for the Palestinian cause. It was completely spontaneous. We saw it as a fun, worthwhile activity. The day was a Red Cross ration distribution day for the Palestinian refugees of Tyre. The idea was that we write up a poster exhorting Palestinians standing in the ration line to reject the rations being offered, declaring, "We Palestinians do not want a handout from anybody. We are a proud people and demand to return to our homes, in our country, Palestine, expeditiously." It was not intended in any way to be an expression of ingratitude to the Red Cross, but rather, we saw the rations as a form of appeasement, a numbing drug, and part of a Western-Zionist conspiracy to lull Palestinian senses into accepting the loss of their homeland. Many of our relatives, in fact, found it very humiliating to have to stand in line, like beggars, for these rations. Essouri was designated to be the scribe, for he had beautiful handwriting. All of us participated in the word composition of the poster. In a couple of hours the several copies of the poster were ready and the two Mahmouds (Essouri and Shublaq) dashed with them to where the ration line formed, a short walk away. I followed behind. I was thirteen years old, while the two Mahmouds were about eighteen years old. Both of the Mahmouds were of large stature, particularly Essouri. Somehow, Ibrahim el-Aswad did not go; Fouad had to attend to the laundry business; Hamadi was not around. As the two Mahmouds were in the very act of pasting copies of the poster onto the wall facing the ration line of refugees, two Lebanese gendarmes (police) suddenly appeared and quickly apprehended both of them. I, seeing what was happening, vanished in the crowd. The two Mahmouds were led to the downtown Gendarme's Station. Stunned at this most unexpected turn of events, I quickly found my way back to Fouad and reported to him what had just happened. Fouad was shocked, for we all innocently viewed the activity as a playful and harmless act. Eventually, the word got out to the grown-up family members of the two Mahmouds who rushed to the Gendarme's Station. Instead of hearing that they got released to their parents, we learned that they had been interrogated, beaten up, and put in jail! In due course, both Fouad and I went to visit them. We found them in a cold and damp cell with hardly any furnishings or even bedding. At the Gendarme's Station, nobody was interested in talking to us, let alone telling us when they might be released. Of course, we were apprehensive that if we showed too much ire or concern for them, we could be thrown into the cell with them. There was no mention whatsoever of a charge or a trial. The two looked pathetic. In succession, several well-regarded Palestinians went to the Gendarme's Station and pleaded their release, not only to no avail, but we kept getting news that they were continually being beaten. The beating along with the interrogation was to force them to divulge which group or organization they belonged to that had sent them with the posters, and to admit guilt! We would go visit, take them food and blankets, but this did not satisfy Fouad who became very restless. He asked "low-level" friends in the Cyclone Club to intercede for them. The effort was not successful. The situation went on for about two weeks as we sought help from higher and higher level individuals in the Tyre community. The matter eventually reached the head captain of Tyre's Harbor Administration; he was also Muhsin's half-brother. He had watched Fouad on the soccer field and developed a special admiration for him. Fouad assured the head captain that the two Mahmouds were good people who were not guilty of any wrong doing, and that they were merely venting the general sense of unhappiness and frustration of the Palestinian community, and should therefore be promptly released. The head captain was very cordial and favorable to Fouad's plea. Within a short time, he approached the Tyre chief of gendarme and made the request. When his request was coldly received, he moved to engage the deputy of the Lebanese Parliament for the Tyre area. The captain essentially asked the parliament deputy to lean on the chief of the Tyre gendarme to release the boys. It was only then that the chief of gendarme finally yielded, and the two Mahmouds were set free. It took the Mahmouds a very long time before they felt somewhat rehabilitated. Based on my observation, one of them, Shublaq (Azzaam), became scarred for life. His back gradually began to hunch down and forward. Last time I saw him, when he was at about age forty, his body was sharply bent over and down. The affair left a very deep and unforgettable impact on me as to how powerless and vulnerable we, Palestinians, had become, and how easy it was to trample over our human rights.

Days passed by; winter followed fall. Palestinians all over, in cities and camps, talked grievously day and night about the *Nakba*. Lots of United Nations resolutions passed—international meetings and pronouncements from world leaders promising this or that to redress Palestinian grievances and to render the Palestinians some justice by returning them to their homes would be hungrily listened to, only to quickly be found hollow and of no avail. Rays of hope turned into mirages. The Red Cross made way to the United Nations Relief and Work Agency (UNRWA), and our refugee status began to sink deeper and deeper into our consciousness.

One day in January of 1949, as I was standing by the front door of the laundry, I saw two boys, my age, going home from school. They were well groomed with books under their arms and talking about schoolwork. Suddenly, a question flashed in my head like lightning: *How come I am not at school like these fellows?* That evening, I asked my mother in a pleading voice, and tears in my eyes, if I could go back to school? The Jaffariyya College, private with some cost, would be my only option. Without hesitation, she said, "Tomorrow, first thing in the morning, you and I will go to the Jaffariyya College registrar to find out what it would take to get you admitted." Fouad, listening nearby in the room, wholeheartedly endorsed the plan, suggesting that tomorrow was hardly soon enough!

CHAPTER 8

THE JAFFARIYYA COLLEGE

The following morning, Mother and I headed to the office of the student supervisor (in Arabic, *annazir*) of the Jaffariyya College, about a mile away. Ushered into his office, Mother did the talking, and the *annazir* listened intently. Mindful of the Palestinian predicament, he told us right away that the college would admit me gratis. After reviewing my academic background, he recommended that I begin in the sixth grade. In Haifa, I had completed the sixth grade and started the seventh grade for about a couple of months before closure. He thought I would need time to refresh and adjust to school life again. Neither my mother nor I questioned his recommendation. In the Lebanese school system, the sixth grade was an important grade, concluding the elementary phase of education. At the end of the sixth grade, students take a national elementary certificate examination. If the student passed it, he was conferred the Lebanese Certificate of Elementary Education, referred to colloquially as *Certificat*.[58] Those who fail it usually drop out of school and are funneled out one way or another into society's labor market. Failing the *Certificat* often constituted the death sentence to further schooling, and carried a heavy stigma. The failure rate of the 1948 examination was quite high, perhaps as high as half the takers. Those who passed it were allowed into the middle high school phase. Even among those who passed it, many chose to end their schooling in the belief that they have gotten all the education needed to begin life in the real world. I then raised my concern about coming from a Palestinian/English system into the contrasting Lebanese/French system, and that I had no knowledge of French but that I had three years of English as a second language. The *annazir* replied, "You will be pleased to know that the Jaffariyya College has just initiated into its program, this past fall, an English section to accommodate Palestinian

---

58 In this chapter some French words come into the narrative. These were in common use in Lebanon's educational system, which was fashioned by the French over the three preceding decades. I have kept them unadulterated to preserve the flavor of the times; where the meaning is not self-evident, it is inserted in the text.

student enrollees." I was elated! He then went on to say, "The Lebanese Ministry of Education had decided to offer, effective the current school year and for the first time ever, two options for the second language in the national elementary certificate examination." The added option was that of English. The Jaffariyya set-up was such that Palestinian students would be in the same class with everybody else for all subjects except for the second language classes; at which time the main group, the Lebanese, would be taught French, while the Palestinians would go to another room and be taught English.

When asked when I could start, *annazir* said, "Right away." The *annazir* provided me with a notebook and a pencil for the day. He then told me that once in class, to try to find out what books I would need for the rest of the school year. Thereafter, I would try to secure them from what might be on hand at the college or buy them second hand. I bade mother goodbye, as the *annazir* walked me over to the sixth-grade classroom. It was in the midst of a mathematics period. I was introduced to the teacher, Mr. Muhammad Issa.(In other words: his name was Muhammad Jesus. One would be forgiven to wonder if such a name was not pregnant with meaning.) He welcomed me into his class and introduced me to everyone. The class had a total of about thirty-five students. As I sat listening to the teacher posing a math problem on the blackboard, I was excited and happy to be in school, but then I was very apprehensive that I might not be able to catch onto the material fast enough to be in sync with my classmates. In fact, I did not quite understand the math problem that was being posed; nevertheless, I attempted it and showed Mr. Issa my work. He thoughtfully corrected my misconceptions and encouraged me to try again. I did. This time I got it right, and he lauded me. In a matter of weeks, I felt in tune with the class. One of the things that early on impressed me about Mr. Issa was the way he conducted himself with a great deal of grace and dignity. Whenever I would run into him outside the class, I would greet him with the utmost of respect. This feeling for Mr. Issa (deceased) is still with me to this day. In hindsight, Mr. Issa was, at the time, a man in his latter twenties and of quite modest academic attainments. He merely had the *Brevet*, the middle high school, i.e., tenth grade, certificate in the Lebanese school system.

When the time for the foreign language class period came, the Palestinian students went to another classroom. While I was relieved to find out that I was not the only Palestinian student in the sixth grade, I was surprised to find out there we were only five others. As the teacher walked in, we all stood up, as was customary in Palestinian schools of those days. "Please be seated," he said, in flawless English. He welcomed me into the class. At some point in the class period, he called on me to read from the English reading textbook and to translate. His reactions suggested that I should be able to manage fine with the right kind of effort. In a matter of weeks, I caught up with the group.

Our English teacher's name was Joseph Layyoos. He was a very young Palestinian (perhaps 22 years old) who had just fled Acre with his family and sought refuge in Tyre. Academically, he had attained the highly-regarded Palestinian Government High School Matriculation. He was not a teacher before, but had worked for the British Mandate Government until the British administration in Acre began to crumble. He was to teach English to all the existing English sections; the fifth grade, the sixth grade, and the eighth grade; there were no seventh grade students. The fifth grade had about the same number of students as the sixth grade, whereas the eighth grade had one student! Months later, I found out that Joseph had two older brothers, Antun and Costa, who lived together with Joseph in the same family household. They were both holders of the Palestinian Matriculation as well.

While I fairly readily caught on to the Arabic language and the general science classes, history and geography presented me with a challenge. Even back in Haifa, history and geography seemed to require a great deal more memorization and outside study than the other subjects. Fearing to fail history and geography in fifth grade back in Haifa; thus meeting a similar fate of having to repeat the grade as brother Fouad had, I hit the books very hard the week before finals. One weekend, I spent virtually all of it studying my history and geography books. I was so glued to my study that my father noticed my abnormal behavior and sudden studiousness, and came by to look over my shoulder to find out what was so intriguing about the books. Since he could not read, he would look at the pictures. In Tyre, however, the history and geography classes focused exclusively on Lebanon in accordance with the national curriculum. Up to that point, I had studied virtually nothing about Lebanon, and I was coming into the school year past the one-third point. Fortunately, the textbooks were well written and illustrated. I studied them diligently alone and with other students to find out what had been covered earlier in the school year.

My study outside class, including homework, was done to a large extent in the schoolyard; there was no lounge, library, or study hall inside the school building. I actually studied quite a bit while walking back and forth between home and school for it was very hard to study at home. For one thing, there was really no place to sit to read or write. On the eve of a major test and in desperation, I attempted to study at home for an hour or so with the aid of a kerosene lamp. Bedtime for everybody was no later than 8:30 pm, and virtually everybody was up by sunrise. Some of my study was done early in the morning before class time or during school recesses. There were very modest sport activities at the end of the class day, which were not officially or formally supervised but freelanced largely by athletic students. They included soccer, volleyball, and basketball. There were no meets with other schools, locally or nationally.

There was more emphasis on art and religion than in Haifa's schools. Drawing was part of the *Certifcat* national examination; religion was not. Our art teacher, who taught primarily drawing, seemed distant and unenthusiastic. Nevertheless, he had us draw a variety of objects such as a pitcher, an apple, grape cluster, etc. We showed him our work, and he would comment on it very briefly. Often, he would merely grade it with a red pen and return it to us. The grades I got most frequently were three or four out of ten. I got no direction or guidance from anybody whatsoever! It was during the art class, while watching classmates, that I began to realize the range of drawing skills and native talents different individuals possess. Somehow, I grew up viewing art and drawing as a frill, and not a bread and butter activity. I did not take the class seriously; I applied myself just enough to get by. It has taken me years to recognize the value of a good drawing, in particular, and art, in general. Worse yet, for many years, I regrettably failed to appreciate the spirit of imagination and creativity that went hand in hand with good art.

I took well to the religion class even though it had a Shiite slant, that is, Imam Ali's role (in Islam) was given a greater focus than in the Sunni version.[59] To me, it was very much the same Islam I had grown up with. I initially did

---

59 Imam Ali was Prophet Muhammad's cousin; he was the second convert to Islam, after Khadija, the Prophet's first wife. He, very early in the Islamic movement, became a major figure in the dissemination of Islam. He married Prophet Muhammad's daughter, Fatima, with whom he had two sons, Hasan and Hussein, greatly revered especially by the Shiites.

not appreciate nor fathom all the historical, political, and theological schisms that lay behind this.[60] As far back as I could remember, I always thought of Imam Ali very highly. I ascribe this to the kind of exposure I had at the Haifa Government School, and to what I had learned from Grandfather Issa, Uncle Mahmoud, and Mother.

My performance in sixth grade was rapidly improving. At the end of the winter term, I ranked in the top twenty five percent of the class. In the English section, out of a six, including myself, I was competing for second place.

As the school year drew closer to its end, our teachers became increasingly mindful of the approach of the national examination day, to be held in the latter part of June. They pressed on to cover the prescribed material in the syllabus while we students, each in his own way, prepared for the big day.

The *Certificat* national examination for the Tyre schools and surrounding areas was administered in Sidon, twenty-five miles up the coast. We were given detailed instructions as to when and where to show up on the morning of the appointed day to board a chartered bus to leave for Sidon. The departure from Tyre was in the early morning. We were driven to the Sidon Maqased School, where the examination was to be given. Each student had been assigned, in advance, a room and seat in which he would take all the examinations for all the subjects—the same single room assignment for the entire day. I had an aisle seat. To my left, by a window at the same bench, was a Maqased student that seemed much more at ease and familiar with the surroundings. During the first break in the day, we chatted together in the schoolyard. He was very helpful in pointing out where things were in the school building. He was very outgoing, well groomed, and seemed to know quite a few of the students around. When the subject of how the first session went came up, he exuded unusual confidence. His name was Muhammad Hussein Saffouri. The rest of the day went according to schedule. At the end of the day and at the appointed place and time, the Jaffariyya students gathered and boarded the bus back to Tyre. On the way home, my general sense was that I had done alright, but I was not sure whether I would pass, for it was my first time taking a national examination and I did not know what it would take to pass. The prevalent view in Tyre was that more students were likely to flunk than pass!

---

60   A subject for another time and place!

Back in Tyre, the school year was over; summer vacation had started, and the suspenseful waiting for the test results was on. It would take at least two weeks for the results to appear. The results would be published in several Lebanese newspapers. The Ministry of Education, the sponsor of the examination, only declared the list of the names of those who passed; no grades nor explanations. Some of my worries were: *What if they made a mistake in grading some of my test papers, or made a mistake in computing my collective average; or, what if I passed but when it came to sending the list to newspapers, my name was inadvertently overlooked or missed.* Finally, the wait was over, the list of the names of those who passed was published; somebody sent word to me at home that he had seen the published list and my name was on the list! At the news, there was a great deal of rejoicing by the entire household. While I was very happy, I did not rest until I went to town, bought a paper, and saw for myself that my name was indeed on the list. It was the first time ever, to my knowledge, that my name appeared in print, and I reveled in looking at it again and again! I further saw that everybody in our English section had passed, whereas in the French section, many did not make it. The English *Certifcat* section was a historical first, and we the students were the first wave! The Jaffariyya College was justifiably proud. The rest of the summer of 1949 I spent swimming, playing soccer, and leisurely helping around the laundry, and taking a trip to Damascus.

The Damascus trip was with Mother, Fouad, and Qasim to visit sister Haliema and family. It had been well over a year since they had left Tyre. Uncle Mahmoud ended up with his family in a small town just outside Damascus, called Duma. He had set up a modest fresh produce grocery business. His presence there served as an added trip incentive. My mother, encouraged by Khalil (Haliema's husband), toyed with the idea of finding a Damascene bride for Fouad. Khalil had in mind a niece of his whom he had praised as good looking and well educated. Damascene women, in general, had the reputation of being good looking and have very fair skin. This was to the displeasure of cousin Fakhriyye, his traditional and as willed to bride. She and Fouad would occasionally and secretly, but very unconventionally, see each other, typically early in the evening, under the cover of darkness! Fouad and Fakhriyye's secret "seeings" were not always harmonious, so Fouad did not close the door to a Damascene bride.

It was our first trip to this famous city of Damascus. Nadiema agreed to cover my mother's laundry duties, which was for about a week. Fouad's absence from his laundry pressing work was also OK'd by Yousef and Hamadi. There was yet some red tape to cut through with both the Syrian and Lebanese authorities. Palestinians were required to have a permit to leave Lebanon, and a permit to enter Syria. With some effort and the crossing of a few palms, the permits were secured.

Our trip to Damascus was full of anticipation. We had heard so much about the city from many sources, most notably, Khalil. Notwithstanding the red tape and slow processing at the borders, the bus rides from Tyre to Beirut (about fifty miles) and from Beirut to Damascus (about seventy miles) seemed to pass fast. While there, we met Khalil's Damascus relatives, older brother and sister and their families, many of whom we had heard about before but did not think we would visit anytime soon, if ever. We moved around visiting the famous city's landmarks, most notably, the Umayyad Mosque. We strolled famous streets like Abu-Rummana's and Baghdad's. We explored Damascus' great Souk (market) el-Hamidiyye, which overlapped the biblical street called "Straight," made famous by Apostle Paul; we sampled the Souk's delights, a wide variety of sweets and *booza* (ice milk of many flavors). Khalil took us on a one-day picnic at a famous park, west of the city, rich with running streams of water that fed the city water springs. He roasted shish kabob on an open fire for most of the afternoon. We took a train ride of about forty-five minutes to Duma. There we stayed with Uncle Mahmoud and his family for a couple of days. One evening, I accompanied Uncle Mahmoud to a Sufi service (termed in Arabic: *Halaqat Dhikr, literally 'remembrance link"*) permeated with chants and whirling dance in praise and adoration of God, to the point of achieving a trance by some. We returned back to Tyre fulfilled, as if waking up from a dream.

As it turned out, the idea of finding a Damascene bride for Fouad was more of wishful thinking and musing than anything else! We did see Khalil's niece, but there was no attempt to follow up. I think Mother felt bound to honor tradition and Father's will. Fouad and Fakhriyye were wed March 1950.

Once back in Tyre, I resumed summer play and work at the laundry with the anticipation that come fall, I would be returning to Jaffariya as a first-year middle school student.

With the fall of 1949, I found out, with sadness, that Mr. Joseph Layyoos had taken a non-teaching job with an oil company in one of the Persian Gulf oil States; and therefore, he would no longer be teaching us English.[61] However, the college hired a new Palestinian teacher to replace him; his name was Arafat Ettaher. He was about thirty years old and a professional teacher back in Palestine. In time, I figured out that he hailed from the village of Etteery, and was in fact, married to the sister of my admired Palestinian military officer, Rashied Jarbou.

Sometime during that school year, the YMCA of Lebanon, headquartered in Beirut, decided to open a branch center in Tyre, as a cultural and recreational outlet for the Palestinian refugees. Mr. Ettaher served as its director. Fouad, Qasim, and I, began to frequent the place.

In first-year middle school (seventh grade), the English section became more separate and distinct from the French section. While in the sixth grade class, the two sections broke away from each other only for the foreign language; in the first-year middle school we had to separate for mathematics and the sciences. The reason was because those subjects were taught in French in the Lebanese curriculum. In the English section, the college decided to follow the Palestinian model and teach them in Arabic. As a result, the two sections, in fact, were together only for Arabic, religion, history and geography. The art class was terminated with the end of the *Certificat* examination. Mr. Ettaher was also entrusted with teaching us general science. Mathematics was entrusted to Mr. Mahmoud Ennana, a new hire. Like Ettaher, Mr. Ennana, about thirty-five years of age, was a professional, matriculated teacher in Palestine who had just sought refuge in Tyre from Galilee with his family. He was entrusted further with teaching Arabic for the combined two sections, the English and the French.

Mr. Ettaher began his English course by introducing us to the content of the seventh grade syllabus according to the Palestinian curriculum. It involved reading English short stories, grammar, dictation, and composition. The English

---

61 Brother Fouad sadly informed me (sometime in 2000) that Joseph Lyyoos had sometime ago, probably in the mid 1960s, been killed in a plane crash while on one of his travels in the Persian Gulf area. He further said that Mr. Layyoos held, at the time of his death, a very high administrative position with the Darwiesh Co. in Qatar, a branch company of the famous Middle Eastern Contracting and Trading Company, widely known by its acronym CAT (Cf. fn 92).

section started with just four of us. Mr. Ettaher followed a similar approach in teaching us science. It was broken down into three distinct and separate areas: biology, chemistry, and physics. We used textbooks that were standard in the Palestinian curriculum. Mr. Ennana also began his mathematics teaching by having us buy Palestinian standard Arabic algebra and geometry textbooks. It was evident that both Messrs. Ettaher and Ennana had virtually a completely free hand as to what and how they taught us. The Arabic instruction involved grammar, dictation, composition, and poetry; reading was presumed, or a by-product. In contrast to English where we read short stories, in Arabic we pored over Arabic poetry; we were required, among other things, to memorize poems that typically had thirty-to-forty lines or verses; some were much longer. In the English short stories, we focused primarily on understanding the literal meaning of the text. If we got the gist of the story, it was satisfactory. In Arabic poetry, considerably more was entailed. In poetry, we learned the different eras during which they were written, pre-Islamic, early Islamic, middle Islamic, etc., up to and including, contemporary poetry. For a given poem, we learned about the life and times of the poet, the motivation and purpose of the poem, etc. In so doing, we not infrequently went over individual lines for both apparent and hidden meanings. We checked the syntax for strengths and weaknesses, and analyzed whether it conformed to sound Arabic structure, rhyme, grammar, and so on.

Except for history and geography, I embarked on all other subjects with a great zest. I found a lot in common with Arabic and English grammar and mathematics. Frequently, on tests, I would get perfect scores. I found geometry fascinating. At the conclusion of the first term, I ranked first in the English section of my class. I retained this ranking for the rest of my enrollment at the Jaffariyya College. The learning gained in all the courses of that year was very rich. I felt very appreciative of what the college provided and the kind of teachers we had.

At the end of the seventh grade school year (spring of 1950), one of the classmates planned to move out to Beirut, and come fall, there would be only three students in the eighth grade of the English section. Very fortunately, Messrs. Ettaher and Ennana planned to stay on for the following year, and come fall, there would be an eighth grade to enroll in.

Late in June of 1950, sister Haliema, well into one of her pregnancies, asked Mother to be with her at delivery time. Haliema, with two young daughters, four and two years old, would need help. There were logistical matters to be worked out for the trip: government permits to travel to Damascus, Nadiema to cover for mother's laundry work and to look after Qasim. Since I was older and could manage pretty much on my own, the choice was made that I would accompany my mother. It was presumed that Mother would be gone at most a couple of weeks, as Haliema had figured the birth was imminent.

The trip time happened to fall during Ramadan in the prime of summer. While Muslim law allows one not to fast while in travel, Mother said devoutly that she would nevertheless fast, and that God would sustain her. She told me I did not need to fast. She would pack me lunch and drink. I told her that if she is going to fast and God would sustain her, I was also going to fast, and God would likewise sustain me. So we both set out on the trip fasting. It was a hot and muggy day. Without Fouad and Qasim to chitchat with, and both Mother and I fasting, the whole atmosphere was different from the last Damascus trip. The bus from Tyre to Beirut was fairly full, with all kinds of people carrying all kinds of belongings including some cages of chickens and a goat or a sheep, getting on and off along the way. It took over two hours to get to Beirut. In Beirut, we got off with our baggage; in addition, Mother had packed all kinds of sweets that she had made. The packages were so many that it took quite a bit of ingenuity to carry them all at once to the Damascus bus station. The Damascus bus did not run on a time schedule, but rather, left when it was pretty full. Once it started, I felt relief. I was ready to enjoy the landscape along the way, the mountains and the Bekaa Valley. Before long, we approached the Lebanese/ Syrian border. First came the Lebanese checkpoint. It was shocking to see the length of the line of busses and cars inching towards it. We inched through it with a few questions by the Lebanese border officer. Insuring we had gotten an exit permit, we were ushered to proceed to the Syrian checkpoint. There, the line got visibly longer and hardly moved at all. It took over two hours, with passengers getting out and back into their respective buses or cars, papers in hand, before our turn came. Mother and I kept tightly and patiently to our seats. The heat would have been quite taxing without the fast. With the fast, it was very trying. Tired and strained, my mother's face increasingly showed her discomfort. I kept assessing how she was holding up. I thought to myself that if she holds up to her fast, I was not giving in. When the Syrian officer reached us, he inquired of mother as to the reason for the trip, etc. My mother answered calmly, factually, and straight to the point. Notwithstanding, he searched our belongings. Finally, our bus was allowed to move on. Before long and rather suddenly, the city of Damascus lay before us. It was dusk. Everybody got off at the bus station downtown. The communication system was such that there was no way to have arranged for anybody to meet us, and there was no one there. Mother had her instructions as to the following steps leading to Haliema's home. We took an inner city electric tram and walked a while before reaching the neighborhood of her home, Shaykh Mohieddine's Quarter. Somehow, on our previous trip, I had paid no attention to these details. Once there, we inquired of shopkeepers around about Khalil Esh-Shatta. We were readily led to the home amidst a maze of narrow streets. It was already dark. Haliema rejoiced and cried at seeing us. A festive dinner was waiting. She did not know that we would be fasting. It was past the breakfasting time. Notwithstanding all the attractively served food, all I wanted, first and foremost, was a drink of water!

Upon settling in, I began to realize that Haliema's home was a small single room unit, simply furnished, with a partially tiled front courtyard (some twenty-five by thirty-five feet). The courtyard was shared with a couple of neighbors and Khalil's older widowed sister. His sister owned the property. From the street, you first entered the courtyard, then the individual dwellings. The homes had neither plumbing nor electricity. In the courtyard, there was a well that provided water for all the tenants. The well's water was from a deep underground spring. It was quite good, refreshingly cold, and clearly superior to Tyre's water. As with the well and the courtyard, the bathroom facilities were shared. Mohieddine's Quarter was one of the oldest sections of Damascus. It was where Khalil had been born and had grown up. He had us meet his older brother again (named Qasim! nicknamed: Shaykho-el-Islam, or Muslim elder). The brother operated a fresh produce grocery shop and was very well known throughout the quarter. Khalil operated a smaller home appliances repair shop, which was a short distance away from his brother's shop.

On this trip, I found myself much more curious about Khalil's family and childhood surroundings, more generally, about what Syrians are like, how they live, their spoken slang, etc. Khalil's brother reminded me greatly of Grandfather Issa in his stature, his beard, turban, and line of business.

As Mother had time to visit privately with Haliema, with me somehow in the background, they soon got into how the pregnancy was progressing, and how she has been getting along. I recall being struck by how eager, personal, intimate, and detailed Haliema was in reporting to mother her ups and downs, including such things as occasional bleeding, baby movements and kicks to her tummy; she even ventured into how Khalil said a prayer before lovemaking, asking God for a good and healthy male heir. Haliema, in her first couple of years of marriage to Khalil, had miscarriages to the point that she was concerned that she might not be able to bear any further children. She had ascribed this difficulty to Khalil's weak seed. Although she already had one girl (Samira) from him, she, nevertheless, was worried that her earlier difficulties might recur. As to when she expected the baby's arrival, she indicated, according to her calculation, it could be coming anytime soon.

As I started to assess my situation, I began to wonder what I might be doing in the meantime. For the first few days or a week, I was not concerned, for there was a lot of sightseeing, both in the Mohieddine neighborhood and in Damascus at large.

As I began to wander in the Mohieddine's Quarter, I was attracted to the several mosques, the ablution courts, and the soothing abundant fresh water that flowed through the faucets and fountains of the mosques' courtyards. Five times a day, I heard the call to prayer blaring out of the minarets. It seemed as though the melodic call to prayer was filling the air all the time; spreading a garment of piety, peace, and tranquility over the entire neighborhood while the faithful went in and out of the mosques performing the prayers at the appointed times. Once a week, on Thursday, there was a shopping fair set up very early in the morning in the heart of the commercial center of the quarter. Somehow, we did not have a chance to savor it on our previous visit. This time, I was told about it by Khalil in advance and encouraged not to miss it. On the first Thursday, I got up early and headed there. It was only a few hundred yards from their home. The crowds were thicker than I had ever seen before. All kinds of merchandise was set up on display and people of all walks of life, men and women, young and old, in multitudinous attires, were engaged in looking, buying, selling, and socializing. A little way from it was also a sheep market. Dazzled, I milled around from one booth to another until about mid-morning when the crowds began to thin out. While I had sort of sensed a return to medieval days on my first visit to Mohieddine's, by the end of milling around that Thursday, I had no doubt that I must have gone back in time many centuries. In fact, the shopping fair on Thursday brought to mind the annual Souk Okaz (pre-Islamic large bazaar market) of Mecca, which I had studied about in Arabic literature. That *souk* enriched all aspects of Meccan life at the pre-dawn of Islam: economic, social, political, and not least, literary. When I went home and happily told Haliema and Khalil, they seemed bemused and delighted.

Having developed a good feel for Mohieddine's Quarter, I began to venture further out into neighboring city sections on my own. Some days later in our stay, it was announced on the Damascus news that a major criminal, who had committed a heinous domestic crime, had been sentenced to death by hanging. The announcement then indicated the day of the hanging and that it would be carried out before sunrise in Marje's (popular alias for Martyr's) Square, the main square in the heart of Damascus. His body would hang at the site for public display till 9:00 a.m. Khalil told me, if I was interested, he would arrange to take time out and accompany me down to the square in time to see the body hanging. Of course, I was, although, he and my mother agreed that it was not a good idea for us to go there in time to witness the actual hanging. On the appointed day, Khalil and I headed for the electric tram terminal nearby and boarded it to Marje's Square. We got there about 8:00 a.m. There the body hung with the head bent over and to the side of one of the shoulders. There was a poster worn over the neck and down the chest with writing on it as to the crime that justified the hanging. The general sense was, let this be a lesson to all who might be tempted to commit such a crime. While there were a number of onlookers, the numbers on the whole were not that large. I was most astonished by the many who briskly walked by, intent to make it to work on time, with hardly a glance at the hanging body. As I strolled around, images of people who, over the years, had been hanged unjustly or for political reasons in that same square, came to mind. With goose bumps, I thought specifically of those Syrian and Lebanese Arab nationalists hanged therein by the Ottomans for striving for Arab independence early in the twentieth century. So much so that the square is appropriately and officially named "Martyrs' Square". Burj's Square, in the heart of downtown Beirut, is likewise and for the same reason named "Martyrs' Square."

I kept myself busy, and a couple of weeks passed by, but there was no sign of Haliema's baby's imminent arrival. Uncle Mahmoud would stop by occasionally, and as always, would have an affectionate brotherly visit with Mother whom he routinely called "his second mother." Duma, where he lived, was a long way to frequently travel to-and-fro. Slowly, but surely, I was getting restless. It appeared that there was not much else to do but wait. Haliema had not been seeing a doctor or a nurse, nor having any kind of professional monitoring of her pregnancy; as such, she went by her instinct. So, I expanded my circle of sightseeing and exploration. With Khalil at work, and not having anybody to fast befriend, I struck out on my own. I walked most of the time. This way I could see and appreciate more of the sights. I took the tram or an inner city bus when the section I wanted to explore was too far to get to in an hour walk or more. Walking also did not entail spending money on transportation. I had neither informative literature about the city, nor maps. I went by what I recalled from my previous visit and what I would hear Khalil suggest. Typically, I did my sightseeing from outside. I did not go into buildings nor did I engage anybody in conversation. I walked around the Syrian parliament, identified many of the government buildings, the Damascus museum, city parks, and such. This went on for a while until one day, while milling in the heart of the city, not far from Souk el-Hamidiyye, I walked by a car service station where I spotted what seemed to be a familiar face. As I approached, sure enough, it was my Haifa school friend and chum, Mas'oud El- Hasan. I could hardly believe my eyes. I walked to him, greeted him warmly, and tried to explain how I happened to be there. He seemed speechless. From his attire, it was evident that he worked there as a junior mechanic. By comparison, I looked very well groomed. After a conversation that lasted utmost fifteen minutes, he seemed too busy with car repairs. I did not want to get in the way. So I had no choice but to bid him good-bye. I walked away telling myself, *but this is my dear friend, my buddy Mas'oud! I should hang around and visit more with him.* Yet, the environment was such that I had to keep moving on. There was a painful sense of sadness; the brief encounter left me empty. It was the last time I saw him.

When I got back to Haliema's home, I did not attempt to tell anyone what had happened. I did not feel anyone was in the mood to listen, not even my mother; again no sign of the baby's coming. In the coming days, I continued what had become almost a routine, wandering the streets of Damascus solo. One day, as I was wandering a wide-open park looking over the international fairgrounds of the city, a husky, good-size man, approximately in his forties, spotted me in the distance. He walked towards me, motioned to me and then to his pocket, rattled something in his pocket as if to say, "I have money (or something) for you." Right away I sensed danger without knowing exactly what kind, and briskly walked away from him and out of the park. Thank God, he made no attempt at following me. It was easily an hour of hard speedy walk before I got back home. Again, I did not bother to say anything to anybody. Even if I wanted to, I did not know where to begin, and how to make myself understood. Despite the encounter, after a couple of days of hanging around the Mohieddine's Quarter, my restlessness prompted me to venture again into the more modern sections of the city. In an outdoor restaurant and café area, near the previous park of a few days past, I spotted the same guy sitting in a sidewalk chair! At about the same moment, he also spotted me. He lifted up his head and stretched out his neck, as if to make sure that it was me again before he got up off the chair and proceeded to walk towards me. I wasted no time and walked away fast. I carefully avoided running, so as not to attract attention; he seemed to do the same. He did not persist though, and I made it safely home.

After that second encounter, I made up my mind that I had enough of wandering. It was, by then, well over a month since we had been at Haliema's. Without trying to explain, I told my mother I could no longer hang around Damascus; I had given Haliema enough time, and still there was no sign of a baby; therefore, the time had come for me to go back to Tyre. Of course, she could and should stay behind. Mother, as usual, seemed to understand. I had never traveled alone before, not even twenty-five miles up the coast from Tyre to Sidon; yet given the circumstance, and that I was fifteen-years-old, I was sure I could handle the return trip to Tyre by myself. She agreed; so did Khalil and Haliema. They gave me a lot of instructions. I stayed one more day to give Mother and Khalil time to prepare things for me for the return trip. On the morning of the following day, which I estimate to have been in the second week of August, I kissed Mother and Haliema good-bye. Khalil and I took the tram to the Damascus-Beirut downtown station. I was laden, along with my clothes and lunch and drink for the trip, with a big basket of Damascus sweets and fresh fruits to take back to the family in Tyre. Though apprehensive as I traveled back, I kept a reserved and calm air. About six hours later, I arrived in Tyre safely and with a big sigh of relief. It was about the middle of the afternoon. Everybody seemed happy to see me and sorry for Haliema's gross miscalculations. I felt like a bird that had just flown out of his cage!

One of the first things I did, shortly after resting from the trip that same day, was to head to the Tyre YMCA to see my friends, catch up on what had been going on while I was gone, and to play Ping-Pong. Within a few days, I settled into a normal summer pattern of activities. It was at least another month before Mother finally made it back to Tyre. Haliema delivered a healthy baby girl; the baby was given the name Khadija, after Prophet Muhammad's first and beloved wife. It was a relief to see Mother back, especially since the new school year was around the corner, and I wanted to count on her, my security blanket, being around!

Late that same summer, one day, around sunset, on my way home from the YMCA, and within a few hundred yards from home, I came upon a fellow screaming and hurling abusive swearwords, such as, "You horrible Palestinian SOBs; you don't belong here. You are ruining our country, etc., etc." at my nephew Rashied, Zahiyye's oldest son. At the same time, he was threatening to beat him up. Rashied, a very meek person by nature, was responding by only saying to the fellow, in a frightened manner, "Leave me alone." Somehow, Rashied did not seem to be able to get away from him. As soon as I was within thirty or so yards, I recognized the fellow. His name was Abdalla (Arabic for worshipper or servant of God). He was of a well-known clan in Tyre. The clan drew a lot of strength from being staunch supporters of the Lebanese Tyre deputy in the parliament; at times, a cabinet member of the Lebanese government. Some of Abdalla's older brothers were known to be henchmen of the deputy. I had known the boy for some time, and I knew him to manifest a mean spirit. He was of the same age as Rashied and me, and physically, about our size. As I realized what was happening, I naturally went to Rashied's help by gently fending off Abdalla with the palms of my hands while telling

Rashied to keep walking toward home. Abdalla shifted the swearing at me and slapped me hard in the face to the point of causing my ear to ring. I knew I could, alone, overpower him and beat him up; for sure Rashied and I together could. He was alone and nobody was in sight. But I had to grit my teeth and not retaliate, for I knew if I did, the matter would not end there. His henchman brothers would be drawn into this in the days to come against my brothers, and somebody would end up badly hurt if not dead, very likely from my family's side. I swallowed my pride, took Rashied by the arm, and kept walking homeward. Fortunately, Abdalla did not give chase; he seemed satisfied that he had humbled us enough. We made it home, otherwise, safely. As I passed by Abdalla in future days, I tried to keep a distance, not make eye contact, keep my head unbowed—deeply hurt, but uncowed!

As the start of the eighth grade was drawing near, I learned that the previous student supervisor of the college, who helped enroll me a year and a half ago, had resigned and moved up to Beirut. Mr. Mahmoud Ennana, in addition to teaching mathematics of our English section, and teaching Arabic for the combined French and English sections of the eighth grade class, had been appointed to be the college student supervisor (*annazir*), a position of power and prominence within the college. Mr. Ettaher continued to teach our English section English language and the sciences, and to serve as a director of the YMCA center.

In the morning of the first day of classes, Mr. Ennana kicked off the new year by addressing the entire student body of the college with an eloquent and resounding speech charging the student body to seek excellence in the pursuit of their education. The students stood silently in attention, and in orderly lines by grade, in the central hall of the college. It felt good to be his student.

My English eighth grade class had three students; Nazmi Kenaan, Mufid Essayyah, and me. Nazmi was a Palestinian from the town of El-Bassa, just south of the Lebanese border. Mufid was from Alma-esha'b, right on the Palestine Lebanese border.

When faced with a problem in algebra, I did not let go of it, if at all possible, until I figured out how to do it, even if it took days and/or sleepless nights. I did the same with geometry. I had more fun with geometry than algebra, and tackled intricate problems that Mr. Ennana described as challenging.

Students of both the English and French sections, of different grades, enjoyed posting hard algebra and geometry problems to each other on the cement walls surrounding cemeteries nearby, amidst ancient ruins overlooking the Mediterranean. Should you figure out a solution of wall-posted problems, then you were expected to post it and sign your name so that you might receive positive or negative comments depending on whether you were right or wrong, and so on it went (a predecessor of the Internet chat-room)! I became diligent about homework and often went beyond what was assigned. Similarly, I approached chemistry and physics in the same way but the subject matter was not presented in terms of solving problems as much as learning facts and rules. Mufid kept pace with the speed with which we were being taught. He was quite studious. Nazmi, on the other hand, tended to drag somewhat behind. I befriended Nazmi and worked to help him keep up. Mufid commuted back and forth daily between his hometown and Tyre. He did not spend time with any one of us outside the classroom. While we were cordial with Mufid, Nazmi and I became close buddies. Nazmi and I also mixed very well with schoolmates of the French section. I slowly but surely became a close friend with Suhayl Niemih, a top student in the French program, and four grades ahead of me. He and I were drawn to each other by the love of mathematics, science, and Arabic literature, especially poetry. Suhayl was only a couple years older. He was preparing for the Lebanese national examination of the Baccalaureate, Part 1, commonly referred to in French as *première partie*. He already was the holder of the Lebanese *Brevet*. The *Brevet* enabled many a holder to become teachers at the elementary grades level, as was the case with my *Certificat* teacher, Mr. Muhammad Issa. If the *Certificat* had some prestige, the Baccalaureate *première partie* had quite an aura, perhaps a bit more than the Palestinian Matriculation. Without exaggeration, it is fair to say that you could count the number of holders of the Baccalaureate *première partie* in the entire city of Tyre on the fingers of your hands. Much less were those who passed the national examination on the first try.

In the eighth grade English, Mr. Ettaher lightened up on spelling and straight reading, and introduced more study of poetry and novels. We studied some of John Milton's poetry, and the works of such writers such as Dickens and Shakespeare. We particularly concentrated on Shakespeare: *The Tempest*,

Hamlet, and *Othello.* We amassed an impressive vocabulary by the end of the school year. Inspired by Mr. Ennana, I delved deeper into Arabic grammar and poetry, with all of its intricacies and subtleties. Given that Arabic was our native language, the medium of our culture and mother tongue, made a huge difference in the thoroughness and depth with which we tackled it.

The Jaffariyya College was in fact, the major center of Arabic and religious studies (Islamic/ Shiite) in all of southern Lebanon. It frequently held literary contests and hosted Arab poetry recitals by major poets from around the Arab world, particularly Shiite Iraqis. Muslim theologians, again especially from Shiite Iraq, were hosted by the college. Some had a residency that lasted into weeks or at times, months. They conducted regular religious classes and/or gave series of lectures. Some of the Jaffariyya graduates went on to further study, often to Iraq, to become religious scholars, clerics or theologians. The college's titular head, Imam Hussein Sharafeddine, was a Shiite theologian revered all over Lebanon. Mr. Ennana (a Sunni Muslim) could not and would not have been given the task of teaching the eighth grade Arabic language course had he not been excellently competent and up to the task. He regularly demonstrated this. The field of Arabic called "I'raab" became a passion of mine. It is a process of dissecting sentence structure to figure the functional role of each word in the sentence, a sort of syntax analysis, identifying, for example, subject, predicate, adjective, adverb; the case, whether accusative, nominative, or dative; verb transitive or intransitive, etc. The process in Arabic, considerably more so than in English, is essential to define the precise meaning of a sentence, where otherwise different meanings would be possible, especially if the sentence is long and not of a straightforward form. I'raab helps determine the vowel ending of each word, among other things. It often provides a key to unlock and pin down the meaning of a seemingly abstruse Quranic verse or a veiled poetry line.

Sometime into my second middle school year, I was selected to recite a poem at a college celebration in acknowledgment of the satisfactory progress of the year and to give thanks for its accomplishments; a type of function that was held occasionally, especially if there were other activities taking place, like the presence of a distinguished guest or significant event in the Shiite calendar. It was held in the largest hall of the college building, the same hall that had housed many Palestinian refugee families about three years before. It usually was a male-only function attended by most teachers, guests of the college, and Imam Hussein Sharafeddine. I do not recall the particulars of the occasion nor the poem that was selected for me. With some nervousness, and completely from memory, I recited the poem flawlessly. Through the delivery, Imam Sharafeddine applauded me a few times with the phrase, "Ahsanta ya hassoun!" a kind of play on words which literally meant, "Well done oh well-doer!" (Hassoun's literal meaning is well-doer). At the end of the recital, I walked to the Imam, kissed his hand, and walked back to my seat amidst the applause of the audience. I was in seventh heaven! None of my family members were in attendance to share in my excitement.

As the school year began to draw near its end, I was beginning to develop a reputation at the college and the Tyre community, particularly the Palestinian one, as a valuable home-grown resource on questions of I'raab, and the deciphering of the meaning of challenging poetry and Quranic verses. Mr. Ennana played a big role in inspiring me to want attain excellence; for in class discussions, after unraveling a seemingly complicated passage or line, he would turn to me for an opinion or input. That image of a budding Arabic linguist gave me a tremendous sense of worth and satisfaction.

Outside class, during that general time period when Mr. Ennana would happen to pass by in a hallway or a corridor, he would stop for a brief and friendly chat. Through some of these chats, I began to learn tidbits of his personal life despite the fact that he usually guarded it judiciously. I found out that while in Palestine, he taught in the Galilee area, in the public school system, until the Palestinians, in 1947, began to arm for the defense of their country in the face of the Zionist threat. At about the time of the general suspension of classes in the country, he became involved in the building of the armed defense of the Galilee area. He later became some kind of a soldier, with a fair degree of leadership and responsibility in the Arab Liberation Army, ALA, headed by the Lebanese-born military veteran of liberation wars, particularly against the French in Syria and Lebanon, Fawzi Al-Qawuqji. The ALA was put together hurriedly by the Arab League as a stop-gap measure in the face of the deteriorating Arab military situation in Palestine vis-à-vis the Zionists. With the onset of warfare shortly upon the UN partition resolution, the ALA became involved in quite a bit of action all over Palestine, but particularly, in the north. Mr. Ennana must have participated in a fierce fight against the Haganah in the battle of Esh-Shajara, a village west of the Sea of Galilee in the Mount Tabor area; for he specifically referred to it often in these chats with evident emotion and first-hand knowledge. The battle was lost to the Haganah. The ALA, despite some successes, eventually ended up in defeat and demise. Thereafter, Mr. Ennana came to settle in Tyre, partly because of proximity to north of Palestine, but also, probably more importantly, because he had close family ties on the side of his wife in Tyre, herself a former Tyrene.

Mr. Ennana's experience with the ALA must have influenced the way he conducted himself as the college student supervisor, as there was a certain military tone in the way he tried to inspire the students and whip them up into shape. I recall once, in the latter part of the school year, as I was walking in the central hallway, I came upon him and a student, a classmate from the French section, having a heated argument over a matter that I no longer recall, at which point the angry student was steeling himself to raise his hand to strike Mr. Ennana. Immediately, instinctively, and absolutely without hesitation, I sandwiched myself between them while facing the student. Firmly, but with a caring tone, I told the student you mustn't! I was amazed how readily the classmate heeded me, and the situation was defused. I had no idea what Mr. Ennana's reaction would be. To my surprise, he seemed very appreciative. Since that event, I seemed to grow even taller in his eyes; it sealed a special bond between us. The student was not disciplined, and the episode was left to dissipate into oblivion. My relation with the classmate also continued to be cordial.

My friendship with my classmate Nazmi Kenaan got close to the point of spending considerable time after school with him. I got to know all five members of his family; his parents, two older brothers, and his older sister. The parents seemed to show a nonchalant attitude towards Nazmi's education and upbringing. Nazmi manifested, at the same time, a bent for mischief. As early as the *Certificat* days, he used to smuggle out cigarettes from his father to a far side of the schoolyard and smoke them. It was an area where other mischievous students walked out to smoke as well. Generally, the "smoking students" tended to be upper classmen, typically eleventh and twelfth graders. My friend Suhayl, in fact, was one of them. As it so happened, there were a few villa-type upper crust homes within view from that side of the schoolyard. In one of these villas there lived a family that had several young women of striking beauty. It was not uncommon that these young women would be in the open-air porch of the villa where they could see that side of the schoolyard and the activities therein, and, conversely, where the students could also see them. The young women's heads were uncovered, for they were, after all, not in public but in their home. So, for these students, in addition to smoking, it was an area to enjoy pleasant scenery, as it were, which was hard to come by elsewhere! An element of showmanship by the smoking students, as if to impress the young women in the distance with their manliness, also crept into the dynamic of the situation. Yet, occasionally, some non-smoking students went there to see what they could see as well. These activities (or games) were common knowledge in the college, but were met bemusedly rather than sternly by the administration, many of whom were smokers. Gradually, in the eighth grade, compounded by curiosity and my own share of mischief, I began to puff on Nazmi's cigarettes. In fact, Nazmi and I did not stop there. We started to walk farther out of the schoolyard to the western side of town, by the sea, to smoke. We found a nearby shop in that section of town that sold single cigarettes rather than packs. We paid dearly for those cigarettes. We further came to know, in that neighborhood, the French-missionary girls' school (it may have been called Saint Joseph) run by nuns; everybody referred to it as the Nuns' School. The terminal school grade was the *Certificat*. The girls, mostly Shiite Muslims, were very well groomed and classy, thirteen-to-fourteen years in age, borderline, age wise, to be veiled. We identified about four of them that looked very attractive and located strategic observation corners nearby to watch them in their goings and comings. Boy, did we ever get a big thrill if we attracted the attention of any one of them, or got a smile! The girls became aware of our antics, and it appeared they were having fun, but very discreetly, too. This went on sporadically for a few months. Through it all, neither I nor Nazmi, at least when I was around, ever attempted to exchange even one word with any of these girls, let alone engage them in a conversation; just distant fooling around. My sisters-in-law, at home, noticed that I was spending inordinate amount of time in front of the mirror combing my hair, etc. They got a kick out of it. Occasionally, they would teasingly query, "What are you up to?" It is curious that nobody seemed to smell the tobacco on my breath, at least as far as I knew.

Away from school, during the two years of middle school, I periodically did things with my cousin Ahmad. He was the second son of Uncle Tawfiq and his fourth child. He was about a year older than me. Ahmad had shown no interest in schools, even before our flight to Lebanon. He was of keen native intelligence, which unfortunately was channeled into mischief. While I was diligently trying to go to school, he was mostly drifting, occasionally doing odd jobs in Tyre. He was known to commit petty thefts, primarily from family members. His parents would sternly scold him, but it did not seem to do any good. Such behavior notwithstanding, and living a short walk from us, it was natural for me to see him and do things with him. After all, he was my cousin. Ahmad frequented some dingy coffeehouses in the heart of Tyre's downtown. He played cards for petty money and played billiards. Every now and then, when school would be closed, he would entice me to accompany him. I quickly learned some of these games and played along with him and others; typically, a foursome. He enjoyed showing me how much better he was than me, both in cards and billiards. He seemed to get a kick out of educating me into his activities and showing me his world. I enjoyed the sense of adventure and excitement associated with it all. While walking back and forth between home and downtown, he would quiz me to find out what I knew about sex. My naiveté was beyond his belief. While at Jaffariyya, we had an hour a week of religious education in which sex and bodily hygiene were touched upon in the context of Islamic duties and wholesome living. Sex was alluded to in a very subtle and indirect way, which to me was very general and vague, and did not sink in very far. So, cousin Ahmad would proceed to educate me about the "birds and the bees" so to speak. I found his "lectures" intriguing and enlightening, and readily verifiable in the animal kingdom. When it came to human sexuality and intercourse, I initially would not believe what he was telling me. In between such exchanges, I would try to check them against what Fouad knew. Fouad had no interest to talk explicitly about these matters with me and would turn me away. It was at least months before I came around to tentatively entertain Ahmad's assertions. It was not until the following year, in my senior high school biology class, that I actually learned about them with precision, objectively, and in a textbook in a school setting.

As the second middle school year, 1950-51, drew to a close, the question of, "What next?" became overriding. Everybody understood that this was as far as I could go at Jaffariyya. I had learned enough material in the past two years in the key subjects of the Palestinian high school curriculum to qualify me to go straight to the senior year. I no longer fit within the Lebanese national/French high school system. Attempts at establishing or developing equivalencies between the French/Lebanese and the English/Palestinian systems for my situation was not readily tractable, to say the least. Therefore, if I wanted to complete my high school education, I would have to look for an appropriate private high school, with a British or American system, probably in Beirut, where with some effort I could adjust and fit. At the end of the school year, my friend Suhayl along with the whole twelfth-grade, a handful number of students, took the Lebanese national examination, Baccalaureate *première partie*. When the results came out and got published, Suhayl was the only student in that group to pass it on a first try. His star in Tyre shined higher and brighter than ever before!

The school year 1950-51 also witnessed an important evolution on the family front. Compounded by brother Fouad's getting married, the laundry income got strained to maintain the full household. Fakhriyye moving into the household, and swiftly becoming pregnant, led Fouad to think in earnest beyond work at the laundry. Early in the summer of 1950, the Union of the Evangelical Congregational Churches of America, with an office in Beirut, set out to provide assistance for the Palestinian refugees in Lebanon. A major thrust of their assistance was the sponsoring of schools, grade one through sixth, in key places of high Palestinian concentration. Tyre was one of the sites. In conjunction with the Red Cross and other pre-existing assisting groups in town, such as the YMCA, a principal and a home for the school were found. A committee of local community leaders was formed to recruit teachers for the school. Since certified teachers were virtually non-existent, the committee set up a qualifying examination, with time and place specified, for anyone wishing to apply for these positions. Mahmoud Essouri, finally out of jail, and Fouad, were among those who applied. They got the two highest scores among all of the applicants. Initially, the committee offered Mahmoud a position at the Tyre school, and Fouad was offered a position at

a similar school being set up in Qana.[62] Mahmoud, being without work ever
since the exodus of 1948, was happy to accept. Fouad declined the Qana
offer. It was just not practical to leave the family household. In a relatively
short time afterward, however, Fouad was also offered a position at the
Tyre school. He readily accepted. The salary offered for these positions was
meager, about $20 per month! One of the classes to which he was assigned,
kindergarten or preschoolers, had to be housed temporarily in a tent on the
grounds adjacent to the building in which space was gradually being rented
and remodeled for the school. The class had about thirty-five students. He
assumed his duties in the fall of 1950. I went to visit Fouad's tent-classroom
shortly thereafter. Later, Fouad needed a substitute for a couple of hours. The
time did not conflict with my Jaffariyya classes. I therefore gladly did it. It
was humbling—how hot the tent-classroom could be! Ever since that time,
Fouad and I prided ourselves that our teaching careers began in a kindergarten
preschoolers' tent-classroom!

Fouad did not altogether drop his work at the laundry right away. The laundry
needed his pressing services, and he could use the additional income. He thus
continued his pressing work after school hours. His pressing, however, could
no longer be done in public downtown, for it would have been in poor taste if
not objectionable to school higher-ups. Therefore, Fouad did the pressing at
home and was paid according to his output of pressed clothes.

Hamadi tried to engage me more in the laundry work after school hours. I
found myself rebelling for the first time ever. One evening, he was scolding
me to my mother for not doing enough at the laundry. I instinctively exploded
at him by pointing out that he hardly touched the iron anymore, and that he
spent quite a bit of time, by his own boasting, socializing with rich spinsters
in Tyre. I was very surprised by my own behavior and utterances. Hamadi,
by then, enjoyed a very high family standing. He was nicknamed Ezza'im,
meaning, the boss. How dare I challenge him? Hamadi, with wide-open eyes,
startled at my unexpected and uncustomary response, remained speechless. I
got up and ran out of the house bare footed for a couple of hundred yards to

62 Site of the April 1996 Israeli-bombed UN compound causing many civilian casualties,
some twelve miles southeast of Tyre; also believed by some to be the biblical El-Kana,
where Jesus performed the water to wine miracle.

a nearby beach. The sky was clear, studded with stars, and the air was on the chilly side. Fortunately, Yousef came behind me and convinced me to go back home and apologize to Hamadi, which I did; for beneath my outburst was a wellspring of affection and respect for him. He in turn was unusually kind and forgiving, which also surprised me. I was glad that Yousef came after me, for I was beginning to shudder at having to spend the night at the beach, bare-footed beneath the star-studded sky above! It was the first and last serious confrontation I had with Hamadi. It was also the only time I attempted to run away from home. Hamadi changed his way of dealing with me and began to show interest in my schoolwork.

Early in the summer of 1951, Mother, Fouad, and I began to think in earnest of my next school. The laundry was clearly not an option. We began to survey potential schools in the Beirut area. Fouad and Mother looked for the highest quality English/American school that was affordable. Through Fouad's newly developed connections in education, one Beirut high school, the Evangelical National Protestant College (ENCP), seemed to stand out above all others, for its compatibility, quality, and affordability. It taught grades seventh through eleventh; the eleventh being the terminal senior high school grade. It had a similar curriculum to that of the Palestinian Mandate System. The college was also an outreach of the Union of Evangelical Congregational Churches of America that was opening the Tyre School for Palestinian refugees, and for which Fouad had started working. The ENCP headmaster, Mr. Kamel Deeb, was a well-regarded and experienced educator from Palestine. The majority of the teachers were also former high school teachers from Palestine. There were, nevertheless, two upfront hurdles: First, the college did not have boarding so my family had to arrange for my housing and food. Second, the tuition fees, though not prohibitively high, still had to be reckoned with.

Mother, Fouad, and I recognized that going to school in Beirut would be considerably facilitated if I had a partner, a classmate from Tyre. In particular, the partner and I would share in the rental of a room and provide companionship for each other. There was one realistic and obvious candidate, namely Nazmi. Mufid was a Lebanese citizen with some knowledge of French, and could switch to the French system more readily than Nazmi and I could. Mother wasted no time. She visited with Nazmi's parents and coaxed them into teaming up with her to send both Nazmi and me to the ENCP. I, in turn, sold Nazmi on the idea. Both Nazmi and his parents were rather lukewarm, but they agreed to go along with it. Mother assured Nazmi's parents that whatever arrangements were made would be for both of us equally.

Part way into the summer, Mother decided that it was time that she go to Beirut to visit in person with Mr. Deeb, the school headmaster. She arranged for an appointment to see him in his office. She asked for a companion from among her older sons. Hamadi, being the most schooled in the family and the "Boss" offered to go with her and to speak on my behalf, and by extension, on behalf of Nazmi. He visited with Messrs. Ennana and Ettaher, who strongly endorsed the plan, and he gathered a fair amount of information about the school material covered the past two years. In addition to securing admission, the purpose of the visit was also to explain our financial situation and the need for some kind of financial assistance to cover tuition, estimated at about $160 for the year. Mr. Deeb was very sympathetic and impressed by what he had heard. Consequently, he offered to waive the school fees for both Nazmi and me. He also agreed to admit us into the senior year on a probationary basis. When mother and Hamadi came back home with the news, we all rejoiced. The next step was to find a rental room for Nazmi and me. Nazmi, his father, my mother, and I traveled to Beirut within a few days after Mother's return from her visit with Mr. Deeb, to rent a suitable and affordable room. As it happened, ENCP was located in Ras Beirut, the same section of town as AUB's campus. Specifically, it was housed in a single building looking over the sea; about fifteen minutes walk from the AUB campus. Student room rental was thus common in the area; however, we were advised to seek the help of a rental broker to expedite the process. By the middle of the afternoon, a room was found for the monthly rate of about $16. It seemed to meet our need very well. Mother and Nazmi's father signed a contract on the spot; the rent was equally split between them. The room was part of a three-bedroom apartment where a widow and her son lived. Her name was Umm Raja, Raja being her son's name.

All along, Mother had reasoned that with the tuition waiver, her emergency reserve (albeit quite limited, about $300), and a projected income from the laundry, she could afford the year.. While my brothers gave me moral support, for which I am eternally grateful, their own family responsibilities were such that none of them was in a position to offer me material support. Mother, as a rule, tended to manage to put away a little money for emergency reserve no matter how puny her income was. One of her quips was, "Only to within the extent of your carpet, you may stretch out your legs." Over her lifetime, she had also built up a sizable collection of gold jewelry, mostly bracelets. She referred to them as her "last resort" and old age security. When a family need would appear overwhelming, she would say, "If I have to, I will sell some or all of my jewelry." She said this to me as we were groping for ways to meet the needs of the upcoming school year. Fortunately, she did not have to.

CHAPTER 9

BEIRUT

M y travels from Tyre to Beirut or vice versa typically were on a bus of the Tyre-Beirut bus line. It had a fleet of three buses owned and managed by Tyrenes. The buses were the old fashioned kind, not unlike the 1940s school buses in the USA. They had a capacity of about thirty passengers and a luggage rack on the roof. Individual windows, pulled up or down via a leather strap, provided the air conditioning. The three buses left the main square of downtown Tyre in succession in the morning, two hours apart; early morning, midmorning, and just before noon. They returned from Beirut in a similar succession; a bit before noon, early afternoon and late afternoon. The departure times were approximate and somewhat a function of how full the bus would be. There was a bus driver and an assistant. The assistant helped passengers to embark and disembark, helped with luggage, and collected fares. There were no tickets; the passenger told the assistant his/her destination, and the assistant pronounced the fare on the spot. The Tyre-Beirut full fare was one Lebanese lira (or one Lebanese pound, roughly $0.35); to Sidon, half a lira; and in between major stops, one quarter of a lira. The fare was not affected by the amount of baggage you had. The bus driver generally allowed for passengers that would be picked up off the side of the road, in the countryside, as he decided the precise time to start the trip. He had a "feel" as to how many to anticipate on a given trip. In general, everybody had a seat, but if the demand was heavy, passengers picked up off the side of the road might have had to stand in the aisle. If the aisle was quite full, then prospective passengers were not picked up. Those unlucky ones had to wait for the next bus (about 2 hours); or, they turned back and went home for better luck another day.

While buses were the primary mode of transportation for the bulk of the population, there was also taxi service. Like the buses, taxis were owned and managed by Tyrenes. Taxis, however, charged two and a half liras per passenger for the full Tyre-Beirut trip. Rarely did they take Sidon passengers.

There were taxis for Sidon only. Taxis, as a rule, did not pick up passengers in between main stops. The taxi cars were often the German Mercedes brand or American car brands that had seven seats. These cars were typically purchased second (or nth!) hand and were at least five and often more like ten years old. Very few people had private cars, definitely less than one percent of the population. The bus duration for the Tyre-Beirut (or vice versa) trip, inclusive of the stops along the way, took somewhere between two to two-and-a-half hours; the taxi took half as long.

I usually took the bus. After arriving at the bus depot in Beirut, I would walk over to the nearest tram stop to Ras Beirut. The electric tram was the primary public transportation of Beirut. I would get off the tram at the stop nearest to the rented room, which was almost right in front of the main gate of AUB; it was an additional couple of hundred yards further to the rented room. The time it took to go from the Beirut Tyre bus stop to my room at Umm Raja's place was easily a half-hour to forty minutes. The time it took to get to my room from Tyre was over three hours. About eight miles north out of Tyre was the crossing of the southern flank of the Litani River known as the Qasimiyya. The Qasimiyya was deemed a militarily strategic crossing. It had a checkpoint. All vehicles were stopped and ID's had to be shown. Passengers with Palestinian ID's were checked more carefully than Lebanese; sometimes even harassed, including myself, for no apparent reason. God help those who for some reason or another did not have their ID's on them. More often than not, they were turned back to their starting point. At times when political disturbances had just occurred or were likely to occur, Palestinians were required to get permits to go back and forth across the river. Obtaining permits was often a very unpleasant, humiliating, and time-consuming affair.

Early on, Nazmi and I traveled together; but shortly afterwards, our travel tended not to jibe, and we traveled separately.

The walk to the ENPC from our new home was about twenty minutes. The school building had a quadrangular central hall surrounded by the classrooms. The kick-off morning meeting for the new school year started at 8:00 am. The students of all grades, about 150, assembled in that hall. The principal, Mr. Kamel Deeb, welcomed the students and introduced the faculty. Some members of the Congregational Church Clergy of Beirut were present and were introduced. Mr. Deeb spoke in English interspersed with Arabic. He then led the assembly with a prayer followed by general orientation remarks. Although the prayer may have been non-denominational, it definitely had a Christian ring to it, in comparison to the prayers and inspirational speeches I was used to at Jaffariyya. I was not bothered in the least. We were told the day begins at 8:00 am with a prayer and an inspirational talk by either a faculty or an outside guest. Classes followed at 8:30 am. To my surprise, I recognized some of the students in the assembly; some from Haifa, some from Tyre, and some from Sidon! At the conclusion of the meeting, we headed to our individual classrooms identified by big signs on the individual room doors. The senior class had twenty-two students. I was filled with apprehension, anticipation, and excitement.

As the seniors entered their classroom, I met Mansour Bardawiel! Mansour attended Jaffariyya and was two grades ahead of me while his younger brother, Abdu, was a *Certificat* classmate in the English section. They had moved with their family to Beirut the year before. While Mansour was surprised to see Nazmi and me in the senior (eleventh grade) class, he did not question it. Abdu was in the ninth grade. Further on, I then recognized Muhammad Saffouri. He was the outgoing, confident fellow that sat next to me at the *Certificat* government national examination hall in Sidon! That was unexpected, given the leap Nazmi and I had made.

Nazmi and I were welcomed readily into the fold. As the other students greeted each other, there was quite a bit of English mixed with Arabic in their conversation although all the students were Arabic-speaking natives. Except for Arabic, English was the language of instruction for all the other subjects, namely: history, mathematics, physics, chemistry, biology, and of course, English. At Jaffariyya, there was very little conversational English. The transition to converse in English was the most challenging in the English and history courses. In these classes, Arabic was rarely spoken. The history course was about modern Europe from the beginning of the French revolution to the beginning of World War I. In the English language course, the syllabus included a recommended list of novels; among these were, *A Tale of Two Cities* by Dickens, *For Whom the Bell Tolls* by Hemingway,

Madame Bovary by Flaubert, *War and Peace* by Tolstoy. I always found myself behind in the reading assignment. I was much slower at reading and understanding than I was expected to be. My knowledge of the vocabulary was adequate, but I often did not understand the meaning of sentences or paragraphs. I made up for that with grammar, spelling, and composition. Appreciating these novels was longtime in coming. The history class teacher lectured exclusively in English and tended to use big and unfamiliar words; the textbook was no different. After some weeks of intensive textbook study with the aid of the dictionary, however, the lectures and the textbook gradually began to make sense. Eventually, the history class helped my English class and enhanced my English conversational skills. One of the early things my mother bemusedly noticed, within a couple of months of being at the ENPC, was that I was beginning to use English phrases or expressions in home conversations.

Nazmi and I made friends readily. Virtually all the classmates were Palestinians who had come from major cities: Haifa, Jaffa, and Acre. Of the entire student body, there was a large concentration from Haifa. It was among those that I recognized a handful that had attended the Haifa government school. To my best recollection now, there were hardly any Jerusalemites. One reason seemed to have been the fact that East Jerusalem continued, post-1948 Nakba, under Arab (Jordanian) control; another, there were no simple land routes from Jerusalem to Lebanon. Escapees from the Jerusalem area tended to go eastward towards Jordan. About two thirds of the ENPC students were Muslims, the remaining third, Christians. With one exception, all the faculty members were Christians; about two-thirds Palestinians, the remainder Lebanese. Even the Lebanese faculty had ties of one kind or another to Palestine. The majority of the faculty members were college graduates (mostly of AUB) and professional teachers. The sole Muslim faculty, Mr. Taher Fydi, was our biology and chemistry teacher. He was from Nablus (biblical Shechem). He had taught briefly in Palestine but chose, perhaps as a result of the Nakba, to pursue a pharmacy degree at AUB. He made it known to all that upon his completion of his education at AUB, he intended to go back to the West Bank/Jordan to practice, either in Nablus or Amman, Jordan's capital city. At the time he taught us, he was in his last year of training, after which he would be able to practice as a pharmacist. Aside from enjoying teaching, which was apparent in how he mixed with students, his part-time teaching at the ENPC helped support him.

Because of the ENPC intimate connection to the American Congregational Church mission, and the background of the faculty, the college adopted a mixture of English and American high school educational systems. This was evident in the textbooks for the courses. One other important factor, however, served to fashion the curriculum: In addition to providing solid general education and preparing the students to enter the labor force of the Arab society, ENPC desired to facilitate for its students admission to the all-encompassing neighbor, that is the AUB. Although both AUB and ENPC had similar church missionary histories, reasons for being, and cultures, AUB did not accredit ENPC to admit its graduates to AUB without an entrance examination, in contrast to the International College (AUB's own preparatory high school), Shweifat National College, and the Gerard Institute of Sidon. The latter three could merely recommend their high school graduates for AUB admission and they would be admitted with no questions asked. Behind this apparent discriminatory paradox was that ENPC was still a nascent college (about three years old; established after the 1948 Nakba) of untested credentials. AUB, however, did not close the door to the graduates of ENPC, nor for that matter, many other high schools in the English/American system elsewhere in Lebanon. It stipulated that high school graduates who desired to be admitted to AUB, without submitting themselves to AUB's entrance examination, could do so by passing the University of London General Certificate of Education (GCE) examination. The latter was offered through the British Council in Beirut twice a year, i.e., two sessions; one in June and the second in November. Typically, it involved a total of six subjects as follows: English, Arabic, history, mathematics, physics, and general science. While ENPC wanted to provide us with a solid education for life, at the same time it wanted us to qualify for university education if we were to choose it. AUB being a standard measure, ENCP, therefore, encouraged its senior class members to submit to the GCE examination in the six mentioned subjects. Unless a male high school graduate of the English/American schools in Lebanon was willing and able to leave the country to seek higher education elsewhere, AUB was his primary option.[63]

In the minds of the Palestinian community of Lebanon, the GCE was treated as a replacement for the Palestinian Matriculation, which had ceased to exist with the end of the British mandate over Palestine on May 15, 1948. Hence, the great appeal and relevance ENCP had to Palestinian refugees in Lebanon. AUB further provided that those applicants for admission, who failed subjects in the GCE examination, could submit to substitute examinations administered by AUB, upon passing which, would then qualify. English was the most frequently failed subject by GCE examination takers in Lebanon. At the time, a handful of GCE examination takers over a three-year period of administration history, could boast passing the English examination on the first try. The explanation often given or heard was that it is quite a task for an Arabic native to perform in English at the level of an English native judged by the University of London. More than a handful, yet a small percentage still, tended to pass five subjects in one session.

The English language examination of AUB was far more passable than that of the University of London. Passing the AUB English examination was also required for freshman admission of all holders of the French-based Lebanese Baccalaureate, *première partie*. Because of AUB's prestige and leading role as an educational institution of higher learning in the Middle East and the greater region surrounding it, the number of applicants to its freshman class exceeded manifold the number of students accepted. Qualifying for admission was no guarantee of admission, but subject to space availability, financial support, and relative academic standing among all qualified applicants. To better appreciate the magnitude of the challenge, the freshman class size around that period was about three hundred and

---

63 Female graduates did have another option, namely, Beirut College for Women (BCW). This should not, however, be construed to mean that female students had a greater choice or more options since the BCW was less than half the size of AUB (enrollment about 3200) and AUB's female student population during that era was only about 20%. In all of Lebanon at the time, AUB was the leading full-fledged institute of higher learning. The Lebanese University was in a preliminary developing phase, and there were a couple of French-based private colleges. Arab Palestine before the Nakba, had virtually no full-fledged university. If anything, it had a couple of small Teachers Training Colleges and one Junior Agricultural College.

fifty, and AUB's student body represented over fifty-five countries, mostly Middle-Eastern and African. It was a major accomplishment indeed, and a cause of great rejoicing of a high school graduate to gain admission.

My mother, at times accompanied by Fouad, visited me weekly the entire school year. On these visits, she would be laden with delicious home cooking in quantities to last me at least three days (there was no refrigeration), as well as fresh fruit, and sometimes, sweets. She would also give me enough allowance to cover the food expenses for the rest of the week, including pocket money. This averaged about a dollar a day. About once a month, I went down to Tyre instead. Nazmi's family worked things out differently. Nazmi's mother rarely came to Beirut to visit. His father and brother, Ramzi, would separately pop up unexpectedly from time to time bringing fruit and sweets. Nazmi had a larger weekly allowance and bought ready-made food. The room had no cooking facility. He was free to go to Tyre as needed, generally biweekly. Nazmi and I shared circumstantially and at each other's pleasure our families' food supplies. My mother consistently encouraged me to treat him as a brother. There was never a problem in this regard.

Nazmi's smoking became more open and frequent. He, nevertheless, continued to conceal it from his parents and kept it away from the school grounds. He and I had smoked off and on in Tyre, consequently, I continued with it, even more so, being largely unsupervised (in hindsight to my shame!). His brother Ramzi's visits were no help. Ramzi was at least three years older than Nazmi; Nazmi was a couple of months younger than me. Ramzi not only smoked, but also bragged about it, and induced us to go ahead and have fun. Additionally, he would brag about his adventures in the big city.

I will never forget the time when my mother, accompanied by Fouad, surprised me on one of their weekly visits by showing up at our room's door somewhat early. I was alone and happened to be smoking! They were inside the room before I knew it, so to speak. With the cigarette in my hand, I was so startled that I did not know what to do. I simply and foolishly dropped it on the room's ceramic floor. Fouad saw it right away. It was still smoldering. Without drawing attention to it, especially mother's attention, he walked to it, stepped over it and put it out, and then, while mother was looking the other way, picked it up and threw it into the trashcan. Mother did not seem to notice anything. If she did, she never let me know. No words concerning the matter were exchanged between Fouad and me until some time later when we two were alone. I was struck and relieved by his forgiving attitude; he merely said, "You should try not to do it; it is not good for you!"

Nazmi gradually explored more and more the neighborhood of Ras Beirut. He managed to find a girls' high school nearby. He began to frequent locations where he would watch his favorite girl or girls in their goings and comings, as he used to do in Tyre. Fortunately for me, I saw utterly no sense in it, though I had done some of it in Tyre. In fact, I felt it was a terrible abuse of precious time that should be spent on schoolwork. I just could not take lightly the sacrifices of my mother and family. Nevertheless, Nazmi persisted solo, and would come home to the room and tell me of his flirting in an exaggerated manner. He seemed to sense that I was not buying into his exaggerations; therefore, one time, he wrote himself a love note, as if from one of those girls, and showed it to me to convince me. I still was not convinced, for I was able to recognize his handwriting and he ultimately confessed.

As the school year unfolded, Nazmi's path and mine seemed to steadily diverge; we associated with different classmates as we did things such as going out for ice cream/gateau shops, movies, studying, bumming around the city, or engaging in the social and political discussions. In these activities among others, I found special rapport with and affinity for Muhammad Saffouri. In addition to having had adjacent seats in the Sidon *Certificat* examination hall, we were both born in Haifa. While my family sought refuge into Tyre, his sought it into Sidon. His father knew of the Hassoun laundry in Wadi-Ennisnas, and knew, though casually, my brother Yousef. I went to the Shiite Jaffariyya College; he went to the Sunni Maqased College in Sidon. We then converged in Beirut about the same time to discover how much of soul mates we have been.

In contrast, however, to my large family, Muhammad had only a single sister; the whole family had moved to Beirut to accommodate his schooling. I further found out that he had relatives in Tyre that he had occasionally visited. I knew one of his cousins. Perhaps more importantly, we both very earnestly aspired to understand the world all around us and impact it positively. It was not too long before other students and teachers began to associate us with

each other. Muhammad's extroversion, studiousness, and assertiveness were
no less evident in his senior year than when I first encountered him in Sidon;
in contrast, I tended to be more reserved and less assertive in my new Beirut
surroundings. Muhammad made friends fast, and he became a catalyst in my
making more friends too. Among these, was Raja Khalil Khouri.[64] Raja's
father, Mr. Khalil Khouri, was our English language teacher. Mr. Khouri's
last home before taking refuge in Beirut was Jaffa, where he had taught high
school English as well. Mr. Khouri, at other times, had also worked for the
British Mandate Government in diverse capacities. He did not have a college
degree, but clearly was very experienced and competent at his teaching. Of all
the classmates, Raja spoke English the most in his interactions with others,
and very fluently. It almost seemed as if it was his first language, although his
Arabic was clearly that of a native. In fact, I soon found out that his mother,
a Palestinian, was also an English teacher in a girls' school in Ras Beirut;
perhaps the one that Nazmi used for his frequent "watchings!" It was evident
from week one that Muhammad and Raja were the top two shining stars of the
senior class. They frequently, on any given test, would have the two highest
scores. I felt it a big compliment to be one of their circle. Muhammad seemed
to be top in mathematics and the sciences, while Raja was best in English
and perhaps, history. They deferred to me in Arabic literature and grammar.
Mr. Taher Fydi, our biology and chemistry teacher, was also attracted to our
circle, and he would mingle and socialize with us three. In fact, it turned out
that he was living at a place not far from where I was rooming, and not far,
as well, from where Raja and his family lived. Muhammad lived in a Beirut
section, virtually across town, from which he commuted daily. Nevertheless,
sometimes, Muhammad, Raja, Mr. Fydi and I would walk together and talk
until reaching the tram station, or where Raja lived, before breaking up. At
times, Mr. Khouri would socialize with us as well. Our relationships gradually
grew stronger and every now and then, Mr. Khouri would ask us to come in
to his home for refreshments. There we would meet Mrs. Khouri (Umm Sami,
Raja's mother), Raja's other and older two brothers, Sami and Nabih, and his
younger sister, the youngest of them all. While I would tread diffidently and

---

64 The name Khouri, also Khuri, is Arabic for priest. A person with Khouri/ Khuri in his/her
    name is a signature of his/her being a Christian or of Christian background.

lightly, and consider it quite an honor to be invited in, the Khouris would receive all of us very hospitably. On these occasions, everybody in the group, whether it was Mr. Fydi, Muhammad, or the Khouris (with the exception of the young sister who usually watched from a distance), had so much to talk about, and talk we did. Both English and Arabic were used interchangeably, depending on which language happened to more expressively convey an idea at a given point. While the conversations often dealt with the individual members' future hopes, aspirations and plans for realizing them, the conversations frequently wound up on the Palestinian Nakba. Mr. Khouri often listened to us youngsters intently, and with very sympathetic eyes.

Among many other things, I learned through these get-togethers that Sami was in his junior year at AUB, preparing to be a civil engineer. Nabih had graduated from ENPC the previous year, and had passed the GCE in six subjects. He was the only student in all of Lebanon that year, among those who submitted to the GCE examination, to have passed English on the first try. Sami had done the same two years before. Because of finances, however, Nabih was holding a job in the city for the year to save enough money to enroll at AUB the following year. He also planned to pursue a degree in civil engineering. Raja expected to go to work for a year after high school before the family could afford to send him to the university; by then, it was hoped that Sami would have graduated and gotten a job. I further learned that Muhammad's family had no means whatsoever to provide for their son's going to the university. His father was unemployed (also unemployable because of a health/back problem) and his mother, through her long sewing hours, was barely able to provide for the necessities of life. To my surprise, my situation began to appear to me to be not too bad! Both Mr. Khouri and Mr. Fydi took special interest in how they might help Muhammad secure financial assistance to get into AUB the following school year. I shied away from talking about my financial particulars. The group gathered in a general way that I had a mother, three older brothers; one a teacher, and the other two in a laundry business. Presumably, I should be able to manage somehow.

As the first quarter of the year came to a close and the grades came in, I ranked fifth in the class. Muhammad was first; Raja, second, Mansour Bardawiel, third, Issam Abu Issa (a Palestinian from a refugee camp, Burj el-Barajneh, on the outskirts of Beirut), fourth. The top two did not come as a surprise to anybody. Naturally, I would have liked to rank better, but at the core, I was not unhappy considering all the hoops I had jumped through. Nazmi ranked about fifteenth. He did not seem bothered.

One of the school activities that I grew to enjoy and looked forward to was the morning prayer and the inspirational talk. It was the only extracurricular activity the school participated in collectively. ENPC had not had time, space, or material resources to develop a sports program, among other things.

The guest speaker of one of those inspirational meetings was the principal of the International College, Mr. Levitt. He spoke in English. He talked about the big challenges that Arab society was and would be facing as it entered the second half of the twentieth century. He went on to tell us of five ills that Arab society, as he saw it, would have to address if it was to catch up and join the advanced societies of the West.

They were:[65]

First: *Ma'alesh*, Arabic for, "It does not matter." This phrase was frequently used to avoid confronting a problem and doing something about it. For example, let us say, a fellow just finished building a wall. For whatever reason thereafter, he looks at it and finds it is slightly tilted from the plumb line. He reacts to the tilt by saying, "Ma'alesh," and forgets about it instead of taking the extra time and effort to straighten it out. A tilt in the wall *does matter;* it should be corrected!

Second: *Bukra*, Arabic for, "Tomorrow." To use the above example, let us say you saw the tilted wall and convinced the fellow who built it that he should correct it. He says, "OK, but *bukra*," when he should do it today and now! Even then, there may be other *bukras*!

Third: *Mashshieha*, Arabic for, "Walk it through" or "Pass it through;" figuratively, "Okay it!" I'll use the tilted wall example again. Let us say you are inspecting the built wall and tell the fellow that the tilt should be straightened out before you sign off on it or approve it. He responds, because he does not feel like fixing it, by saying, "Mashshieha!" Instead of recognizing that it should not and must not be "passed through!"

---

65 The example and illustrations given here are my own for simplicity and conciseness. Mr. Levitt's illustrations were more varied and from real life situations; but made substantially the same points.

Fourth: *Inshallah*, Arabic for, "If God wills." Again, using the above wall problem, let us say you convinced the fellow it should be done right away. Then, you ask him to do it that same afternoon. He grudgingly agrees, but then he follows his agreeing by saying, "Inshallah." The afternoon passes, the task is not done, and you ask him, "Why not?" He responds, "God did not will it!" Or worse still, he might say, "*Bukra, Inshallah!*" I should hasten to note here that the issue is not that God's will should have been overridden: that could open a religious Pandora's box. The issue is that when he verbalized by injecting *Inshallah* to his agreement, was he saying it to express a religious conviction, or, was he, by injecting it, diluting his promise and commitment to get the job done that afternoon? Unfortunately, as most (conscientious) people who have lived in that part of the world would tell you, the use of *Inshallah* has been sadly corrupted to dilute commitment and give delinquency a way out.

Fifth: *Min Allah*, Arabic for, "From God." Continuing with the tilted wall example, let us say it is not straightened, and the edifice of which the tilted wall is a part, collapses, resulting in great harm. Confronting the builder-fellow as to how he could have allowed this wall to collapse, he says, "*Min Allah*," that is, "It is from God!" In other words, it is not his fault!

Throughout my senior high school year, it became a habit with me to share some of the messages I would hear at the morning meetings with my mother and the extended family during my visits back to Tyre. In this instance, the sharing was met with considerable receptivity. Yousef would look for a funny twist, while Hamadi wanted to hear the narrative in English.

There was one off-school experience that I had trouble sharing with anybody for a long time. It took place on a warm sunny day early in the spring term of the school year. I did not manage my allowance well that week and my money ran out two days too soon; before I received my next allowance. As it happened, there was no food of any kind to be found in the room either. Suddenly, I was faced with a problem I had not anticipated before, namely; being without money or food for the next forty-eight hours. I did not know Nazmi's money situation, yet I could not bring myself to tell him of my problem. He did not seem to notice it either. I could not bring myself, in fact, to tell anybody else, or explore or seek to borrow money from such. So, I simply drank a lot of water and got hungrier. As I was walking home from school at the end of that day, this time alone, I saw a sandwich with lettuce, tomatoes, and sausage that had been bitten off a couple of bites, placed on the top of a wall-fence of a family residence. Without hesitation, I walked to it and picked it up. I checked it out for cleanliness. It looked clean. I said to myself, *Some spoiled kid discarded it.* I was glad it was not thrown out onto the ground. I bit into it, it tasted good, I ate all of it as I continued my walk home. As I was eating, the thought did come to mind that the sausage might have been of pork, but it did not deter me. Since then, I've wondered at times, *Was that God's manna for me that day?* Relief did come the next day when Mother arrived. It was many months later before I told Mother or Fouad. There it rested; at no time did I tell anybody else for many years.

As the month of June drew nigh, the end of the school year seemed rapidly approaching, and everybody at school, seniors and faculty, were thinking of the GCE examination. My ranking in the class stayed the same, i.e., fifth. The rank was less on my mind than how well I was learning the course material. I frequently felt I had it within me to do much better, if only my external environment was more conducive.

The school final examinations and the GCE examinations were held in the third week of June 1952. All seniors took the GCE's six subjects examinations. The results of the GCE examinations would not appear until late in July. The school examination results appeared a few days before commencement, set for June 24. When the scores were posted, my rank again was still fifth. I further found out that the top two students in the class, Muhammad and Raja, would be graduating *with high distinction*, while the next two, Mansour and Issam, would be graduating *with distinction*. Further, the word somehow got out to me that I was a border case, and the decision not to include me with Mansour and Issam, made by Mr. Deeb, was a hard one. I felt slighted and shared my feelings with Muhammad Saffouri. He took my side and agreed that I deserved to graduate *with distinction*. We then both decided the matter deserved to be taken up with Mr. Deeb. Muhammad offered to go with me. I welcomed this. We did not waste any time in going to see him. He met us, as was his habit, very cordially. As soon as we brought up the matter, he smiled a big smile saying how happy he was to have us as students of ENPC and confirmed how hard it has been for him to draw the "distinction" line. Then, to my deep relief, he said, while looking at me, "On further assessing the matter, Ghazi, I think you deserve this honor. I will get to work on it right away so that the words, *with distinction* will be on your diploma in time. However, since the program had already been sent to the printer without the words, *with Distinction,* appearing next to my name, he said that during the commencement ceremony he would announce from the podium, as I come up to receive the diploma, that I was graduating *with distinction* though the program erroneously did not reflect my honor. Muhammad and I were satisfied and happily left his office.

While my particular ranking had not been a big thing for me, as noted herein before, I felt a great uplift in my morale when Mr. Deeb determined to grant me the honor; perhaps not so much for myself, but for my mother who had worked so hard to get me to this point. For economic and practical reasons, only Mother and Fouad attended the commencement. They joyously saw and heard Mr. Deeb confer upon me the high school diploma *"with distinction!"*

In Tyre, the entire Hassoun household was very happy with my accomplishment. They all recognized that this was a history-making event; the first of the Hassoun clan, or Aswad clan for that matter, to finish high school, and *with distinction* no less! There was also virtual unanimity at home that I should not stop here, that I should seek entry to AUB. Our attitude concerning financing was buoyed by past successes with a spirit that might be characterized by the saying, "If there is a will, there is a way."

If I was to secure admission to AUB, I had to prepare myself to pass the entrance examination, should I fall short in the GCE examination. So until the results of the GCE came out, the safe course of action for me was to knuckle down and prepare for that eventuality. It was economically out of the question, and probably emotionally inadvisable, for me to stay in Beirut during the summer. In Tyre, I had to find a quiet, peaceful place to study. In the meantime, I gathered as much information as I could about the nature of the examination and purchased books that were recommended by a variety of sources as most pertinent for the examination.

Tyre had no public library in which to study. The YMCA had a reading room, but it was not far from the games room. It was not quiet enough; there were many distractions nearby. As I surveyed my options, there were a few walls erected on the second floor of our Tyre dwelling, but no roof. The landlord had hoped, as noted earlier, to put up a second floor, but stopped short for lack of money. The second floor was accessed by the rail-less stairway underneath which where my mother and brother Yousef did their laundry washing. It could serve as a study space for the summer. There was one negative, because of the absence of a roof, I would have to follow the wall shades to protect myself from the direct summer sun. I decided it would have to do. I put up a simple chair and a small table that were quite mobile and rain resistant; though rain in the summer was quite scarce. It worked pretty well. It was quiet, private, and even enjoyable. I had the freedom to come and go as I pleased. I kept in touch with some of my Beirut classmate friends, most notably, Muhammad Saffouri.

The weeks of suspense eventually passed. The British Council finally announced the GCE examination results. Nobody in all of Lebanon had passed the English examination for that session, not even Raja or Muhammad! Only four students of all takers in all of Lebanon passed five subjects. They were all students of ENPC! They were: Muhammad, Raja, Mansour and **me**! Issam Abu Issa somehow stumbled on one examination, and he passed four subjects. Nazmi passed two subjects, Arabic and history.

I was regretful about failing English, though in good company with Raja and Muhammad, but euphoric about passing five subjects and being one of the four students in all of Lebanon! I felt redeemed and vindicated concerning my with distinction graduation. The examination results got published in many Lebanese newspapers. My celebrity in Tyre jumped an order of magnitude. I put away studying for a while and partied. Mother served sweets and drinks for several days as the family and friends came to congratulate. AUB looked close at hand; there remained only the AUB English entrance examination and the finances.

As the rejoicing subsided, my attention turned, in addition to passing the English examination and the finances, to the choice of a university major. My passionate interest in Arabic and religion at Jaffariyya tempted me at times to think in terms of becoming a writer or a Muslim scholar and/or Imam. I thought in terms of studying at the Cairo Al-Azhar University, the worldwide leading center of Islamic scholarship. I had frequented the Sunni mosque in Tyre, attended many of that mosque's Imam's teaching and preaching and found them fascinating. The Imam, Shaykh Musa Zuhair, was well regarded in the community; he was a graduate of Al-Azhar. However, I was quite mindful of the many logistical obstacles. Additionally, even before getting serious, brother Hamadi would pour cold water on such pursuits. He would say that writers, in the Arab World, are a dime a dozen. His political left leanings at the time also made him scoff at religion-related careers. He would often quote Lenin's famous line, "Religion is the opium of the people." If I were to mention political science, he would say, "You don't need to go to a university to study about politics. You go to coffee shops for that!" Also, Mother fully distrusted the Arab political arena. According to her, most likely, you'd end up either dead or in jail or, if lucky, banished! Law was far fetched because Palestinians in Lebanon, being refugees, had no opportunities to practice law. Going to a military college, like my admired Rashied Jarbou, assuming it was an option, which it was not, at the time, for Palestinian refugees, was way too dangerous for my mother's taste, not much different from her opinion of politics. Going into broadcasting, inspired by my admired Raji Sahyoun, seemed to lead, like going into law in Lebanon, to a dead end. Engineering and medicine, though venerable, were unappealing to me; they were too applied, along with other applied fields. They did not deal with the big questions of the day, that is the Nakba and colonialism, questions that were weighing heavily on my mind. One notion that kept coming up in the discussions of the causes of our predicament was that Arabs and Muslims had lagged way behind the West in science and technology. This lag, the assertion went, was a big contributor to the vanishing of the glory of Muslims and Arabs. Ah! "The glory that was," in the first several centuries after the rise of Islam in North Africa, in Spain, in the Middle East, and so forth. Granted, all this is somewhat simplistic and general, but it was the prevailing accepted view and appealing. The outcome of World War II and the role of science, especially physics, in the development of the atomic bomb and its deployment, seemed to underline and accentuate these arguments and give them credence. So, to confront the challenge head on, I reasoned, I had to work for the revival of science and technology in the Arab realm. Physics, being at the foundation of the sciences, seemed to be a natural choice. At ENPC, these notions got even more articulation. Muhammad Saffouri[66] and I resonated with them. Mathematics, being the platform needed for physics, was folded in our choice of a major. Saffouri, Mansour, and I took the AUB English examination a couple of weeks before the start of the school year, passed it without a hitch, and received admission. I had, by then, made up my mind to be a physics major, so had Saffouri. We were the only two of the ENPC graduates of that year to choose physics. After postponing his enrollment for a year to work and save money, Raja planned to go into medicine. Mansour chose mechanical engineering. Issam Abu Issa decided to forget about higher education and left Lebanon to go to work in one of the Arab oil Gulf states, as did several other classmates.[67] Nazmi got a teaching job in one of the UN elementary schools in the Tyre area. [68]

Each of the three of us had to fend for himself in securing the finances. The freshman tuition fees alone were of the order of $500 a year. Fouad's teaching salary, by then, was about $25 a month, as an example. There was no way I could raise the kind of money I needed within my family. At the time, I was so inexperienced and uninformed about the ways of the academic world that I did not even know how to go about identifying and applying for scholarships. My mother decided again to take the bull by the horns in her own "old fashioned and tried way." She decided to call upon some Anglican acquaintances she had known back in Haifa who had sought refuge in Beirut in 1948. They were close relatives of the late Muallem Boulous Duwani. Somehow, my mother knew their whereabouts. These people agreed to arrange for her to visit the AUB registrar, Mr. Farid Fuleihan, at his home. They seemed to know him well, probably through their church. Mother had Hamadi accompany her to his home. I was left behind. According to Mother's report back, Mr. and Mrs. Fuleihan were most gracious hosts. Mr. Fuleihan genuinely wanted to help. He had nothing to offer in the College of Arts and Sciences, the college of my intended major. The best he could offer was a scholarship that covered

---

66 For brevity, henceforth, Saffouri

67 Issam, working in the Gulf, achieved a very successful career in banking.

68 One other classmate, Michael Effarah, did manage to eventually get admission to AUB. However, I did not know the particulars of how he did it nor did I know his choice of major. He always impressed me as a diligent and earnest classmate.

the full-year tuition, made available through the Ford Foundation, to students intending to enroll into the College of Agriculture. Mr. Fuleihan further indicated that freshman-year course work was basically the same for both of the two colleges. "So," he suggested, "Why not give the matter a try, and see how Ghazi feels by the end of the freshman year? In all cases, there is a gain of one university year and not much to lose." Mother and Hamadi came back saying, "Well, agriculture is better than nothing." Mr. Fuleihan arranged for forms to be sent to me to fill out and return promptly back to him. I received the news, as expected, with mixed feeling. Matters boiled down to either I try this way, or not enroll at all. I decided that I was not going to enroll under a false pretense, but that I would give agriculture honest consideration. With that, I was able to enroll as a freshman, October 1952. Muhammad and Mansour managed, through their own channels (unknown to me), to secure enrollment in their respective colleges of choice.

While the securing of the tuition removed the big hurdle, I still had the hurdle of room and board expenses to jump. Nazmi had put himself out of the picture. The university did have room and board services, but the cost appeared prohibitive. Mother, Fouad, and I looked for possible options. Happily, while in Beirut during senior high school, I got reconnected with my Haifa school pal, Illyas El-Jisr. Illyas was finishing high school at the Shweifat National College (SNC). While our encounters were very few and far in between during the preceding year because of our schools being physically quite apart, I did visit him and his family at his Beirut home, and got caught up on their travail since leaving Wadi-Ennisnas/Haifa. They had a huge share of pain and suffering. Illyas's older and only brother, As'ad, had passed away back in Haifa at the young age of about seventeen, of a seemingly mysterious illness that drained the family's resources. With the exodus, both his father and sister lost their jobs. When they finally managed to make it to Beirut, they rented a modest three-bedroom apartment in a building in a section of Beirut called Furn Eshshubaak. His sister, Blanche, succeeded to get an administrative job at SNC, and his father opened a modest grocery store in their new home neighborhood. Their new abode was about halfway between SNC and AUB. I also found out from him that he hoped to enroll at AUB after his high school graduation, if his family's finances permitted it. I told him that I hoped to enroll likewise if I was admitted and the family finances permitted it as well. He seemed to have no concern about getting admitted because of the accredited status of SNC, knowing he was sure to get the admission recommendation. He, in fact, did not bother to take the GCE examination.

In my desperate search for feasible, affordable housing, the thought came to me to explore the possibility of rooming with Illyas's family for a payment, should Illyas decide to enroll into AUB. My payment to the family could help defray some of Illyas' expenses; at the same time, Illyas and I could become not only classmates again, but also roommates. I explored the idea with Illyas informally. He and his family were open to it. I told Mother. She and the household said it is worth trying. A meeting was set up for my mother to visit Illyas' family at their home to work out the details. My mother and I called on them on a Sunday afternoon. We all agreed that I would share a room with Illyas, and be given daily breakfast for fifty liras (about $17) a month. I would have to manage on my own lunch and dinner. I would move in the weekend before school started.

In the summer of 1952, Hamadi decided to apply for a teaching job with the UN Agency for Palestinian Refugees (UNRWA) in the Tyre area. He had seen an ad for a position opening at the Rashidiyya refugee camp (some five miles south of Tyre). Applicants were to submit for a qualifying exam. Hamadi took the exam and ranked second among a handful of applicants. The first ranked, upon getting an offer, declined it; he had, in the meantime, found a good paying job with Aramco Oil in Dhahran, Saudi Arabia. Hamadi was then offered the job. The pay was quite modest (about $30 a month). Hamadi found this offer to be an opportunity to change the course of his life. After some consultation with mother and Yousef, it was decided he would take the job. It was further decided that he would not drop out completely from the laundry. Rather, he would continue his managing work after hours and on off-school days, and he would be paid accordingly. Hamadi became a full-time elementary school teacher in the fall of 1952, and remained a part-time laundryman on the side.

CHAPTER 10

AUB

"AUB IN THEE WE GLORY, MAKE US TRUE AND BRAVE!"[69]

The kick off of my freshman year was quite different from what I had been used to before. There was the choice of an academic advisor before registering. With the advisor, you selected the courses for the semester in contrast to high school, where everybody took the same set of courses. I stuck to core mainstream freshman courses; English, Arabic, college algebra and trigonometry, college chemistry, and college physics. The registration was a tedious lengthy process that involved standing in a long line: it took a couple of hours to go through it. I then found out that virtually every course classroom was apt to be different from every other course classroom, and were often in different buildings. I had to study the campus map to learn where buildings and classrooms were. It was the first time I saw and used a campus map. Then, there were several social and orientation parties—with food and refreshments! There were get-acquainted social and mixer parties. This was all unfamiliar. I made the effort to go to some. The presence of women students, even though they were only about one-fifth of the freshman class, made things all the more novel. It seemed their presence at these get-togethers was proportionately larger than men students. Even from a distance, I could tell that the women students generally had a certain air of cultural sophistication.[70] They seemed considerably modern, more western looking, and seemingly came from the upper crust of Middle Eastern societies. All of this made me uncomfortable and I wondered how well I was going to fit in. I was reluctant to talk to them one-on-one. I was too gender and class conscious; I was not sure what to say, how to say it, and I was definitely concerned that I might sound foolish, or backward, or both.

---

69 Line from AUB's Alma Mater song.

70 Clearly this was my subjective perception at the time.

The start-up of classes was for the most part not too unfamiliar. The freshman Arabic instructor, Professor Anis Freiha, however, was well known in all of Lebanon as a writer and social critic. He was unusually dynamic. The course material was Arabic/Islamic medieval philosophies and philosophers: Ibn Siena (Avicenna), Al-Farabi, and Ibn Rushd (Averröes) of the golden era. He prodded us to participate actively in class discussions. The subject matter would take up such things as predestination, free will, science, religion, and their interconnections; and, trying to relate Muslim philosophies to Greek philosophies such as those presented by Plato and Aristotle. Until then, I was only vaguely familiar with this wealth of Arabic/Islamic literature. I remember, before then, telling myself that such pursuits would have a great appeal to me. I wanted to know more about the nature of God. I thought to myself, *This would be the place where we can delve into such issues.*

I found the approach to the study of chemistry refreshingly different from High School, which had often been by rote. Professor Adib Sarkis, the chemistry professor, tried to reason out chemical behavior logically from basic principles. He encouraged us to find logical answers to chemical behavior in terms of the electronic structure of atoms rather than memorizing such behavior at face value. I was readily drawn to this modern way of studying chemical behavior. He backed his explanations frequently with demonstrations. In addition to being a very caring teacher, Professor Sarkis was an eloquent communicator and a showman.

Physics seemed to delve even deeper into space, time, matter, motion, and energy. One of my physics instructors was Mr. Fateen Boulous. I had heard of Mr. Boulous before I met him in class. He had a reputation, particularly among Palestinians, of having been an outstanding student, a genius. He hailed from near Acre (Kufr Yaseef), Palestine. His pre-college academic excellence earned him a scholarship to study physics in England. He studied there and received a B.Sc., Honors, before teaching physics at AUB. Upon seeing him in the flesh, so to speak, I was rather surprised to find out that he was very much a human, not unlike me, except for being about twelve years older. Some of the distinguishing qualities that he evinced were his precise articulate manner of speaking and a passion for the subject. Simultaneously, he was very kind, humble, and friendly. I related to him.

A practicing civil engineer taught my section of freshman mathematics. He was a part-time instructor. He was very methodical, focused, conscientious, but to a large extent, impersonal. He drove to campus in his little Fiat, and parked it just outside the chemistry building where the class was taught, visible from the classroom. He taught his class and assigned homework and got back into his car and drove off; a life-style unknown to me heretofore. He had no office on campus or any office hours. Except for an occasional few minutes after class to respond to questions, he was nowhere to be seen on campus. However, very soon it became apparent that if you faithfully attended his classes, studied the assignments, and did the homework, you did well on his weekly tests, and eventually, the course.

The English class was the most novel of them all. An American lady in her early thirties, a well-groomed and nice looking blonde, taught my section. She was a part-time instructor, a wife of a campus professor. She did not know any Arabic to speak of. She did not seem to have any cognizance of the backgrounds of the students she was teaching. Initially, she appeared to be quite apprehensive standing before us. She looked new to the role, and she may very well have been. Gradually, she became more relaxed. The students, as a general rule, were polite to her. The course involved considerable readings of contemporary American writings. I found the course challenging; most of the time I did not know what was being talked about. The readings dealt with American subjects and themes. The textbook was written for American college freshman students; implicitly assuming the students had grown up in America (specifically, the USA). Early on, we were told that we would be required to write a term paper of approximately two thousand words in length, about a subject of our own choosing. This requirement sent shivers down my spine. The notion of a term paper was, like lab reports, very new to me. The teacher tried to sketch the format for the term paper, indicating elements such as an abstract, introduction, and a bibliography. However, because of the newness of these concepts, most of her explanations went over my head. I don't think I was alone in this predicament. Outside the class, students huddled and discussed among themselves what a term paper was all about, and what it entailed. Seeing them as confused as I was, the matter began to slowly clear up, and the apprehension lifted somewhat.

Early on, it was a breath of fresh air that our teachers dealt with us as mature and responsible adults. We were expected at almost every turn, to think and figure things out for ourselves. We were free to be ourselves. Not being informed was not an acceptable excuse; we were expected to have initiative and seek things out.

Chemistry and physics had laboratory practice as an integral part of their courses. Weekly, we had to perform experiments, collect data, analyze it, relate it to theory, and submit a report. In high school, things were more often than not spelled out in detail and delivered to us on a silver platter. Rarely, in high school, were we shown a demonstration, much less given the chance to do experiments on our own.

In contrast to my experiences at Jaffariyya and the ENPC, we were required to take a one-credit hour physical education course in each of the two semesters of freshman year. In the first semester, each student chose the sport of his/her preference from among a set of options. I chose soccer. Soccer was not open to women. There were enough enrollees to make four teams. After some preliminary practices, our instructor assigned me, to my surprise, captain of one of the four teams. The reason for my surprise was that I enrolled in soccer because I had figured, with all the informal soccer I have had, that I would pass the course with minimal effort. Instead, I found myself assigned more responsibilities! I was also on the select freshman class soccer team. Although I had no problem doing reasonably well in these positions, our soccer coach could sense by the end of the semester that soccer was not high on the list of my priorities. Consequently, I did not make the varsity team, and I had no regrets. The second semester I took swimming; it was mandatory for every male freshman. For women freshman, swimming was optional; in deference to Arab and Islamic mores, they could substitute some other athletic activity. With my swimming background in Tyre, passing the course entailed very little effort. Dressing and undressing before and after a swim as well as showering after a swim, nevertheless, gave me an initial cultural shock. The male shower stalls as well as the dressing rooms were not privately partitioned; you stripped off on one side of a big area and walked naked across to the open showerheads along with other classmates. It took a while before I overcame my sense of modesty. The fact that everybody else was doing likewise made it easier.

All in all, it was obvious that I was entering a new world at AUB.

At the start of the freshman year, I had initially and subconsciously assumed it would be an extension of high school. My high school successes lulled me into thinking that I could continue to do well at the same level of effort as I exerted in high school, if not less. Images from movies led me to think of college life more as play and socialization than very serious hard work. Somehow, I thought that learning would take place by osmosis. Nobody had stirred my thoughts to expect otherwise. This was further exacerbated by my living conditions. Early on, rooming with Illyas, within his family's apartment, presented me with a variety of challenges. The family apartment, as noted earlier, was across town from the AUB campus. I had to walk daily from the apartment to the tram station, a few hundred yards, then pick up the tram and ride for about thirty to forty minutes before I got to the campus. The process was reversed in the evening. Once back in the apartment, there was no chance of doing any schoolwork. The apartment was small in the first place; in the second place, the atmosphere was nonconductive to serious study. There was a certain amount of daily, ritualistic evening socializing among the family members. It felt rude to shun it and intrusive to participate in it. The socializing transpired within the climate of their strained financial situation, and against a background of sadness that Illyas' mother perpetuated over the loss of her older son, As'ad, several years before. With the passage of a few weeks, it became apparent that I was likely to be heading to a grand failure academically. In fact, if I had any doubt, it was removed by Illyas' declaration within a little over a month of the start of the school year that he no longer desired to go to college; that he would soon be dropping out to look for a job.

In thinking to myself, I had one option: *Move out. But how and to where?* I must hasten to remark that through it all, I was shown nothing but love, affection, and hospitality.

As I contemplated the how and where of my move, I decided to approach my Tyrene and Jaffariyya College pal, Suhayl Niemih. Suhayl was in Beirut attending *The Centre de Recherche Mathématiques, Chimie, et Physique* (Center of Mathematical, Chemical, and Physical Research). It was a center set up by the French, during their mandate over Lebanon between the two World Wars, for the benefit of scientifically outstanding and gifted Lebanese students who otherwise would have gone without the opportunity of university education. Suhayl was in his third year at the center. The location of the center, a mere single building, was in the Furn Esh-Shubaak section of town not far from Illyas' family home. Suhayl had a room with a kitchenette not far off from there, an area called Sinn el-Fiel. Suhayl quickly understood my predicament and graciously agreed to have me share his place with him. I, in turn, would of course share in the cost, at about twelve dollars monthly. His apartment was initially unfurnished. Suhayl had furnished it almost primitively; one chair, one small table, a mattress that rolled out onto the floor at night and rolled off the floor during the day, and bare minimum cooking utensils. I procured a similar mattress, a chair, and a table. Mother was not significantly involved, but did visit the place shortly after my move. She had only known Suhayl and his family casually in Tyre before then. In support, she reached out to befriend Suhayl's family in Tyre with the idea of teaming up with them to provide some distant care along the lines she had with Nazmi's family. Suhayl's family did not show much enthusiasm, he being already in his third year.

My rooming with Suhayl markedly changed the scholastic milieu, none of the depressing home surrounding of Illyas' family existed. We enjoyed each other's company. Suhayl was fun-loving, and of a caring nature. We talked about Arabic literature as we did at the Jaffariyya College, especially poetry. We recited favorite and interesting verses or poems to each other, reveling in their beauty, fascinated and intrigued by the respective poets and their times. When it came to mathematics and sciences, however, being at two different levels and in two different systems, the French and the American, inhibited meaningful and stimulating exchanges. The remoteness of the AUB campus and the daily time and energy spent in commuting continued to bother me further. I was beginning to feel as if I were living two lives; on one hand, the modern American life at the AUB campus, and on the other at the apartment, an extension of the Tyrene, Jaffariyya College type of a life, with a French flavor. There were additional problems, cooking and cleaning. Suhayl was good at cooking, but neither one of us was good at washing dishes or home cleaning. Frequently, the place would get very untidy and unsavory. Suhayl also smoked; I smoked along with him, but less frequently, and with considerable guilt. Suhayl, being of a relatively fairly prosperous Tyrene family, had a lot more pocket money to spend. I tended to bum cigarettes from him. Not too infrequently, on weekends, friends came to the apartment, cooked a big meal, and enjoyed it with liquor, mostly wine. Some of these friends, Tyrenes as well, were considerably older. One of them was a former history and geography teacher of mine at the Jaffariyya eighth grade. It was very hard not to be part of these parties, yet I had serious misgivings being party to them. Occasionally, they would even get together at one of their homes in Tyre for a big meal with drinks, and I would be included.

Against such living conditions, I managed to keep up with my course work at the university, but not as excellently as I had aspired. My performance was slipping. I was managing passing grades, but not much more than that. Brother Hamadi was keeping a distant watch; he was not happy with my association with Suhayl and his friends, especially, their smoking and liquor parties. He wanted me to dissociate from them. Increasingly, I began to look for another arrangement. From conversations with a variety of classmates on campus, I gathered that the Dean of Students, Dr. Harvey Beatty, was good at helping students deal with problems. In time, and feeling a dire need, I mustered enough courage to go and see him in his office. He listened, with a big smile on his face throughout, as I painfully tried to present my problem. Frankly, I went to see him partly out of desperation, partly just to convince myself that I was trying, and partly to oblige what others had suggested I do. I did not expect anything to come out of it. In fact, I felt awkward seeking his help thinking that it was my problem and not his. In hindsight, how wrong I was!! I simply did not understand the working of the American university system or the job of the dean of students, though Dr. Beatty was still exceptional. As I concluded speaking, he agreed that I did need to change my rooming situation. He said he would look into finding a place for me in one of the dormitories on campus! He further said I could pay for the room in installments, and that he would find me some work on campus, a few hours a week, to defray some of the cost. "In the meantime," he said, "keep the faith, work hard, and check back in a week's time." While I did not get an instant solution, I felt very good as I left him. His compassion and kindness during the visit was unusual and unforgettable. It was qualitatively different from any thing I had experienced from a person who was not a family member heretofore in my life. The notion of working on campus was also new to me. Somehow, I had separated the role of a student from the role of a worker in my mind, a trait prevalent among my peers of the time!

The next time I was with Mother, I put her in the picture. She said that she would try to raise the needed room-rent come what may. On my next visit with Dean Beatty, he told me that he found a place in one of the dormitories, sharing a room with two other students and that I could move in at the beginning of the second semester. It would average about twenty dollars a month. He also asked me if I would accept the job of taking attendance in chapel twice a week for a sum of about seven dollars a month. He wondered if I could raise the remainder from my family, or perhaps through selling refreshments on weekends at athletic events, particularly soccer meets. I was happily excited with what I heard, "It suits me fine," I said. I readily agreed to the chapel job, but made no comment about selling refreshments. Typically, chapel services were non-denominational, and I was required to go to them anyhow! We agreed to plan accordingly. In his usual way, Dean Beatty was very cheerful as I left his office. Alone with myself, the notion of selling refreshments in a public place did not sit well with me. Somehow, within my social value system of honor and false sense of pride at the time, it implied poverty and low life. It just did not sit well with the image I had built up for myself, either in Tyre or in Beirut. Selling refreshments at campus-wide athletic events seemed as if to advertise my family's poverty out in the open. Being a captain of one of the freshman soccer teams made it all the more difficult. As a Hassoun, perhaps I had a false sense of pride and an ego just like my Grandfather Muhammad. I was very grateful that selling refreshments turned out to be not essential to getting by financially. Dean Beatty did not push it, and I tried not to bring it up with him; hence it was never reconsidered. Reflecting on it from my present perspective, I can say how unfortunate it was that I could not overcome a perception deeply ingrained by my clan and society. In the Arab social setting and the mind-set of the time, it just was that hard!

Once the room question was headed for resolution, I could concentrate more on schoolwork; I made the honor list on one of the periodic chemistry tests; it felt very good. My final overall average for the semester hovered at about 80%. However, my English class did not go well; the term paper on

René Descartes, whom I had chosen for the subject of my term paper, fared poorly. I was shocked upon getting it back full of red ink. The teacher had penalized me severely for plagiarism. It took considerable explanation from the teacher before I understood what I did that was so wrong? The word and the whole notion of plagiarism were foreign to me. She may have explained it in class, but it didn't register with me. She insisted on the penalties despite my protestation that I didn't do it knowingly or on purpose. Ignorance was no excuse. I did receive a passing grade on the paper, however, but just barely. I tried hard to make up for it in the other components of the course.

With the start of the second semester, it felt good to live on campus. I gradually began to realize that not all students living in the dorm were financially well-off. In fact, a sizable percentage was wrestling with a variety of challenges, and I was not singularly different. The second semester was fairly uneventful. My performance was not significantly different from the latter half of the first semester; I continued to underestimate the level of effort I needed to fathom the courses' materials.

My moving out of Suhayl's apartment was cordial and harmonious. I continued to see him from time to time, more often in Tyre than in Beirut. Since I admired both Saffouri and Suhayl, I thought it would be fun to have them meet each other. I managed to arrange it once, but it was brief. They did not hit it off well; they seemed to be of very different "chemistries." I made no further effort to bring the two together again.

My occasional goings to Suhayl's parties continued to vex and worry brother Hamadi, until one day Hamadi walked over to Suhayl in Tyre, introduced himself, and asked him outright not to include me in any of his future parties. Suhayl felt deeply offended; the encounter chilled our relationship. I have always regretted what Hamadi did and felt there should have been a better way to go about it. I apologized to Suhayl for Hamadi's behavior. Nevertheless, the damage was done![71]

About halfway into the second semester, shortly after I had gotten onto the downtown Tyre bus heading to Beirut after a weekend stay with the family,

---

71 Suhayl went on after Beirut to study in France. He became a chemist and worked there, but maintained strong ties and frequent visitation with his family in Tyre.

Nadia[72] appeared, accompanied by her father. Her father put her on the bus and bade her farewell. She sat in the bench right behind me. Nadia was headed back to her school,[73] after a vacation with her family in Tyre. We had known each other before, but mostly from a distance. Before her school north of Beirut, she had attended the Union School for Palestinians where brother Fouad had taught. In fact, Nadia was Fouad's former student. Fouad had talked about her a good deal. She was very attractive and an excellent student. At the Union school, she had many admirers among her classmates and teachers. I was also attracted to her.

As the bus started out on the journey, I felt a special thrill that here we were within talking distance with no chaperones. As the bus was clearly well on its way out of the city, I turned around and began to chat with her. She seemed as happy to talk to me as I was to talk to her. The conversation seemed also to generate its own momentum. The seat next to her on her bench was vacant and I naturally offered to come and sit in it. She expressed approval. We chatted on sundry matters, mostly about my school experiences in Beirut and hers north of Beirut, for the rest of the trip. I talked to her on that single trip more than I had talked to her over the several years I had known her, and probably more than most of her Union School admirers had talked to her throughout their years at school together. Alas, society severely frowned on one-on-one conversations between unmarried individuals of opposite sexes. Within a few days after the trip, I continued to feel the thrill of the encounter and decided to write her a letter at her school, where she was boarding, to express my appreciation of the time we had on the bus. The letter was affectionate, but not outright amorous. I never received a response. From time to time, I would wonder why I had not heard back from her, as I was sure she knew my address just as I knew hers. I could not figure it out until the next time I went back home to Tyre. Following the first night, my brother Fouad took me aside and very privately said to me in a scolding but caring voice that I should not be writing love letters to young women, for it could bring trouble to me and even to the family. Also, it could tarnish the young woman's image and her family. Genuinely not thinking of

---

72 Not her real name.

73 Actual place is deliberately left out.

my letter to Nadia, I said, "What do you mean?" Fouad went on further to say, "The letter you sent to Nadia was intercepted by her school's principal and was sent to Nadia's family in Tyre, whereupon, Nadia's father brought up the matter with me, being your brother." Fouad further explained that Nadia's father was very unhappy with my behavior even though he basically thought well of me and the family. He went on to tell Fouad, "If Ghazi has intentions (to marry), he should approach us through the proper channels." I was flabbergasted! I was glad it was Fouad who was approached, not Hamadi. Hamadi might have been sterner. Fouad and I agreed that this was no time to think of marriage, and I pledged not to repeat it. I faithfully honored the pledge. Some years later, Nadia married an AUB graduate and a classmate. I was not invited to the wedding!

Late in the freshman school year, as I was visiting in Tyre over a weekend, I was walking with Hamadi in the main square of town, nicknamed el-Bawwabe (literally, the gate). A short distance off, Hamadi spotted one of the laundry clients who owed the business a significant sum of money for work previously done.[74] Hamadi, trying to seize the moment, walked over to the fellow and reminded him of the debt, nudging him to pay up soon.[75] I had known the fellow before. He was of a large Tyrene clan that was known for its loyalty to the Tyre/South Lebanon deputy member in the Lebanese Parliament, for brevity, MLP. It was a clan different than Abdalla's, cited earlier, but of even greater influence. The fellow was known for being the rebellious type. His name was Yousef. He turned to Hamadi and angrily said, "Don't you dare ask me for money again!" Hamadi firmly replied, "But you owe me money, I need it, and I want it." The fellow reached for a nearby short chair by an open air coffee shop and charged at Hamadi with it, shouting, "I am going to break your neck; you... (a bunch of foul swearwords)." Instinctively, I ran and put myself between him and Hamadi with my hands raised up to shield Hamadi and to hold the fellow back. I was careful not to make any threatening moves whatsoever toward him, knowing full well that any such move would further aggravate the situation. Fortunately, other people nearby saw what was

---

74 Recall that Hamadi at that time was managing the laundry business part-time while teaching elementary school at the Rashidiyye camp.

75 It was customary in those days to chase debtors in this manner.

taking place, came forward to hold back the guy, and take the chair away from him. Among those in the crowd was a friend, Ali Y. El-Khalil, who was also attending AUB, second-year political science, from the family of the MLP.[76] He, realizing who the combatants were, and well known to him, proceeded to calm the situation with a quiet authority. The fellow went one way; Hamadi and I went the other way. As we got a ways off, Hamadi whispered, "See how hard it is to eke out a living here, especially if you are a Palestinian refugee!" I doubt if that fellow ever paid up the debt.

As the freshman year was nearing its end, and students were earnestly looking ahead to arrange for food, housing, etc., for the following school year, Dean Beatty let it be known that a self-help student cooperative program was being planned for the benefit of students of demonstrated financial need and proven academic ability; these students would constitute The Student Cooperative Group (SCG). The student-run program would have three components, all of which would be run, for the most part, by the members for the benefit of the members. The first component had, at its core, renting a building adjacent to the campus for a dormitory to provide inexpensive housing. The second; a vacant room in the basement of the Student Union (West Hall) would be refurbished and converted into a cooperative cafeteria that would serve three meals a day, five days a week, Monday through Friday, with zero rental cost. A non-student full-time cook would be hired; however, the SCG members would carry out all other services. Third, a primarily student-operated sporting goods shop, near the campus administration building, would open for business the upcoming fall; the profits of which would go into a reserve fund to meet the SCG unforeseen financial needs. The SCG members were to pay equally apportioned fees for room and board. The dean's office would handle the paper work and secretarial services related to the total program. Student members were expected to put equal number of service hours a week towards the operation in one or more of the three components with no reimbursement, that is there was an equal sharing of responsibilities to the total undertaking.

---

76 Ali, years later, became an MLP himself, representing the Tyre South, and subsequently occupied at different times several cabinet posts in the Lebanese national government. Over a span of many years, Ali's path and mine crossed, including the time when we both were students in the US. Sadly, he was killed in a car accident in Beirut, April 2005

Naturally, I was enthusiastically for it, and qualified as a member. I offered to manage the laundry services in the dorm, and to be a dishwasher three evenings a week at the cafeteria. Somehow, I did not see myself of any use in the sporting goods shop. With that, my room and board for the sophomore year seemed secured. For reasons unknown to me, I was not asked to do any preparatory or groundwork for getting the program going during the summer, and I was not sure I could afford to stay in Beirut to offer any.

The summer of 1953 was spent in Tyre living with the family. Only occasionally, and for a reason, did I go to Beirut during that summer. In Tyre, I mostly took it easy. I swam often in the Mediterranean and frequented the YMCA for a game of Ping-Pong, or backgammon, or domino, or cards. The notion of finding work to earn money (assuming such opportunities existed) for the following school was, unfortunately, absent. I was, in the eyes of everybody around me, too educated to help at the laundry. From time to time, I would check out a book to read from the very modest YMCA library collection. It did not exceed a total of fifty books. I was fascinated by Ghandi and read the three books or so about him in the collection. Alternatively, I reveled in the admiration accorded to me by the local Palestinian refugee community for having made it into AUB; they saw it as a breakthrough, for I sprang from among their ranks to make it into the most prestigious university in the Middle East. At the same time, I was very mindful within myself of how I made it, the good and the bad, the help of many, and the hurdles that still laid ahead. Interspersed with all of this was the discourse I would have almost daily with the community members over the Palestinian problem. The questions most often asked were: When are we going back to our homes? When will we have our rights restored? Older Palestinian folks, with very little education, particularly looked for me to provide answers to their thirsty questions. They thought that since I was so much ahead of them in schooling, and since I was interacting with Americans in Beirut, I would be able to answer their simple and natural questions, or at least shed some light on them. AUB's faculty was predominantly American; those who were not often had received their higher education in the USA. Alas, I hardly knew anymore than the people of my community. One day, a Muslim leader in the el-Buss camp approached me to find out if I would be willing to lead a Friday service there and deliver the *Khutba* (Arabic, for sermon).

While I was deeply touched by the gesture, I felt compelled to decline; I did not feel qualified for the task. I had not been performing such basic Muslim duties as prayer and Ramadan fasting since going to Beirut for ENCP, in the fall of 1951. My refusal was a must; it seemed hypocritical to do otherwise. However, I did attend occasional Palestinian political gatherings and rallies; at some of which, I would make short speeches. Afterwards, I would go home thinking, *I barely scratched the surface*!

While my heart was in studying physics, mathematics, philosophy, and religion, I felt morally bound to give the agricultural scholarship a fair chance. So, I enrolled as a sophomore in the College of Agriculture.

The cooperative's dorm building was remarkably pleasant and close to campus. It was three stories high with a lot of windows, high ceilings and large hallways. It had occupancy of about thirty students. I shared a room with two other fellows on the main floor. The pay was at about $10 a month. The laundry facility was also on the main floor. It was a simple room with a washtub, dryer, an iron, and an ironing board. My job was to be more of a consultant than anything else. I advised individual students how to wash, dry, and press things, to clean up after the work is finished, and to be considerate of others' needs. My job turned out to be much easier than I initially thought. Many students, particularly those who went home over the weekend, rarely used the facility; they took their laundry home. Dean Beatty saw fit to hire a full-time non-student building custodian. The cooperative dorm was God sent. It quickly became a home away from home. The cooperative cafeteria was less satisfactory. The cook turned out to be unimaginative in his meal preparation, though he was on a very limited budget. His meals were nowhere near as good as Mother's cooking. He relied heavily on canned foods and cold meats. However, I was not about to complain. For the money we students paid (about $18 a month), it was a bargain. Washing dishes gave me considerable satisfaction. It was done privately and quietly in the kitchen after dinner. I felt doing so was the least I could do for all the benefits. With the income from the chapel attendance job, I was able to minimize the help from my mother to about $20 a month.

As the school year got underway in earnest, I found myself separated from my old freshman group of friends by course work and daily activities. I was enrolled in a general agriculture course that included weekly field trips. These trips took the first year agriculture students to select model farms all over the countryside by bus. Also, I was required to take courses such as biology, agricultural chemistry, and economics. Not unlike my agriculture classmates, my course load was nineteen semester credit hours and included no physics. I took a calculus course as an elective. While initially I tried to convince myself that these courses are going to be fun, I increasingly began to feel that I was out of my element and headed away from where my heart was. The conflict deepened as the weeks passed by. I knew that to keep my sanity, I would have to find a way to either transfer to the College of Arts and Sciences, or, if not financially feasible, to drop out of school. About the same time, I became aware that the UNESCO office in Lebanon had a program of scholarships for needy Palestinian undergraduate university students. I further found out that my classmate Saffouri, among other Palestinian students, had been already receiving the scholarship. The scholarship was quite generous in that it paid for full tuition, books, and a room and board allowance of $50 a month. Somehow, I had not heard about it. I decided, in due course, to check it out and learn who to talk to and how I might apply. It turned out that the campus person in charge was Professor Ishaq Al-Husseini, a Jerusalemite,[77] in the Department of Business Administration. I went to see him, explained my predicament and my wish to transfer. However, I would not be able to do that without financial assistance, and therefore, I asked to be considered for the UNESCO scholarship. He was most hostile to my request, and sternly discouraged me from applying! He seemed to think that my change of major was expediently motivated, that I am after the more generous scholarship. I was distressed, and for a while I did not know what my next step should be. Nevertheless, I was determined to finish the semester as successfully as possible. Nothing would be gained from dropping out before completion. If I were to drop out of AUB, I reasoned melancholically, I would probably find a teaching job like Hamadi, Fouad, or Nazmi. If not, I would seek a job in one of the Arab oil states. At least, I would have a year and a half of AUB education.

Out of desperation, it flashed through in my mind that before making such a major step, I should go and talk to Mr. Fuleihan, the registrar, who had gotten me into AUB in the first place. He received me most courteously as I walked into

---

77 Is of the Jerusalemite Al-Husseini family of the Grande Mufti.

his office. I explained what had been happening over the past year and a half, with some allusion to the problem I was having with Professor Al-Husseini, and what I had been contemplating of late. He listened very sympathetically and seemed to have some knowledge of my dilemma. He said, "Let me see what I can do," as the visit concluded. Within two days, I received a letter from him in the campus mail with a scholarship offer for the second semester of about $150 that would pay a little more than half the tuition fees, and expressing hope that I would find other sources to pay the remaining sum. I cried tears of happiness. I returned to Tyre to inform my mother. She was very happy too, and assured me that she would manage to provide me with the rest of the fees herself, by the due date. The dropping out was averted, and I enrolled in the College of Arts and Sciences as a physics major beginning with the second semester. My former College of Science and Arts classmates and friends welcomed me back into their fold, even though I was a semester out of sync.

Since I had some catching up to do in the second semester, I enrolled in as many physical science and mathematics courses as were open to me. That still left me able to take two elective courses. I took a course in philosophy of science and a course in Arabic literature of the Abbasid period. I relished those courses so much. The philosophy of science course expanded my precepts of what physics is about beyond formulas and numbers. Physics, after all, was termed in the Middle Ages "natural philosophy," in Latin, "philosophia naturalis." The course traced the view of nature and its evolution, from pre-Greek times to the end of the nineteenth century. The Abbasid course was approached from a modern analytical and critical point of view. Up to that time, I studied literature playfully and traditionally, for enjoyment, like music and singing. The course teacher, Khalil Hawi, a poet and writer in his own right, was often digging to compare and contrast the Abbasid period with contemporary Arabic literature. To him, the literature of the people tells what the people are like; it encompasses their inner soul and values. He frequently dissected the Arab soul in a cold-blooded, analytic, and scientific way. He seemed to focus more on what was wrong with contemporary Arabic literature.[78] He would

---

78   Mr. Hawi was so depressed by the incursion into Beirut of the Israeli army during their invasion of Lebanon in 1982, short though it was, that he did commit suicide. He seemed deeply disenchanted with the Arab World for allowing such a thing to happen. He was sixty years old.

ascribe this to the degeneration of Arab literature as a whole in the nineteenth century and early twentieth century under the Ottomans' rule.

The AUB community, students or faculty, tended to feel rather privileged, even somewhat elitist, and for a good reason. AUB had a rich history of producing many of the leaders of the region; occasionally, it was referred to as the "Harvard of the Middle East." There was, among students, a sense that we were the future leaders.[79] Somewhat relieved after the transfer, I expanded my circle of friends. In particular, I came to know several of the male Jordanian students. There was a women's group as well. However, I got to know some of them mostly from a distance. Most of the male students were actually Palestinians from the West Bank, from Hebron, Tulkarem, Nablus, and Ramallah. A majority of them were high achievers in their respective home high schools, and managed to come to AUB on Jordanian government scholarships that covered even their travel expenses from Jordan to Lebanon and back. At the same time, they had to commit to go back to Jordan and teach in public schools upon graduation, for an equal number of years. Most memorable among these were Rasmi Mahmoud, Falaah Essaghier, and Izzat Zahedi. They were on "education" scholarships, that is, they had a double major: One of their majors was mandated to be education, and the second, science or mathematics, of the student's choice. Rasmi and Falaah had physics for their science major, whereas Izzat had chemistry. Being Palestinians, we had a lot in common to talk about. There was a rather strong Islamic current of thought and leaning among many of the Jordanian/Palestinian students. The Islamicists were often of the Islamic *Tahrir* (Arabic, for liberation) Party (ILP). The party's central theme was to revive and return to the Islamic state. Their slogan was (and is): "Islam is the solution." Also, there was the Arab Nationalist Group; the Nasserites were most prominent: these were the supporters of Gamal Abdel Nasser of Egypt and his program of liberation and unification of the Arab world, not based on religion, but on a sense of national belonging. Their slogan was (and is): "From the Gulf to the Ocean;" the gulf being the so-called Persian/Arabian, and the ocean being the Atlantic. There

---

79 As the UN was being launched at the conclusion of World War II, AUB alumni were the most represented of all the world institutions of higher learning at the first opening session ever of the UN General Assembly.

was almost constant pull on me to side with one over the other. I resonated with the nationalists. The Islamicists were nonviable medievalists as far as I was concerned.

There were other active political currents and groups clamoring for followers and assertion. Of those, three noteworthy ones were: The Syrian Socialist Nationalist Party (SSNP), The Arab Baathist Party, and the Communist Party. Most of SSNP followers were Lebanese, Palestinians and Syrians, with active Christian presence. The Baathists, were basically Arab nationalists, but with a socialistic economic program. The Iraqis and the Syrians were in the lead. A prominent Iraqi Baathist student of that period was Saadoun Hamadi, later to serve as prime minister of Iraq under Saddaam Hussein. Even as a student, he was noted for his stirring oratory. Baathists and Arab Nationalists worked closely together and often organized joint events. Among Saadoun's close friends and classmates was the noted Arab nationalist Shafiq El-Hout, later to become the head of the PLO office in Beirut for many years. The Iraqi Baathists tended to be among the most passionate and doctrinaire. The communists or communist sympathizers on campus were few in number and did not readily reveal themselves. They tended to attract people that scoffed at both religion and nationalism, and were disenchanted with the policies of the West in the Middle East. They predominantly tended to be of a socially and intellectually avant-garde class of Palestinian and Lebanese Muslims and Christians. Some of them, to my wonderment, hailed from financially fairly well-off families.

Amidst this crucible of many ingredients, I made sure to look ahead, beyond my sophomore year, for financial support. A few weeks into the semester, I went back to Professor Al-Husseini and updated him with the steps I had taken, and my renewed interest in being considered for the UNESCO scholarship. He again was not encouraging, but at least allowed me to apply. I did not waste any time; I filled out an application in which I stressed my financial need and that I qualified in every respect. I handed it in person to him and asked him when I could expect to hear back. He said, "Later in the semester," but was not precise. I did not wait too long before I stopped by at his door again. I did this periodically, perhaps to his great displeasure. This went on till almost the end of the semester, whereupon one of these stops, he rather grudgingly informed me that I had been selected for the scholarship effective the fall of my junior year. I could not hide my elation, thanked him profusely, and walked away anxious to send a word to my mother and family in Tyre.[80]

With the UNESCO scholarship, I felt, as long as I maintained a respectable academic standing, my financial troubles were over for the next two years. I also tried to assure my mother of the same. I finished the second semester of my sophomore year with an overall average in the seventies percent. I was not too unsatisfied with that; however, I felt I could and should do better. At the end of the school year, I unexpectedly received a diploma certifying I had satisfactorily completed the requirements for the two-year program of study in the College of Arts and Sciences; called the "Intermediate." The intermediate diploma was soothing and reassuring. It was framed and hung up on the wall at home next to my Lebanese *Certificat*, the ENCP High School Certificate, and the London University GCE!

It was not practical to stay on campus for the summer of 1954 for a variety of reasons. First, none of the required courses for the B.S. physics program were offered. Secondly, while I could room cheaply at the cooperative dorm, there was no cooperative food service, and I would have had to eat out a good deal of the time, an expense I did not need. I had no imminent job prospect and I was not about to turn to my mother for help after all the money she had provided to finish the second semester. So, I chose to spend the summer in Tyre again, probably reading and socializing at the YMCA Club.

Within a couple weeks in Tyre, while hanging around at the laundry downtown, a client stopped by to inquire if his laundry was ready for home delivery. In the course of the inquiry, he started a friendly chat with Hamadi as he had done with him periodically before. His name was Sliman Eddada, alias Abu Daoud; his oldest son's name being Daoud, Arabic for David.[81] Abu Daoud was a well-to-do member of the Tyre (Muslim Sunni) upper class, and a landlord. He owned large tracts of land in and around the town of Saddiqin, a town of a few hundred people about half an hour drive (some 15 miles) up

---

80   On reflection, much later, I developed the sense that Mr. Fuleihan very likely had something to do with it.

81   Sliman is the easy way to pronounce his actual name: Suleiman. Suleiman is Arabic for Solomon. It is hard to resist wondering if, in this name (in view of the Prophet/King David and his son, the Prophet/King Solomon), there is a profound biblical message to ponder, or is it just a hollow and pure coincidence?

a narrow hilly road southeast of Tyre. Hamadi and Abu Daoud got to talk about family and children. Abu Daoud had four children, ages twelve through seventeen. They were all attending the Sidon American boarding school, The Gerard Institute; boy, girl, girl, and boy, respectively, in descending age-wise order. Abu Daoud complained to Hamadi that his three younger children had not done well that past school year, and they needed to undertake remedial study in science and mathematics during the summer before they would be allowed to proceed to their respective next grades. Hamadi, pointing to me, said to Abu Daoud, "I've got the perfect answer for your problem," offering me to tutor Abu Daoud's children. Hamadi then proceeded to praise me to high heaven. Abu Daoud's eyes got bigger as he listened to Hamadi.[82] Abu Daoud became most impressed when he found out that I had just received my intermediate diploma in physics and mathematics from no less a place than AUB. Abu Daoud then divulged that he had the highest regard for American schools, that he had completed the freshman year at AUB some twenty-five years back, but had to quit to take care of his father's business. He wanted his children to get the best schooling Lebanon could offer. Before I could digest the exchange between the two, Abu Daoud in a serious tone of voice asked me, "When can you start?" Hamadi jumped in, "Right away," he said. I followed, "I would like a few days to think it over, and check out some of the details." Abu Daoud elaborated his children would be spending the summer at the family country home in Saddiqin. He did not think they would agree to come to Tyre for tutoring; Tyre was too crowded and restrictive for them. He thought, however, he could talk them into being tutored if the tutor were to come to the country home in Saddiqin. He said I should think in terms of a live-in tutor. He did not think it practical for the tutor to commute daily; public transportation was irregular and messy. In those days, my having a car would not even enter anybody's mind. He thought he could arrange a housing quarter for me within their family's country home, which he implied was large enough, and that I would have my meals with my students, his children! The weekends would be off. I would be chauffeured to Tyre on Friday afternoon to spend it with the family, and chauffeured back to Saddiqin on Sunday afternoon. He

---

82 It was not uncommon during that period that Hamadi would take me along to some of his special laundry clients or friends to show me off.

then added, "I'll make sure you are treated right." His laundry was ready, and Hamadi arranged for their delivery. Upon leaving, Abu Daoud said to me, "I'll get back to you soon."

At first, the idea of being a live-in tutor in a very little rural town, living with strangers under the thumb of a landlord for about two months, seemed unappealing. Yet, it offered room and board and some salary that could be used in the fall for a variety of needs; it allowed plenty of time for being with family and friends on weekends. It would also give me something worthwhile to do— private tutor, a novel experience. If I were to choose to remain in Tyre, the time might be ill utilized, and I would be dependent on my mother, even for pocket money. I would also be living in a crammed up household of twenty-two people. The choice to accept the offer, if confirmed, was not hard to reach. Within days, Abu Daoud came back affirming his interest in having me do the job. He also said that whatever reasonable salary I would ask, he will try to meet it. Hamadi, without consulting me, decided on the equivalent of forty dollars a month,[83] over and above room, board and transportation, was a reasonable salary. Abu Daoud readily accepted. Abu Daoud picked me up in his chauffeured car that following Sunday afternoon. It was a scenic drive, and he and I got better acquainted!

Upon arrival, I was introduced to the children, Daoud, seventeen years old, had finished the eleventh grade; Amal, sixteen, finished the tenth grade; Raja (the name can be a boy's or a girl's name), fourteen, finished the eighth grade; and Zuhair, twelve years, finished the sixth grade. They were all dressed very fashionably and welcomed me per protocol and in good taste. I was then shown my room and private facilities, which were located in a corner of the main floor, set-aside and private. Next to it was another room, which would serve as a classroom. The family lived on the second floor. The house was indeed large, situated on top of a hill that looked over fields of wheat, barley, lentil, tobacco, grapevines and a scattering of fig trees. It was about a mile out of downtown Saddiqin. There were a couple of families that worked the land, who lived on the main floor also, in another section of the house.

Daoud was eager to tell me right away that he was not in need of tutoring because he had passed his junior high in all subjects; only his two younger

---

83 About as much as he himself was getting at the UN school at the time, with no room nor board nor transportation!

sisters and brother needed it. I met their mother from a distance; she looked dignified with a scarf over her head. At dinnertime, sure enough I ate with the three youngest children, my students to be. A maid served the food and waited our table. The parents and Daoud did not join us. At the dinner table, we talked about the plan for each day of the working week. The girls were mostly interested in algebra and geometry, but also wanted to go over some topics of science in their textbooks that they had difficulty with during the school year. Zuhair, it turned out, was mostly in need of help in the English language. We agreed that at 8:00 am sharp, we would all show up for breakfast, dressed, and ready to go. At 8:30 am, we would start class work. We would stay with class work until 12:00 noon, with intermissions as appropriate. Lunch would be from 12:00 pm to 1:00 pm. In the afternoon, 1:00 to 4:00 pm, everybody would study and do homework and other assignments on his/her own, in their private quarters. I would be available for consultation and/or assistance in my own room. We agreed that two months would be ample to do the job.

The basic plan was closely followed, and everybody cooperated. I initially feared they might be difficult, spoiled, and uncooperative, but it turned out not to be true. I let them tell me what they wanted to learn and where their difficulties were. I was open and straightforward. The only thing I noticed that contrasted with my student experience was that they did not study with passion, nor did they hunger for knowledge. I did bring a variety of books and materials along with me that occupied me while not working with them. Abu Daoud, from time to time, would have a meal with us to find out how things were coming along. He also, as we carried our work earnestly and diligently, would reward us (tutor and students) with an all-day Saturday fun trip to Beirut or the mountains, east of Beirut, in the chauffeured family car. There, we would go sightseeing, have a lunch in an open air restaurant over a scenic hill, engage in a lot of playful, leisurely chitchatting, then return before dark. On these occasions, I would stay in Saddiqin Friday night, dropped off in Tyre at the end of Saturday's excursion, while the children continued to Saddiqin. I would be chauffeured from Tyre to the village by the Sunday schedule.

Generally, I noticed Abu Daoud was always on the move and did not seem to take time out to relax. He was accessible only briefly, and when there was a need. He seemed to manage his time carefully and efficiently. Occasionally, there was time for me to visit with the working families on the main floor and with some of the folks in town. One time I happened to be nearby when a man of one of these families approached Abu Daoud to tell him that his wife, a few months pregnant, was not feeling well and needed healthcare in Tyre. He asked Abu Daoud for permission to take his wife to Tyre for the needed care. He then, in a roundabout way, asked for extra money to meet the expenses of the trip. Abu Daoud granted him his request. However, I could not resist thinking of the feudal system of Europe in the Middle Ages, which I had studied about in my senior high school history class. I wondered if I was living in one here and now!

On occasions of special events or gatherings, when with the town's people, I seemed to end up conversing with the town's Imam. He loved poetry, and of course, the Quran. He enjoyed testing my knowledge in both, asking me to explain a poetry line or a Quranic verse. More often than not, I surprised him. Once, there was a wedding celebration in a nearby community about a couple of miles from the family home. The community was most directly reachable by walking or donkey trails. Everybody in the household of Abu Daoud, including the working families, were invited and expected to attend, no exception. I decided I would attend too. The wedding happened to fall on a beautiful sunny summer day. It was early afternoon when many of us headed to the wedding. The countryside was so serene and glorious as guests were converging onto the place amid all the farm fields. It brought to mind those fond days in my childhood, when my family would go to a wedding of a relative in Etteery. The thrill was awesome and inspiring. I marveled at the glory of the creation.

Summer was running out fast; the two months were up. Except for pocket money, the bulk of the cash earned was turned over to my mother. The three students felt confident about taking their make-up exams at the start of the new school year. The summer tutoring bore good fruits. Amal, Raja, and Zuhair passed onto the next grade and for which I was very grateful!

Back in Tyre for a few weeks before the start of my junior year, I would run into Ali El-Khalil, my fellow AUB-ite, and we would find how the summer was going for each other. I would hear about some of his pursuits in the community. He was clearly preparing himself for public service on the national level. Among other things, he was taking interest in the city's sports, not least of which was soccer. The Cyclone had disbanded upon the execution of Antun Sa'aadeh. The *Tadhamun,* or "Solidarity", team became the 'primary game in town'. Many of the Cyclone players simply joined the Solidarity Club; Fouad included. In a couple of years it became the undisputed leading team in Tyre, to be reckoned with on the (Lebanese) national stage. Ali desired to have another team to compete with it. There was also a partisan political motive behind it. The Tadhamun was identified to lean towards the As'adi's clan, which rivaled for prominence the Khalili's clan, to which Ali belonged. Naturally, he hoped that the new club would identify with his clan. He proceeded to organize a new soccer club with some of his friends and followers. The newly-organized club was to be named The Torch (Shu'li, in Arabic) Club. Because of my connections with the Palestinian community, Ali coaxed me into joining the group, not as a player, but to serve on an executive committee for the club, which was about to be elected. He further thought I could help with attracting good soccer players among the Palestinians to join, not least, brother Fouad. I was really not interested, even couldn't care less. I went along out of politeness. After all, we were two out of a handful of AUB students in all of Tyre at the time. I also crossed paths with him frequently on campus and in my goings and comings between Tyre and Beirut. In short order, an organizational meeting was called at an appointed time and place, which I attended. At the meeting, after Ali was nominated and elected a president, I found myself nominated and elected as vice-president. I said, *Whoo Whoo!* to myself, but outwardly was speechless! I felt awkward and that I really had no business being elected; still I accepted. Ali and I could not have been in more different frames of mind. I held the position very passively. As the school year in October arrived, we both headed to AUB; he was a senior, and I was a junior. The cares of the school year got the upper hand, I found many excuses to disengage. As we got deeper into the school year, my vice-presidency gradually was forgotten. The Torch Club never managed to get off much above the ground. The Tadhamun/Solidarity team reigned supreme.

The summer of 1954 brought about a major change in the Hassoun household as well. Hamadi had become increasingly aware that our current dwelling had become way too small to accommodate the three growing families of Yousef, himself, and Fouad; and my mother and Qasim. (It was assumed that I was virtually on my way out.) The crowded existence tended to generate friction, and sometimes outward and unpleasant quarrels, particularly among the wives. Typically, it would be sparked by some of the children of the three families fighting among themselves that would spread eventually to engulf the brothers. Hamadi's ulcer would flare more frequently and more painfully. His level of tolerance with family members and others was on the descent. Consequently, Hamadi asked his school administration to facilitate him a transfer, preferably, to the city of Tripoli. He had heard a great deal about the city of Tripoli (about 100 miles north of Tyre), that it was larger and more dynamic with many more economic opportunities, but not so big as to be overwhelming, as Beirut might be. A large Palestinian refugee community had settled there, and the UN had some schools. Hamadi's request was granted and he was offered a position like the one he had in Rashidiyye, in the suburb of El-Mina (literally, the harbor), contiguous to the southwestern edge of Tripoli, along the seacoast. Within weeks, it was time for Hamadi to part irrevocably with Yousef and the laundry business. Hamadi gave up his interest in the laundry to Yousef and mother with no compensation. Mother went with Hamadi to Tripoli days in advance of the start up of the school year to help him find a suitable apartment to rent. They both returned to Tyre after having lined up a place. Hamadi stayed in Tyre long enough to pack up his meager belongings and head back with his family to El-Mina to settle down. Hamadi, for the first time in his life, was essentially on his own, with a wife and five children, solely dependent for livelihood on the income from his job as a grade school teacher, with a monthly salary less than $50.

On my occasional visits to Hamadi in El-Mina in the three years to follow, Hamadi would look back to his time as a laundryman and would express a desire to return to it somehow in the Tripoli area. He would remark that his teaching salary was woefully inadequate. He confided to me once that on occasion, he would be hurting so much for cash to provide for his family that, at the sight of cash in circulation in the marketplace in El-Mina, he would be tempted to snatch the cash away from the hand of whomever! He would then add that it was the deep sense of honesty ingrained within him, self-respect, and turning to God with recitations from Quran, that enabled him to dispel the devil and fight off these temptations. Mindful of his need, my mother would come loaded with food gifts on her periodic visits. On a couple of occasions, during my junior and senior years, I spared some of my UNESCO allowance to share with him. Hamadi rarely was able to visit Tyre, and conversely, Yousef was rarely able to visit Tripoli. Hamadi tried to befriend some people in the laundry business in Tripoli, thinking he would find his way back. His large family responsibilities, his refugee status, and his over-all bad health[84] deterred him from giving up the security of a teaching job, measly as it was, and risking the unpredictable "waters and currents" of a laundry business in a town he could not claim as his own.

Simultaneously, Fouad's school had been adding higher grades to include the *Certificat*. His teaching, as well as his devotion to the job, were being recognized. He was informally designated as deputy principal of the school, and was being proportionally given added responsibilities to teach the higher grades mathematics and science. In the fall of 1954, he was offered and accepted, though it involved juggling his schedule, a part-time position teaching mathematics and science at the *Certificat* level at the Jaffariyya College, over and above his full-time job at his home school. To keep up with the new added responsibilities, and to secure his hard won gains, he began to upgrade his formal education to earn, in steps, the London GCE in the same five basic subjects that I had earned. Fortunately, the GCE examination had these built-in flexibilities and twice a year sessions.

A top priority of my junior year was to pick up those required courses that I would have normally taken in my sophomore year, had I not been in the College of Agriculture for the first semester. Most notable among these was a two-semester course, six credit hours each, in general education, titled, "The Individual in Society;" nicknamed, Gen. Ed. It was required for graduation from the College of Arts and Science. Its offering was interdepartmental, with many faculty members and guest lecturers participating. The College of Agriculture did not require it. It constituted one third of my total course load for the year. There were three general lectures a week for all of the class' students assembled together, alternated with three discussion meetings of smaller student sections, of about twenty students each. The course began with ancient world civilization and concluded with the present. It covered virtually

---

84 Hamadi, specifically, nursed since his teens a chronic duodenal ulcer.

all aspects of the individual in society, in art, music, architecture, economics, politics, philosophy, literature, science, etc. The lectures were delivered at, what seemed to most of us students, a very fast pace. The joke was that if you dose off for a minute, you could miss a hundred years of human happenings! Concomitant with each lecture was a long list of required and recommended readings. The reading assignments were heavy, even if it had been the only course I was taking. I still had to take, in addition, two mathematics classes and two physics classes; a total of eighteen credit hours each for the two semesters. The Gen. Ed. reading assignments tended to be of a very high and scholarly caliber, requiring a lot of thinking. The challenges were reminiscent of those I had in my senior high school English class. This time, I wanted to take the assignments much more seriously. I invested a lot of time and effort. Yet, I continued to meet, a good deal of the time, a cultural wall, for the material was written by western authors on western society. When all is said and done, I did manage to attain a grade in the mid-seventies, which was about average for the class. In hindsight, I realized that my predicament was not at all unique.

Benefiting from the UNESCO scholarship, I left the chapel attendance job for a more needy student. However, I continued to live in the cooperative dorm. In the previous year, I was in a room with several roommates, with whom I interacted very little. In the junior year, I managed to have a room with only one roommate. His name was Adnan Mroueh. He was beginning his sophomore year, preparing for admission to the AUB College of Medicine. He was of the rather famous Mroueh family of Southern Lebanon. Kamel Mroueh, an uncle, was the founding father and chief editor of *Al-Hayat*, a leading Beirut newspaper. *Al-Hayat*, back then, was considered "The Times" of Beirut. He let me know that his nuclear family was not particularly affluent, and the medical course of study was long and expensive. He turned out to be one of the nicest and kindest people you would ever want to have for a roommate. We both understood our circumstances and the importance of our undertakings. We made sure to maintain a clean, quiet, and peaceful atmosphere for each other, conducive to study. And this was the way it was for the rest of the year.[85]

---

85 Many years later, I learned with joy and a sense of pride that he became a prominent member of the Faculty of Medicine at AUB in obstetrics and gynecology. He also became active in the Lebanese Government and served as a Minister of Health, Labor and Social Affairs.

Through Saffouri, I met Emile Asfour. Emile was a junior in Business. He hailed from Haifa. Like us, his family sought refuge in Lebanon. The three of us did a lot together, going to movies and sweet or coffee shops, sightseeing and mountain camping, and of course, discussing politics. He also was a gentleman, very accommodating, and of a very delightful and kind disposition. Occasionally, the three of us would get together at Emile's home in East Beirut, at Saffouri's home, in West Beirut, or at the cooperative dorm. We continued this camaraderie until our graduation. When we would get together, we would never run out of things to talk about. Saffouri continued to excel in his course work, breaking AUB student grade records, and receiving increasing acclaim from the campus community and beyond. Emile and I felt special being close friends with him.

At the start of my junior year, I came across my Haifa grade school pal, Uthman Abu Ghayda. He had just enrolled as freshmen with the intent of studying agriculture. The two-year difference was largely due to my leap after Jaffariyya as a senior at ENPC. There was always a special feeling of a cherished special bond, when we crossed paths on campus, even though it was evident that our life-paths were diverging.

During that same year, I also came across another Haifa grade school pal. It was Salah el-Ouri. The encounter was most pleasant and thrilling, as if it had fallen from heaven! Salah was not enrolled at AUB, but showed up occasionally, and I think only for a brief period, at a popular coffee shop, *Feisal*, just across the street from the AUB main gate. *Feisal* was a famous meeting place of the elite among AUB Arab Nationalists and Baathists. Until my junior year, I had rarely gone there, simply because I could not afford it. I was struck by how impeccably well-dressed Salah was. Unfortunately, the encounter was brief. We quickly updated each other on happenings since leaving Haifa, with the hope we would have a more leisurely visit at a later time. His family had sought refuge in 1948 in Beirut, where he was residing at the time. Alas, that time never came, leaving me with a note of regret and sadness.[86]

---

86 Many years later, circa 1975, while I was on a short visit to Kuwait, I saw Salah's name on a local TV show among those involved in its production. I got an emotional lift and wished I could learn more, never to be!

Early in the second semester of my junior year, there was a lot of agitation on campus and in Lebanon at large about a political pact that the Americans and the British were concocting for the region. It was to be centered in Iraq and to include as many Middle Eastern countries as were willing or coercible to join. They called it outwardly, *The Baghdad Pact,* under the auspices of Iraq's prime minister at the time, Nuri Essa'id.[87] Its declared intent was a Middle Eastern alliance with the West to stem the tide of communism in Southeast Asia and to prevent it from spreading to the Middle East. Lebanon was pondering it with some interest. Egypt, under Nasser, was vehemently opposed to it. Egypt and Nasser argued that it was a Western plot of division, imperialism, and domination in the guise of defense and security against communism. The many political groups on campus, in coordination with groups all over Beirut, decided on a major rally to demand the Lebanese government not join; a date and place was set for it. The AUB contingent was to gather on the northern side by the "Medical Gate" and proceed to a major rally at Martyrs's square, downtown Beirut. The activists on campus worked hard to encourage a good turnout for the rally. I was among those who reluctantly agreed to join the march. My reluctance stemmed from, among other things, my experience the year before when I participated in a lesser downtown political rally, the particulars of which I no longer recall, and was pick-pocketed out of about three days allowance. This time, however, the cause seemed bigger, the groups more organized, and the passions were greater. The Lebanese Government put out a stern word banning the rally. Camille Sham'oun was the president. The organizers were not dissuaded; they thought they could successfully challenge the ban. As the AUB contingent approached the Medical Gate with banners, and shouting slogans, we saw Lebanese army units in position just outside the gate, intent on preventing our exit. Ali El-Khalil was a few yards away from me in the rally as well. As the group moved out of the gate, the army tried to physically push us back. They were not very successful. Thereafter, we began to hear gunshots. The students retreated back. The word got out that some students had been hurt! I did not see any, nor did I hear right away how many, nor how seriously. I was in the midst of the crowd and could not see what

---

87 A few years later (1958), he was killed and his body dragged by a mass mob through the streets of Baghdad following a military coup.

was happening at the firing line, so to speak. Slowly, we disbursed back to the campus. At the cooperative, all that the students talked about the rest of the day was the rally. We heard that there was firing at other student contingents in town. The following day, I found out that one of our contingent students was shot in the spinal chord and paralyzed. I knew the student fairly well, and did not want to believe it![88] He was a junior in business or political science, a very fine chap from southern Lebanon (from around the village of Ettaybe). It was very tragic. I thought to myself that it could have been me. I visited him at the hospital a few times. After the hospital, he was taken back to his hometown for further recuperation and I saw him no more. Thereafter, the students went back to their classes and studies, with business as usual.

About the middle of the second semester I seemed to be falling ill to an attack of abdominal pain. The pain came suddenly in the afternoon. It felt serious. I was guided to go to the student infirmary, about fifteen minutes walk from the co-op's dorm. I was given tests right away. I was quickly diagnosed as having an inflamed appendix. I was transferred forthwith to the university hospital. They needed my approval to operate. I gave it without hesitation. I was rolled right away for anesthesia. The surgeon chatted with me about the courses I was taking at the university. When he found I was studying physics, he seemed impressed. When he further found out that I was taking a course in thermodynamics, he asked me to explain the concept of entropy to him, because he had trouble with it as a student. Entropy is one of the more difficult concepts for most students. I was surprised he would ask me about it in the setting I was in. Before I knew it, I was waking up a day later without an inflamed appendix. It took some years before I appreciated why he engaged me in the discussion the way he did. He was trying, successfully I might add, to take my mind off the pain, relax me, as I was being anesthetized for the operation; very clever! The word got back to my family in Tyre within a day or so. Fouad was the first on hand. He spent a few hours by my bedside before he returned to Tyre. I, in turn, tried to assure him that all was well, and to make sure to report accordingly to our mother. I was happy that the inflammation was diagnosed as it was and where it was, and that I received the excellent care

---

88 Regrettably, I no longer remember his full name: Hussein...?

the AUB hospital was famous for. I was never billed for any of the expenses incurred, nor did I ever know how they were paid! The following weekend, Mother came with Fouad to see for herself. Despite my initial apprehension about the class time I had missed, and that I might not be able to catch up with the classes, I slowly got back into the groove, and things began to become under control. The school year was successfully, but not excellently, concluded. Under the circumstances, I could only take a sigh of relief.

After a deep breath following the end of the semester, I began prospecting how I might spend the upcoming summer. There was, however, a five-semester-credit-hour junior chemistry course in quantitative analysis that was thought to be very desirable for physics majors. It was being offered in the summer. It had a reputation for being very demanding. Even the best of the students were having difficulty doing well in it during the regular school year. Everything in my situation that summer said, go for it! Make it a test case for what I can do, my inner sense would whisper. The questions that continually popped into my head during my college years were: *How good am I, really, academically? How fit am I for advanced studies?* Because of my relative excellence in the three years preceding college, I often felt I was underperforming in college. I had secretly maintained to myself that were it not for the many challenges; cultural, financial, social, among others—while living in the big city and away from home (particularly, Mother's care and emotional support), I would be performing academically at a much better level. That summer seemed to offer me conditions, in terms of relative comfort at the co-op dorm, though the UNESCO scholarship did not extend to summer school, that would enable me to test these claims, if only in part. The course professor, Dr. Bruce Martin, was the same professor who offered it during the school year. I enrolled with everybody's blessings; family, friends, and academic advisor.

For a couple of weeks, the time period between the end of the school year and the start of summer school, I was mostly in Beirut at the co-op dorm, psyching myself up for the summer session. The dorm was fairly abandoned. Brother Fouad was in Tyre wrapping up his preparation for the early summer session of the GCE examination in physics and mathematics. With me in recess, Fouad would visit me from time to time to update me on his preparation for the GCE exams in math and physics and for us to have some fun together in the big city.

My quantitative analysis class had about two-dozen students. The professor was a no-nonsense superb teacher, the syllabus was extensive, and the course was not going to be a summer picnic! There were five hour-lectures and six hours of laboratory every week, for eight weeks. I kept virtually all other activities and distractions for the duration to a minimum. I found myself enjoying the lectures and looking forward to the labs. Every student was assigned a laboratory station and given an unknown-project analysis to perform weekly and independently. I constantly surprised myself by getting A's on the laboratory projects with commendations from Dr. Martin. My performance seemed at the top of the class. Dr. Martin showed an appreciation of my work as well as personal interest; he encouraged me. When I voiced my possible interest in doing graduate work in the USA, he seemed to signal an unqualified green light. When all the work was done and I received the final grade for the course, it was better than any grade I had achieved heretofore in any of my physical science or mathematics courses; the heavy demands of the course notwithstanding. My secret claims to myself were vindicated, and I was overjoyed!

Fouad took the GCE exams in physics and mathematics on schedule that summer. The results did not come out until early October. When they did, Fouad had passed. His passing was a major turning point in Fouad's life.

The remaining weeks between the end of the summer session and the beginning of the following school year were spent, for the most part, in Tyre doing what came naturally; playing at the YMCA, looking for a book I might read in the new books section of the library, socializing in the Palestinian community, and swimming at the beach across the street from the Tyre home.

It was time to move out of the co-op housing. With the UNESCO scholarship into its second year, I no longer needed to live in the co-op dorm, nor did it seem fair not to make room for another student of a greater need. A classmate, Fouad El-Hajj (Fouad E., for distinctive identification) and I met in a modern algebra class in the second semester of junior year. We found we had a lot in common to share and exchange so we planned to room together the following year. We jointly found a room in a private rooming house on Hamra's Street, about a ten-minute walk from campus. Fouad E. hailed from Sidon. He showed an unusually free mind with a good mathematical bent that evoked my admiration. He was, at the time, unsettled on a major but leaning towards mathematics and physics. He and I were out of sync in most other courses, so we saw each other primarily at the room. All along, we recognized our different backgrounds, he being Lebanese Christian, and myself, Palestinian Muslim. We discussed all kinds of topics of the time. It was not uncommon that we had different views on things, but they were never expressed, I recall, in an angry way; we truly respected each other's views. We worked very harmoniously to maintain a clean room and a quiet environment so each could do his schoolwork without distractions or inconvenience. In time of illness, such as a cold, etc., we tried the best way we knew how to care for each other. On some weekends, when both happened to be going home, we would ride the Beirut-Tyre bus together. He would get off in Sidon while I continued on to Tyre. Brother Fouad got to meet Fouad E. early on and the two Fouads hit it off very well.

Shortly after having taken the GCE exam in physics and mathematics the previous June, and finding out he had passed them, Fouad turned his attention to taking the exams in general science and Arabic in the October session, which he did. When the results came out that he had passed them as well, Fouad was four-fifths of the way to qualifying for admission to AUB, except for the English language entrance exam. The remaining fifth was passing the GCE exam in history. He scheduled that for the next June session.

During the second semester of my sophomore and the just-passed junior year, I had alternated between Drs. Byron Youtz and Salwa Nassar as major advisors. Dr. Nassar seemed to be off campus often, so I tended to visit more with Dr. Youtz. Gradually, Dr. Youtz became my official advisor, while Dr. Nassar continued as an informal advisor. As I progressed through the grades, sophomore to senior, the classes got smaller and the relationship with the advisor, and to a lesser extent, course professors, got closer and less formal.

Dr. Youtz had joined the Physics Department in the summer of 1953. He was a rather recent PhD in cosmic rays experimental physics, which was also Dr. Nassar's specialty. Dr. Nassar was at least ten years his senior. In fact, Dr. Nassar was a celebrity in Lebanon, in that she was the first Lebanese woman to earn a PhD in physics at a time when you could hardly find a Lebanese or Arab man holding a PhD in physics. She had further spent the World War II years doing cosmic rays research in the U.S. Initially, I would interact with her with a considerable awe; gradually, however, my relationship with her got more relaxed, and she appeared increasingly human. Dr. Youtz had assumed the chairmanship of the physics department in the fall of the school year. He replaced Dr. Nassar, who wanted to be relieved of the chairmanship to pursue other interests involving travel.

Dr. Youtz, with his young wife, had come to AUB motivated by a sense of service, which he had acquired, at least in part I believe, through his church affiliation.[89] He also wanted to experience the "world" outside the U.S. His declared intent was to spend, at most, four years at AUB. He was not unique in this respect, although more often such transient American professors would spend two years, and some still less. Dr. Bruce Martin, my chemistry professor of the just-passed summer was similarly motivated. Moreover, Drs. Martin and Youtz knew each other well, became good friends and socialized together along with their families. A somewhat similar example was Mr. Owen Gingerich, who also was contemporary with Drs. Martin and Youtz and befriended them. He came with his young wife and their newly-arrived baby, to serve for a couple of years. He was a recent recipient of an M.S. in astronomy from Harvard. AUB had a special attraction for him in that it offered an unattended observatory with a telescope well located on campus for sky observation. It sort of was a case of an observatory and a department (astronomy) in need of a caretaker. He became and managed the one-man astronomy department. I interacted with him, but casually, as astronomy seemed to me at the time to be a far-out field. What is especially noteworthy about Mr. Gingerich is that after his AUB service, he went back to Harvard to earn a PhD in astronomy. He rose rapidly to full professor at Harvard. His contributions to astronomy and history of science have been recognized worldwide. AUB, acknowledging his outstanding achievements, conferred upon him an honorary doctorate degree in 2011.[90]

My senior year was heavy in physics and mathematics courses. I knuckled down to serious work for the entire year. There was one course in the first semester, Introduction to Atomic Physics', taught by Dr. Nassar. In that course I began to realize that the logic of atomic physics differed markedly from nineteenth century classical physics. It ushered in a new physics called quantum

---

89 Most frequent of those churches were the Congregational and the Presbyterian.

90 He was not unlike the famous Cornell University's Carl Sagan of the TV series "The Universe" in popularizing its study.

physics or quantum mechanics. That course was followed in the second semester by an introductory course, Quantum Mechanics, offered for the first time in the physics department and taught by Dr. Youtz. The rationale was that it would help in further study of atomic physics, in particular, and modern physics in general. It was felt to be a must for those contemplating graduate study in related physics areas. Dr. John F. Randolph, a visiting mathematics professor from the University of Rochester (U of R), N.Y., taught the second semester of the senior advanced calculus class. Dr. Randolph, chairman of the mathematics department at U of R. was on a one-semester leave. For a long time he had had an interest to live and travel in the Middle East, and his visiting position with AUB fit well in his plan. He only taught that one course (three hours a week). He planned to travel with his wife throughout the area after the end of the school year. He was in his mid fifties. It was all to AUB's good fortunes and the students in the advanced calculus class.

The quantum mechanics course had only three students; the smallest class I'd ever been in at AUB until that time. The three were Saffouri, Sa'id (henceforth, Said, for simplicity) Mughabghab, and myself. All three of us were senior physics majors, yet the senior physics class had another four students: Khalil Dagher, Jamil Katul, Rasmi Mahmoud, and Fahd Wakiem. For a variety of reasons, these four chose not to take the course. Nevertheless, since quantum mechanics was thought to be the basis of modern physics, and by implication, the modern age, we came to be viewed as the avant-garde of the class. The smallness of the class brought all three of us even closer to Dr. Youtz; we got to do other things with Dr. Youtz outside the classroom that were social and cultural in nature, including visiting his home. The more I interacted with him, the more I saw a compassionate, decent human being. He showed tremendous interest in many aspects of the Middle East, and asked lots of questions. The three of us tried, in the best way we knew how, to provide answers. From time to time, he would reveal a debate within himself as to whether to settle permanently at AUB and in Lebanon. The course also brought me closer to Said. Said's performance and mine were comparable, whereas Saffouri's was generally distinctly higher. We both tended to marvel at the intensity with which Saffouri pursued his course work in particular, and academic goals, in general.

Dr. Randolph's advanced calculus class had about a dozen students. Several of us recognized a master at work as he taught the class. He was very engaging and stimulating. He would present mathematical questions, and give individual students a chance to answer them. I was strongly drawn to the course and Professor Randolph's ways. One time, he asked a question that seemed to silence the class until I jumped up on my feet with the answer. He asked me for the reasoning behind the answer; I presented it. Unbeknown to me at the time, it was a well-known theorem in calculus. He wrote my answer on the blackboard, and gave it the name, "Hassoun's Theorem," and underlined my name. It was the only time any of the students in the class got such recognition. I was in high heaven for at least a week, basking in my classmates' admiration. Come the semester's end, my final grade in the course was at 90%.

Dr. Randolph socialized with the students outside class. He shared some of his planned travel during the summer at the end of which he would return to the University of Rochester to resume his regular duties there. Before he left the campus, at the end of the school year, he took my name and address and gave me his address, should he be able to be of help to me if I came to the States for graduate study.

One course, in the last semester of the senior year, that did not quite pan out was Introductory Electronics. Normally, the electrical engineering department would offer it, but it was not being offered at the time. The physics department decided to offer it to give seniors basic working knowledge of the field. Virtually all the seniors enrolled, as I did. A young recent AUB M.S. graduate in physics/mathematics, Bino Robush, was assigned to teach it. The course was heavily lab oriented. The teacher was very lively, energetic, but inexperienced and stuck up on himself. He tended to be sarcastic and condescending. In one of the early lab periods, as I was setting up equipment for an assigned experiment, he looked over my shoulder to find my set-up was wrong. So he began to openly make fun and ridicule what I was doing. I was very offended, but carried on with the work until the end of the period. The course was desirable and recommended, but not required for graduation. I had no background in it whatsoever, was not psychologically in tune with it, and had a latent apprehension of it. With all these factors coming together, I got turned off on the material and the teacher. I decided to drop the course. At the next chance, I went to see Dr. Youtz, my advisor, and asked him to allow me to drop the course. Dr. Youtz tried hard to talk me out of dropping. Unfortunately, I was in no mood to change my mind. Dr. Youtz reluctantly approved it. It was the only course that I had dropped out of in my undergraduate years.

One good thing did come out of the electronics course experience. I got to meet another physics major who was about a year ahead, except for being a few credit hours short of graduation. His name was Hanna Nasir from Ramallah, Palestine. He was the son of the famous Musa Nasir, founder and president of Beir Zeit College/University. Hanna happened to be in the class and stayed the course. Thereafter, Hanna and I had something to converse about whenever we would cross paths on campus. Our conversations were always informative, stimulating, and friendly.

Another worthy occurrence took place in the senior year: it was the formation of a Physics Majors Club, intended to study and report back to the group, or in a public presentation, on current problems in physics and Arab society. It was short-lived. During its short life, however, I researched and reported to the club, in an open campus presentation, on "The Capacity of the Arabic Language to be a Modern Scientific Language." At the time I chose this subject, there was a widely-held view among some (Westernized) Arabs that Arabic had stagnated for several centuries heretofore, while Europe and the West were engaged in industrial and modern scientific revolutions. As a result, Arabic was rendered unfit to be the vehicle for progress and modernization. In many Arab universities of the time, the advanced sciences and mathematics were being studied in either English or French. My presentation was to refute such claims. The basic point I made was that the language of a people is a reflection of those who speak it. If the Arabs seek to progress and modernize, and they can and will, the Arabic language will progress and modernize with them likewise. Arabic was the language of scholarship, philosophy, and science when European languages and Latin were not! My presentation, delivered in Arabic, was well received by those present, primarily students, with a few Arabic-speaking professors. Dr. Nassar, though not present, complimented me with some encouraging words on the presentation, as she had heard about it from others. Her comments told me something more about Dr. Nassar that I did not realize before; namely, she cared not only about physics, but also about Arab issues!

Rasmi Mahmoud, my Palestinian/Jordanian physics classmate also roomed in the same building that Fouad El-Hajj and I roomed in. Rasmi hailed from a small town called Enebta, between Nablus and Tulkarem in the West Bank. This proximity of dwellings during the senior year brought us even closer together than otherwise would have been possible. On one weekend, I invited him to visit my family and the Palestinian community in Tyre, which he gladly accepted. A major reshuffling in the household was necessary to provide him with private overnight sleeping quarters. From all appearances, he had a very rich and enjoyable time. It was a memorable experience for all concerned.

Rasmi, active in the ILP, worked hard to interest me in it. Rasmi, who was a couple of years older than I, tended to assume the role of protector against what he thought corruptive influences, secularism and materialism. He also periodically cautioned me not to allow myself to be brainwashed or dazzled by America or the West. At one time, to my great astonishment, the head and founder of the ILP, Shaykh Taqiyye-Eddine Ennabahaani, a renowned scholar and prolific writer, and author of many books on Islam and the ILP, was staying with Rasmi overnight! Rasmi even introduced me to him and let me visit with him informally! Despite my sympathies to certain aspects of the movement and well-meaning aspirations, I was never able to buy into the concept of a religious state, no, not for our time!

On the romantic side of things, I did feel affection for one of my classmates in several mathematics classes. I first met her in my second semester of the junior year. She was of a very fine Palestinian Christian family, and a good student. With the exception of my most intimate confidante, brother Fouad, I kept my feelings to myself. Society or peers did not treat kindly or understandingly, "Being in love." In fact, it could become an object of ridicule and mockery. For a woman, it was even worse; it could be a cause of disgrace and shame! As a result, I never dared to even entertain the thought of hinting any of this feeling to her. For if she were favorable, the societal pressure would not allow her to express it, and if she were unfavorable, the pain of rejection would have been too much. I was not emotionally prepared to deal with it, and could not afford the distraction it would mean from my studies. Whenever we encountered each other, for example, in the library, we talked about course work, homework assignments, and the like. I knew so very little about the opposite sex that I had no idea how or what she felt. If I had to guess, I would be inclined to guess that she reciprocated my feelings, but this is only based on instinct and little things such as her manner of talking, or her occasional seeking out help on a homework math problem, even though she was perfectly capable herself. Dating was not an option. It was not permitted nor practiced among Arab students to my knowledge, even at AUB. In fact, I did not know what dating was. There was also the view that if I were to profess affection, I would have had to follow it by declaring my intention! But what kind of intention would I have been able to declare? I was too green emotionally and socially. Financially and economically, I was in no position to declare any intention; and in terms of future plans, I was merely beginning to contemplate going abroad for graduate study while she seemed to be heading back home to teach math in a high school. And so the mystery hung on until we both graduated and moved on our separate ways. One thing, however, I did feel: True love does not die; it might fade away, but very, very slowly!

The senior year was finally over. My overall grade average was highest of all the four years heretofore. I could say that I completed my undergraduate work on a fairly positive note. Several parties were scheduled by the administration for the graduates and their families over a two-day period, culminating in the commencement on the afternoon of June 25. It was to be followed by an evening "finale" party for the new and the old graduates, in honor of class 1956, hosted by the AUB alumni club at their center, a short walk off campus.

There was a lot of excitement at our Tyre household as graduation time approached. Mother thought that I would need a brand new suit to wear for the celebrations. Brothers Yousef and Fouad endorsed her thought and facilitated the process. She bought me a top quality English wool yard-good and had it tailored into a suit at the tailor shop next door to the laundry. I felt it was the best suit I could hope to have.

Mother and Fouad attended the Parents' Reception given by AUB Acting President, Constantine Zurayk, the evening before the commencement. It was held at the president's home garden on campus. I was initially concerned that Mother, with her traditional Islamic white scarf about her head, might be out of place in a very Western setting. My concern turned out to be quite baseless. I was pleasantly surprised by her ability to socialize gracefully with many of the guests. A very memorable encounter occurred when she found Dr. Sa'd Mussallam, our Haifa family doctor to be among the guests; his daughter was in the same graduating class! Dr. Mussallam and Mother rejoiced at seeing each other and reminisced over the old times. She also visited with other parents of some of my classmates whom she had heard me talk about over the years. The hours passed quickly and harmoniously before it was time to leave to prepare for the next day.

The following day, Mother and Fouad attended the commencement exercises. The actual diplomas were conferred right there on the stand. Dr. Zurayk was, ex-officio, the master of ceremonies, and Dr. Charles Malik[91] was the featured speaker. The exercises were held outdoors. It was a beautiful sunny afternoon that brought together a large assembly of people including many dignitaries from a broad spectrum of Arab and non-Arab societies.

Dr. Zurayk spoke in English on the obligations and responsibilities of the new graduates to their society and the homeland. His speech rang in my head for a long time afterwards. He wanted us to be leaders in our communities and catalysts for change in a society that sorely needed change to meet the challenges of the modern world. One exhortation that has lingered in my thought for all these years was, "You cannot afford to betray the high hopes that your nation has placed in you."

Dr. Malik spoke in Arabic about the role of the individual and his or her fundamental importance in society. He stressed that society is made up of individuals, that the individual is the elementary building block, and that a healthy society begins with a healthy individual. To some extent, he seemed to be alluding to the Arabic ill of not giving the individual his or her right to be independent, free, and equal before the law with every other individual. He further seemed to be saying that Arab society should desist from interdependent and clannish living, which constrains and inhibits individual excellence, and move towards a society wherein the individual, not the clan, or the tribe, is at the heart of what we hold dear and for whom we legislate and plan.

---

91 One of the most accomplished AUB alumni, he served for a time as Lebanon's ambassador to the UN, and served one term as president of the UN's General Assembly. He also held on and off academic positions in the philosophy departments of several prestigious universities, as well as AUB.

Mother and Fouad left for home after the commencement, whereas I stayed behind to go to the alumni party later in the evening with the understanding that I would head home to Tyre within days. Mr. Emile Bustani[92] was the president of the club at the time and master of ceremonies for the evening. Mr. Bustani took time to mix and socialize with many of us amid an abundance of food and soft drinks. He recognized, in his comments from the podium, the most accomplished of the graduating class. Top among these was Saffouri, who had graduated with "high distinction;" and further; had set a new grade record among all AUB alumni, past and present. He broke the record set, until then, by Charles Malik. Saffouri was in seventh heaven, a major achievement indeed! I missed the "distinction" honor by several percentage points in the overall four-year average. The Ramallah math coed-classmate graduated with "distinction." If I had felt any disappointment in myself, it was mild and it quickly vanished. I excused myself. I was convinced that the accomplishments we all were celebrating far exceeded and overshadowed any disappointments endured. I saw the glass more than half-full. *I will always feel this way!*

Within a couple of days after the festivities, Saffouri and I somehow got the idea that it would be nice, as an expression of appreciation, to invite our American physics professors and their spouses; particularly, Dr. Byron Youtz who had done so much to guide us on, to come and spend a day in Tyre with me as their host and tour guide. Saffouri would be their companion on the trip since he lived with his family in Beirut. The idea was irresistible. We went with it to Dr. Youtz. He gladly received it. There were two other American professors in the department who were invited and who accepted. One of them was Dr. James R. Heirtzler, and a second professor whose name, regrettably, I no longer remember. Both of these professors were married, transient, and had no children.[93] Dr. Heirtzler was finishing up a three-year

---

92 He was another illustrious alumnus who achieved great wealth and fame as the CEO of the "Contracting and Trading" company (acronym: CAT, with a black cat for its logo), a leading and dominant company in construction, throughout the Middle East and parts of Africa, for many years.

93 All three professors were moving back to the States at various points in the summer, including Dr. Youtz. Dr. Youtz had accepted a position at Reed's College Physics Department in Portland, Oregon beginning with the fall of 56. Dr. Heirtzler accepted a position as senior physicist at General Dynamics Corporation. The size of the AUB Physics Department was about six. The three professors on the trip, thus, constituted half the department.

term at the physics department; the third professor was there only for a semester. Their wives were able to join them. Dr. Youtz' wife was pregnant and near the end of her term. He thought that she would not be able to come. He jokingly added that he hoped the baby did not decide to come on the day of the trip. A day was set, which was a mere few days off. While I initially offered that the group have lunch at our home, Dr. Youtz insisted that would be too much for my family. He suggested limiting it to coming into the house to congratulate the family, and for sweets and refreshments. For the rest of the time, they would sightsee and perhaps do some swimming and/or scuba diving.[94] As a good advisee, I accepted. Thereafter, I left further logistics and details of the trip for Saffouri to work out with Dr. Youtz. I headed for Tyre to set the stage for the visit.

The family received me as a victorious soldier coming back home from battle! Ever since Mother and Fouad got back from the graduation ceremonies, many of our neighbors, relatives, and friends had come to congratulate us on my graduation, some with presents—the family busily doled out sweets and refreshments. Brother Yousef gave me a hug and a gold-plated Parker ink pen for a present. More congratulators continued to come. In due course, I broke out the news of the impending visit of the three American professors and two of the wives, accompanied by Saffouri, whom they had met before. Mother simply said, "*Ahlan wa sahlan*," which is Arabic for "Welcome." I then went over the details of the visit. Fouad and his wife offered right away to vacate their bedroom, which was spacious and looked to the sea, and to convert it into a reception room for that day. It had partially been that for the past few days anyhow. The family further decided to give the house a thorough cleanup job and some painting as needed.[95] There was further, the question of furnishing the reception room befittingly. It was decided to borrow a set of summer wicker chairs, a love seat, and sofa from our next-door neighbors. When the day of the visit arrived, the reception room looked very nice and was adequate to seat the group plus more. The house as a whole never looked cleaner since it became

---

94 Tyre is rich with ancient ruins and had good beaches. Some years later, the UN had declared it, "A World Heritage City."

95 There followed a beehive of activities and preparations behind the scene that I could not keep up with.

our refuge in 1948. The kitchen and a back room (where Mother, Qasim, and I usually slept) were full of drinks, sweets and fruits. Everybody worked hard and cooperatively with everybody else, especially my sisters-in-law, Nadiema and Fay (Fakhriyye). The little children were sent away for the day to be with nearby relatives.

The company arrived on the appointed day, about 10:00 am. The car carrying the guests pulled up straight across from the house on Tyre's main road and they disembarked. The car was in full view from the house's verandah, where some family members were watching in anticipation. The weather was sunny and pleasantly warm. My feelings at that point were a mixture of high excitement and deep apprehension. The excitement had to do with seeing these wonderful people from the new world, with advanced education (three PhDs in physics), and modern ways, walking right here in an ancient little town of a medieval society. They were coming to our simple, modest, and undoubtedly crowded home to meet the family and to celebrate my graduation and that of Saffouri! The apprehension stemmed from my eagerness to insure that nothing untoward took place that could blemish or even spoil our collective joy. I have no doubt that all my family members felt similarly on that day. My mother, Fouad, and I went out to meet them and walk them to the house. There were the introductions, the shaking of hands and the smiles. All of them had carry-on bags of one kind or another. The car left, but was to be back in the town's main square for the return trip later in the day. They were ushered to the house, up the verandah and, with one right turn, into the reception room. There they met the rest of the family present; in particular, Yousef, Nadiema, and Fay. Yousef, with his indomitable spirit, tried to crack few jokes. Some of the family members sat down; some began serving the drinks. There was a lot to talk about, and for a time the room was full of chatter. When drinks were served, they opted for pop rather than lemonade. At the time, we did not appreciate the reason. In hindsight, they were concerned about drinking local water. They enjoyed the sweets. They liked baklava, and said so. One of the wives particularly socialized with Nadiema and Fay. She told me that her grandfather was Armenian, and that she always hoped for the opportunity to see this part of the world. When it came to fruits (pears, apples, melons, etc.), the wives asked that they wash the fruits with soap before they were peeled and served. Both Nadiema and Fay were quite surprised, especially when they, themselves, had washed them before.

They spent about an hour or so before it was signaled to me that it is time to start sightseeing. I excused them to the family, and left with them to begin the next activity. As they walked out, the family pressed all to come back for refreshment before they headed back to Beirut. Initially, they did not think it necessary, but because the family asked them to do so, they agreed.

At first, they seemed most interested in finding a secluded beach to do some swimming and scuba diving. I knew just the right place; somewhat rocky, but fairly private and possessing an interesting sea floor. It was behind major ruins, to the south of the city. We walked over there. I chose a path that was least walked over. I wanted to shield them away from the crowds. When we got there, they pulled out their gear, and many of them discretely put on their swimming suits, goggles and other paraphernalia. Foremost among them was Dr. Youtz. I was happy to see them feeling free enough to want to swim and/ or explore the beach. Those who did not swim, myself included, did quite a bit of talking. About one o'clock, they pulled out bag lunches and drinks of their own. About two o'clock, they decided it was time to get dressed and see more of the town. They seemed to mostly want to see the ruins, which was what we did. Then came the subject of seeing the residential sections of town and the old city. They left it up to me to decide what else I would show them. I think they wanted me to do what I was comfortable with, while I wanted to do what they were interested in doing and were comfortable with. After a brief discussion, we all agreed that it would be fun to walk them through the old city with its narrow and meandering streets. Dr. Youtz made sure that I felt it was safe (perhaps because of possible anti-America feeling), and that I was at ease in doing so. I told him that I saw no problem.[96] The day was a normal business day; the town was lively. So all seven of us proceeded with me in the lead. We walked by many little shops; yard goods, grain merchants, fresh produce, the fish market, the butcher, the tailor, the shoemaker, the barber and, the Hassoun Laundry! We stopped at the laundry and chatted a bit, then

---

96 I might have been naïve, but the saying, "Better be lucky than smart!" perhaps described the occasion, and all was well.

continued onward until we emerged out of the old city into the main square (el-Bawwabe) downtown where the return trip car was waiting. Throughout the walk, the people of the town were probably as intrigued by the Americans amongst them as the Americans were intrigued being amongst the most humble of working locals! I greeted quite a few of the people as we walked by, for most of them knew me or some member of my family. It was about three-thirty in the afternoon when they all got into the car. I was squeezed in as well. In no more than five-minute drive, we were in front of the house, as agreed upon. The family welcomed them back. Drinks and sweets were served on the run as the party bade everybody goodbye. It was about four o'clock in the afternoon when I saw them off! Everybody seemed happy. I was filled with gratitude that all had gone well as I walked slowly back to the house.

At the house, the family asked if I had noticed anything different in the reception room on the group's second visit. I said, "No." Fouad explained the wicker set of chairs, the love seat, and sofa were no longer the borrowed ones from the neighbors. He had decided the set had added so much to the house and was needed. While we (the company and I) were gone, he went to the furniture store in town and bought a set similar, but not identical to the one the family had borrowed. He had it brought to the house and placed in the reception room in the same arrangement of the borrowed set; and, he had returned the neighbors' set! In my excitement and absorption of being a good host, I had not noticed the changes. Whether anybody else in the company had noticed, I'll never know![97]

Early into the second semester of my senior year, my intention to pursue graduate study in physics in the USA became firmly anchored. I was no doubt influenced by many previous AUB graduates who had done so, as well as conversations with my teachers. Conversations with classmates were also another incentive; for typically, the good and ambitious students talked in terms of further education in the U.S., if not immediately, at least at a later date. The notion of becoming a high school physics teacher in some Arab country rapidly lost any appeal it may have previously had for me. My classmate and pal, Saffouri, was advised and urged to pursue graduate studies in the U.S. In

---

97 Fouad informed me at the time of this writing that the transaction had cost him the sum total of about $40.00. In those days, it was close to a month's salary of his.

fact, with his distinguished record, it was inconceivable that he would not do so, not withstanding the manifest absence of financial means. Saffouri, sure of his continued excellence and with guidance from the physics faculty, started the process of applying for admission and financial assistantship to leading U.S. universities quite early in the senior year, whereas I took a wait-and-see attitude until well into the second semester. Even then, I was still not used to planning too far in advance. Anything beyond three months seemed far in advance. By April of the senior year, it became common knowledge that Saffouri had been admitted, with a research assistantship, to the California Institute of Technology, "Caltech," and that he planned to go there. For the following year, I declared my intent to enroll at AUB as a first year graduate student, ostensibly working for the M.S. degree, provided I could get some assistantship to support myself. Said Mughabghab seemed to be in a similar situation. Much later, near the end of the summer, I became aware that another physics major classmate was going to enroll as well; namely, Jamil Katul. All the others were headed into different places in the Arab physics teaching market. Jamil, though very capable, was a very quiet person, a bit older than average, and somewhat aloof. The notion of a graduate teaching assistant was not well developed in the physics department at the time. Dr. Youtz offered Said and me a half-time assistant instructor faculty position at a pay of LL200.00 (roughly $65) per month each, over a twelve-month period, beginning with the new academic year. It would start in October 1956. The amount was intended to be just enough to meet our basic needs. We both accepted the offer readily. Our duties were to teach freshman physics laboratory and recitation sections. For the summer, there was a research project that Dr. Nassar had received a money grant for. It had to do with building and operating a neutron monitoring station on campus in connection with the International Geophysical Year of 1958 for the study of solar spots.[98] Dr. Nassar was away on a semi-sabbatical in the U.S. during the second semester of the senior year, and was not getting back until the fall of 1956. The project somehow fell in the lap of Dr. Youtz in a "care-taking capacity" for the summer's duration, as he was finishing up

98 It is known that solar spots have a cycle of activity about eleven years in duration. The year 1958 came at the peak of the spots' activity. The monitoring station was to study any correlation between neutron intensity on the earth's surface with the spots activities on the sun.

his stay at AUB and leaving by the end of the summer. In his characteristic conscientiousness, he was eager to get the work on the station going right away. Be that as it may, he asked Said and me if we would be interested in being summer research assistants to help launch the project at the same pay as the half-time assistant instructorships. We both gladly accepted. With these two jobs, I felt financially secure for the next fifteen months.

Early that summer, Fouad took the GCE exam in history. Should he pass it, it would put Fouad in position to qualify for admission, except for the English entrance examination. Fouad wasted no time and filed an application for admission to AUB, which I hand-delivered to Mr. Fuleihan. He had gotten to know me fairly well by then.[99] At the time, I explained to Mr. Fuleihan, Fouad's eagerness and potential to become a civil engineer, his excellent aptitude in the sciences and mathematics, and I provided him with a brief biographical sketch. The thrust in Fouad's case was to initially secure admission. The financing part was to cross over later. As with my case, Mr. Fuleihan listened carefully and sympathetically. Within a few weeks, Fouad received conditional admission, subject to passing the GCE history exam and AUB English entrance exam. The English entrance examination was set later that summer. Fouad settled down for the rest of the summer to prepare for it. The result of the history examination would not come out until late that summer.

Aside from summer work and shepherding Fouad's progress towards admission to AUB, I socialized often with Saffouri and Emile Asfour. Emile had graduated with us in business and gotten a job in Intra Bank, headquartered in downtown Beirut. Both Emile and I were very mindful of Saffouri's impending departure to Caltech. We visited his parents from time to time to provide them with some emotional support, as Saffouri was an only son with one sister. To his family, who had hardly traveled more than a hundred miles from their birthplace, Saffouri's going to America was a very major step, a journey into the great unknown. Saffouri encouraged us to keep in touch with his parents after his departure. In the company of his parents and some immediate relatives, I saw him off as he sailed out of Beirut's harbor about the middle of August. The scene was gut wrenching.

---

99 In fact, Mr. Fuleihan hired me, as a junior, to tutor his son, Amin, in a freshman math course.

My work on the neutron station began by boning up on what it is supposed to do, its significance, and studying the blueprints for building the monitoring pile, as it was then called. The pile was to be built by blocks of lead and paraffin layered in such a way as to embed and shield neutron counters from background spurious radiation, yet capable of detecting neutrons from the sun. The pile was cubical over a meter to the side. It required lead and paraffin blocks of certain dimensions. These dimensions were not readily available on the market. A great deal of effort was spent before we found somebody in Beirut who had the wherewithal to make the lead blocks. As for the paraffin, we ended having to buy it in large blocks, melt them, and pour them in molds of the required dimensions. All this took time. The counters, from the States, were also slow in coming; so were the electronics to process the neutron counts. By the end of the summer, the pile and counters were in place, but not the electronics. Dr. Youtz' time to leave for Reed's College had come. Just before departure, Dr. Youtz invited Said and me to join him at an open-air classical music concert in Baalbek, a famous Roman city in the Bekaa Valley, about forty miles across and over a mountain range and east of Beirut. A very memorable time was had by all three of us.

With Dr. Youtz gone, our research assistantships terminated. Said and I assumed our new teaching jobs as assistant instructors. The project was put on hold. Dr. Nassar returned from the States just in time to start the fall semester. We never got back to the project, except for preparing two articles in the fall, describing the project, for the two leading Beirut daily newspapers, *The Daily Star* (English) and *Al-Hayat* (Arabic). They were readily published.[100]

Fouad was allowed to take the AUB English entrance examination in advance of the outcome of the history exam, which happened to have been abnormally late. He took it and passed it. His admission became thus conditional only on the outcome of his GCE history exam. Within days, Fouad back in Tyre, the history exam result finally came out. It was a "Pass." Fouad's admission became unqualified. I telegraphed him the code phrase, "come and register."

---

100 Said's name and mine appeared as joint authors of each of the two articles. It was "a first'" for both of us. Said prepared the English version while I prepared the Arabic one. Dr. Fouad Sarruf, vice-president of AUB at the time, guided our efforts; his encouragement and kindness were very valuable.

He knew it is all clear! Fouad had a wife and four children aged five, four, three, and one, and the wisdom of giving up his teaching jobs, to reckon with. His total assets at best could not have exceeded a few hundred dollars. Even with all of this, Mother still managed not to tap into her "old age security," her gold bracelets.

CHAPTER 11

LAST YEAR AT AUB; FAREWELL TO *ARABY*[101]

Most of those who knew Fouad met the news of his impending enrollment into AUB with disbelief. How would he give up his teaching, support the family, and meet college expenses all at once? Some of his colleagues who knew him as an eighth-grade laundry man even jested at the news saying mockingly that he was being admitted as a sophomore! Fouad, nevertheless, without hesitation, tendered his teaching resignation. I, in the meantime, found a room for both of us within walking distance to the campus, just off Alhamra Street. It was a good-size room with an annex, like a walk-in closet or half a room, and a balcony for the sum total of 120 Lebanese liras; the equivalent of $40. I was going to be making about $65 monthly, I would be able, with the remainder, to manage my other basic needs, food and pocket money. I counted on some of my summer work savings to make up for any deficit. Fouad liked the rented place and felt that it was big enough to house a third person. He had just learned that Ka'yed el-Maari, a Palestinian from Ein el-Hilwe refugee camp, a few miles east of Sidon, a starting freshman, was looking for housing. Ka'yed was a graduate of Sidon's prestigious American High School: Gerard's Institute. He also had taught for a couple of years at a Palestinian UN school in the Ein el-Hilwe area. Fouad asked me if it was all right to invite him to live with us and share in the rent. It was fine with me. The annex became my private quarters, while Fouad and Ka'yed shared the room. With Kayed's contribution of one-third the rent, I did not have to dip much into my summer work savings. Fouad, from his own savings, and with some help from Mother, provided for his food, pocket money, and university tuition, as well as the support of his wife and children. Mother also provided emotional support for Fouad's wife and the children who lived within the same household, along with Yousef and his family. The housing expense for Fouad's family in Tyre was next to nothing, if anything at all. We were off to a good start. However,

---

101 "Araby" is an Arabic adjective meaning that which is Arabic.

we all knew that Fouad could not sustain such expenses for long. We were betting that once Fouad's foot was inside the "university door," he would be able to secure some kind of financial assistance. For me, this school year was to be the springboard to graduate study in the U.S.

To simplify our life, Fouad and I subscribed for all meals at the East Hall Restaurant; a short walk from the campus main gate. It included three meals a day, seven days a week, for $25 each, per month. The food was quite good, far superior to that of the cooperative. Typically, the more affluent students subscribed to eat there. Some faculty ate there as well. It was a meeting place of a diverse AUB population. During meal times, the place would be throbbing with dynamism and chatter. I look back at those times as some of my happiest at AUB.

Fouad seemed to adjust remarkably well to being an older than average freshman. The AUB culture did not seem to shock him anywhere near as much it had me. Yet, one hurdle surfaced the first week of classes. The mathematics lectures seemed to go over his head. This was particularly disturbing to Fouad because of a lifelong excellence in math. It got to the point that he started doubting the viability and wisdom of his going to the university. That of course got my attention; there was too much at stake. I knew right away that his self-doubts and fears were not well founded, and that he was amply up to the task. Bino Robush, being his math teacher, compounded the problem. Yes, the same "Robush" that I clashed with in the electronics class of the previous year. The kick-off for the course introduced some modern concepts of math that, back in those days, were never touched upon in high school (involving such things as set theory and vector spaces). They presented a higher perspective of math of a greater abstraction. It would take time and effort to develop and appreciate such a perspective for one stooped in the traditional approach such as Fouad was. I counseled patience to Fouad, and right away offered to tutor him on the material and the homework as long as he felt the need, which he accepted. Fouad quickly began to catch on, and in short order, no longer needed my tutoring. Eventually, Fouad and Robush, who was very likely younger than Fouad, developed a friendly relationship. Fouad did have other, but less, threatening challenges, notably in English, not unlike some of mine. Overall, however, the school year for Fouad progressed well. He secured a financial student loan from the Palestinian Aid Fund that paid his tuition for the second semester. He made many friends and readily made the soccer teams of the freshman class, the College of Arts and Sciences, and the varsity. He distinguished himself in all three, which got him coverage in the AUB weekly paper, *The Outlook*. Rapidly, he became a campus-wide celebrity. As he played on the forward offense-line, his speed and his successful dogged pursuit of the goal gained him the nickname, "AUB's scorer."

Fouad's circle of friends grew and developed so fast that at times he was manifestly socially more active and freer than me. I recall deciding one weekend evening to live it up with my friend and colleague Said Mughabghab by going to a dinner nightclub in the famous Zaitouni district of Beirut, looking over the Mediterranean. It was the sort of thing that I had rarely done before. The club had a particularly relaxing atmosphere with a live band and Western and Arabic dancing. Said and I made the decision reluctantly, both of us mindful that it was going to take a big bite out of our monthly salary. As we were ushered in, I saw Fouad with a lively bunch of friends at a large round table covered with hors d'oeuvres and drinks. I contained my sense of surprise, greeted those at his table, and proceeded to a separate table with Said. We all had a good, relaxing time. The next day Fouad and I chuckled at the coincidence and acknowledged that life has to have some fun as long as the cost does not lead to irreparable damage.

Looking ahead, Fouad and I turned our gaze towards a UNESCO scholarship for him, like the one I had for the past two years. If we could only capture the scholarchip, we reasoned, Fouad's financial hurdles would be greatly diminished. Fouad, feeling that I was the more experienced, delegated its pursuit to me. I got no positive response from UNESCO-liaison officer (no longer Mr. Husseini) on campus on the grounds that the scholarship guidelines forbade two members of the same family from getting the scholarship. I was advised to take the matter to the Beirut UNESCO office in Beirut's UNESCO headquarters. To my pleasant surprise, the liaison officer was Raji Sahyoun.

I had run into Raji the year before on the AUB campus. I had introduced myself to him as Hamadi's and Fouad's brother. He acknowledged them and politely inquired about them. I voiced my long-held admiration, especially of his work as a broadcaster of Radio Palestine during the war of 1948. He humbly, and with a bittersweet mixture of emotions, appreciated my sentiment. As we chatted further, I found out that he was trying to complete some course work to earn a B.A. degree. I could hardly believe what I was hearing. I had assumed that he was far too accomplished and famous to be an undergraduate student at my level of academic pursuit.

I presented Fouad's case at length to Raji. He listened patiently and sympathetically. I stressed the point that while we were brothers, Fouad was the head of his own family of wife and children, and that this was the case even before I enrolled at AUB. After a couple of visits, Raji, unable to act on the case, arranged for me to see his superior, who he referred to and addressed as "His Excellency, Mr. Touqan,"[102] in person whereat I again presented Fouad's case. In the end, we amicably parted with the understanding that he would get back to me with the decision in a timely manner. When the answer came, it was to my great disappointment, negative.

Disappointed and rejected was how both Fouad and I felt, but not defeated! Fouad and Mother could draw on their reserve a little longer. I impressed upon Fouad that he needed to do whatever was within his power to get into the second year. By then, it was clear I would be leaving for the States in the upcoming summer; I thought out loud and told him, "While I may not be able to help the first year of my going over, I will do whatever is humanly possible to help the following years."

Somewhere along the line, Mr. Shamma, College of Arts and Sciences athletic officer, offered Fouad a full-tuition scholarship for the sophomore year if Fouad stayed in the College of Arts and Sciences. Mr. Shamma wanted Fouad to be on the college's soccer team. Fouad and I, early in Fouad's freshman year, had discussed what might be his major. I was uncompromisingly opposed to his going into the College of Arts and Sciences. His most likely major would be mathematics. I could see little point in it, for all it could lead to would be becoming a high school math teacher, which he was advancing towards anyhow before his back-to-university enterprise. Going to graduate school was

---

102 I was struck by the degree of reverence shown by Raji to Mr. Touqan. While I did not know or hear of this particular Touqan, I certainly was familiar with the Touqan family he belonged to: a prominent Palestinian family in Nablus, made especially famous by the great Palestinian poet of the 1930s and 1940s, Ibrahim Touqan, and his sister poetess, Fadwa.

out of the question for him, given his family situation. I had also seen some of my successful classmates, and of admired families, go into engineering, often civil. It was common knowledge on campus that the opportunities for civil engineers in the Arab World, especially the oil-rich states, were abundant and virtually unlimited in potential. In a short time, the prospect of Fouad becoming a civil engineer caught fire with him, even though intermittently, he would revert to thinking of going back to teaching. Fouad eventually declined Mr. Shamma's offer and secured student loans from various sources to cover tuition for the sophomore year in the College of Engineering.

Ka'yed's fortunes, sadly, were not as good. He seemed to be struggling with several courses and experiencing a strong financial pinch. His second semester proved even harder. He was performing especially poorly in chemistry. His prospects for financial aid looked very slim. He decided to drop out by the end of the freshman year. I regret to say that he and I had very little interaction beside the formal. Consequently, I did not get involved in his difficulties, nor did I appreciate them. He went back to teaching at a Palestinian UN school in the Sidon area.

As an assistant instructor, I taught freshman physics laboratory. It had many sections. I taught three of those and a couple of problem solving recitation sections. When the matter of distribution of laboratory sections among instructors came up, I chose, unwisely, among my assigned sections, one that Fouad was in. Fouad, thus, became my student! Early on, Fouad realized it was not a good thing. I seemed to be more demanding of him than others and stricter in grading, lest I appear partial. Fouad, wisely, and without consulting me, requested that he be transferred to another section; his request was granted. It was definitely for the better!

Teaching came easy to me; it was almost a second nature. I taught from the heart and loved to connect with the audience. Since I was not much older than the students, sometimes younger, I availed myself generously to them; I identified with them and quickly established a rapport. I relished in my newfound sense of importance.

During this last year at AUB, Said Mughabghab and I became buddies. We enjoyed each other's company. We did a variety of activities together. I spent time at his home in Beirut, met his mother, some of his brothers, and spent one memorable weekend in his mountain home village of Ein-Zhalta. Said was more receptive to things Western, such as classical music and boy-girl dancing. He encouraged me to be open to them. I was too self-conscious, stiff and clumsy at the dancing, not that we had many occasions to do it. I am sure my traditional Islamic upbringing, in contrast to his Lebanese Christian upbringing, had a lot to do with it.

In fact, because of my view of the West's role in the Palestinian Nakba, I subconsciously developed a strong resistance to, and a wary eye of, things Western. I wanted Western education, but not its culture and values. I wrestled with this dichotomy intensely and for a long time. It caused inner conflicts; religious, cultural and nationalistic related to who I am. I knew inner conflicts could impair an individual's ability to function at their highest potential. Above all, I insisted that I wanted to be able to live at peace within so I could live at peace without. This was also a part and parcel of my pursuit to be a modern day physicist.

The Palestinian Nakba was at the core of my being. Any activity of significance was weighed against its relevance to alleviating the Nakba. Perhaps this effort of writing down my story is still, at least in part, an expression of this proclivity. I keep asking myself: How may I shine the sunlight of truth to heal this problem?

With the new school year, it became obvious that Jamil Katul was in the same boat as Said and I, assistant instructor/graduate student. As such, I came to interact with him more often, and to appreciate his camaraderie.

As a graduate student, I enrolled in three courses, one math and two physics, totaling nine credit hours. As an assistant instructor, I was exempted from any tuition fees; a big help, perhaps not sufficiently appreciated at the time.

The graduate courses had small enrollments, typically three to five students. The interaction with the professor was close and generally collegial. It was rarely a case of passing the course. Rather, it was how well you were going to pass, and what you were going to do with the acquired knowledge. Since I strongly felt that the AUB's physics graduate program was in its infancy, and that I should be pursing a graduate degree in a larger university in the U.S., I looked at my course work as interlude of enrichment in math and physics that would be useful once I got to the U.S. In fact, there was, that particular year

(1956-1957), only one viable subfield, had I decided to pursue the MS at AUB, namely, Solid State Physics.

Until the fall of 1956, the physics department was housed in a small corner of the College of Engineering building. Through the generosity of Emile Bustani, the physics department received its own building, named after him. We moved into it during the midyear break. There were several vacant offices, and we assistant instructors each got a private office. During the second semester, over and above my normal assistant instructor duties, I was called upon from time to time to give a general lecture to one of the freshman physics classes, to substitute for an absent professor. My success and enjoyment at these undertakings reinforced my intended goal of an academic university career.

Trouble was brewing on the Middle East political front in parallel with the school year (1956-57). Nasser's problems with the Americans and their pullout of the financing of Aswan's High Dam made the Lebanese government more nervous than normal. Travel restrictions between Tyre and Beirut became more stringent; permits would be required of Palestinians. Soldiers on the Litani/ Qassimiyya River crossing indulged in derisive comments about Palestinians. Once, when aggressively interrogated of my rather frequent goings and comings between Tyre and Beirut, I decided to show off by saying, "I have family in Tyre and am a teacher at AUB." The soldier seemed taken aback as if to say, "How could this be?"

Nasser's nationalization of the Suez Canal, July 26, 1956, electrified the Arab masses' aspirations for independence, freedom, fraternity, and unity. With the Palestinian Nakba in the background, we were very hungry for a leader, a Saladin,[103] to rise amongst us, to take on the West and humble it, to eradicate the Zionist entity, and erase the shame of 1948. When the tripartite, Anglo-Franco-Israeli attack on Egypt was launched on October 29, 1956, many of us were again ready to march in rallies and demonstrations in support of Gamal Abdel Nasser, and in denunciation of imperialism and Zionism. Offices for volunteer fighters to go to the front to repel the tripartite aggression sprang up around Beirut, among many cities in the Arab World, including the AUB campus. I found myself spontaneously standing in line to register as a ready volunteer

---

103 He was the medieval Muslim leader to recover Jerusalem from the Crusades.

even though I had no military training of any kind. There are times in one's life, I must have reasoned, when one has to stand up for what one believes in, be willing to fight for it, and if necessary, die for it. This was such a time. All other considerations: Mother, America, education, were put on the shelf.

Fortunately, the two superpowers of the time, the USA and the USSR, with Eisenhower and Khruchev as their leaders, were strongly opposed to the tripartite invasion. Within a matter of days, they were able to bring enough pressure to bear on the attackers to stop the invasion, and pull out their armies from the field of battle. Slowly, our life began to return to normalcy, as did life on campus.

Having ruled out pursuing the MS degree at AUB, I diligently, and early on, started a survey of pertinent U.S. universities to apply to. As a result, I applied simultaneously for admission and teaching/research assistantships, even though research assistantships were hard to come by for first-year students, particularly those from abroad. Without assistantship, admission, even if granted, meant nothing in practical terms. Said and Jamil planned on sticking it out for their MS degrees.[104]

I sought the advice of my teachers and some elder acquaintances. Most notable among these were Drs. Salwa Nassar and Tony Zahlan. Dr. Zahlan was from my hometown, Haifa, and an AUB MS chemistry alumnus. He was a recent PhD from Syracuse University, majoring in solid-state physics. He had just joined the faculty at the start of the school year. He taught me my first course on solid-state physics. The subject matter was too applied to appeal to my theoretical bent.

I was guided not to target the very top places, such as Princeton, Harvard, Caltech, etc. Among the oft-cited reasons were: "You will get lost there! The competition is fierce and you will have many adjustments to cope with. Your grades don't measure up." Consequently, I aimed at the next layer, the "Big Ten:" University of Michigan, University of Wisconsin, Ohio State University, University of Minnesota, etc. In fact, I also included in my targeted places, Cornell and Rochester universities. Since I had a connection with Professor John Randolph, I decided to apply to the physics department of the University

---

104 They, eventually, did pursue further graduate work in the U.S.

of Rochester. He was kind enough to serve as a reference in many of my applications. I applied to about fifteen places. Some rejected me outright, others accepted me for admission but not assistantship, yet others accepted me for both admission and assistantship, or had me on a waiting list for assistantship. The University of Rochester denied me admission. Cornell University had me on a waiting list for assistantship, but later informed me that all positions were filled before my turn came up. Of the universities that gave me assistantship with admission, the University of Minnesota ranked best, as explained to me by Professor Nassar. I got the news by the first week of April and had about a week to answer. Initially, there was some concern about the weather, as virtually everybody who knew anything about the place said the winters were bitterly cold out there! It did not take long, nevertheless, before I accepted the "cold, snowy way!" Promptly, I got a welcoming letter from the Foreign Student Advisor Office with a fat package of literature about the university, the Twin Cities, the state of Minnesota, how to plan for the trip, the clothes I'd need, etc. With the arrival of the welcoming letter from the University of Minnesota (U. of MN), planning for the big leap got seriously underway.

The assistantship provided a monthly salary of $180 for the nine-month school year, September 15 through June 15. It did not, however, provide waiver of tuition, nor did it provide for school supplies, notably books. As I checked the facts and figures, as to cost of living and related expenses, it was designed to meet the bare minimum. I had also to raise the travel expenses. At the most economic level, by sea, it came to about $325 for the ship's fare from Beirut to New York. Traveling by air was out of the question, it being too expensive at about $550. I further figured that I should have at least $125 for miscellaneous expenses to get me from New York to the university, and to last me through to the first paycheck. The university payments were bi-weekly, the first of which was due at the end of September. Many general suggestions were offered by a variety of individuals towards finding a travel assistance source. None of the doors I knocked on looked promising.

Alternately, I realized that my assistant instructor salary extended over the months of July, August, and September (about $200), if saved, would be a good start towards the total of $450. I also had an emergency savings of about $50 in a bank account that I had opened early in my junior year. It was the first time ever that I had an account to my name. Hence, the actual unmet need was more like $200. I thought in terms of a loan, but I was a risky borrower! My mother, to put my mind at peace, let me know that she had managed, in the intervening three years, to build a reserve of cash for extreme exigencies. She would avail it to me; it was enough to do the job.

My mother was very somber at the prospect of my going away to the U.S. Her emotions were against it. The prevailing wisdom around our Tyre community in those days was that people who go to the U.S. rarely come back. They are lost to their people, country and religion. Yet, my mother never discouraged me from going. She would say, "If that is what you want to do, then go in safety, and may God facilitate things for you." (Literally, in Arabic, "*Ma essalaami, wa Allah ysahill alayk.*"). We both felt the pain; nevertheless, we both realized that it had to be. Conditions in the Middle East left so much to be desired. My consistent response to her, to some extent subconsciously on my part to lessen her pain, was that once I completed my graduate work, I would come back to see her to celebrate the accomplishment together. I had estimated, based mostly on hearsay from others, that it would take me at least four years to earn the PhD degree, if things went quite smoothly.

At the end of the freshman year, Fouad, trying to make every penny he could, landed a summer teaching job with his former Union School. The principal seemed to take pride in having Fouad, with one year to his credit at AUB, back at work, in his summer school. Fouad further helped Yousef and mother in the laundry business. Fouad, over the many years in the business, had become an accomplished presser, and Yousef almost always welcomed his quality services, which he carried out at home, away from the public eye!

As for me, I had one focus: to be ready for the trip. The foreign student office of the U. of MN recommended I make it to the campus no later than the first week of September. So, I set out to make travel arrangements accordingly. First, I had to get a student visa for the U.S. This meant I had to get a passport. Being a Palestinian refugee, I could only get a document of travel issued by the Lebanese government. Every time I needed something from the Lebanese government, I would get very nervous and apprehensive; for you never knew the angle from which they would review your application, the time it would take, and the action they would come up with. Nevertheless, I went through the process, applied to the Ministry of Interior, Department of General Security, and within a couple of weeks, I got the document. It was valid for a year from the time of issuance May 4, 1957. While I was glad to get the document, when I saw the one-year term of validity, I said to myself, *Before long, I will be trying to renew it*! Then I noticed that the document was valid only for the Arab countries and the USA. Somehow, it would not allow me a non-Arab stopover anywhere between Beirut and New York (a distance of over eight thousand miles), the "would-be" natural port of entry. As the travel route became clear, it required two non-Arab stops in Europe: Italy, and Portugal. I had no choice but to go back with the document to the Lebanese Department of General Security. I explained that I needed to have those countries added to the countries already listed to make my travel feasible. Fortunately, they gave me no argument and obliged. They, in fact, added the one word, Europe, without specific mention of countries and making absolutely no distinction between east and west of those days, and without being precise as to what the word *Europe* exactly included.

As for the student visa for the U.S., I had to first submit to a general health examination administered at the AUB hospital, and turn over the results, along with the visa application, to the U.S. embassy in Beirut. After reviewing the application, a date was set for a personal interview with the American Consul. I did not know the purpose of the interview. I must have done all right, for my application was approved and I was issued a student visa on June 12, 1957. The visa was valid for four years, multiple entries, four times longer than the validity of the document on which it was stamped. Many years later, I learned that the consul's interview was to establish my bona fide student status, rather than an impending immigrant.

Within a matter of days, through a travel agent, I was booked to leave Beirut on a Turkish ship (it may have been called the *Denizyollari*) on August 21, 1957, destination Napoli, Italy. I would change ships in Napoli, and board the Greek liner *Olympia* (of Aristotle Onassis' fleet) with its final destination being New York City, two weeks later. Mother and I were able to put together enough money to pay for the ticket.

With my travel papers and ticket in order, Mother and I decided we should try to go to Syria to visit my two sisters, Haliema and Munawwar, and their families, and to say goodbye.[105] As before, we needed a permit to travel to Syria. So, we applied for a permit in the usual manner. Since I needed a timely action on our applications, I engaged a facilitator,[106] an acquaintance of Uncle Tawfiq, to follow up the applications and expedite a positive outcome. Within days, I received back word that my application was denied with no explanation. Mother's application was approved. I tried to explore a way around this refusal, but to no avail. During that period, Syria had been experiencing frequent military coups d'état. Adieb Shieshakly, a Syrian Army officer, was the head of the military junta in power at the time. It was a short-lived junta; nevertheless, too long for my immediate need. I was never able to ascertain if the denial was arbitrary or had any basis in fact. Since I could not think of any reason to be denied a permit, having never engaged in any hostile activity towards Syria, I tended to think it was a paranoiac arbitrary action. One thing has continued to intrigue me ever since, namely: I got a visa to go to the USA, multiple entries, valid for four years, even though I had participated in mass protests against U.S. government policies in the Middle East; but I could not get a permit to nearby Syria, a country that I loved and felt strong cultural affinity to, and that I never protested against, to go say goodbye to my sisters before my big leap— sisters I had not seen, at that point, for six years; it would be at least four more years henceforth before I could even entertain the thought of seeing them!

As the time of departure approached, pressured by conditions all around me, I continued to explore, notwithstanding my sense of uselessness in the pursuit, finding a possible travel grant source or sources to lighten Mother's burden. I frequently traveled back and forth between Tyre and Beirut, knocked at various doors, and voiced my need. I felt demeaned by the whole thing. One day as I was checking my mail at AUB, I found, seemingly out of the blue, a hundred Lebanese liras cash (about $32) enclosed anonymously in an envelope with my name on it and a note wishing me a successful sojourn in the U.S. I was touched positively and negatively by it. On the one hand, somebody

---

105 For them to come to Lebanon would have been much harder, the red tape was much thicker and the expense forbidding.

106 A person who has no official position per se, but through his wits, gratuities (briberies) and public relations' skills with government employees can push, for a fee, the paper work, or cut through the red tape, more expeditiously than otherwise. Such facilitators were common around government offices of those days.

cared enough to do this and it augmented my meager cash; on the other, it was a personal gift, possibly a form of charity. I did not want that.[107] Since it was anonymous, it was very awkward to guess the person and try to return it. I kept the money with much gratitude to the unknown source![108]

Mother encouraged me to buy whatever was recommended to me by the foreign student office of the U. of MN; in particular, warm clothes. She would say, "We managed thus far; we will manage the rest." Brothers Yousef and Fouad, and their families, were very supportive in every tangible and intangible way. Their hospitality within the household knew no limit. About two weeks before travel time, sister Zahiyye came to see us at home in Tyre from her home in the el-Buss refugee camp. During her visit, she handed my mother a hundred Lebanese liras, on behalf of herself, her husband, and children, towards my travel expenses. My initial reaction, filled with self-pride, was not to accept. Mother, with her eyes, urged me to be a grateful recipient; I obeyed. As Zahiyye got up, bidding to leave, we hugged in tears.

It is traditional in the Hassoun family, and generally in the Arab setting, that when a member is embarking on a trip of significant duration (several weeks or more), for example, the pilgrimage to Mecca, that members of the extended clan, as well as neighbors and friends in the community, make a special effort to call on the family member about to travel to wish him or her a successful and safe journey. Suddenly, I found myself engulfed in this ritual. Even some of the town dignitaries came to our home to do so. The elders tended to want to leave me with an advice or to quote the Prophet Muhammad, "to bless my steps." Most common were the two sayings of the Prophet, "Seeking knowledge is a duty upon every Muslim; male and female," and, "Seek knowledge even unto China."

Many members of the family, including cousins, nephews, and nieces, wanted to see me off at the Beirut harbor; yet, they had no means of transportation. Not wanting to be unaccommodating, yet within practical limits, my brothers Yousef and Fouad chartered a bus, and whatever arrangements were needed, to

---

107 Alas, our society and culture, particularly of those times, did not readily provide the means or encouragement for self-help in this situation through work, no matter how menial. My preoccupation, emotional or otherwise, compounded the hurdles.

108 My instinct strongly pointed to Professor Salwa Nassar as the benefactor. At AUB, she was most aware of my pursuits for travel assistance, and showed the most concerned interest.

allow those so eager to make the trip and back. And so, on the morning of the August 21, 1957, amidst over twenty-five members of the extended family, I headed from Tyre to the Beirut harbor. So many wanted to help with my bags that I was at times afraid to lose track of them. At the harbor, we were met by brother Hamadi. He had come from Tripoli to say goodbye. The atmosphere was tense as I checked in my bags, and proceeded towards the stairway leading to the ship. Many were in tears, especially the women. My mother, whose eyes were fixed on me, was very somber but not in tears; neither was I, as I repeatedly looked at her. I embraced many, kissed my mother's hand, and walked up the stairway to the ship. The group was following me with their eyes up the way. As I got on board, my papers checked out and found in order, and still in full view of the family, I spontaneously and without aforethought, reached for my copy of a permit for crossing the Litani/Qassimiyye bridge, and with a shout of, "I don't need it anymore!" tore it up into pieces, and scattered it to the wind; ultimately, for the pieces to settle down over the harbor's water. It was perhaps the way my subconscious wanted to say, "Farewell to *Araby*."

The family continued to watch from the pier as the ship sailed out of the harbor just before noon. I, on the ship's deck, in turn, looked back at them as we receded slowly and painfully away from each other. I had never before felt so much pain run through my veins. It was like my heart was being drawn out of me in strings, one string at a time.

Part II: USA

CHAPTER 12

FARING TO THE USA

The farewell party faded in the distance. With a heavy heart, I turned my attention to my luggage, finding my way on the ship, and locating my "stay-quarters" for the trip to Napoli, Italy, where there would be a ship change. My luggage was two large suitcases and a big bag made of heavy creamy-white cloth that contained a variety of things that did not fit in the suitcases, and needed to be more accessible. It was with difficulty that I managed my entire luggage on my own; but I did, as I had to.

One of the early discoveries I made on board ship was that my ticket was class 3B. That meant, the least expensive. I had no private quarters such as a cabin. Rather, I had been designated a bed (a narrow bunk bed) in a large hall at the lowest level of the ship hull. The hall easily had about thirty beds arranged in a manner not unlike that of an army barrack. The hall looked dark and dreary, but the bed coverings looked clean. Having never been on an overnight sea trip before, or on ship of that size (with several hundred passengers), I could not tell whether the quarters were good or bad. I simply figured that it would have to do. So, I brought my luggage down and placed them by my designated bed. I proceeded, thereafter, to look around the ship, eventually making it up to the upper deck where I could see the sea. I was alone, knew nobody, feeling the pain of separation and the thrill of the start of a major adventure toward a major dream; yet, with apprehension of all that was unknown, and how I might fare. The ship seemed like some I had seen in movies, an old and rather run-down vintage, perhaps as old as one voyaging at the turn of the century and not unlike what my father might have known as a soldier in the Ottoman army. It plodded along with loud engine sounds and vibrations in the background. I knew our first stop, the following morning, was going to be Alexandria, Egypt. We would be allowed to get off there and sightsee for a couple of hours. *Ah, Alexandria, Egypt!* I thought to myself, *noted (along with Cairo) for movies, music, sentimental and passionate songs, and of course, belly dancing.* Ancient Egypt was not so much on my mind; it was common knowledge that Pharaonic ruins were further south. I began to anticipate seeing the city with a great deal of curiosity and suspense. *Will I run into some of my favorite movie stars or singers there*, I naively wondered?

In Alexandria, I instinctively knew that I would not want to wander on my own, so I proceeded to find possible companions. Before long, I identified two Jordanian lads. They were a couple of years younger than me and heading for Italy. They had been studying there for two years and were returning from a summer vacation with their families. They were at ease with the surroundings and sort of the happy-go-lucky types. They readily accepted my interest to accompany them in sightseeing the city. The morning of the docking, I joined them for breakfast and let them guide me in the disembarking. They decided for the time available, they would hire a horse carriage (*hantour*, in Arabic) and let the driver of the carriage take us around. The cost, they assured me, would be modest (a dollar or so each!) and I agreed. In the carriage, we were filled with laughter and chatter throughout. Right away, nevertheless, I saw that Alexandria was no Beirut despite all the romantic stories I had heard about the city before. It was more crowded, and the buildings rather drab, and nowhere as clean as I expected. The people were not as well-dressed on the whole as those of Beirut, and not as prosperous. Nevertheless, I found the sights interesting and thought provoking, especially the dark, African-looking Egyptians in their famous *gallabiyas* (overall gowns). The ride along the sea corniche was especially pleasant. The sights were more African than Levantine. I enjoyed hearing the Egyptian dialect. I was very mindful that for the first time in my life, I was in the land of Gamal Abdel Nasser, the hero of the Suez. Ah, Mr. Nasser!—hope-giver for my people, the Palestinians, was tickling my spirit. Mr. Nasser, the one who was stirring up the imaginations and aspirations of the Arab masses from the Persian Gulf to the Atlantic Ocean!

Back on ship, I continued to reflect over what I had just experienced. I was already farther than ever before from my mother and the family. I was breaking new ground. I also felt that the two Jordanian companions, while at ease in their travel, were rather superficial and immature; this gave me encouragement and some confidence that I should be able, if I had to, to manage the rest of the trip all on my own. Napoli was three days hence, where the Jordanian lads and I would part company. I thought it wise to try making new friends for the rest of the journey. I proceeded to meet more passengers on board. Sure enough and to my good fortune, I recognized a fellow about my age, who in fact had been an AUB student a while back, and that I had come across on campus. I readily engaged him in a chat. He told me that he left AUB a couple of years or so ago to study in the States; that AUB was too hard for him! He had been visiting his (Lebanese) family for the summer and was returning back. He was also traveling with a friend in a similar situation. I then met that friend. The two appeared veteran travelers and gentlemanly. They accepted my overtures to befriend them. I explained my reason for the trip and that it was my first time leaving home. As we socialized, I was further encouraged after hearing them say how flexible and accommodating the system of higher education in the U.S. was. They implied that since I had made it at AUB, I should have no problem in the U.S. I sighed in relief. Happily, I further found that they would be transferring to the same ship in Napoli, the *Olympia*. In Napoli, we were scheduled a day of sightseeing. I asked if I could sightsee with them. They said, "Sure!" As I inquired further as to how we might get along in Napoli, since I knew no Italian, I found out that the second fellow's mother was of Italian descent and that it was his first tongue, even though he spoke Arabic and English beautifully. He assured me not to worry. The sightseeing went very well.

In Napoli, I had a lot to process and think about. I felt the city was a different ballgame from both Alexandria and Beirut; the architecture, the streets, the shops, the traffic, the cars, the people, and the language. It was Italy, the land of the Romans. It was also Europe, an altogether new flavor!

At the end of the day, my newly acquired pals further helped me with my baggage as we headed to the harbor and boarded the *Olympia*. My mind was busy twirling and sorting out all that we were experiencing; I was filled with gratitude for my new companions.

The *Olympia* was also a new ballgame compared to the Turkish liner. It was considerably larger, perhaps as many as a thousand passengers. I shared a private room and bathroom with one other passenger on one of the lower decks. The linen was very clean and pressed and I had my own daily set of fresh towels. There were several swimming pools on the upper decks. The dining room was big and elegantly furnished. The first meal was a buffet dinner. The variety was dazzling—meats, salads, soups, beverages, and desserts! It was definitely beyond my expectations and transcended anything I had experienced before. The following morning, breakfast, with all the choices, was also quite impressive. I sensed in short order that I was in for eight days of luxurious "high-life." Among the passengers were many American families returning home from summer holidays in Europe. It was striking how colorfully and diversely dressed they were. Throughout the journey, as it turned out, the weather was typically sunny and the sea very blue and calm. I kept in touch with my Lebanese friends and we exchanged our room numbers. We chatted here and there, but respected each other's freedom to explore individually as well. As I milled around the different decks and at meal times, I met more and more Arabic speaking passengers; one in particular was from Bethlehem and about my age. We chatted on and off through the journey. I was surprised that he was not a student. He had some family already in the States and expected to work there. Nevertheless, he seemed excited and anxious. In many of these encounters, I was learning that there were people "in the same boat" as I was in terms of anxiety and fear of the unknown. My level of apprehension steadily went down, though my wonderment and amazement remained as peaked as ever.

On board the ship, there was a calendar rich with daily events: games, programs, and activities. Among other things, there were movie and slide showings and lectures. There was a series of lectures by a sociology professor passenger about life in America, which appealed to me. The professor, perhaps in his early fifties, looked like some of my AUB ones. Right away, we connected. He was happy to teach. There were only about eighteen passengers in attendance. The smallness of the group allowed for informal questions and answers and lively discussions. I was not bashful at participating.

Additionally, I occasionally went to a movie or a slide show. The time on ship seemed to pass quickly and the enjoyment level was great. Within a few days, we were approaching Lisbon, Portugal for a stop, before embarking on the last leg of the trip, crossing the Atlantic.

As we docked at Lisbon, I joined one of several groups of passengers, expressly organized to tour the town for the few hours while the ship was in port. The cost seemed very modest and my curiosity great. The group I joined turned out to have none of the passengers that I already knew. I recall being most impressed by the size of government buildings, the city parks, the wide boulevards, the level of cleanliness, and the street peddlers with all kinds of merchandise; particularly as they flocked us, the tourists! Most memorable were rural Portuguese women peddling beautiful linen embroideries and needle-knit laces. For the most part, I was a passive tourist. I did buy a cone of ice milk in one of the parks and had a small lunch in a downtown restaurant. I recall the main dish included lamb kidneys spiced and sautéed in butter or olive oil, a delicacy that I enjoyed in Beirut. Before long, we were back on ship and leaving dock for the new world! As the land receded out of sight, the serenity, grandeur, and majesty of the all-encompassing ocean seemed to overshadow and overwhelm everything else in my thought. There was a lot to contemplate and marvel at.

For the remaining days of the journey, I continued the activities already initiated on board, while the level of anticipation of seeing America continued to rise. Rising anticipation seemed to be shared by many. The day before arrival (Sunday, September 2, 1957) we received forms to fill out for the U.S. customs, and general instructions for disembarking. A sense of down to earth realism and uneasiness came over me; realism that the joy of the days on the *Olympia* was coming to an end, and uneasiness that I had to get my luggage all in order, to handle things all by myself, disembark and move on to the next step without a hitch.

At some point of that day, I was approached by the Bethlehemite fellow and asked if I had much to declare at customs. I said, "Not really." He told me that he brought quite a few gifts from Bethlehem, such as rosaries, cross-necklaces, mother of pearl boxes and the like. He wondered if I would carry some of them across customs lest he pay some duty if he were to carry all of them himself, as they would exceed his allowable custom-free limit. I uncomfortably agreed. So he handed me a bunch, which I tucked away in one of the suitcases. We further agreed to get together right after we are checked through to return them back.

On the morn of September 3, passengers had early breakfasts and got their belongings out for landing. We were told that we were arriving on a national holiday called Labor Day; much of the city would be shut down. As announcements indicated landing was imminent, passengers milled around to catch a glimpse of land. After about a week of seeing nothing but water, people were eager to see land. The sky was cloudy and a thick fog hung in the distance. It was perhaps the only day, since I left Beirut, when the blue sky was all blanketed over. As I looked out through clouds and fog, I could see nothing for sometime, to the point that I assumed land was still a long way off. But then, and all of a sudden, the Statue of Liberty and its base island emerged as if to be a stone's throw away. It was just like I had seen it in pictures and movies. A big stir swept over the passengers and it was evident that we were at the end of the journey and about to enter into the new world. For me, I knew deep in my soul that I was embarking on something really big. People began to gather their belongings and to bid their friends or acquaintances farewell, and I did likewise, particularly the two Lebanese lads and the sociology professor.

CHAPTER 13

THE NEW WORLD

O nce on land, we were channeled to different custom lines or lanes. The customs hall was thick with people. By the time I was cleared through, the Bethlehemite fellow and I got separated and lost track of each other.

About the time I had received a welcoming letter from the foreign student office of the University of Minnesota (UMN), back in Lebanon, I also received a welcoming letter from The Institute of International Education (IIE) in New York City in which they offered, upon arrival, to arrange for me to be met by one of their volunteer corps members; usually a college student who would be waving an IIE welcoming poster. The IIE service of meeting incoming international students was common knowledge among seasoned AUB faculty and students, and I was urged to avail myself of it. Naturally, I accepted the IIE offer, and supplied them with the details of my arrival. Thereupon, the institute further sent me a few phone numbers to call, in a recommended order, should there be a mix-up of some sort.

Cleared by the customs, and officially admitted into the country, spotting the institute's poster or sign became my primary concern. I found myself preoccupied with finding the IIE party and lost track of the Bethlehemite fellow. My mobility, with two large suitcases and my cloth-bag, was very limited. I reasoned, rightly or wrongly, that the Bethlehemite should be the one to try to locate me, rather than the other way around. As time passed, I was unable to locate the Bethlehemite or the IIE welcoming party. My level of anxiety mounted steadily as the crowds began to thin out, departing from the scene. The time already was about 1:00 p.m., as I stood virtually alone by my luggage pondering the next move. The ship had docked at port about 9:30 am. I finally decided to give up looking for either of them, and to pull out the paper that had the IIE phone numbers, in order to begin calling. I maneuvered myself to the nearest phone booth. As I entered the phone booth to make the call, it did not look anything like what I was familiar with back in Lebanon. The dialing instructions meant very little. I had not used a telephone much in

Lebanon except within the AUB campus, which was fairly straightforward. In the booth, I was in no mood to try to decipher the phone instructions or puzzle them out. I looked out for help. As it happened, there was a lady nearby that seemed to be waiting. She looked friendly, clearly an American, and about thirty years old. I asked if she would help me in calling a number, pointing to the paper in my hand. She readily agreed by trying to guide me through it. She proceeded by saying, "You need to first insert a dime in this slot..." My concealed reaction was, *a dime in a slot, what is that*? I had never before heard of the word *dime* let alone have one on me!" She quickly realized the extent of my helplessness and said, "I have a dime and I will dial the number for you." I said, "Please do." Sure enough, a lady on the other end of the line answered; I was handed the phone. The lady on the phone understood my need. I carefully described my location to her and she told me to stay put and she would send somebody right away to meet me within the hour. I thanked the lady that dialed for me with her dime. She graciously smiled acknowledging my thanks. Although a lot was going through my mind, there was not much time to process or savor it. The next overriding question was, *Will it really happen? Will I be met within the hour*? With my background in the Middle East, logistics like this invariably tended to have a glitch of one kind or another. More often than not, arrangements like this did not pan out smoothly. Thank God, not this time! A college coed met me pretty much as I was told over the phone. She recommended a stay in New York for a few days of sightseeing, courtesy of the IIE, if my time permitted. My schedule did. We loaded the luggage into her car and headed for a Columbia University dormitory by Harlem, where I would be staying. I had heard the word Harlem before only in relation to a world leading basketball team. I did not know anything about Harlem as also being a predominantly black, even rough, New York City neighborhood. The dormitory was empty except for smithereens of some international students. The new school year for Columbia University had not yet begun. I had to register at the dorm and declare how long I would be staying. I was given brochures of programs and guided sightseeing tours of the city, organized and provided by the IIE. After looking over the possible tours and activities, I decided to stay until Friday, September 7, for there was nothing scheduled for me to do on the campus of the UMN, or in Minneapolis, that week. I was responsible to pay only for the dormitory room, which was a nominal couple of dollars or so a day, and my meals. I signed up for tours and activities accordingly. By then, it was past 3:00 pm, and I was still running without lunch. I was given a brief orientation and a list of a few places to eat nearby; the dorm's food service was not open. I was left to settle down and refresh for the rest of the day. The activities of the following day started at 8:00 am. It further turned out that the coed that gave me a ride to the dorm would be in charge of the following day's tour group.

As I sat down in my room to catch my breath, the matter of the Bethlehemite and the gift items came back to haunt me. I felt guilty that I had somehow not tried hard enough to locate him. We did not work out details of finding each other afterwards, should we get separated in the process. We did not even contemplate that eventuality. He left me with no full name, address, or means of contacting him. There was not much I could do at that point, and there were a lot of more important things for me to look after. Looking back, it had been a very unhappy and unwise activity, and I executed it very poorly. [109]

While the finer details of my four days in NYC are not as vivid as I would like them to be, the highlights remain so. In particular, I signed up for tours of the Statue of Liberty, the Empire State Building, the *New York Times* publishing house, the New York Stock Exchange, and the United Nations (UN) headquarters. At the Statue of Liberty, I climbed to the highest point inside the body and head of the statue and looked out. I saw the panorama of the landscape and grounds below. I marveled at the architecture, the narrow winding stairs, and engineering thereof, which went to the head. We did the same at the Empire State Building, except for taking the elevator to the top instead of climbing. It

---

109 As it turned out, nine months later, as I vacated my dorm room at the end of the school year, I forgot these items: mother pearl rosaries, crosses, etc., in one of the drawers of a clothes cupboard that was in the dormitory room, along with other important papers, including my Palestinian birth certificate. The latter, I had carefully guarded through thick and thin, ever since my family became refugee into Lebanon. When I returned for them a few days later after realizing what had happened, I was accompanied with the dormitory officer in charge back into the room, I found the room had already been cleaned out and the particular drawer was emptied clean. The items in question had not been turned in to the dorm's office either. The officer indicated that it would be hard to try to track them; the process could generate a lot of headache. Yet, I left my contact address with the officer, should the items get returned. Alas, it was not to be. Except for my Palestinian birth certificate, for the rest of the items, it did not bother me not to have them back. The loss of my birth certificate, however, was a bitter pill.

was a scary feeling to ride up the elevator and to think about all the floors I was ascending. As we rode up, the thought, *What if the elevator cable gives out?* came to mind, but I quickly dismissed it. I experienced the proverbial butterflies in the stomach. It felt very eerie to walk on the top balcony and look over the city and down onto the streets below. It was amazing how small people and cars looked at the ground level below. I was struck by the height of the many buildings (appropriately named skyscrapers) all around. How could these buildings have been built, I wondered? I could not fathom the know-how and technology or the driving spirit behind them, nor the minds and associated imagination that would design and build such mammoth structures. I never recognized heretofore that humans would be so ambitious, daring, and persevering. I wondered along similar lines at the bridges and subways that the tours took us to. The word *mind-boggling* was no exaggeration. At the sight of the first European city, Napoli, I felt a "new ballgame" in relationship to the cities of the Middle East. In NYC, I felt it to be yet another "new ballgame" in relationship to Europe. At the *New York Times* publishing house, we were walked through the presses and offices involved in the different phases of the publishing process, and were shown the imprints on the daily-prepared metal plates in this vast and mass production operation. I gained a greater immediacy to the great importance and significance of the printing press. At the Stock Exchange, from an overlooking balcony, we saw people on the trading floor down below who were as busy as bees in a beehive, with white slips of paper scattered all over. I must confess much of the detail of the explanations both at the Stock Exchange, and to a lesser extent, at the *New York Times* publishing house, went over my head. The UN building looked just as I had seen it in pictures; tall, sleek, and elegant. One of the first thoughts to come to me, as I was about to enter it, *Hmm, this is where the tragic and unjust resolution to partition Palestine* (November 29, 1947) *was cast!* We walked in large hallways, looked at many art exhibits and gifts from different countries on display. We ended up in the visitors' auditorium overlooking the General Assembly Hall. It was explained to us how, by using earphones and dials, one could listen to a speaker's presentation simultaneously translated to one of the major UN world languages.

During these tours, I met quite a few international students from many countries. I remember being somewhat surprised at meeting an Englishman, for example, in the group. My naïve thinking at the time was why would an Englishman want to come to the U.S. for study, since he had good universities in his own country? I reasoned that in my case it was different since I was coming from a far less developed country. Long ago, I slowly but surely outgrew this naiveté.

I gravitated towards Arabic-speaking students as I met more international students. In particular, one student from Baghdad, Iraq, seemed heaven-sent! He was going to the University of Wisconsin in Madison to do graduate work in biochemistry. He was traveling alone and had done undergraduate, and some graduate work, in England. He seemed at home traveling in the West. By his appearance and mannerism, he was evidently far more traveled and experienced than me, and seemed to be from a prosperous and quite cultured family as well. I reached out to befriend him. I introduced myself to him and told him my destination. As it turned out, he was planning to head to Madison by the end of the week with a stopover in Chicago for two days, to look around. It fit my schedule well. I told him that I would like to join him in the travel and that I would look around in Chicago along with him. We would part ways on Sunday, he to Madison, and me to Minneapolis. He was quite agreeable. I explained my tight travel budget. As we checked into the train vs. the (Greyhound) bus as to cost, the bus significantly won over. By choosing a bus trip that traveled all Friday night, as we did, we saved the cost of a night at a dorm or a hotel.

The ride from NYC to Chicago, which started Friday afternoon, was the longest bus ride I had ever been on. Except for a couple of hours at the start, it was too dark to see much. Although the bus seats were quite comfortable by comparison with those in Lebanon and Syria, I slept very little that night, and wished I could see the countryside we were going through. Upon arriving in Chicago the following morning, my Iraqi friend and I headed straight to the YMCA, which had a dormitory facility. It was downtown and a major gathering place of international students. We somehow knew about it well beforehand, and its inexpensiveness and convenience. The YMCA dorm was about eight dollars a night, considerably more expensive than the dorm in Harlem.

Shortly after we checked in, to my utter amazement, I bumped into a former AUB student. We had known each other only slightly before, but enough to shake hands and inquire into the circumstances that brought us together there.

Our chat was brief as he was in the process of checking out. Nevertheless, I learned that he, like the Lebanese lads on the *Olympia*, had left AUB after two years, eschewing its rigor and competitiveness, to continue his studies in the U.S. I said to myself, wow the USA is not as far-off a place as I was thinking, and it is a small world after all! My level of confidence got a further boost.

In Chicago, my Iraqi friend and I mostly milled around downtown, looked at city parks, shops, probably visited a museum, etc. We walked up and down Michigan Avenue and admired Lake Michigan. Lakes in the Middle East are scarce. Seeing Lake Michigan for the first time, being a huge body of fresh water, was quite an impressive sight.

On Sunday afternoon, we headed to the bus depot. His bus trip to Madison, of a few hours duration, left about 4:00 pm. We said goodbye and wished each other well on our planned studies as he got on his bus. He had somebody to contact in Madison upon arrival. In my case, I saw no point in traveling to Minneapolis too early. The trip duration was about nine hours. The only contact I had was the foreign student office at the UMN, which would not be open until Monday, 8:00 am. Thus, it seemed best to take the overnight bus, which left the depot at about 9:30 pm. In so doing, I would, further, not worry about where I was going to stay for the night and the cost incurred.

While alone at the bus depot, I looked around, not far away from my luggage, to see what I could see. I bought myself a hamburger and fries for supper, to the tune of fifty cents. After a while, I settled down on a bench by the gate of the Minneapolis bus. As I was pondering my surroundings, a church minister with a white round collar, in his late forties or early fifties, came into the depot. It was about 7:30 pm. He was carrying a small briefcase and a couple of medium size bags. He walked over and sat next to me. Before long, we started chatting. "Who are you? Where are you from? Where are you headed and what for, etc.?" Our conversation evolved rapidly and got into all kinds of topics; education, religion, the Middle East, etc. I found out he was headed to a small town not too far from Chicago. He was taking a bus from the same gate (or nearby gate) as my bus, an hour earlier. We conversed until the call came for him to board. By then, quite a few passengers had gathered at the gate and formed a line. As he got up to go into line, I instinctively stood up and offered to help him with his bags. Initially he declined, but I assured him that it was no problem, and I was happy to do so. As he stepped up into the door of the bus and I handed him the last bag, he pulled out a ten-dollar bill from his wallet and pressed it into my hand. I was really taken aback, as remuneration was the farthest from my mind. But he insisted and told me to use it towards buying school supplies. We were blocking the passengers' flow into the bus; I therefore gratefully accepted it and wished him a safe journey as I walked back to my bench seat. Yet, I had a mixed feeling about getting the money. I wondered if I had, in some inadvertent way, evinced my tight finances and led him to feel sorry for me. I could not think of anything that I had said that would have done that, and certainly I would not have thought of doing it deliberately. Whatever it had been, it was an act of kindness and appreciation on his part. It was a significant addition to my total liquid assets! Years later, I relished telling close family members and friends how I made my first ten dollars in the U.S.

The bus ride to Minneapolis, while shorter from the previous one, was nevertheless quite taxing. Again, I got very little sleep and it was too dark to see much as I strove to look out the bus window. The bus arrived at the Minneapolis depot about 6:00 am on Monday. The place was virtually empty. I had figured out by then that my next step was to go to the UMN Foreign Student Office, which was housed on campus in Eddy Hall. I had looked at the campus and city maps and knew that it was of the order of five miles from the bus depot. Although it was theoretically possible to get there by bus, there were some hurdles. I would have to figure out where the bus stop was and which bus, out of several, went closest to Eddy Hall. I also would have to carry my luggage from the depot to the bus stop, into the city bus, and out of the bus to Eddy Hall. With all the question marks about the practicality and even the feasibility of all this, I opted for a cab. By then, I had an approximate idea of what it would cost. There were some cabs outside the depot. I called on one, asked him if he would take me to Eddy Hall on the UMN campus. I thought I might have to explain to him where Eddy Hall was and prepared myself to do that, but he needed no explanation and knew exactly where Eddy Hall was. I readily loaded my luggage and got into the cab. By about 7:00 am, my luggage and I were delivered to the front doorsteps of Eddy Hall! The fare came to about a dollar and a half (with tip). The city bus fare would have been fifteen cents.

Eddy Hall was still closed. The office would open at 8:00 am. Hardly anybody was around in sight. Across from Eddy Hall was a wooded area, like a small park with benches. So I carried my luggage near one of the benches and sat to wait for 8:00 am to come. As I sat, I felt a chill in the air that seemed to foretell the cold weather that Minnesota was famous for. In a strange way, I sensed I was in a different climate zone from anything I had experienced before. The sight of what seemed to be a bushy-tailed rat, as I sat inspecting the trees and the vegetation around, startled me! *How could this be?* I asked myself in revulsion. Before long, I saw another one, and then another one, running around freely. Though the campus looked pretty and the buildings impressive, I could not figure out how the campus could be so infested with such rats. *What happened to agricultural know-how and pest control that the university must have?* I wondered. *Maybe they will disappear mysteriously into hiding when 8:00 o'clock strikes*, I tried to reason. After all this travel, about nine thousand miles, to be met by these rats seemed terribly unfair! As the time was approaching 8:00 am, the campus began to stir and I began to see people coming to work from all sorts of directions. The rats did not go into hiding and the pedestrians did not seem to pay attention to them. I decided to keep calm; *There must be an answer to all this in due course*, I thought to myself. Sure enough and in due course I was told that they were squirrels of the gopher family, the mascot of the university! It has taken me quite sometime to train myself not to cringe or be uneasy at their sight. I continue to marvel at those who playfully feed them!

CHAPTER 14

THE UNIVERSITY OF MINNESOTA

"Minnesota, Hail to thee! Hail to thee, our college dear!
Thy light shall ever be a beacon, bright and clear."[110]

Ido not know now the condition I was in when I walked into the Foreign Student Office that morning of September 10, 1957, after a week of hectic sightseeing and travel with not a lot of hygienic care, but it did not cross my mind nor deter me from going in.[111] The office was on the second floor and I lugged my baggage up the stairs with me. I introduced myself to the young woman at the front desk. There were other women in office, but the advisor was not there. His absence did not deter the young woman from addressing my needs. She pulled out my file and informed me that there was a single room reserved for me in Pioneer Hall, one of the men's dormitories on campus. Pioneer Hall was well over a mile away. Seeing my baggage, a woman from the office drove me there.

I was advised to go into the dorm's business office by the lobby to check in. There I chose a room and board contract and set up a payment plan to allow me time to begin receiving wages, twice a month, from my teaching assistantship. I did the same thing when I registered as a graduate student. Out-of-state teaching assistants, including international students, were charged tuition fees at the state resident rate, which roughly was half of the non-resident rate. I was assigned a room on the second floor that had a window that looked onto the front yard and main entrance of the dormitory as well as Centennial Hall, another men's dormitory. I could readily see people coming in and out of the dorm building. Right away, I liked the room, it was about ten feet by twelve feet, quite adequate, the first private room I had ever had. In short order, I walked around the dorm, and got acquainted with the various features and

---

110 UMN lead song.

111 Students like me were tagged as foreign students. Many years later and generally across higher education in the U.S., the label "foreign" was deemed negative and changed to "international."

facilities, in particular the laundry room. I already had some laundry to do. With my laundry background, I felt a sense of familiarity and home there. I then walked over to a nearby branch bank, upon advice of the foreign student office, and opened an account and deposited most of my cash (about $100).

The contract food service did not begin until one week later, when classes would begin. Right away, I was eager to walk around the campus to see where things were—the student union, the university library, the physics building, and so on. Walking had always been a happy activity; I looked things over at my own pace and it cost nothing, I figured how to walk to downtown Minneapolis. It took about an hour, but did not seem to bother me. The primary and most direct path was Washington Avenue. As I walked, I inspected, with fascination, the roads, the cars, the buildings, the shops, the people, the Mississippi River, the bridges, the underpasses, the overpasses, anything and everything that I laid my eyes on; in brief, the whole shebang! Some sights were impressively positive, others were not. I remember saying to myself, even back in NYC; not all cars are shiny and new like the impression I must have gotten from American movies. The streets were not that crowded with cars, there was no comparison with the messy traffic of Beirut. The density of people on the streets was considerably thinner; some places, woefully thin. The environment, physical and otherwise, looked quite different and unfamiliar from what I was accustomed to both in Palestine and Lebanon; it definitely looked foreign.

One day, on one of my early excursions along Washington Avenue, as I reached downtown, a man, in his late thirties and seemingly healthy, approached me asking for a dime to buy a cup of coffee. Not familiar with the phenomenon, I was startled by him and hurriedly and fearfully moved away. My reaction was so stark that it even bothered the poor fellow so much that I could read his face telling me, "All I want is a dime. I am not trying to hurt you!" This experience started me thinking about bums and the social forces that produce them. It is a phenomenon that is distinctly different from begging, the former, i.e., bumming, is absent while the latter, begging, is common in the Middle East. With my past background, the notion of evils of capitalism and its cruelties began to rush into my mind.

One thing that struck me in my early wanderings around Minneapolis was that I was having trouble determining directions: east, west, south, and north.

After some introspection, I realized that, in Lebanon, it was quite easy to tell directions for at least two important reasons: First, the presence of the sea, often visible from my stomping grounds, served as unmistakable reference; second, the sun in the sky. Being lower in the sky, the Minneapolis sun was quite a bit more southerly. Also, the Minneapolis sky was often a lot cloudier than Beirut's to the point where the sun was not readily and accurately localizable. A lesser reason, perhaps, was the familiar and rather unique Beirut landmarks of varied shapes and designs, e.g., minarets, schools, winding streets, and uncommon intersections. Landmarks, at least at first, did not seem to have a counterpart in the new sights.[112]

Early on in Minneapolis, I missed the sea and longed for it. The lakes in and around the Twin Cities offered no substitute for the Mediterranean; they were less visible and hard to locate as a pedestrian.

On one of my early wanderings, I decided to take the inner Twin Cities bus to the end of the line in St. Paul and then come back, just to see what I could see. It was a practice that brother Fouad and I, even as far back as when we were kids in Haifa, employed to learn about our town and nearby surroundings. The Minneapolis-St. Paul bus cut across campus on Washington Avenue where I picked it up. On the way back, granted it had gotten late in the afternoon and turned somewhat dark, I saw surroundings that looked like the place I had gotten on. I therefore got off the bus only to find out I had gotten off at least two miles too soon! Rather disgusted with myself, I foot-paddled to campus.

Preceding the start-up of the school year, the campus of the university was in a phase one might describe as the calm before the storm. Gradually, more students were arriving; initially, mostly foreign students, but slowly, American students as well. It was thus quite natural in this circumstance to meet many students from China, Japan, Korea, France, Philippines, and other countries, as well as Americans from all over the States. Sometimes we would interact in large groups around a lunch table in the student union, and other times in one-on-one encounters. An exchange of a wide and diverse range took place during those times. It was also natural to interact more with those that were in the same dorm. In fact, an early bird freshman student moved into a room

---

112 Sights in Middle East cities and towns tend to be generally more distinctive than their counterparts in the U.S.

across the hallway from my dorm room, an eighteen-year-old named John Mitchell. His room had three or four beds, but almost until the start of classes, he was the only occupant. He was from a town in Illinois not far from Chicago. We hit it off well from the start and found a lot of fun things to talk about. He was tall and handsome and seemed to me unbelievably mature for his age. His mannerism seemed reminiscent of the movie star Robert Mitchum. I wondered why he chose to come to UMN. He said that his father owned a funeral home business that he was going into after graduation, and wanted therefore, to study mortuary science. UMN had a program in it that his father thought very highly of. It was the first time I had heard of such a thing as "mortuary science." I thought it very intriguing that people go to college to learn how to bury the dead. John enjoyed talking about fun places to go to, locally as well as world-wide, foods to experience, and of course, women and romance. I was happy to share some of my knowledge about the Middle East, and Lebanon in particular, as well as my fresh travel experience just gained in coming over. He was shocked almost beyond belief that I did not know hardly anything about dating. It was evident that he had dated a fair amount in high school. We agreed that I will be his consultant on world affairs and that he would be my consultant on U.S. social affairs. I think he got a big kick from being a social advisor to a physics graduate student from the Middle East.

One day I was inquiring of him about a place that had some real food— meat-vegetable stews with rice, not just hamburger or hot dog with fries. He thought he knew "the place" and recommended a Chinese restaurant not far from the dorm, on Washington Avenue. I told him that I had never had any Chinese food before. He said that it was time I had some. He was sure I would like it; the servings were large at bargain prices. He might even have mentioned I should try beef chow mein. So the next day at noon, I decided to go there for lunch. I had not had any breakfast that morning and was ready for a hearty meal. I was seated in a booth and readily ordered beef chow mein. From the menu, it was priced at a dollar and twenty-five cents or so. Shortly, the waiter came back with a big plate heaped with noodles and beef-celery type of stew. As I dug in my fork and took the first bite, my taste buds revolted. The flavor was so foreign and it did not at all sit well with me. The celery was a vegetable that I had not had before and it had an offensive aftertaste, or so it seemed. The oil or grease used was also off my palate. My first thought was to send it back and ask for something else. However, I was not sure that I would not be charged for it; it was exactly what I had ordered and I had already taken a bite. *If I am going to be charged, can I afford to order something else and be charged further?* I asked myself. Besides, how would I know that the next thing I ordered would be any better? After some self-debate while looking at the plate, I decided that I better not make waves or cause trouble,[113] and that I should suppress my revulsion and try to eat it, or the greater portion anyhow. I would further help myself by washing the food down with a lot of water. That was what I ended up doing. I ate enough of it to last me to suppertime. I consoled myself that it was a learning experience after all.[114]

The foreign student office had what they called a "brother/sister program." Foreign students were assigned individually to a brother or a sister local student to orient them around campus and town, and to help them with whatever sundry matters that foreign students needed help with. In fact, I was assigned a sister and was given her name and phone number to get in touch with her at my convenience, and as needed. When explained to me, I did not take it seriously, primarily because it was so unfamiliar to the way I did things in the Middle East. It was so foreign a notion that I could only be bemused by it. Of course, in hindsight, I was simplistic, cynical and plain wrong. It was a few weeks into the school fall term before I, upon urgings of some friends, phoned my assigned sister and asked her how we might meet. She sounded happy to hear from me and arranged to meet me in short order, initially, in the physics building. She was a senior in political science and business administration. It is no exaggeration to say that she was a strikingly good-looking coed. After the preliminaries, we walked over to the student union and visited for an hour or so. She inquired how I was getting along and how she might help. By then, I could not think of anything. She offered to spend the following Saturday with me to show me around the city and to have me meet her family. Her family lived in St. Louis Park, a suburb of Minneapolis. She had her own car. I readily welcomed the offer. As it turned out, she was not only strikingly

---

113 Being a foreigner and new, I was not sure I would get by with it.

114 Two years after that experience, I became a connoisseur of Chinese food.

good-looking, but also of very impressive personality.[115] I could not help but see in her a broad mental horizon and a high degree of cultural sophistication. On Saturday, she picked me up from the dorm around nine in the morning. She showed me department stores and how to shop for things there. She drove me to the Minneapolis Art Institute where we took a look, and then to Walker's Art Center. We broke for lunch with her mother at their home. Her mother and their house looked prosperous. However, since it was the first American family home I had been in, I had no meaningful reference frame for comparison, and therefore was in no position to judge, nor did I care to.

I was delivered back to the dorm late that afternoon. It was a very lovely and memorable day. Thereafter, I saw her on campus a few times; they were brief, formal encounters. As time passed by, I was becoming more and more involved in my own living and academic affairs and the "brother/sister" bond gradually faded away.

The week before the start-up of classes required me, among other things, to show up in the physics department, get assigned an academic advisor, go to orientation events, register, and attend a kick off teaching assistant (TA) meeting. I was officially on the payroll as a TA as of September 15. Unless incoming graduate students had advanced inside knowledge of the faculty and had a previous specific advisor choice, they were routinely assigned to the associate chairman, as a temporary advisor. He met me at his office and made course recommendations. I was enrolled in three graduate courses, two physics and one math. All of these had continuation courses in the winter and spring.[116] Thus, my course work for the year was pretty much set, and I needed not to wonder any further about it. He told me that for the first term I would be expected to get to know who is who in the department and their research interests and programs, in order to choose an advisor in line with my interests and goals. "The sooner you do this the better, but certainly by the end of the second quarter of the school year," he said. It was the first injection of specific demands and obligations as to why I was there in the first place, namely; to become a professional physicist at the highest level I am capable of.

---

115 Looks-wise, she resembled somewhat Natalie Wood, the famous movie star of the 1960s and 1970s; albeit a bit taller.

116 UMN ran on the quarter system at the time.

As I pursued the different tasks, it was abundantly clear that UMN was indeed a very major university, a member of the Big Ten,[117] and the physics department was big in facilities and faculty, and well respected nationally and world-wide.[118]

At the kick-off TA meeting, about fifty-five *new* TAs showed up! They were from all over the U.S., with concentration from the Midwest, and only a handful was foreign. There were no women TAs and only one black American.[119] Except for me, there were none from the Arab States. We met in a large lecture room. A red-faced professor, beaming with a smile, and a full head of white hair, walked in and introduced himself as the director of the department's TA program. He was Professor Clifford Wall, who was in his late fifties. As if to emphasize his role, he was wearing a gray lab robe. After a get-acquainted preliminary, whereby each one of the TAs stood up and introduced himself and where he was from, he went over a long list of items; our roles, duties, responsibilities, etc. We each received a copy of the lab manual by Wall and Levine, Professor Wall being the senior author, and a stack of mimeographed instructions and guidelines, as well as our lab teaching assignments. We were told that additional information would be sent to us through departmental mail, in the main office. We each had a mailbox and were expected to check it regularly. He also had two senior TAs typically having had at least two years experience as TAs in the department, assisting him, to whom we could go to for questions and further guidance. One of the things he said was that he could not stress enough the need to be well prepared beforehand for each lab session, two hours in duration. He recommended that we do the experiment of the week in advance of the first lab meeting, especially if the experiment was one we had not done before. It was a must that we familiarize ourselves with the apparatus and equipment before each lab session, to check that they were in working order. He informed us of the procedure to follow if things were, or should go, out of order. Each TA was assigned, on the average, four lab

117 I.e. of the top ten largest universities in the U.S.! The enrollment at the time was around twenty-eight thousand with two major campuses, the second being in St. Paul. At this writing, it has more than doubled in size.

118 About fifty in number at the time, in contrast to AUB's physics faculty of five or six!

119 The situation of white women TA's changed slowly in succeeding years of my stay, but not so in regard to black TA's.

sections of the same lab experiment a week.[120] Consequently, the preparation was kept to a reasonable level. A section had about twenty-four students; two students to each experiment station. A typical TA had therefore to grade about a hundred lab reports a week. Had I not been an assistant instructor at AUB the year before, not much unlike the role of TA that I was entering into, I would have found the first TA meeting quite intimidating.

The TA meeting catapulted me into a serious work frame-of-mind. I was assigned an office desk in a large room, twenty feet by thirty feet, on the second floor that had six TA or RA (Research Assistant) office desks. It was fifty feet or so from Professor Wall's office, a location that I liked. It was also fairly centrally located in the physics building. The stage was set for the school year.

---

120 At times, a TA would receive grading duties in lieu of lab teaching; this was especially done if the TA showed little aptitude for teaching or had inadequate command of English communication skills.

CHAPTER 15

THE NEW COLLEGE LIFE

As the school year started, I found myself in graduate classes in the order of forty students in size as compared with two or three at AUB. The class on mathematical physics had large contingents of mechanical and electrical engineering students, and was quite international in composition; but still none, other than me, from Arab States. Before long, however, I made acquaintance with two Iranian classmates, Parviz Mahmoodi and Mahmoud Sayrafiezadeh. Very quickly the acquaintance evolved into a close camaraderie. They both had been in the States a few years and seemed at ease with the surroundings. Parviz was four years older than me, and in the latter phases of his work on his PhD in mechanical engineering. He was in the course because he strongly held the view that the more physics you know, the better engineer you will be. Mahmoud, on the other hand, was about two years older, unsettled on a major, torn between physics, mathematics, and philosophy. Professor Edward L. Hill taught the course. He was an internationally renowned theoretical physicist and an early contributor to quantum theory.[121] Parviz was unpretentious, gregarious, and very pragmatic. Mahmoud was very idealistic, somewhat unfocused, and a dreamer. He smoked a pipe and often wore corduroy jackets with leather elbow patches. He looked and acted scholarly. When the three of us got together, invariably, we would wind up talking about conditions in the Middle East; medieval existence, ignorance, poverty, bad sanitation, corruption, ineptness, the terrible Shah, the American foreign policy and the CIA,[122] the Palestinian-Israeli conflict, etc. Little did we fully fathom at the time, the profound influence they were having on us, the region, and the world; issues that continue to rock the world. Notwithstanding, we all knew that our

---

121 He was a PhD student of Professor John Van Vleck, a 1977 Physics Nobel laureate, formerly of UMN, later of Harvard. Some of Professor Hill's PhD students have attained international prominence, among them Josef M. Jauch.

122 The CIA had a mere few years back (~1955) reinstated to the throne in Iran the deposed Shah and arrested those behind the toppling of the Shah, most notable the very popular Prime Minister Mossadeq.

primary and immediate objective was to succeed in our studies. They spoke no Arabic, though they had good familiarity with simple and common words and phrases resulting from our common Islamic tradition. I spoke no Persian. So, English was our medium of serious communication. At times, we studied and did homework together. During these sessions, I found that AUB had done a good job preparing me for graduate school; that success or failure was going to depend on me, and how I managed the opportunities before me.

Parviz and I had quite a bit of fun when we two got together; he kidded me a lot and we laughed and laughed at our anomalous cultural condition.[123] He had a car and was very generous in giving me rides; I did not drive. He introduced me to a lot of inexpensive eating joints such as the White Castle, where we had twelve-cent hamburgers, and drive-in AW root beer stands with their novel root beer taste and root beer floats. Since it was my first year and a lot depended on my schoolwork, I had to fight hard the temptation to indulge often in these activities. In due course, I found out that both Parviz and Mahmoud had girlfriends and were not much around campus on weekends. Coincidentally, Mahmoud's girlfriend was my foreign student office assigned sister! Parviz's girlfriend, later to become his wife, was studying for a master's degree in library science at the University of Michigan in Ann Arbor. She had done her bachelor's degree at the UMN. On holidays and longer weekends, he often drove to Ann Arbor to be with her, a distance of about seven hundred miles, one way. Such activities were well beyond what I was used to back in Lebanon, where a fifty-mile trip was a big deal!

Shortly into the fall quarter, Professor Wall walked into our (TA/RA) office looking for someone to proctor a make-up final exam on the upcoming Saturday, in the early afternoon. A student in one of his introductory physics spring classes, of the past school year, had skipped the final exam to be the bridesmaid in her older sister's wedding. Saturday afternoon seemed to be the only time he was able to work out with the student to take the make-up; she was a home economics major and spent most of her time on the St. Paul campus. I was the only one in the bunch who seemed to have nothing conflicting, so I enthusiastically offered to do it. It made me feel good that I was going to be of

---

123 He got in the habit of calling me affectionately, "Azizi Arab Boy," Azizi, Arabic for dear, and I reciprocating by calling him, "Azizi Persian Boy!"

special service. He described the coed to me, gave me a copy of the exam, and told me he would have her come to my office at the appointed time. I would return the worked-out exam to him the following Monday.

On the appointed time of that Saturday, at my office, the coed showed up. I gave her the exam and seated her at one of the TA desks; while I, at my desk, did some schoolwork. I recall she took up the full time allowed when she turned in the worked-out exam and left. Very few words were exchanged.

That evening Pioneer Hall held a social mixer in its main lobby where all residents of Comstock Hall, a woman's dormitory minutes of walk away, were invited. I had discussed the mixer earlier that week with John Mitchell, my social consultant, and he strongly recommended I go to it. Consequently, I planned accordingly though with apprehension. He even recommended various scenarios as to how I might strike a conversation with a coed, and possible follow-ups. He recommended initially milling around to meet many coeds. "If you settle on one for the duration, however, and have an extended conversation and some dancing," he advised, "be a gentleman and offer to take her back to her dorm as the mixer winds down." He said I could also invite her out before that for a beer at some pub nearby, perhaps the popular one, called The Big Ten. "As a general rule," he further explained, "you should not attempt to kiss the girl at the goodnight point unless you sense a clear interest or encouragement. Should you decide you would like to see the coed at a future time, you would then politely ask for her phone number. If she gives it to you, it is likely that she would be interested in a future date although there may be other variables in the equation; if she does not, move on to another subject, don't press or feel rebuffed. End the evening on a friendly positive note!"

After supper, I cleaned up and dressed appropriately within available options, and nervously headed to the dorm's lobby. In addition to wondering what I would say to a stranger coed, I was worried if I could bring myself to dance. For all intents and purposes, my Western dancing skills, especially with an American coed on American turf, were practically nonexistent; but I would try, I reasoned I must. I seemed to arrive early to the party. After being there for some minutes, I helped myself to a soft drink (alcohol was off limit), and as I started a casual milling about, I thought I spotted the same coed that had taken the make-up exam earlier that day; she was alone.

Initially, I was not even sure if it was really her. The lobby was dimly lit, perhaps for effect! So, I walked over and asked her if she was the one. She nodded, yes. That gave me a break, and I did not have to think hard of what to say next, the words flowed; at first we talked about the make-up exam, then school things in general, then tidbits of personal histories. With the music, I attempted feebly at some of the slow dances. I am sure she figured out quickly that I was no Fred Astaire. As the evening progressed, I did not wander far from her, nor did she from me. As more students came in, the lobby got crowded and noisy. So, I suggested we go outside to get some fresh air, where we could talk and hear each other better. She agreed. We wandered out and around the grounds of the dorm. It was a pleasant evening weather-wise. I then asked if she cared to go to the Big Ten pub for some beer. She did not care for that. For a moment, I felt stumped. John had not told me what to do in such an eventuality. Fortunately, perhaps sensing my bewilderment, she suggested we simply walk around a bit more along Washington Avenue, on campus. I said fine, and we did. As we walked by The Big Ten, I could see from the outside that it was packed full with students. So, I was glad I did not have to elbow my way inside and order beer for two. I had not done this sort of thing in a pub before anyhow, crowded or empty. I had beer only very rarely back in Lebanon with male AUB classmates. After strolling for a while, it was time to walk her to Comstock Hall, which I gladly did. As I was departing, I asked if I could have her phone number, perhaps we would get together again. She obliged, and I was relieved that there were no hitches. Throughout, there was no physical contact of any kind, not even trying to hold her hand. Her name was Virginia Louise Schultz. She was a senior in home economics, in the subfield of textile and clothing. Her parents and family lived in Bismarck, the capital city of North Dakota.

On my walk back to my dorm, I felt all in all I did not do badly. Granted I did not interact much with other coeds; yet, I did not make a fool of myself. In time, I reported back to my consultant, John, for evaluation. He was very tactful and supportive. Since it was a first, I got a passing grade! I recall we laughed a lot about my being "broken-in" into the dating game. John, though a freshman, was amazingly tactful and sensitive to know that I could use a lot of positive feedback and encouragement.

My life as a student living in a dorm grew fairly quickly to become multidimensional. The circle of acquaintances and friends continued to expand among classmates in the courses I was enrolled in as well as the TA/RA office mates. The office mates were a mixture of first year to fourth year graduate students.

At the office, in addition to studying, grading and maintaining office hours for our lab students, many discussions and exchanges took place; virtually all were physics-related or career-related. Out of these discussions and exchanges, much was learned. Some graduate students were content to attain a master's degree and go to work afterwards. These tended to be the work-oriented and down-to-earth type. Most of them expected to work in industry or government. Many made the case for industry as a more rewarding area, both in terms of professional advancement and financial rewards. These office-mates were unlike my AUB classmates in terms of plans and expectations. Back in the Middle East, there was hardly any industry of the kind that would hire physicists. It was more so when it came to governments, especially if you were a Palestinian. Erroneously, I saw them as the less ambitious in a setting of many opportunities. Among those going for the PhD, there were many that held the view that they would be lucky to complete the work in six years, and not without hard work and perseverance. In fact, I found out that was the average number of years for recent PhD graduates in the department. It was quite discouraging. Back at AUB, the figure most often mentioned was four years, the figure I had mentioned to my mother and family. When I would go around polling and questioning senior graduates about the six-year time length to check its validity, I typically was told that only the very good finish in four to five years; they were few and far between. Then, after deeper probing, I would hear of unusually bright and well-prepared students who were able to earn the PhD in even less than four years. I wondered where I would fall.

Other exchanges involved talking about the different faculty members, good or bad, tough or easy, their research specialties, and the projects they were pursuing. There were discussions of research funding. Well-funded research meant graduate students could get research stipends and move from being TAs to RAs. RAs advanced more rapidly toward graduation than TAs.

These exchanges were generally very casual, informal. Once in a while, some faculty member would pop into the office for a variety of reasons and participate. I often marveled at some famous faculty members who chatted leisurely, humbly, and amicably with us. Yet, when faculty was present, the exchanges became more thoughtful and reserved. The degree of formality or informality in the graduate student-faculty interaction depended a lot on the people involved, both faculty and students. Nevertheless, there was, on the whole, a definite sense of collegiality between the two groups.

The food service for Pioneer residents was combined with the Centennial residents, in the basement of Centennial Hall. The food we had was generally very good, generously served, of large variety and healthy. You could have all you want of some things, I recall; in particular, milk and bread. Bag lunches were provided for people whose schedule did not allow them to make it to the dorm for lunch. My least favorable food day was Friday. On Friday, the primary dishes included fish, a food I have never been able to like. However, there were enough other substitute things that I did not go hungry.

The food area was quite large and a great deal of human interaction took place there. I got to know a handful of physics and mathematics classmates, residents at Centennial or Pioneer, better in this setting. One of these, in the mathematical physics course, also a first year TA but assigned a different office, was a black American physics graduate student. His name was Tannie Stovall. Somehow, it was several weeks before the two of us got into substantive conversation, after which we socialized often. He had grown up in Atlanta and was schooled there before coming to the UMN. When I innocently asked him why he came all the way north to Minnesota to do graduate work, his answer was unexpected. He said, "I'm tired of the stigma of being a Negro down in Georgia." He wanted to get away from that. I asked him how it felt in Minnesota? He said, "Better, but there is a lot more room for improvement." It was my first direct encounter with the problem of racial discrimination in the U.S. The depth of his feeling and its effect on his personality got my attention; he seemed to carry his blackness on his shoulder. Every now and then we would walk together back and forth between the dorm and the physics building. At times, we would sit next to each other in the classroom. He was tall, sleek, handsome, and walked fast! It was a challenge to keep up while walking with him. As our socializing grew more informal, about halfway into the fall quarter, he hesitantly asked me how often I showered, and if I washed my feet when I did. Taken aback but not offended, "Why do you ask?" I responded. He said, "For your own good, I should tell you that your feet have a strong stench that I can smell sitting next to you in our math-physics class; it is not good!" As I thanked him for pointing this out to me, I realized that although I showered daily at the dorm, it was often a quick rinse rather than real wash with soap and a scrubber. I did not change my socks everyday, partly out of habit and also because I had only a few pairs of socks and I wanted them to last until the weekend, when I would find time to do my laundry. Furthermore, I had only two pairs of shoes and was not faithfully alternating them. I realized that Tannie paid a lot more attention to his appearance and body hygiene than I did; he used very aromatic soaps and shampoo as well as after shave. Though it had been deeply inculcated in me that appearances were not important, and that the inside of a person was what really counted; nevertheless, hygiene and cleanliness were altogether a different matter. Henceforth, I decided to be more attentive to these issues, bought more socks right away, and was ever grateful for his nudge. Tannie and I became good friends and did a variety of activities together during our graduate years at UMN and well beyond.

One day into October, I went to bed at about midnight, having last seen the outdoors to be normal and the grass fairly green, only to wake up the next morning and find that the outside was all white, covered with snow! I was amazed at the sudden change; what further amazed me was the sight of students headed towards Centennial Hall for breakfast and carrying their books to classes without the slightest hint that anything unusual was happening. I thought surely there would be no school, as would be the (rare) case if this were happening in Tyre or Beirut. So, I went excitedly to John's room across the hallway to find him already moving about. I said, "John, is there school today?" He retorted, having not had chance to look out yet, "Why wouldn't there be school?" I said, "There is snow outside!" He nearly fell back into his bed in laughter! He said, "It is likely to be this way until next spring; according to you, we would not have school for months to come. This is Minnesota, and you better get used to it." Like somebody had knocked me out of some stupor, I left his room saying, "I better get ready for the day, then."

Early on, after the first snow, I realized that despite my mother's best effort and all the information I got in advance, I did not have the right kind of clothes for Minnesota weather. I had no head covering of any kind. My shoes had hard leather soles that were dangerously slippery on ice. The top leather, after having gotten wet and dried over the heat register, began to crack up. I had no long underwear, no heavy overcoat, etc. At various times, Parviz and Mahmoud advised me as to what I ought to have for winter clothes, and where to buy them. However, I did not take their advice seriously until hit by the chill and stark reality of it all.

Well into the fall quarter, I found myself dealing with many issues; making sure that my schoolwork, both as a student and as a TA, was satisfactory was a top priority. Adjusting to life on campus and Minneapolis became increasingly challenging as the temperature continued to drop. The contrast with Beirut's weather and landscape was hard to ignore. I also found myself far removed from all those who were near and dear, and not knowing when and how I would be able to see them again.

The notion of six years as the average time for the successful student to get the PhD was disquieting; at the same time the notion of not making it and going back to Lebanon in failure was not only unacceptable, but also unthinkable. *How would I face my mother, family and friends?* was a recurring question. There were emotional temptations to question the wisdom of having left Lebanon to pursue graduate studies. The state of misery, humiliation, and helplessness that we Palestinians lived, in Lebanon, was still vivid in the back of my mind. Therefore, at the rational level, I readily dismissed such questioning; I would not allow myself to indulge in doubting that I was doing the right thing. I knew deep in my heart there was no turning back.[124]

Two weeks after the dorm mixer encounter, I decided I would try to ask Virginia Schultz for a full-fledged date. I talked it over with John in advance and worked out the finer details of the call. The date was for a Friday night.

---

124 I recalled the lines from the Muslim General Tariq bin Ziyaad's address to his troops as they landed upon the southern coast of Spain, from across the strait now named after him (Gibralter; derived of the Arabic 'Gabal Tariq'), at the turn of the eighth century, "The enemy is before you and the sea is behind you, and you have by God only the truth and the perseverance.... your means to victory..."

Virginia accepted.[125] On the date, we took the bus to downtown Minneapolis, where we saw a movie. I tried to let her choose the movie because I did not want to pick one that she might not like. The movie was some kind of a mystery, an Alfred Hitchcock type, which I did not understand, but she did! Of course, I tried to conceal it. After the movie, we went for an ice cream sundae nearby. I found out that she loved hot fudge ice cream with nuts, and that her parents owned a creamery in Bismarck, North Dakota, which manufactured ice cream and butter. After that, we took the bus back to campus and to her dorm. At the dorm, I hung around for about fifteen minutes, and then headed to my dorm room. Aside from courteously stretching out my hand as she got off the bus or opening doors, I was too nervous, to make any physical contacts with her.

While at times I was at a loss for words, however, our time together was pleasant and enjoyable. I was befuddled at the number of boy-girl pairs that hung out around different parts of the lobby or hallways of her dorm. Some were just chatting and flirting, others were necking and petting, oblivious or indifferent to all that was around them. It seemed preposterous that they should have such freedoms. I did not think, if I were to have that kind of freedom, I would behave in that manner so openly.

Again, at an opportune time I reported back to John. By his and my evaluation, I did all right. Nevertheless, I was faced with many questions: Did I want to do this as an occasional pastime or make a habit of it? Should I try dating other coeds and not settle on the first one that had come along? How was dating going to bear on my schoolwork? Can I manage to separate romance from academic pursuits? Or, am I going to mix and mess things up? Of course, by then, John was too careful to make hard and fast rules, although he tended to counsel me to stay cool and go slow!

In truth, I did not logically work out answers to these questions. I followed my instinct. I found myself seeing her more often as time went by. She was

---

125 Sometime later, she divulged to me that a short time before meeting me, she had been out on a date with a foreign student and had difficulty understanding his English. Consequently, she was not of a mind to date me had I asked her shortly after the mixer evening. It was too strenuous to converse. Since it took two weeks before I called, she was taken by surprise, and had nothing planned for that Friday evening. As a result, she could not think of an excuse fast enough to say no, and thus accepted. It was on that date that she realized my English was understandable after all, and that she would go out with me again if asked.

filling a big void, and I was enjoying her friendship. She seemed to stabilize my situation.

As Thanksgiving Day approached that November, and having had four or five dates by then, Virginia considered inviting me to go with her to Bismarck for the holiday. Her family expected her home at Thanksgiving. She had never before skipped being there for the occasion, and was not about to this time. It seemed to both of us premature for me to appear with her in Bismarck. As circumstance would have it, Professor Wall, who had in the intervening weeks taken a sympathetic interest in me, invited me to join him and his wife at their home, along with a small group of friends, for the Thanksgiving dinner. I gladly and excitedly accepted. Hence, the question of going or not going with her lifted off both of us. Virginia and I agreed that there will probably be another and better time to go to Bismarck.

Professor Wall and his wife were a very kind and caring host and hostess. The Thanksgiving dinner was in the early evening. It was preceded by hors d'oeuvres and wine. It was the first time a professor of mine had offered me wine. Instinctively, I declined and limited myself to a soft drink. The conversations of the evening were highly stimulating, and quite memorable.[126] We talked a lot about world affairs. Professor Wall and his wife had a very broad range of interests and astute knowledge of the human scene. Months later, I realized that he was a fervent advocate of a world federal system of governance. He either belonged to or sympathized with a group known at the time as The World Federalists Union. He, as well as some of the company, seemed to get a big kick out of my uninhibited (very likely, simplistic) views of world events, particularly as related to the Middle East. The Suez war was still fresh and subject of a lot of interest and discussion; specifically the roles of the U.S. and the USSR in bringing about a halt to the war, and the subsequent pull-back of the invading forces. There was also mention of the Joe McCarthy era and the purge of the physics department of presumed left-leaning members. Most notable among these was Dr. Frank Oppenheimer, brother of

---

126 Aside from being a very able and helpful supervisor, Professor Wall was an amazingly humble man. It was a couple of years later before I realized that he had been years back the recipient of the Oersted Medal in physics from the American Association of Physics Teachers, the highest national award in the field of physics education.

Robert Oppenheimer, the head of the Manhattan Project. Frank Oppenheimer had been fired from his job in the UMN department a few years earlier for alleged communistic leanings and/or contacts. Gradually, I picked up, from overhearing others, a deep sense of betrayal by many physics faculty members of the university administration for allowing such a purge to take place.

Many years later (early 1970s), as fate would have it, I was among a group of physicists going to tour The Exploratorium in San Francisco, a hands-on physics museum that had recently been launched and headed by Frank Oppenheimer. The American Association of Physics Teachers organized the tour. Professor Wall, retired by then, was among us. I sat next to him on the bus that took us from our hotel to the Exploratorium. When we got off, Frank Oppenheimer was meeting the group at the door. Upon seeing Professor Wall, he dashed to greet him warmly, as I stood by. It was clear that they were good old friends. I then had the pleasure of being personally introduced to Frank Oppenheimer by Professor Wall. We spent several hours touring the Exploratorium that day with Oppenheimer as the primary host and guide.

CHAPTER 16

TRYING OUT MY WINGS: ON AND OFF CAMPUS

Virginia and I continued to see each other, at times more than once a week. She had enrolled as a freshman majoring in music to become a professional flutist. She was less interested in music education, or for that matter, in the teaching profession. Her mother had attended two years at the UMN and was a few credits short of graduating with a bachelor's degree in education. Virginia's family was practically minded; particularly her father, who took pride in maintaining his creamery machinery. Her brother was a practicing mechanical engineer. "Those who can't do, teach," was one of the notions she seemed to have. She had considered becoming a mechanical engineer herself, except for the fact that society at the time did not look favorably at such a role for women. She reasoned that UMN music program was of such quality that it would launch her off to a good performing career.

Virginia had been a first flutist in the Bismarck high-school band and a second flutist in the UMN band. She had attended major national music camps, including the prestigious Interlochen Camp in Michigan, and was very well traveled in the U.S. However, during her second year at the UMN, she was advised by her flute teacher to drop out of the music program. She was found, upon being carefully tested, to have had a tone-hearing defect, a mild form of tone resolution, yet significant enough to handicap her from realizing a professional flutist career. Up to then, the defect had gone unnoticed. It came as a major blow to her. She first transferred to the College of General Studies, where students of undecided major usually enrolled. After some reassessing and soul searching, she transferred to the College of Home Economics to major in clothing and textile. For a time, she considered dropping out of the university. However, she recognized that led to nowhere. She wanted to prepare herself for a self-supporting, respectable, and independent living. Her parents made it clear that all their children would be supported during their four-year college education, after which, they would be expected to be on their own. She thought textile and clothing were sufficiently interesting and would provide her with a fulfilling career. On my part, I told her about my Palestinian background and my hopes and aspirations for the Palestinians in particular, and the Arabs in general.

Before long, we found ourselves drawn to each other in more ways than one. We found security in each other's company. However, each still had concerns and unanswered questions. Early on in our relationship, she expressed concern about religious compatibility. On my part, what I was most concerned about was cultural, social, and political compatibility. We were mindful of our widely different backgrounds.

I was concerned about such matters as: Are her marital values and expectations, being an American, in harmony, or can they be made to harmonize, with my values and expectations, being raised in a Muslim/Arab home? Would she be receptive to live in the Middle East, if that was where my work would demand of me to be? How hard would she be willing to try to make the marriage work? Divorce has always been a most unpleasant option to me. My opposition to it was deeply ingrained in my upbringing.

Yet, I was not about to settle back in the Middle East at all costs, or without a careful assessment of the pros and cons. There were plenty of negatives to living in the Middle East that I knew only too well. Furthermore, in the case of marriage, certainly her welfare would have to be carefully considered. The Middle East meant a lot to me, the desire to make a difference there was great, but common sense and survival came first. One thing was very clear in my thoughts; namely, if we were to get married, then I would have to be responsible for her welfare at least as much as I would be for mine. It was deeply embedded in me, thanks to my beloved mother, that marriage is a two-way, very serious and sacred spousal commitment and obligation.

She was a member of the Christian Science Church. I had not heard of that faith before. She let it be known that any place she would consider living would have to be such that she would be able to practice her faith freely. She said that any man she would consider marrying would be expected to become familiar with her faith, and would not get in the way of her practice of it. It was clear that Christian Science was central to her life. I was relieved when she did not insist, however, that her husband would have to be a Christian Scientist; that would have been a nonstarter.

I had reasoned with myself that, with my fairly liberal religious upbringing and education, my mother's significant associations with, and affection for, many Christians, and my AUB exposures and experiences, I would not have a problem with her living her faith as she chose; I had always understood that Islam is a religion of tolerance; it wants for mankind "ease and not dis-ease" (as I would put it in my own translation).[127] I expressed these feelings unambiguously to her; she nevertheless, continued to be concerned about her unhindered practice of Christian Science. To further reassure her, I began to learn more about her faith by accompanying her to some of the church services. She in turn gave me the textbook of the church to study; namely, *Science and Health with Key to the Scriptures* by Mary Baker Eddy.

As I undertook learning more about Christian Science, I found it indeed quite different from anything I had encountered before. I found the textbook hard to read. It made statements that went against many things that I thought were self-evident or I had taken for granted before; for example, the unreality of matter and the physical world and the unreality of evil and death! Additionally, I learned that Christian Scientists generally choose prayer to treat illness rather than medicine and medical doctors. In fact, they do the same in encountering and overcoming all kinds of discord, including social, economic and political. Virtually every problem is tackled first with a prayer. Slowly, I began to understand her concern about religious compatibility, for she knew that these ideas do not sit well with many people. While I expressed my initial disagreements with those notions and ideas, I nevertheless granted that it was her right to believe them. I also agreed to continue to think and rethink over and reassess my views, to be open-minded, if she would be willing in return to do the same for me. I felt there is always room for evolution through sincere analytic study, evaluation, and persuasion.

Virginia and I wanted to be positive and constructive. She would comment that in many instances, it might take time to begin to see through and appreciate her beliefs, that it involved a higher level of (metaphysical) thinking, and that I needed to allow myself that kind of time. It seemed far-fetched, but I was not going to rule it out. If she allowed me the time, I would be willing to learn and expand my horizons. Simultaneously, there was no way around the fact that

---

127 The Quran, S.II, v.185

Islamic values were deeply ingrained within me, and an integral part of my cultural heritage and affiliation. I felt it was only right to be quite plain as to where each of us stood. In matters like these, we had to be open and honest.

Alternatively, what boggled my mind after much was said and done in our theoretical and hypothetical discourses, that the many Christian Scientists, whom I had met in the meantime, seemed very kind, well-mannered, refined, reasonable and just like everyone else in discussing mundane matters; and a majority of them were quite successful members of society. They eschewed tobacco, alcohol and gambling, which happily, are in accord with Muslim teachings.

As we spent more time together, we did not find our religious differences to be much of a hurdle in enjoying each other's company. Our humanity seemed to rise above old-fashioned and traditional stereotypical religious sectarian divisiveness. We found great comfort in each other's company and got along very well; she worshipped her way and I, mine. As long as we both respected the differences, we were fine. It was, and still is today, a fundamental fact to me that rituals and methods of worship are not basic or absolute, but are rooted in history, culture and circumstances, which are subject to change, and are subjective. It is what is in one's heart of human goodness as translated into one's dealings with others that is the "proof of the pudding."

The question of future children and their religious upbringing was a natural follow-up. To me the answer was obvious; namely, we both expose them to our beliefs freely and without maligning the other's faith, and when they become adults, they decide what they want to practice and how they want to live. It was perhaps a departure from Islamic orthodoxy; nevertheless, it seemed fairer (in our world and times), and I was comfortable with it. The best sermon is setting the example. This sat well with Virginia. We both detested emotional and self-righteous arguing. We concurred that with love all things are possible. We increasingly saw a bright prospect for success.

Against such a background, we began work on the social mechanics of getting married. We felt it was too soon and unwise to rush and make public pronouncements. Even though things were evolving fast, we decided to at least be deliberate. By Christmas time, she was ready to invite me to spend Christmas in Bismarck, meet her family, and learn about her community. Her family gave her the green light. I also gathered the courage to accept.

The school fall term rapidly came to a close and the Christmas/New Year holiday was upon us. The course work went quite well, two As and an S (for satisfactory) for final grades. In order to accompany me on the trip to Bismarck, Virginia decided to wait in the Twin Cities until I was free of all lab grades' figuring, and finished buying appropriate things for the trip. In fact, she went downtown with me to help me buy supplies; socks, gloves, shoes, hat, overcoat, etc. Dayton's department store, downtown Minneapolis, was our favorite shopping place. I found myself plunged into such an unfamiliar world that I could only foggily discern it; yet, I had only one option, to keep on looking forward and moving!

The most frequent and convenient mode of travel between Bismarck and Minneapolis was the train. We chose a Northern Pacific train and boarded it in the morning at about 9 am. A train trip of about four-hundred and fifty miles was a first for me. I was filled with curiosity and anticipation. I had been on streetcars (tramways) in Beirut and Damascus, but not on a steam engine train of many cars traveling over hundreds of miles. For a while, I sat by the window, and looked hard at the landscape and the little towns. Virginia tried to provide as much information as she could about what we were seeing. Some of the towns we simply passed by, at others, we made a short stop; St. Cloud, Wadena, Fargo, Valley City, Jamestown, among others—new and unfamiliar names except for Wadena, which had an Arabic ring to it, and meant "our valley." Whether there was any real historical basis for this name, I have yet to know.[128] I was always looking to find something that would connect my past roots with my present. The countryside was largely covered with snow and the trees leafless and dreary. The towns looked rather drab and pretty much alike. Every now and then, I would get up and walk from car to car and look over who else was on the train. We made it to Bismarck at about five in the afternoon. At the train depot, waiting

---

128 It is not beyond the realm of possibility that there may have been some historical connection. There is another town, in central North Dakota, named Medina, pronounced for a time alternately Medeena and Medi-na (Medīna, a long 'i' as in the 'i' in sublime), which evoked similar queries. Eventually, a city council resolved, to my dismay, officializing the second pronunciation. In fact, years later I have come to know that indeed there have been significant Syrian settlements in the late nineteenth and early twentieth centuries in many Midwestern states including North Dakota; further, I learned that the first mosque to have ever been built in the U.S. was in fact, built in North Dakota. There are towns and places scattered all over the US named Lebanon and, to a lesser degree, Palestine.

to meet us, was Virginia's mother, Caroline, and her younger sister, Carole, a senior in high school. We were warmly welcomed in weather that was so cold that steam visibly streamed out of people's mouths and nostrils. We unloaded our suitcases off the train and into the family car and drove to their home.

At the house, a room was set for me on the main floor. The house looked typical. There were two bedrooms on the main floor and two on the second floor. Shortly after arriving, we had dinner. Virginia's father came into the house just before dinner from the Schultz Creamery, which was literally next-door. All five of us sat around a big table that could easily seat twelve. The meal was roast beef, mashed potatoes, vegetables, apple pie and ice cream. It was a classic meat and potato American meal that the Schultz family often had. We chatted politely and reservedly at the dinner table and afterwards. Carole was the friendliest and tried the most to put me at ease. She looked happy to meet her sister's boyfriend. Later that evening, we watched TV. It was black and white, recently purchased, and a novelty to the family. It was also a first for me to actually see and watch a real TV.

The following day, there were many errands and last minute shopping to be done by everybody in the family, except for Virginia's father, Enoch, who was at work in the creamery. Virginia was given the use of the car to show me around, do last minute errands, and have me meet some of the relatives in town. I met Virginia's Aunt Margaret first, Caroline's sister, who ran a grocery store, Pioneer Groceries, on Main Street. Their father, John Yegen, had founded the store many years ago. John had emigrated as a young man from Switzerland. Margaret never married and lived by herself in an apartment in the house, back of the store. There was a table set inside the store with a couple of trays filled with a large variety of cookies, a coffee pot and a hot cider pot, for whomever walked in, usually clients, to enjoy. It was a traditional feature of the Christmas season that went back for many years. That atmosphere touched a very receptive chord within me; tradition, family, community, and hospitality. After chatting for a little while and helping ourselves to the refreshments, Margaret asked Virginia to take me into the house in the back, and show me her apartment with all the Christmas decorations and other cherished items and artifacts. It was a lovely experience. After that we drove around town, and stopped at a couple of stores for Virginia to do some last minute shopping or pick up something her mother asked her to buy. Then we headed back home for lunch and a bit of leisure. Later in the afternoon, we went on a tour of the creamery. I found out that her mother managed the office of the creamery. Yet, there was also a secretary that dealt with routine business. Her father was more into the technical side of the operation; the manufacturing, packaging, and distribution of butter and ice cream. He oversaw the running and maintenance of all the different machinery involved, including refrigeration. They also had, as an annex, a meat storage locker service that some of their milk and butter farmer clients used.

Christmas Eve, by tradition, was at Virginia's parents house, where we would be joined by Uncle Bill, Caroline's brother, his wife, Aunt Lena, and their two sons, Bill Jr. and Jimmy, both grown-up bachelors, and Aunt Margaret. Christmas Day was at Uncle Bill's and Aunt Lena's house. An older lady, Julia, who lived alone in a little apartment nearby, a friend of Aunt Margaret and a member of the Christian Science Church, and who had worked for years as a secretary in a bank in town with no family around, was included. She was commonly included in holiday family gatherings.

Uncle Chris, the oldest sibling of Caroline, was married to a former widow, Aunt Lydia. She had two children from a previous marriage. Chris and Lydia had no children of their own; they celebrated Christmas separately with the families of Lydia's children. Uncle Chris owned a dairy milk and cottage cheese processing plant, Yegen Dairy, which he ran with Aunt Lydia. It was a few minutes' drive from Schultz Creamery. Virginia's father, Enoch, and Uncle Chris started out as partners in a joint ice cream, butter, and milk enterprise, but chose to split after a few years, allowing each of them to have more focus and independence. Uncle Chris also had a large dairy farm that supplied a good deal of the milk for the Yegen Dairy plant. I was told that he was a very progressive dairy farmer and milk processor. He kept up with the latest dairy technologies and introduced them expeditiously into the farm and the plant. He stopped by the house and we met. He was a very outgoing and dynamic person. His stop was brief; before he left he told Virginia to make sure to take me to tour his farm and the plant.

The Schultz family; Virginia's parents, Virginia and Carole, were the host and hostesses for Christmas Eve dinner. Virginia's oldest sister, Margaret, who had been married for a few months, was not there. She lived in Marion,

North Dakota, about 140 miles away. Virginia's brother, John, fresh out of North Dakota Agricultural College (later becoming North Dakota State University) as a mechanical engineer, had been working for a few months in the Los Angeles area, and was too far away and chose not to make it home for Christmas. Uncle Bill, Aunt Lena, Bill Jr., Jimmy, Aunt Margaret, and Julia all arrived in close succession. The main dish for the evening was lutefisk, a Scandinavian tradition. Caroline's mother was a Swedish immigrant. Virginia and I knew beforehand what was coming. Virginia, knowing of my dislike of eating fish in general, let alone lutefisk, which is particularly of strong fishy odor, put in a request for a couple of lamb chops instead. There were still many side dishes, and cookies and ice cream for a dessert. So, nobody left the table hungry unless he or she wanted to. After dinner, we all moved to the living room. The dirty dishes were dealt with in a hurry. In the living room, there was the lighted Christmas tree and a pile of gift packages under it. Virginia and Carole were assigned the task of pulling out the packages and delivering them to the named persons on the respective tags. Everybody present got one or more gifts. Nobody was overlooked. It was remarkable that I got several gifts when in fact I had not expected any, and I did not give out any. I was at a loss as what to do. Virginia must have known what was coming, but probably did not know how to prepare me in advance. I must confess the whole event was quite unlike anything I had experienced before. I wondered how uninformed I must have appeared to some back then. Yet, I believe they must have understood. I recall I got a tie from Virginia and a billfold from Santa Claus. I did not know who that was. In time, I found out Santa Claus was actually her mother. She gave me a billfold because she was aghast at the way I handled money, how I reached for it out of my pocket and how I stuffed it into my pocket. It was the first billfold I ever had! I have not been without one ever since. I was struck that night by the many acts of generosity and thoughtfulness from so many present, and the individual attention each got from the rest.[129]

---

129 The reality of the matter is that where I grew up families tended to have many children, and that they could not be given anywhere near the attention that children in smaller families in the West got. The same can be said in regard to observing birthdays. In my family, my birthday would be verbally noted at some point in the day, usually by my mother, but that was about it.

Uncle Bill was very sociable. He was the manager of the water treatment plant for the city of Bismarck. He was quite interested in the sciences and the environment. The cousins, Bill Jr. and Jimmy, were curious about how Virginia and I met, and what it was like to be as far away from home and family as I was. Bill Jr. worked as a salesman in a hardware store in Casper, Wyoming. Jimmy worked for a car dealership in Teaneck, New Jersey. A cousin of the Yegens owned the dealership; his name was also Chris (for Christian) Yegen.

On Christmas Day, around one o'clock in the afternoon, Virginia, her mother, sister and I dressed in festive clothes, got into the car and headed for Uncle Bill's house. Virginia's mother had boxes of cookies and a couple of ice cream buckets, of different flavors, to take along. Virginia's father did not join us. He did not enjoy too much socializing was the explanation given. Virginia did the driving. I learned that her mother did not care to drive unless she had to.

Uncle Bill lived on the outskirts of the city, about five miles away, overlooking the Missouri River. It was a small but immaculate home. Aunt Margaret and Julia were also at the party. The meal was turkey with all the trimmings, and many side dishes. It was a deliciously prepared and elegantly served meal. Uncle Bill gave a demonstration on how best to carve the turkey and the right tools to use. He even showed us how he sharpened the tools before use, and how he cleaned and stored them after use. After the meal, some of us played cards and socialized. Others worked in the kitchen and socialized. Jimmy was especially good at card games and was happy to tutor me. The atmosphere was quite jovial. We stayed there until almost dark.

In the remaining couple of days of my visit, Virginia and I did more sightseeing. We visited Yegen's Dairy and farm. It was fascinating how machines milked cows on the farm. No human hands touched the fresh milk from the cow's udder all the way to being homogenized, pasteurized and bottled for distribution. I learned that at the farm they kept a thorough record on each cow; how much milk it produced and a measurement of the different quality factors of the milk. The data collected was utilized to learn more about the various factors bearing on better milk production, a far cry from the milk that was delivered to our home in the morning in Tyre by a rural lady who had hand-milked it that morning and loaded it on the back of her donkey for delivery into our neighborhood.

Virginia found occasion to take me to the North Dakota State Capitol. It was an impressive high-rise building. She walked me into the hall of representatives, where state affairs are debated. She explained the system of representation in the state, the different roles of the legislature and the governor. We concluded the tour of the building by stopping at the governor's office. He was not in, but we were able to walk into his office and see the desk at which he sat when in office! I was struck by how accessible and open the building and its many facilities, including the office of the governor, were to the citizens and visitors, in contrast to anything comparable in Lebanon or Syria at the time. On the way out of the Capitol, we walked the large grounds around the building, and Virginia pointed to the house of the governor nearby. It looked respectable and nice; however, it was not pompous nor out of the ordinary, nor ringed by armed guards, as I thought it might be.

I returned to Minneapolis alone; Virginia stayed behind with her family for the rest of the holiday. I took the train back to Minneapolis at about nine in the evening. Virginia drove me to the train depot. Before leaving, I thanked her parents and sister heartily for their magnificent hospitality. At the depot, Virginia and I bade each other a tender goodbye. The train arrived in Minneapolis early the next morning. I did not sleep very much on the train; I had a lot to ponder and reflect upon. Looking back, the trip to Bismarck and the stay with Virginia's family during the Christmas holiday unmistakably deepened our relationship and widely broadened my horizons. Virginia's kind and gentle nature repeatedly manifested itself. I got firsthand knowledge of her background. It became a lot easier for Virginia to discuss her family matters with me, and for me to intelligently listen.

Chapter 17

Back to the Grindstone!

Well into the winter school term, I explored the possibility of more work within the department to meet increasing expenses. I started earnestly thinking about a more appropriate advisor in line with my research interests. The department offered me lab teaching in evening classes for the spring term, subject to continued satisfactory progress as a graduate student. It would bring in about an additional hundred dollars a month for teaching two lab sections; over a fifty percent jump in my income. I accepted. The advisor's choice was not so straightforward. I was very impressed by Professor Hill, but he was a theoretical physicist. The thought was, experimental physicists are better agents for technology transfer to the Middle East than theorists. Nuclear experimental research seemed to fit the bill. So I surveyed my options in the department along those lines. There were two major groups: the low energy group, also the smaller of the two, using the Van de Graaf accelerator within the building; and the second, the higher energy group, using the Linear Accelerator (LINAC) Laboratory, which was housed separately, a bit off the central campus and the physics building. The LINAC group seemed too large, rather impersonal in terms of the student and faculty make-up, and intimidating. I decided to go with the Van de Graaf group. I expressed my interest to the director, Professor George Freier. He thought I could join his group of RAs. He recommended that I begin to spend time at the lab, as my time allowed, getting to know "who is who" there, both graduate students and faculty, and learning what experiments were being carried out, with the idea of arriving in due course at my own proposal for a research project. We agreed that it would be good to start the process with the spring term. In the initial, trial phase, I would receive no remuneration. Other first year graduate students were doing similar things. The winter term wound up, courses-wise, as satisfactorily as the fall term.

As winter progressed and Virginia and I steadily saw each other, it was no longer whether we would get married, but rather, *when*? As Valentine's Day approached, the residents of Comstock Hall planned a dinner and dance on that evening at a downtown hotel. Participating coeds would invite their respective Valentines to the event. I was Virginia's invitee. Therefore, I went back to my consultant John to find what it all entailed.[130] Other than being on my best, dress and behavior wise, and practicing some dancing, I was told that I would be expected to present Virginia with a flower corsage for the event, which I gladly did.[131] That evening I learned she had purchased a party dress expressly for the event. She looked stunning, and I was in seventh heaven!

In the spring term, Virginia and I decided it was time to make our marriage intention public. First, it was natural and foremost to try to secure Virginia's parents' approval and blessings. As far as my side was concerned, I was quite sure of my mother's support and trust; the rest of the family would follow suit. Virginia and her father seemed to have a special and close relation. In the final analysis, he stated that it was her life, and she was the one that was going to have to live with me; what would make Virginia happy would make him happy too. Virginia's father was not a Christian Scientist. He was raised Lutheran, but generally lukewarm about traditional religion. Virginia's mother was a different story. While she was properly hospitable, at Christmas time, she had many reservations, some very strong. She was concerned that I might take Virginia to live in the Middle East, which would take her a long way from her family and cultural environment. It was very unlikely that would provide her with the kind of life she had in the States, both economically and from the standpoint of individual freedoms. She felt one would have to be out of his or her mind to leave the States to live in another country. With me being a Muslim, I might adversely influence her daughter's religious life or beliefs. She viewed Muslims in general with apprehension. It was Virginia's mother who was the ardent Christian Scientist in the family, and had raised the children accordingly. Lastly, I was dark and from a third world country, a likely misfit in American social fabric.

I was not surprised by her mother's concerns, nor did I take offence. I simply felt that was the way it was, and I hoped she would be proven wrong in due time.

---

130 Virginia by then had gotten to know of my consultant John Mitchell. When I showed ignorance of the occasion, she smilingly recommended that I get John to help me!

131 It was the first time I heard of a thing called "flower corsage!"

Virginia engaged her mother in a drawn out exchange over these issues. Neither one convinced the other of their respective stands. Virginia, in the meantime, let me know that if her mother stuck to disapproval, it would not stop her from going ahead with the marriage. I felt uncomfortable about that. It was against my upbringing, where my sisters would not think of going against their mother's wishes. Nevertheless, it was a reassurance of her level of commitment to our relationship. Yet, I did not want it to go that way if I could help it. Eventually, I think, Virginia's mother saw the signs on the wall and decided to relent, and granted that Virginia would have a full-fledged wedding in Bismarck, like her sister Margaret. Virginia and I decided on the date of September 7, 1958, a Sunday, as the day for the wedding.

As my dating with Virginia was going on a steady, harmonious, and reasonably firm track, I decided to reach out to get to know more about Arab students on campus and their activities. I found out there was an Arab-American student club that numbered over fifty student members. Its objective was to promote all kinds of interaction among Arab students, and between Arab students and the university community at large. They met regularly in the student union. I began to attend some of the meetings, but quietly. As I gained more confidence, I had Virginia accompany me to some of the meetings. I felt it was a healthy and educational exposure to my world for her!

At one of these meetings, I saw almost in disbelief, Hanna Duwani, son of Muallem Boulous, brother Yousef's milk brother! In contrast to previous encounters when I was too shy, I made up my mind that this time I was going to introduce myself to him. As I told him my name and who my parents were, I tried to follow up with further proof to authenticate my claim. He quickly put on a smile, and said you don't need to prove any further, I believe you for you look like Yousef. I then introduced Virginia to him as my fiancé. He further proceeded to ask me about the family and how they were getting along in southern Lebanon. While I knew that he was in the U.S. to work for his PhD, it was the farthest from my mind that he would be pursuing it at UMN. I found out during the encounter that he was in the final phase of writing up his PhD thesis and expected to be done in the summer. Before parting that evening, he took my address and phone number, and told me that he would want me to come to his home and meet his wife and two children.

Toward the end of the spring term, Virginia and I were invited to a Sunday dinner at his home, a short walking distance from Pioneer Hall. Both he and his wife really rolled out the red carpet for us. I had not expected to be met with such affection, even though I knew of the affection he had for my mother especially, and the family in general. His plans beyond graduation were that he would be leaving with his family in a few months for South America (Brazil or Argentina?) where he already had a job. Within a few short years from his moving to South America, word came back to me, via Mother in Lebanon, that he had fallen ill there and passed away.

At the end of the AUB school year 1956-1957, I met an American student from Red Wing, Minnesota on campus who was finishing up a year of study at AUB as part of some international exchange program. [132] His name was Bud Belden. He told me that he would be enrolling in the fall in the UMN medical school. Wow, isn't it a small world after all, was my reaction. By then, I knew of my plans vis-à-vis UMN. We both were excited at the coincidence. He took down my dorm's name and said he would contact me. For a time, there was no contact. Then, and unexpectedly, he showed up at my dorm's room to say hello and, "I haven't forgotten you." He expressed hope that at some point before the school year was up, I would visit his hometown, an hour or so away by car, and meet his family. He found, in the process, that I already had a girlfriend who I was serious about. With a grin, he said, "Of course, she would be included."

It was late in the spring term that I heard from him again. We settled on an upcoming Sunday for Virginia and me to spend a day with him in Red Wing. He had his own car, and said he would pick us from our dorms in the morning and drive us back before evening. He concluded by saying something to the effect, "Let us pray for good weather." On that Sunday, sure enough, we were picked up. The sky was cloudless blue, the air nice and warm, the drive pleasant, and the countryside lush green. At Red Wing, we did early sightseeing until noon. Red Wing turned out to be a very charming town, beautifully located on the Mississippi River. At noon, we headed to his family home for lunch. There, we found tables in the backyard arranged for a picnic style lunch, a peaceful setting. Clearly, other people were coming to the party.

132 Actually, it was through another AUB student, who became aware of my plans to go to the UMN, and who had previously met and befriended the Minnesota exchange student..

Before long, young people began to show up, mostly college men and women dressed in beautiful, colorful clothes. For a while, it was get-acquainted time with soft drinks and hors d'oeuvres, followed by lunch, sandwiches and sweets amidst lively chatter. There was a lot to share: Bud and his time in Lebanon, and me and my time coming over to the UMN. Early that afternoon, I found out that the group, about a dozen, was going to join us on a boat cruise of the Mississippi. The boat was a good size, more like a yacht. We all fit comfortably on deck, and were able to mill around and enjoy a lot of socializing. We went back to land late afternoon. Thereafter, after saying goodbye to all others, Bud drove Virginia and me back to campus. It was like being in a movie, or a dream, where you would rub your eyes a few times to make sure it was real!

The spring term found me battling on several fronts; additional teaching in the evening, defining the future course of my relationship with Virginia, choosing a research field while spending time at the Van de Graaf Lab, and reaching out for the campus Arab-American club. My course work went satisfactorily, though my grade in the math course dropped from an A to a B. The Van de Graaf group was unbelievably supportive of my joining them. Notwithstanding visible inadequacies in hands-on technical skills, I was granted a summer research assistantship, RA, which paid me about $220 a month, a jump of over twenty percent from the TA stipend. I ascribed some of this good fortune perhaps to my eagerness and bravery at wanting to learn, and some to the big-hearted people at the lab. The RA would be automatically extended to the school year if my progress at the lab was satisfactory; Professor Freier officially became my advisor.

At the end of the spring term, Virginia was due to graduate with a bachelor's degree in home economics. Her mother came to the graduation celebrations, commencement exercises, and took many pictures. Her mother felt strongly about graduation before marriage. Privately, Virginia confided, she was short one three-hour credit course, specific to her major. Yet, her name was on the program as a graduating senior. Because of the large number of graduates, degrees were not handed out as the graduates walked on and off the stage of Northrop Auditorium; rather, they were handed a formality card saying that upon meeting all the requirements, the degree would be conferred and the diploma would be delivered, usually by mail. Virginia could not fulfill those three credit hours in the summer; they were not offered. Virginia and I, however, pledged to each other that she would do so at the earliest date. Virginia completed those credits the following school year and got her diploma.

As for me, the end of the spring term meant it was time to vacate my dorm room and say goodbye to my friends there, in particular, John Mitchell. He knew of the planned wedding and was sent an invitation, but he told me in advance that he would not be able to make it because he would be in his hometown in Illinois, about eight hundred miles away. I found a temporary room in a house, owned and lived in by a widow, a couple of blocks east of "Dinky Town." The rent terms were flexible and Dinky Town, with all its amenities, enabled me to survive without a car. Virginia would be in Bismarck most of the summer; but when in town, she could be accommodated for on a reasonable daily rate basis at the rooming house.

CHAPTER 18

THE ROAD TO MARRIAGE

There were several tasks that required addressing that summer (1958). Three primary ones were; research at the Van de Graaf Lab, locate and prepare a place to move to upon marriage, and take a math course that was being offered in the first summer session, and thought of potential merit to my program of study. Virginia would be in touch and would come as needed, particularly to partake and help in the finding and preparing our future love-nest.

Additionally for the wedding, I needed to come up with somebody to be my best man. In Muslim weddings, all you need are a couple of witnesses who are trustworthy family elders or members of the community. For a best man, the natural person was Parviz Mahmoodi. Of all individuals I came to know that past year, he was by far the one. He got well acquainted with Virginia, and she got a big kick out of his constant humor. When I asked him if he would be my best man, Parviz agreed. We thought, in view of his love for driving, that he and I could even drive together to Bismarck before the wedding, and that he would then drive back by himself; or if we could interest another person to come to the wedding, perhaps Mahmoud Sayrafiezadeh, then that other person would accompany Parviz back. With that general plan in place, I turned my attention to other matters.

I enjoyed the math course. I got an A. I reaffirmed to myself once more that when I apply myself and the external conditions are right, I have the ability to perform at a high level.

The research at the Van de Graaf Lab proved to be quite challenging in an unexpected way. The accelerator was often not in running order. The repairs required being a mechanic, an electrician, an electronics wiz, and a plumber all at the same time; skills that were not at all in my psychological makeup or home environment and experience. My group associates saw much of these challenges, sometimes bemused, but nevertheless were understanding and considerate. My thought, and perhaps others around, was to allow myself time.

I was drawing a salary and wanted to earn it. I fought valiantly. I did all I could to assist others in running their experiments. I thought in so doing I would learn by example; I might also count on their help when my research project got going. Sometimes I would go home looking dirtier than a car mechanic from crawling up and down the Van de Graaf machine; a big space of about ten feet in diameter and thrity feet high, full of electrical and mechanical hardware. It would take me quite sometime, after getting home, before I was adequately cleaned up. Well into that summer, though, I was not progressing much towards developing my own research, and my aptitude for experimental research was in question; still, they extended my RA for the fall term. For the time, I felt that was good enough, and I hoped things might yet turn around.

Virginia came back to Minneapolis once that summer, around the middle of August. In a relatively short time we located an adequate efficiency apartment in a brand new apartment building; a good twenty minutes walk to the physics department. We contracted it right away, at $80 a month, and proceeded to furnish it with the most basic needs, just enough to function when we came back after marriage. We planned on a one-week honeymoon immediately after the wedding. The Van de Graaf group allowed it; theoretically, my employment was half-time. I could make up for the hours upon return. In practice, nobody really counted hours, because everybody put in considerably more hours at the lab than were expected. Virginia told me that her parents offered us the use of their one-year-old Chevy for our honeymoon. I thought that was great. I did not have a driver's license nor did I drive. I could get a driving permit that would allow me to drive accompanied by a licensed driver, which I did. We decided to honeymoon in the Black Hills. We could afford the week, but our finances were such that Virginia would have to find work soon afterwards.

A few weeks before the wedding, Parviz came up and told me that he and his fiancé, Sue, had been exploring for a time for their own wedding, and could not come up with anything other than the same weekend of our wedding! He apologized for having to pull out at that late hour. While upset, there was not much I could say. I proceeded to search for an alternative. I tapped Subhi El-Qasim, a Palestinian PhD student in agriculture, from Tulkarem, that I had befriended a few months earlier through the Arab-American club. Subhi, who by then had gotten to know Virginia as well, felt happy to be asked, but on such a short notice and because of other obligations, he could not manage it.[133] At that point, my bag of viable prospects looked empty. I had underestimated the magnitude of the task. I called up Virginia with the unfortunate news and encouraged her to find a solution on her end. Within a day or so, she called back and said that she had asked Uncle Chris if he would serve in that role and he had agreed to do it. It was with a mixture of relief and failure that I received the news. I was relieved that we had a solution, but unhappy because I had failed at doing my part and had to impose through Virginia on Uncle Chris.

Virginia and her parents took care, for the most part, of all the arrangements and expenses for the wedding. There were a few minor exceptions like paying the minister for conducting the marriage vows, which were the groom's unambiguous responsibility. Needless to say, we each bought the other a wedding band, with the wedding date carved on the inside. Earlier in the spring, I had given her an engagement ring with a yellow topaz stone, which she personally picked. A diamond ring was beyond my means, and she understood that. Aside from these, all I had to do was show up on Friday with my suitcase (traveled by train) two days before the wedding. Over a hundred guests attended the wedding. With the exception of a couple of Syrian American families who lived in Bismarck, with whom I had made acquaintance in a hurry,[134] all were guests of the side of the bride.

I had bought a brown suit and a new pair of shoes for the wedding ceremony, but found out a few days before the appointed hour that Uncle Chris did not have a brown suit to match, but could wear a blue one. The thought was that the groom and the best man should wear suits of the same color. Luckily, I had brought from Lebanon the blue suit I wore for my bachelor's degree graduation at AUB. So, Virginia told me to bring it along with a pair of black shoes, which I had, and that was what I did.

---

133 Years later, Subhi became dean of the College of Agriculture of Jordan's University in Amman Jordan, then minister of Agriculture, eventually went into private, agriculturally related, business.

134 One of the guests was Mr. Nayef Saba, a Bismarck judge. He was very kind toward me right away and fluent in Arabic. When he learned of my best man story, he retorted, "You could have asked me." Alas, I actually did not think of it. Years later, his son, Michael, and I socialized together on occasions in Fargo.

As I reflect on this many years later, I feel a sense of disenchantment, embarrassment, and inadequacy with myself. So much good was shown me by so many; yet, I wonder if I had ever tried to show proportionate appreciation and gratitude.

As to a place for the wedding ceremony, Virginia, sometime in the spring, had taken up the subject with me. The Christian Science Church does not conduct marriages, for they have no ordained clergy. Consequently, neither Virginia nor I were under any particular religious pressure to marry in a church. She mentioned that we could get married in a public place, like a hotel, if marrying in a church was likely to evoke disapproval from my family's side. Somehow instinctively, I felt that it might be better for all concerned not to deviate from common practice if we did not have to. For Virginia's sake, I wanted the wedding to have all the semblance of normality and appropriateness. There was nothing in my background, or in how my family felt, that forbade me from marrying in a church. We were not hung up on mechanics; it is all in what is in your heart. There was mention that the First Presbyterian Church in Bismarck had a good facility for the ceremony and the reception. It was a common choice by some relatives and acquaintances of Virginia's family. In Beirut, I had formed a high opinion of Presbyterians. They were also close to the Congregationalists, who have done so much for my education in high school and at AUB. We settled on it for the wedding place.

With the help of a friend, Virginia carefully hid our going away car lest it be tampered with and decked with clinking cans and "Just Married" signs by mischievous friends! We were in no mood of such advertisement, no matter how playful. A friend stealthily drove us to it after the reception. The reception was joyous and by evening we were off on our honeymoon! We were so tired from the hectic pace of the days leading up to the wedding that we only drove across the Missouri River into a motel in the neighboring town of Mandan, a mere five miles away, to stay for the night.

The first day of the honeymoon, we spent meandering in western North Dakota. Virginia took me to her Grandfather John Schultz' homestead house and farm near the town of Glenn Ullin, fifty miles or so west of Bismarck. I found the house to be impressively large and well-built. It was no longer lived in, and in a state of disrepair and abandonment. Virginia's father had largely bought out the farm of about seven hundred acres from his siblings; it was farmed by tenants. It is quite unforgettable to see the zeal and affection that Virginia held for the place. The place was full of memories of her father's childhood that she had heard at his knees and also memories of western pioneers settling the land in a harsh environment against many odds. We then pressed on further west and south to the Black Hills of South Dakota. The sound of names of places like Hebron, the Badlands, Belfield, Spearfish where we had stopped in and wandered about carry happy melodies for me. The beefsteaks we enjoyed in Belfield were outstanding, taste and size-wise. The sight of Mount Rushmore National Monument, where the heads of presidents Washington, Jefferson, Lincoln and Theodore Roosevelt are carved in the mountain, lingers on.

During the honeymoon, Virginia did virtually all the driving. She was a very good and careful driver. She had gathered all kinds of maps and information materials for the trip and she used them very competently. I tried hard to read the maps as she drove, but could not help but feeling like I was retarded in the skill of finding the places and roads to take as compared to her. With the driving permit that I had, I did some driving, but only in the wide-open spaces and in daylight. She was not keen on me driving and did not want to teach me driving, least of all on our honeymoon!

The week slipped away fast and the day soon came to get back to Bismarck to collect our belongings and wedding gifts and head on to our new home in Minneapolis. The trip to Bismarck seemed long and arduous; it was Saturday evening when we made it to her parents' home. I was shocked by the size of the pile of presents awaiting us to open and take to Minneapolis. The following morning was spent opening presents and packing. Virginia's parents looked on, more so her mother than her father, sometimes from close, more often from a distance.

Late that afternoon, we seemed ready to make our next move. I will never forget the moment that Virginia's father, Enoch, walked into the living room and asked me how I planned to haul the stuff off to Minneapolis? I don't remember if I said anything back to him, but I am sure that all that I could have responded with must have been a mumble and a blank stare, for I did not have clue as to what to do next. Knowing now his ways, he must have chuckled in wonder at me. Then, calmly and gently talking to Virginia and me, he offered to drive us to Minneapolis (some 440 miles) himself with all our belongings, including gifts, in his green Ford pickup truck. I was speechless. I did not have an alternative to counter with. We took early supper and loaded the pickup accordingly. It was early evening that we set out on our journey. Virginia sat between her father and me. The conversation was for the most part light and sporadic. Enoch did a good deal of the talking. It seemed mostly centered on how to survive driving on the highways with special emphasis on winter and night driving. I was amazed how much thought Enoch had given to driving over the years. I gained insight into why Virginia was such a good and careful driver. All three of us stayed awake throughout the whole drive. Virginia and I periodically suggested stopping for rest. Enoch accepted stopping only once, for coffee, somewhere near Valley City, 140 miles east of Bismarck. We made it to our apartment around five in the morning. We unloaded the pickup and Enoch would not even sit down for a breather, let alone a breakfast that we tried to press on him. He took a glancing look at the apartment, got into his pickup, and headed back to Bismarck, where he presumably had some business to take care of that day!

CHAPTER 19

MARRIAGE AND THE M.S. DEGREE

Alone together and just married, we had many things to take care of. Virginia would initially focus on the apartment to make it functionally livable. I was eager to head back to the Van de Graaf Lab, lest I miss too much work time and appear delinquent. I also wanted to gear up for the new school year. The Van de Graaf group warmly welcomed me back and with wedding presents.

I got fast to work and enrolled in four graduate courses, three in physics and one in mathematics. Also I applied for the master's degree. My enrollment in four courses was ambitious when you add to it research work at the Van de Graaf Lab. Being married seemed to imbue me with a new spirit of optimism. There was a new sense of stability and peace that I had not known since becoming a refugee in 1948. I felt more secure and better anchored to face challenges.

Virginia and I were positive and forward looking about what we had just accomplished. I took her unhesitatingly into my loving confidence. We yearned for and sought to the extent we could the unadulterated truth in our discussions and relationship. From time to time Virginia would express a sense of hurt and disappointment for having had to give up a music career. She wanted time to soul-search. I was happy to see her take the time. On the subject of children, we readily came to the conclusion that children would have to wait until we were economically secure, that is, after I earned the PhD degree and had a regular, stable job.

Virginia loved to go to Sunday afternoon concerts performed by the Minnesota Symphony Orchestra, typically in Northrop Auditorium. She also loved to go to plays performed on the UMN campus, Como's Park and Zoo, and joyous movies. I too enjoyed partaking in them.

Of concern, was the need to have sufficient income to pay our bills and to have a little extra for unforeseen challenges and activities. My research assistantship (RA) was clearly insufficient. I hoped that with Virginia working, we could also help my mother, and those with whom she lived. My first year at the UMN went without any financial help to the family back in Lebanon. My mother was working for Yousef in the laundry and earning her way, but she was getting older, the business was meager, and Yousef had a wife and eight children. I was also mindful that, with Fouad at AUB and his wife and five children under the same roof with mother and Yousef, things were extremely tight. Hamadi's situation in Tripoli was no better. My mother meant a great deal to me and had sacrificed so much for me and others that I simply felt that I had to do all I could to help her, even if only to the tune of forty to fifty dollars a month, which by "back-home" standards would be a significant shot in the arm. In hindsight, it was sad that I had to heap all this on our just launched marital life. Virginia was, however, very sympathetic, understanding, and respectful of my sense of duty towards my mother. She never questioned nor belittled my urge to help. Within a matter of weeks, she proceeded to look for a job. She initially tried to find work in textile and clothing, but nothing seemed to turn up. We both were very averse to taking loans and falling in debt. Therefore, she proceeded to consider other jobs of a lesser level and desirability. Within a month or so thereafter, she got an offer for a job as a lab technician in a beer brewery, a few miles from home and accessible by bus. Owning a car was out of the question. The job was not at all what she would normally have considered. It was clearly below her qualifications and abilities. Far more importantly, it went against her religious beliefs, being Christian Scientist. Yet, she agreed to take it.

The pay was $240 a month, twenty dollars more than what I was making. We definitely viewed the job as temporary until something better turned up. We reasoned that if we managed our money wisely, we should get through this period all right.

As I settled down for the fall term school work, it became increasingly clear that while my course work was going well, my research was not getting off the ground. My typical day would begin at six in the morning and would not end before midnight. I did not seem to progress well enough into the Van de Graaf's research to initiate my own project, nor did I seem to develop the experimental skills or aptitude needed to independently conduct the kind of experiments others in the group were conducting. Toward the end of the fall term, it became abundantly clear to me that despite my best efforts, I realistically had no worthy future in the Van de Graaf Lab. On the brighter side, I was showing promise in a year course with Professor Hill, in atomic and molecular structure, and doing well in a year course with Professor Wall, the director of the TA program, on statistical mechanics and thermodynamics. My interest in Professor Hill's course was clearly the greatest. In light of all this, there was one sensible thing that I needed to and could do, and that was to change my research area from experimental to theoretical, and accordingly, change my research advisor. Humanly, it was difficult to do, particularly because of all the support and kindness I had received from Professor George Freier. But I had to face the realities, and I succeeded in doing so without hard feelings at all, and with a good deal of understanding. Giving up on the Van de Graaf research meant no more RA stipend. I needed to secure a TA, though there was an expected drop of about 10% in the stipend. This was not automatic and depended on availability. Luckily, Professor Wall assured me that I would get one. Professor Hill welcomed me as an advisee effective of the start of the winter term. With such, I was charting a new track to earn the M.S. degree.

During the Christmas year-end school break, I embarked on a crash self-study program of French to take the scientific French competency test offered in mid-January of the following year. Passing the test enabled me to fulfill the one foreign language competency requirement for the M.S. degree. It further satisfied one of the two foreign language competency requirements for the PhD.

Once an advisee with Professor Hill, I speedily drew up a plan for my master's degree program. Because of loss of time in the summer and fall pursuing experimental nuclear research, and a good accumulation of course credits, it was more expeditious and secure to pursue the Plan B master's program over the Plan A. Plan A was called the thesis option and Plan B, the three-review papers option. The thesis option emphasized original research whereas the three-review papers option required more course credits and a broader exposure to the field. One of the papers I decided on related to the atomic and molecular structure course. A second paper was related to the course on statistical mechanics and thermodynamics. I still needed a third paper.

The previous courses with Professor Hill had already given me a good background in quantum mechanics, its historical roots and philosophical precepts. I had also attended several seminars on the philosophical difficulties in the subject conducted by local and guest professors in physics and philosophy, which I thoroughly relished. Furthermore, at AUB, I had already taken a course on the philosophy of science, which dealt, however, primarily with the philosophy of classical physics. I consequently decided on a paper critiquing the philosophical foundation of quantum theory for the third requirement. To top off my background for the project, I took a couple of pertinent courses in the philosophy department, one on metaphysics in the winter term and another on modern physics philosophy in the spring term.[135] I got A in each of these courses. By early July of 1959, I had all the papers submitted and approved and all the course credits completed, plus some more. I took my final MS degree oral about the middle of July and was granted the M.S. degree on August 20th, 1959. My mother-in-law came from Bismarck expressly to attend the graduation ceremony.

My friends Parviz Mahmodi and Subhi El-Qasim completed their respective PhD work, the former in mechanical engineering and the latter in plant pathology, and took their final exams for the degree within days from my final exam for the M.S. Alas, Mahmoud Sayrafiezadeh continued to drift without settling down on a serious plan or program of study for a degree.

Particularly during the first year of my marriage to Virginia, and for the remaining years of my graduate study, I must record here, a heart full of gratitude for the considerable generosity showered upon me and Virginia by her parents, in terms of gifts of home furnishings and food. Such gifts undoubtedly enabled us to enjoy a significantly better life than otherwise, as well as occasional luxury.

After about three months at the beer brewery, Virginia found a better job with General Mills as a lab technician. The pay was about fifty percent more. With such, we were able to help my mother to the level I had hoped for and save some for the future.

---

135 My passion for the philosophy of modern physics course was such that my friend, Subhi El-Qasim (writing his PhD thesis in agriculture at the time), sensing my enthusiasm and looking for a fun course to expand his thought with, decided to take it as well.

CHAPTER 20

FULFILLING A PROMISE TO MOTHER: THE PhD

A ttaining the M.S. degree added to my sense of security and confidence within and without the university. I had something to show for my effort and it gave me breathing space to explore, without undue pressure, possible research projects for the PhD degree. I thought in terms of continuing my research pursuits with Professor Hill. By then, I was aware that his uppermost research preoccupation was the foundation of quantum theory in all its aspects; physical, mathematical and philosophical. It was natural that I would choose to continue with him and use my third M.S. paper as a springboard. Professor Hill welcomed the sentiment, inferring it was worth further pursuit. He, however, warned that this track was not fashionable, that progress might be slow and hard, and that he did not have grant money to support it. Initially, the warning did not seem to deter me. The absence of support was made up for by being offered a senior TA position where I would teach a couple of sections of modern physics lab and help junior TAs as a trouble shooter, and as a liaison between them and Professor Wall. The pay was about the same level as an RA. A fringe benefit and a "sort of duty" of the position was to attend a couple of meetings a week, mid-afternoons, with Professor Wall in his office. The meetings included another senior TA and the chief labs' technician. In these meetings, we went over problems that came up in the freshman-sophomore labs of that week and how to best deal, or to have dealt, with them. Almost always, these problems came as no surprise to Professor Wall and he had something helpful to say about them; nevertheless, he welcomed our input. The meetings were quite informal. Following these meetings was "tea time" and cookies, wherein we were joined by some of Professor Wall's campus friends who paid him a visit. Several of these were almost regular, among them the head secretary in the university president's office, some college deans and former colleagues. When the big wigs came in, the peons went silent and listened. Invariably, the chatter was collegial, broad in scope, and quite informative.

For the following school year, 1959-1960, I was to complete the remaining courses required for the PhD, as well as formulate and get into the PhD thesis research. The conclusion of the research would be written up as the thesis. The thesis would have to be reviewed and approved by a Graduate Advisory Committee, appointed by the Graduate School, and chaired by my major advisor. After thesis review and tentative approval, there would be the thesis defense in the form of a final oral exam before the Graduate Advisory Committee. Upon successful defense of the thesis, the PhD degree would be conferred upon me. By the spring term, the course work was virtually completed. I followed it by taking the qualifying PhD exam,[136] passed it, and was officially admitted as a candidate for the PhD degree. For the thesis research, I took it upon myself to examine critically the wave particle duality of matter. I aimed to give it a conceptualized comprehensible basis, not unlike that of classical physics. I did extensive review of the literature on the subject. I learned a lot about the character of these (quantum) waves and their existing interpretation, but did not succeed toward formulating a deeper, visualizable meaning for them to think in terms of. When I would explain to fellow graduate students my research pursuits, I would invariably be met with the reaction that it was too ambitious, too general, it needed narrowing down, etc. In those days, I had somewhere, somehow, the view that a PhD thesis had to be a revolutionary type of work. Historically, there have been times when this was indeed the case; most often, however, it is considerably of more modest originality and impact. After arduous probing and digging into the nature of wave particle duality without results to show, I shifted to study photon interaction with matter.[137] Photons are energy bundles called quanta constituents of electromagnetic radiation. Professor Hill was interested in learning of a more detailed description or picture of the mechanism of photon absorption or emission by matter. Again,

---

136 This exam administered by the department was the last major hurdle, outside the thesis, toward the attainment of the degree. It usually had written and oral parts. Professor Alfred Nier, famous for his work on enriching uranium during World War II and playing a role in the production of the first atomic bomb, was a member of my oral examination committee. Graduate students tended to approach this exam with a great deal of trepidation.

137 In time, with greater insight, I found it readily demonstrable that the quantum mechanical waves, as commonly used, were really not physical waves in the sense of water waves, but abstract probability or statistical waves. In a sense, Professor Hill and I were trying to swim against the current.

the questions often heard were, "Just what is the photon like?" "What kind of time-spatial configuration does it have?" "How can we glean answers to this from its observed behavior?" Tough questions. I came up with no answers. Professor Hill, for a variety of reasons, left me alone and to my own devices to wander in the wilderness if I must, to stumble and fall if need be. In a real sense, I was self-supporting the research; as a result, nobody was breathing heavily down my neck to produce results. Yet, the process could not go on forever, or too far beyond the norm. Professor Hill was available for advice, but I had to seek it. He did not want to direct or restrict my pursuits. He also never pretended he knew how to tackle these issues. As time passed by and I discussed my research with other students and occasionally with other faculty, I began to get discouraged. Most of the advanced graduate students were RAs, grant-supported. Professor Hill, though very highly regarded and secure in his accomplishments, was seen by many as too idealistic and not pragmatic or expeditious enough in "producing PhDs." Chatter of this sort was rather unkind and not well thought out, yet it gets to you. The reality was more complex. At no time did I allow myself to think negatively of him. He commanded my high regard and esteem, and that will always be so. One important aspect was that he thought of me (or hoped I was) at a certain level of knowledge, creativity, skill, initiative, and maturity, and I was not. Because of my cultural background, I did not fit the typical American graduate student mold. My emotions and motivations were complex; I did not understand them well enough myself at the time to make him realize that. Somehow, I may have needed to be led by the hand more, but that was not his way. I respected that. He enjoyed telling me the story of a PhD student of Paul Dirac, the famous Nobel laureate physicist at England's Cambridge University, who walked over to Professor Dirac one time and asked him to suggest a problem to work on for his thesis, a problem that was well-defined and doable. Dirac answered, "If I knew of such a problem, I would do it myself!" On a couple of occasions, when he would see me somewhat distressed, he would say, "Maybe mathematics research would suit you better," but I knew that would not be so. I loved mathematics, but I saw it as a tool to solve problems. Historically, mathematics grew out of the need to solve real practical human problems. Some may assert that in his latter years, about the time of my association,

Professor Hill was turned off on quantum theory.[138] Even if that is true, he definitely was not alone; he was in the company of some physics giants like Einstein, Schrodinger, and De Broglie.

By the end of that school year, I started contemplating an advisor change and research area. On one hand, I had been aiming high and very idealistically, but not making the kind of progress expected. On the other, I had by then a working wife, who was making big sacrifices for me to complete my graduate studies. I had to consider this and weigh it in the balance. Also, I had a mother expectantly waiting for me to succeed in attaining the PhD degree. The more the days passed by, the greater the urge to travel to Lebanon, crowned with the success of a PhD in hand, and to have Virginia meet my mother and the rest of the family. Virginia and I wanted, sooner rather than later, to go to the Middle East and explore living possibilities there. Consequently, I began to think more and more in pragmatic terms. In the meantime, in June of that year, I decided that the least I could do while thinking on these things was to fulfill the second foreign scientific language competency requirement. With German as the choice, I applied myself intensively to its study. I passed the test on the first try the next exam offering.

After my marriage and attaining the M.S. degree, I felt like getting more involved in the campus Arab-American club affairs. Since I had hoped to serve the Arab World in scientific development after the completion of my graduate work, the least I could do was to test the waters and participate in the campus Arab-American club affairs. I attended meetings regularly, debated issues, appeared on public panels on campus dealing with Arab and Islamic world issues in general, and with the Palestinian-Israeli conflict in particular. I worked on inviting expert Arab public speakers for Arab-American social and political events, mostly on campus. Virginia was guarded in her support and endorsement of these involvements; particularly, when they led to differences or disputes among club members. Some bloomed into lengthy, frequent, and heated, emotional follow-up phone calls to me at home. Often I would find

138 My association with Professor Hill eventually did bear fruit, two papers in particular, one published alone in the American Journal of Physics: AJP. 49, 143, (1981), a second with Don Kobe (also Hill's student!): AJP 57, 658 (1989). There were other fruits less discernable on the surface, but quite valuable, nevertheless. The first paper was in fact dedicated to his memory; sadly, he was deceased by then.

myself in the middle of an exasperating conflict resolution effort. Toward the end of the school year (1959-1960), I was nominated for the office of the president of the club, effective the following school year. It was then that Virginia raised a red flag. Being a more detached observer, she saw more clearly than I did that assuming such a position would seriously jeopardize my PhD pursuit. At the election of the executives meeting, Virginia, by then a voting member, voted against my election in favor of an opposing candidate; he won and I was then elected vice-president. As a vice-president, I could lie low and let the president do the heavy lifting. It was a compromise between her wishes and mine. I tried hard after that to curtail my club involvement in deference to Virginia and in my dispassionate assessment that my graduate study should come first. The Arab scene, particularly as it bore on the Palestinian problem, and what one could do about it, continued to burn unabated inside me, and demanded my interest and attention. In fact, it was during the school year 1959-1960 that I developed symptoms of what turned out to be a (chronic) duodenal ulcer followed that summer by hay fever allergies and psychosomatic health problems that bothered me for many years thereafter.

In the fall of 1959, I had enrolled in a year course in advanced quantum mechanics, often termed "quantum field theory;" the most advanced course in the department. Professor Donald R. Yennie was the course teacher. He was relatively young (mid-thirties) and belonged to the modern school of quantum physics, and a practitioner thereof. Professor Yennie had joined the department in the fall of 1957, and had come from Stanford University. He was already forming a small group of theorists, he being the director of the group. He had gotten his PhD from Columbia University, working under Yochiro Yukawa, the famous Japanese Nobel laureate theoretical physicist. He practiced physics research more as a team player than an ivory tower sage. He collaborated with physicists from all over the world. He, off and on, would invite guest physicists to the department; typically, from major physics centers in the country.

While I was active in class discussions, I was much less so in seminars, and the weekly departmental colloquia; where the atmosphere was august and commanding, especially the colloquia, when a large number of the departmental luminaries were apt to be present. Unless you really knew what you were about to say, it was wisest to listen, ponder, and be quiet. Professor

Yennie seemed to enjoy my uninhibited class participation and encouraged it. The class enrollment was about half a dozen, which aided the informality. In hindsight, Professor Yennie saw me bringing a healthy different perspective to the subject and welcomed it.

For a while Professor Yennie and I did not entertain research under his tutelage, I being Professor Hill's advisee. The feeling began to change toward the end of the school year. Professor Yennie let me know, usually by inference, that I have the potential to do a quality thesis in the field, and that he would accept me as his advisee if I so chose. He already had several PhD students to his credit, some graduated, and some making good progress towards graduating. I saw that he worked closely with his advisees, socialized with them, was goal-oriented, and did not allow his students to stray too far afield. These features seemed to be what I needed, but at the same time, aroused considerable trepidation in me. On one hand, I wondered whether I would live up to his expectations, or whether I would flounder and not rise to the challenge. He was, after all, the leading theorist in the department; if I failed with him, there would be nowhere else to go within the department. On the other hand, there was also the consideration of how to disengage graciously from Professor Hill, though I felt by then that Professor Hill would understand. To be on the safe side, I decided for a while not to make any decisions or moves. My TA was secure for the summer of 1960 and the following year, and I decided to give myself more time.

By the fall term of 1960, the urgency to change was great. I made the necessary moves in as kind a way as I could. Professor Yennie became my major advisor. However, I did not seek RA status, though his advanced advisees typically were RAs. Professor Yennie had research grants that enabled him to do that, but I did not seek one, unsure if I would and could deliver the goods. The Van de Graaf experience probably influenced my conduct, and the matter rested there. My relationship with Professor Hill remained cordial. Professor Yennie decided not to assign me a thesis project of a calculational nature, which usually had a research grant, particularly since I was managing a senior TA position. Calculational thesis projects usually required operational skills with equations to obtain a numerical answer to be tested against an experimental measurement. It was not as much conceptually innovative or fundamental in character. Some of his students were doing theses in this category. Based on his evaluation, he chose to steer me toward a fundamental pursuit, and encouraged me to do more study of the mathematical foundation of quantum theory. He thought, in so doing, he and I might stumble on something quite noteworthy. We essentially spent a year in this pursuit. Unfortunately, the year passed and I had nothing concrete to show for except learning theoretical methodologies in field theory. During that year, Professor Yennie obtained a Senior Fellowship to do research at the Nuclear Research Center in Orsay, France for the school year 1961-1962. He was excited about the prospect and considered the fellowship a great feather in his cap. He, in the meantime, arranged for the hiring of the physics faculty member, Dr. Steve Gasiorowicz, who was at University of California, Berkeley. Dr. Gasiorowicz made it to the department just before Professor Yennie left for France. Professor Yennie introduced me to Dr. Gasiorowicz and recommended that I seek his assistance, as needed, in my research pursuits. He did the same with another student, Bob Oakes. Bob Oakes was a stellar graduate student. He had an undergraduate degree in electrical engineering from UMN, did his master's degree work, Plan A, with Professor Alfred Nier, in experimental spectroscopy[139] before changing to field theory. Professor Yennie offered Oakes and me RAs. He thought it would allow us more time, and incentivize us to work unencumbered on our theses' research, an offer that I could not refuse. I gave up my senior TA. In the fall of 1961, to facilitate things further, Dr. Gasiorowicz offered a course on high-energy elementary particles, generally within the context of quantum field theory, that I took along with a handful of other interested students, including Bob Oakes.

   In the spring of that school year (1960-1961), both Bob Oakes and I learned about a six-weeks summer institute in theoretical high-energy elementary particle physics to be held at Brandeis University in Waltham, an outskirt of Boston, Massachusetts. The guest lecturers were on the cutting edge; they included some Nobel laureates, and some on their way to becoming one. It could not have been more timely and appropriate for our career development. We applied to be student-participants; we were both accepted and granted

---

139 Cf. fn136

financial support, including travel and living expenses. I recall Professor Yennie being quite happy. For me, it was a bright moment in an otherwise uneventful year.

Both Bob and I had wives but no children. We independently decided that our wives would go along. For Virginia, who welcomed the opportunity, it meant asking for a leave without pay; she was granted the leave. Bob and his wife drove there. Virginia and I, having no car and not of a mind to have one and drive that far, decided to go by train. We were provided with a list of housing places and possibilities by the institute's staff. We were led to a furnished apartment in Waltham. A church minister and his wife were the regular occupants; but they were going to be away for that summer. We rented it sight unseen, in advance of our arrival. It turned out to be quite respectable, and superior to our own in Minneapolis. The only drawback was the distance to walk to the campus, which was about two miles. Under the circumstances, I felt that the walk was manageable, considering my dexterity and love for walking. As the summer progressed, however, my enthusiasm for walking was dampened by the presence of multitudes of loose dogs on the streets of Waltham that at times trailed behind me in packs. My unease about this was compounded by the fact that in my childhood and adolescence, in Palestine and Lebanon, dogs generally ran loose, unclean, owned by nobody in particular, and cared for very little. Some could get aggressive. The dogs in Waltham seemed to have collars on them, yet apparently were not required to be on a leash.[140] Fortunately, I survived the stay, despite some anxious moments, without any bites or otherwise physical harm.

The daily lectures at the institute were extensive, typically three in the morning and two in the afternoon. The attendees numbered about fifty, from around the world; mostly advanced PhD students or post-doctoral researchers. The largest contingents were from the USA and Western Europe in that order, yet there were Russians, Japanese, Chinese, Indians, among others, as well. There was a handful of Israelis. They were readily recognizable to me by their use of Hebrew and growing up among them in Haifa. I was the only one from the Arab World at the Institute. It was a while before any of the

---

140 If they were required by law to be on leash, it was not being heeded or enforced.

Israeli members recognized my presence as a Palestinian. The encounters were distant, but civil.

The lectures were advanced, stimulating, and demanding. I absorbed some better than others. I made friends and engaged in helpful discussions with many. I gained a firsthand view of what active forefront researchers in field theory and high-energy physics were pursuing and the major issues of the day.

There were a few members, attendees and faculty, who lived in the Boston area and would drive up to Brandeis on a daily basis. Every now and then I would hitch a ride back to our apartment from one of these attendees. One memorable and steady ride provider in particular, who took a personal interest, was Frank Von Hipple. Occasionally, after a ride, I would invite him into the apartment to socialize. Virginia typically would serve coffee and whatever was available in the sweet department. He was most kind, friendly, and willing to take the time. I learned that he had grown up around MIT where his father, Arthur R. Von Hipple, a member of the Applied Physics Department, was of world fame in the field of materials research. I could not resist but reflect to myself on our vastly different backgrounds; yet, I did not give much thought as to what kind of (bright) future may lie ahead for him. In later years, it was thrilling for me to see him advance to become a world figure in the field of energy resources and the environment. Whenever we would run into each other at future physics meetings, he would stop by to say hello and chat.

Virginia loved the time in Waltham. She had been to Boston before. The Mother Church, headquarters of the Christian Science denomination, is in Boston. She had participated in a variety of church activities, particularly as a college student, that took her there. She relished the Sunday morning and Wednesday evening services in the commanding edifice of the Mother Church. Briefly put, in an analogous frame of reference, it was like Mecca for Muslims. She was also aware of the rich history of the area that went back to the revolutionary times and the formation of the country. Virginia made an excellent tour guide. Wherever we traveled, she got maps and travel information and studied them well, usually well beforehand. On weekends, we spent as much time as I could afford sightseeing and learning about the area. We did cultural things—museums, historical landmarks and trails, attended a Boston Pop concert, and more. I also found out that there was a sizable Arab-

American community there. We went to a great length to get familiar with it.[141] I further looked up my UMN buddy, Parviz Mahmoodi, who, after his PhD, got a research fellowship in the applied physics department at Harvard University. One weekend, he generously drove us around and took us for a swim in the Atlantic. The swim in the Atlantic was quite different from the Mediterranean, the water being much colder, and the bottom rapidly dropping deeper.

As the institute folded up, I was impressed by the participants' strong passion for, commitment to, and deep involvement in their research. If there were things that stood out as common among so many of them, they included clear, uncluttered single-mindedness, intellectual courage, independence, focus, and perseverance. For example, my friend Bob was already thinking in terms of a specific research problem for his thesis, and was building his skills and knowledge to tackle it. In my case, I was still unsettled about a specific research problem. Perhaps I was timid to take one on and fail to carry through with it. I found my mastery level of skills and tools for research in the quantum field theory of high-energy physics was still lacking. I made up my mind that summer that if I hoped to succeed in this pursuit, I had better settle down to really upgrade my skills and sharpen my tools.

Upon Virginia's urging, our return to Minneapolis included an excursionary train detour, of about a week, into New York City and Washington, D.C. The Washington visit was a first for me; it opened my eyes wide to the magnificence of the city with its mammoth government buildings, notably the Capitol, the White House, the Mall, important memorials, museums, and their layout.

By the time I got back to the UMN, Professor Yennie had left for his sabbatical in France. While Bob settled down on his PhD research in close association with Professor Gasiorowicz as advisor, I kept a distance except for occasional visits. In the meantime, Virginia went back to her job with General Mills. Professor Gasiorowicz did not apply any pressure nor try to coax me into a project; rather, he left me alone. I decided to use the time of Professor Yennie's absence to improve my mastery of the methods of quantum field theory, which I figured would be handy once a specific project was undertaken upon Professor Yennie's return. So for the school year 1961-1962, while on

---

141 Boston was also a major home for the famous Lebanese-American, Khalil (alternately written as Kahlil) Gibran, author of *The Prophet.*

a research assistantship (RA), that was basically all I did, except for periods of discouragement and or distraction, often by events in the Middle East. During that year, I shared an office with another PhD candidate, Don Kobe. Don had been a classmate for the past three years, but we did not do much with each other until then. He was doing research in low energy theoretical physics with a different advisor, Warren B. Cheston. The methods of his research were rather different from the quantum field theory. As a result, we did not discuss our work beyond generalities. Yet, he and I had the right personal chemistry. For his part, he was single and rather shy; he did not make friends easily at the time; for my part, I was still in some sort of wilderness, research-wise, and needed the empathy and support he provided. We developed a good friendship. From time to time he would visit Virginia and me at our apartment. Don's father was a professor of chemistry at the University of Texas, Austin.

By the end of the school year, both Bob and Don completed their PhD research and graduated while I was still learning methods I might need to do the research. Bob went to Stanford to be a post-doctoral research fellow and Don went to Taiwan to teach and do research there. I was genuinely happy for both of them and wished them well, but I became concerned about what the future held for me.[142]

Late in the spring of 1962, Professor Yennie came back from France to find me still not having started a specific project. He had a long visit with me. The visit was cordial. Through it all, I never felt any kind of censure or scolding. He merely said that I needed to start something specific soon; that I couldn't just study methods forever and that it wouldn't get me anywhere. He said that I needed to meet with him at least once every two weeks; but preferably more often as warranted. I agreed, though I felt some discomfort, but knew that the plan was for my own good.

With the return of Professor Yennie, the theoretical group shifted into a higher gear of seminars and individual research activity exchanges. I had become, by then, a full member of the group and was expected to participate actively in its proceedings, including some of the social functions. One of the early guests to

---

142 Both Bob and Don have developed into highly regarded, internationally recognized physicists.

come was Professor Sheldon Glashow, at the time, of Harvard University.[143] Professor Glashow talked about the latest discoveries in extremely unstable particles that were called resonances and their decay schemes. Among these were two termed the rho and omega resonances, their decay schemes did not fit predictions of pre-existing models. He conjectured a coupling mechanism that could explain this unexpected behavior. He then provided a sketchy procedure by which he was able to quantitatively estimate the observed seemingly discrepant decays. It was felt that there was merit and perhaps even a need to develop formal and detailed quantum mechanical derivations by which the calculations could be methodically and unambiguously carried out. Professor Yennie turned to me to work on the problem. He and I met separately thereafter whereby he handed me a couple of pages of handwritten notes pointing how I might approach the task. He told me to report back before long as to how well I was progressing. Within a few days I got back and reported accordingly. He seemed pleased and asked me to continue along these lines further till we could get to the goal of a detailed derivation for the calculation of the decay schemes. The effort lasted about four months. I managed to carry out all his suggestions and at times, go well beyond them. I reported my work in a couple of seminars to the theoretical group; they were well-received. My methods shed light on how to use methods of quantum theory to describe coupled unstable particles, and the influence of the coupling on their decay schemes, hitherto undone before. It was toward the end of 1962 when he told me to write up the work as part of my thesis, and also, prepare a journal article based on the thesis write-up for publication. "The *Nuovo Cimento Journal* would be a good place for its submittal," he said. "You will be the sole author, since you did most of the work, and this will help you professionally."[144] He was not ready, however, to declare the work sufficient for a full PhD thesis.

About that time, a private communication from Professor Lawrence C. Biedenharn, Jr. of Duke University, North Carolina, to Professor Yennie,

---

143 1979 Nobel Laureate in physics with Abdus Salam and Steven Weinberg.

144 Sometime in 1962, about the time I was wrapping up the couple resonance research, a paper by J. Bernstein and G. Feinberg appeared in the Nuovo Cimento Journal which dealt with the same basic problem and worked out similar answers, although using different methods: Nuovo Cimento 25, 1343 (1962). Professor Yennie, nevertheless, felt my work was still publishable because of its different and more general methods.

inquiring of him about the magnitude of the angular momentum of the radiated field in electron scattering from nuclei, the radiation termed bremsstahlung.[145] He seemed to suggest that it would be infinitely large. If so, it would violate the important physical principle of angular momentum conservation, as well as being physically contradictory. Professor Yennie had earlier published an important paper dealing with other aspects of the scattering of the electron off nuclei, but not with the angular momentum. Professor Yennie shared the communication with me and asked me to consider how we might respond to Professor Biedenharn's concern. I took Professor Biedenharn's communication and read and reread it several times. After considerable thought, I decided the surest way to deal with the question was to try to find a way to calculate directly the angular momentum of the radiated field in the electron scattering process. Could I formulate a method of calculation, I asked myself? The study of methods that I engaged in the previous year finally came in handy and I was able to formulate a procedure, but did not carry out the details. It was time for consultation, so I went to Professor Yennie and showed him my plan. He was clearly impressed and gave me the green light to go ahead and work out the details. For the next several months, I embarked on carrying out the details of the calculations. I reported the work to the theoretical physics group in a couple of seminars. I also submitted, with Professor Yennie's consent and his advice, an abstract for a paper presentation of the preliminary results at the 1963 annual winter meeting of the American Physical Society in New York. I flew (first time ever on a plane) to New York City for the meeting and made the presentation. I briefly discussed the paper at the meeting with Professor Julian Schwinger of Harvard University.[146] The upshot of the calculations showed that angular momentum was not divergent or infinitely large. The calculation of the square of the angular momentum, however, did diverge to infinity, but signified physically meaningless, non-measurable fluctuations, in view of the incoherent emission of the radiation. There was no violation of angular momentum conservation, and the apparent contradiction was explained away.

---

145 Biedenharn is a world-renowned physicist for his work on angular momentum in quantum mechanics. Non-technically speaking, angular momentum can be thought of as quantity of rotation or twist.

146 Was awarded the Physics Nobel Prize with Sin-Itiro Tomonaga and Richard Feynman, in 1965.

By the end of February 1963, Professor Yennie gave me the green light to write up both works; the one dealing with the coupled resonances, and the one dealing with the calculation of the angular momentum of the radiation field, to submit as my PhD thesis. I eagerly did so. A Graduate Advisory Committee was formed and a date for the defense of the thesis was set toward the end of May 1963; the thesis defense is called "final oral exam."

On the appointed time and day, I appeared before the advisory committee. I successfully defended the thesis, thus passing the final oral exam. In so doing I had fulfilled *all* the requirements for receiving the PhD degree. The feeling of relief and exhilaration I felt immediately after walking out of the exam room, and the congratulations of the committee members, chaired by Professor Yennie, were indescribable. I was done! Thank God Almighty! I was done! I went straight to our apartment, where Virginia was waiting. No words were needed; she read the news written all over me. We rejoiced and partied—a dream come true, a promise to my mother and family fulfilled; perhaps two years late; but late is far, far better than never!

The final exam time was a bit too late for my graduation to be included in the June commencement of the university. Instead, it would be honored in the July commencement. The question arose as to whether I should stay around campus to go through the July exercises with the appropriate cap, gown and hood conference. I was far more interested in going to Lebanon to celebrate with my mother and the family than staying for the graduation ceremonies. It would have been desirable to go through this "once in a life time" event— invite special people to it, people who played an important part toward achieving this end—but my yearning to see my mother after six years of separation, and to take Virginia to meet the clan won the day.

Sometime in the spring when it was becoming clear that the end is near, Professor Yennie urged me to start applying for postdoctoral research fellowships. I applied in several places. Professor Yennie, in particular, and other members of the theoretical physics group, notably Professor Gasiorowicz, supported my applications with strong recommendations. Sometime in April, I received an offer from the Physics Department of the University of Michigan, Ann Arbor, to be a research associate in theoretical physics. It was clearly superior to most other likely offers that may have been in the pipeline, but were not in hand. I, therefore, gladly accepted it. It was to begin in September 1963. As things later unfolded, I never regretted the decision.

With a heart full of gratitude, I acknowledge the evident and important role of Professor Yennie in my attaining the PhD degree and the job I got at the University of Michigan. In many ways, he tried to open doors and acculturate me to the research community of quantum field theory and high-energy physics. He encouraged me to attend regional conferences pertinent to our research such as those that were annually held at the Argonne National Lab.[147] During his tutelage, Virginia and I were often guests at his home. Typically, the invitations were to receptions given in honor of some of the visiting guests to the theoretical research group. I met, or were in the presence of, many leaders on the research frontier.[148] At a Thanksgiving dinner we were invited to at his house, we were among some of the top brass in the physics department; among them was the director of the Linear Accelerator (LINAC) Lab, Professor John Williams and his wife.[149] To further shed light on the kind of person Professor Yennie was,[150] he at times would agree to meet me on campus on Saturdays to discuss and review my research progress. The two of us would break for lunch to have pizza at Dinky Town or on Washington Avenue. On one occasion, as we were finishing up a session on a Saturday afternoon, I asked him if he would be interested in coming to our apartment to have a cup of coffee with me and Virginia. With a smile, he said, "I would love to," and he did.

147 Is a major government Lab outside Chicago.
148 e.g. Bob Karplus, Steve Frautchi, Sheldon Glashow .
149 Professor Williams was a member of the Manhattan Project during World War II.
150 Deceased, 1993.

CHAPTER 21

ANOTHER PROMISE: THE RETURN

Anticipating that we would not stay for the graduation ceremonies, Virginia and I drew up a tentative plan for a round trip to Lebanon and back to Minneapolis by air, with various stops in countries on the way going over and coming back. Departure and return times were set for the middle of June and middle of August respectively. Professor Yennie had recommended that I should spend the last two weeks of August back in the department to prepare a draft of a paper, based on the angular momentum thesis work, for publication in the *Physical Review Journal*, before I started my job on September 1 in Ann Arbor; I fully concurred. I also felt that he should be a co-author, and he accepted.

Virginia engaged Thomas Cook Travel, an international travel agency with offices all over the world to access help should the need arise. Ever since we got married, we initiated a program of saving for this long awaited day. By travel time, we had savings to cover the trip expenses and manage for a few months afterwards. With a job upon return, we could afford to treat ourselves better. We got rid of all the apartment furniture and belongings except what we needed for the trip. Our important books were boxed and stored for later retrieval. We planned to buy furniture as needed upon arrival in Ann Arbor. We allotted six weeks of the two months travel for our stay in the Middle East.

In reality, I was not too enthusiastic about the stops, particularly the ones on the way over to Lebanon. I was very eager to get to the family as soon as possible; but Virginia, who used her head more than her heart, saw the additional opportunities, at modest additional cost, and did not think it smart to let them pass by. On the appointed time and day, we took off from the Minneapolis Airport.

On the way over, there were stops in Madrid, and Alicanté in Spain; Oran and Algiers in Algeria; Cairo in Egypt and finally, Beirut. The way back had stops in Cairo again; Athens, Greece; Rome, Venice, Italy; Munich and Frankfurt, West Germany, with Zurich, Switzerland, sandwiched in between; London, England; Paris, France, and then back to Minneapolis.

Madrid was a beautiful, modern, vibrant European metropolis, rich with history, art, and culture. We visited, among many things—museums, war memorials, national parks, the square and café frequented by Ernest Hemingway.

The flight out of Madrid to Oran was on a relatively small plane; it had an intermediary stop in the small Spanish coastal fishing town, Alicanté, before we proceeded to Oran. We hit our first snag in Oran, Algeria. In the excitement of the moment as we got off the plane, I left my raincoat, which I had just bought in Minneapolis, on the plane. Although I recognized my oversight in the lobby of the airport, I was not allowed to go back onto the plane, which was still on the ground and in view, nor could I get anyone from the airline staff to help me retrieve it; all in the name of security! I filled out a form for later mailing once it turned up. I never saw it again. We had scheduled a stay of two days to look around before the flight to Algiers. After settling down in the hotel, Virginia and I decided to take a stroll outside the hotel to see what we could see. It was early afternoon. It did not take long before I realized that things did not look right. The surroundings seemed charged with social and political tension. The streets were virtually empty and eerie looking. I saw a fellow sweeping and cleaning in front of a house, he looked Arabic. He was in his early twenties. I decided to greet him with the traditional *"Salamu alaykum"* ("Peace upon you.") greeting and see what I might learn from him. Sure enough, he spoke good Arabic.[151] He essentially told me that Oran was no place for tourists and sightseeing, that there was a lot of killing going on in retribution against those who collaborated with the French during the long and bloody war (1954-1962) of independence, formally concluded less than a year before. I calmly explained to Virginia what I understood, and we both walked straight back to the hotel. With Virginia's clearly northern European features, I became concerned that we could become targets, albeit mistakenly. We decided it was better to stay put in the hotel. I bought a couple of Arabic newspapers to learn more about what we were into while we contemplated our next move. Fortunately, the hotel had a coffee shop where we could eat. The menu, however, was extremely limited, and the cost substantially higher than

---

151 Most Algerians in those days, shortly after independence, spoke a north African dialect that was a mix of Arabic and French that made it hard for me to communicate with them; particularly those who had not had much schooling, nor were practicing Muslims.

even the bigger cities in the U.S., an obscene inflation as a result of the war. We found out that there was a Thomas Cook Travel office nearby. We stopped by to see if we could leave Oran sooner than was planned. They could not oblige us; there were not many flights in and out of Oran in any given week. We impatiently hung around the hotel for the two remaining days of our stay. Then, we headed to Algiers, our next scheduled stop.

The atmosphere in Algiers was less eerie, but we could still tell, not "touristic!" We had previously allotted a three-day stay. However, as soon as we got there, I started finding out how we might continue onto Cairo sooner. I had no luck at the airport. There were only two flights a week to Cairo; the earliest was not early enough, and all were booked anyhow. Thomas Cook was not of any more help than it was in Oran. After we checked into the hotel downtown Algiers, which looked over the Algiers Harbor and had a rather charming overview, I started looking around to see what I could find out in terms of a quicker departure to Cairo. There was a small United Arab Airline office nearby. The office head turned out to be a friendly Egyptian in his mid-thirties. It was not hard for me to quickly fraternize with him. I explained our situation. Initially, he told me there was not much he could do to help; yet, he was sympathetically touched by my presence in Algiers with an American wife to look around, and where I was and where I was going. He then offered to come to the lobby of our hotel for his coffee break. He would look me up and we would think about the problem together in a more private and relaxed way. I welcomed his offer. In a short time, we got together in the hotel lobby; Virginia came along. We socialized and had a few laughs for a while before we got into the business at hand. During our chat, I told him how proud I was of the Algerians getting their independence, and the role Egypt, under Nasser, had played. I said, "Algeria's heroic accomplishments made me want to see the country for myself, that is why, when the opportunity presented itself, we put Oran and Algiers on our travel itinerary; but now, we find there is not much we can do but spend a lot of money sitting in a hotel!" He listened carefully. He then quietly told us that there was a United Arab Airline flight scheduled to Cairo the next day. The flight, however, was chartered by the Algerian military. The Algerian military was before independence the fighting force within the Algerian National Liberation Front, for brevity denoted by the acronym FLN

(French for "Front de Libération Nationale"). With independence, the FLN became the governing body of Algeria. The chartered plane was to transport Algerian army officers (formerly rebels) to Egypt for training. He then said that he would check with them to see if they could spare two seats for Virginia and me, if that would be agreeable to us. I looked at Virginia to see what she thought. We both felt that anything that would get us out and onto Cairo as soon as possible was OK. With that he excused himself, saying: "I'll get back to you a little later." In a span of a couple of hours, he called to inform me that he got two seats; he would stop by in the evening to give us further details. In the evening he made sure that we knew when, how, and where to be at the airport to go for the flight the following day. I thanked him profusely as he bade us farewell.

The flight to Cairo was all men (except for Virginia) ranging in age from their twenties to their forties. It took off around 9:00 am. There was hardly any service on the flight, or stewards. The officers had individual food and drink supplies for the trip. We endured the lack of service quietly. During the flight, nobody spoke to us. We made it to Cairo late in the afternoon. The flight was rough and bumpy and aroused concern for our safety. I attributed it to the poor skills of the pilot, as the weather was good and the sky clear. There were two stops for refueling, one in Bizerte, Tunisia, and the second, in Benghazi, Libya; both landings were in military bases. Notwithstanding the bare bone roughed-up character of the flight, I took pleasure in being in Benghazi, albeit briefly, because of its name, "Son of Ghazi," and because of its prominence during World War II!

In Cairo, we had a stay of three days before our flight to Beirut.[152] The hotel we stayed in, the Continental, was right downtown. In Cairo, both Virginia and I had a culture shock. The crowds were everywhere. You had to elbow your way to walk many of the streets. The public transportation was virtually inaccessible to us and cabs were hard to come by. When you got a cab, you had to bargain, and still pay a high price. We nevertheless decided to make the best of our stay. Except for one cab ride to see the home of President Nasser, we did not see much outside the immediate surroundings; not even the pyramids.

---

152 Our "going over" stop in Cairo was short by design because we had planned a longer stop on our return trip.

Everything seemed complicated. We did not want to make a flight change to cut our stay there, and thus, get to Lebanon sooner. The change would have been hard to communicate to the family in Lebanon, who had planned to meet us in a big way at the Beirut airport on the previously designated time. On the day of the flight to Beirut, via United Arab Airline, we found out that the flight was going to be several hours late. We stopped at the airline office to find out the particulars for the delay. We encountered Mr. Ahmad Shuqueiri, a prominent member of the Palestine High Commission during the 1940s, a real historical figure, sitting at the office in wait of service. He was a lawyer by education, an eloquent orator and champion of Palestinian causes, in particular, and Arab causes, in general. He had a regular radio time on *Voice of Palestine*. I recognized him right away from pictures I had seen years before. He was distinguishably and impeccably dressed in a white linen suit. It was a memorable thrill. The office secretary had not much to tell us about the flight other than its rescheduled time of departure.

Our excursionary adventure to see the home of President Nasser turned out to be amusing and memorable as well. It was motivated by my great admiration and irrational childish zeal to see President Nasser and to shake his hand; may be also to say a few complimentary words. When we got there and got out of the cab, we asked the cab driver to wait for us, and walked to the gate. At the gate, an armed guard in uniform met us. I explained my desire to see the President in a very affectionate and passionate way. I further explained that I had just gotten back from the USA and that it might be my only chance. The guard had a big bemused grin on his face and apologized that he couldn't let us in. I then asked how we could arrange to see him. He simply said he did not know; all he knew was that we could not go in. We then turned back to the waiting cab, somewhat let down; the cab took us back to our hotel. It was nothing like the experience on my first visit to Washington, D.C. (summer of 1961) where it was straightforward to tour the White House, and if you were lucky, bump into the President, and maybe even shake hands with him.[153]

The flight to Beirut arrived late in the evening; it was supposed to arrive before noon. There was no simple way for me to relay the delays to the family in

---

153 Security concerns since then, particularly after 9/11, have made things much less straightforward.

Lebanon on such a short notice. Telephones were hard to come by, international calls were expensive, and none of my immediate family had a phone. Yet, when we walked into the airport lobby, there was my mother still waiting to meet us. She had stuck it out at the airport all day for the flight to arrive. Uncle Amin and his wife had kept her company. They had been kept informed by the airline of the flight delays. Many of the family members who had come in from Tyre to meet us at the scheduled arrival time couldn't wait and had to go back to Tyre to attend to their families and to sleep in their homes. Sleeping in hotels did not come easy to them, and would have been turned to only as a last resort. The meeting as expected was very emotional, but joy-filled. Mother's sticking it out at the airport all day did not surprise me; that was my mother all right! She welcomed Virginia with an embrace and a few English sentences in a British accent. There was absolutely no reservation in my mother's embrace of Virginia, physically and figuratively; she was simply her daughter-in-law in all respects. We stayed overnight in Beirut with Uncle Amin and his wife.

The next morning, after a typical local breakfast, e.g., tea, olives, *zatar* (a mixture of herbs like thyme, sage, with salt and sesame seeds) *labane*, olive oil and pocket bread, we hired a taxi service, and headed straight to Tyre. In those days, the taxi service fare for the trip was about ten dollars, to me by then, quite manageable.[154] In Tyre, at the home that I had left six years ago, we were met by lots of relatives, many of whom had before doubted that I would ever come back. There were two live lambs in the front yard waiting to be slaughtered at the front steps of the house before Virginia and I could enter. This practice, that approximates a religious ritual, was customary when a family member comes back home *safely* after a long absence. The sacrificial lamb signifies an offering to God in gratitude. Doing the same for Virginia was saying that she was a fully-cherished member of the family. The meat is generally given away to the poor and denied to the "returnee" and his or her immediate household. The butcher, who was also a cousin, slaughtered the first lamb right on the front step as I crossed over it going into the house, followed by the second

---

154 Taxicab service, henceforth "service car," in many countries of the Middle East worked differently from the U.S. Often it was a one-man operation, with the driver and the car owner being one and the same. Fares for customized service, off normal routes, were routinely negotiated.

slaughtered lamb, with Virginia doing likewise. Shouts of joy and ululations were sounded by some of the women on the scene as we went into the house.

Virginia showed sensitive awareness of the significance of the moment, reciprocated the warmth with which she was received, and was a good sport. Of course, over at least the two years before the trip, I had gone to great lengths to explain to her how the family lived, the facilities, particularly bathing and washroom facilities; that toilet seats are more rarity than common; absent in our home. To defecate, one squatted over a hole in the floor. "Toiletries" in bathrooms, public or private, such as tissue paper, napkins, soap, etc., could not be counted on to be available. We further went over things such as water pollution and "drink-ability," general sanitation and hygiene, or lack thereof, the "dos and don'ts" of the culture, and so on and so forth.

In hindsight, Virginia was better equipped than I had tended to credit her for. In fact, I tended to underestimate her ability to rough it. As a teenager, she was an avid camper and a Girl Scout. She had slept in tents and cooked on open fires, using gathered firewood. She was an avid moviegoer, and had seen many western movies. Her father was an avid hunter, and she grew up around hunted deer carcasses, geese, ducks, etc. Also, through her avid religiosity, she could relate some of what she was experiencing to some of the bible stories she had read.

The first week we were there, she offered to make pies for the family, apple and peach. She thought it would be fun and gave her something to do. The family did not have an oven to bake in, but that did not deter her. In short order, she put up one together using things around the household; e.g., bricks, aluminum sheet reflectors and firewood; just like she used to do in scout camp. Unfortunately, to my surprise and hers, most everybody was unwilling to try the pies. A little bit of ashes had fallen on the pies' top and seemed to many to be a big objectionable hurdle. Only a few brave ones tried them, and fewer less, complimented her.[155]

As for housing, the family, however, did everything within their power to provide us with private quarters to sleep in, and with clean and comfortable bedding. As a home economics major, Virginia took special interest in, and

[155] Many family members did not, at least in those days, master the art of social grace when it came to comment on the food and clothes of others; many of them did not mince words if they did not like something. Yet, these things were not meant to injure.

was very observant of, all sorts of practices around the house. In years that followed, I was continually amazed by the things she would mention that she had observed or learned during that time, that heretofore I had paid little attention to, or simply took for granted. She was struck in a big way by the absence of refrigeration in the house, particularly in regard to preserving meat and leftovers. Almost everything had to be consumed in a span of twenty-four hours. Also, she was quite struck by the amount of visitation that Arabs indulge in with each other, and the coffee and cookies served. After the first week, she would tire of, "So and so is coming to greet us," because we had to make sure to be home and ready to receive him or them at the appointed time. Thanks to some of my grown-up nieces who could speak English, I was able to let Virginia go with them to look around Tyre, while I received many of my old friends and shared with them some of my experiences in America. One day I was taken quite by surprise when, alone with my mother, she pointed out that I was neglecting my wife, and that I should try harder to pay her more attention. When I reflected on it, I realized how right she was. The thing that surprised me most was that she was so perceptive across cultures, even to understand subtle interactions between Virginia and me. She cared so much for our welfare, and was ready to admonish or correct me if and when I strayed.

My return to Lebanon, after almost six years, found brother Fouad at work in Qatar, on the Persian Gulf. He had graduated as a civil engineer from AUB in June 1961, and was busy earning a living there. Upon graduation, he moved his family, wife and six children to live in Tripoli. He had rented an apartment for them in a building next to the building where brother Hamadi with his family, wife and eight children, had a rented apartment. It was the customary course of action in those times, particularly for Palestinian men with special skills, to seek work in the Arab oil rich states by the Persian Gulf. Typically, the wife and children stayed behind. It was felt that Hamadi would oversee the daily needs of Fouad's family as a father substitute. In those days, it would have been viewed quite unwise and irresponsible to leave a wife and a bunch of children alone in a community to fend for themselves without some sort of access to a male protection and guidance. Hamadi was happy to do it. Fouad's wife and Hamadi's wife were sisters; the thought was, therefore, the combined families would function like one big family.

It was inconceivable that Fouad and I would not find a way to get together before the end of my stay in Lebanon. The timing of my coming back did not jibe well with his work situation; he nevertheless applied for a family emergency leave, which was granted. When Hamadi and Fouad came together from Tripoli to see me and meet Virginia in Tyre, the housing accommodations did not allow them to stay any extended period. Thereafter, Virginia and I went to Tripoli and spent time with the two brothers and their families as well. Mother accompanied us. It seemed right to include Yousef's wife, Nadiema, in this trip. It was the least we could do to show appreciation for her hosting us in Tyre. This we did, and we had a few days of magnificent time in Tripoli before returning to Tyre. Hamadi took great pleasure in showing us around Tripoli, and showing us off to his friends and acquaintances as well. He frequently told Virginia that he was taking her to places off the beaten track that tourists rarely get to see. Virginia loved the tours into the narrow alleyways with the little shops such as the butcher, the baker, the shoemaker, etc. With camera around her neck, she took numerous pictures. The sweet shops were particularly impressive. Many were of high quality and displayed a large variety of sweets. We took time and chatted with the proprietors and workers. A master sweet maker recalled to us a famous Arabic proverb: "Not everybody who shuffles sweet trays is a sweet maker." The implication being that it is an art form, a lot more than busy mechanics. Just before departing Tripoli, we took a brief trip to the mountains nearby and admired old cedar trees of biblical fame.

Back at the time when Virginia and I were planning our trip to Lebanon, as I was finishing up my PhD thesis, Carole, my sister-in-law, expressed serious interest in traveling along with us, at least part of the time. Carole had graduated in the spring of 1962 with a B.S. in home economics from North Dakota State University (NDSU) and was in her first year of graduate study at Michigan State University of East Lansing, Michigan (MSUEL). She was working for her M.S. degree in "Foods" as a major. My mother-in-law encouraged the prospect. Virginia and I welcomed it with the proviso that we go ahead of her for a time and that she catch up after Virginia and I had a chance to settle and get somewhat comfortable with the family. Carole decided she would take a ship rather than fly to Beirut. In so doing, she would catch up with us in Beirut two weeks after we arrived there. This seemed to suit us fine. Carole took a passenger freighter ship from New York City with stops in Cadiz, Spain; Marseilles, France; Napoli, Italy; Alexandria, Egypt; and then Beirut. We had a hearty reception for her as she disembarked at the Beirut harbor. In addition to Virginia and me, I had my nephew (also, milk brother) Qasim accompany us. Qasim was single and by then was a grade school teacher on summer vacation. He was happy to avail himself to us. He was fun to have around, a trusted companion, and a security blanket for me. I had been out of the country six years and was not as at ease in dealing with cab drivers, vendors, coffee shop waiters, etc. as he was.

It was a lovely sunny summer day as we loaded Carole's baggage in our accompanying service car and headed all four of us to Tyre along the coastal road. The coastal drive with its beauty, charm, and richness of memory, had meant so much to me over the years, and it was once more a thrill to be doing it in the company of very special and close people, with a service car (and its driver) at our command. Somewhere between Sidon and Tyre, we stopped at a beach café for refreshment; Carole rejoiced at the scenery.

Before Carole's arrival, I had briefed Qasim about Carole and strongly recommended that he treat her as a sister. I knew, without a doubt, that he would honor my expectations. Even though age-wise, they were not far apart, Qasim being three years older, culturally, they were. From the outset of her arrival, her being with us was for me a mixture of pleasure and anxiety. I thought it wonderful that she would get to meet and know the family, and be introduced to the Arabs through me. Conversely, my family and friends would meet Americans that have become family to me. My biggest concern was that she was coming to an environment quite foreign to her, and she had not been adequately prepared for it beforehand. I worried as to how she was going to react to the lifestyle she was about to enter into, of a Palestinian refugee family with twelve people living in a three-bedroom house, the primitive bathroom facilities, and the overall level of sanitation and hygiene. I wondered if my brother Yousef, his wife, and children were capable of hosting all three of us in a manageable manner, satisfactory to all within the available space. I could see no way in time or place for a crash orientation; the only option open was to let things unfold and to deal with situations as they arose, one situation at a time! The financial part was not a major issue. Carole, of course, had her own budget for the trip. I let Carole know she would be monetarily charged with things that I incurred for her in the activities outside the home; here and there were some grey areas, but never did we have even a mild argument in this regard. At home, however, she was a welcome guest. It was rather the adequacy and comfort of the physical facilities, and the human interaction among the individuals coming under one roof, that concerned me the most.

After our stop over at the beach café, we headed straight to Tyre. Everyone there met us joyously. Carole quickly tried to adapt to the new situation and took cues from Virginia and me. Carole was of an especially big physical stature and seemed to dwarf some of the girls her age there. I once recall brother Yousef, with his indefatigable love for joking, whispering to me that Americans are like their watermelons, bigger, and better! I may have said back, "It is the milk and ice cream." Carole was moved into the same bedroom as Virginia and me. It was the most sensible and viable arrangement under the circumstances.

We stayed in Tyre and southern Lebanon for a few days, sightseeing and taking advantage of opportunities for meaningful activities. We visited nearby refugee camps, ancient ruins, an irrigation dam, and went swimming south of Tyre by the lovely, open, sandy beaches of the Mediterranean, away from the crowds and in privacy, especially because women in bathing suits in public would go against Islamic mores. Both Virginia and Carole were well-trained and graceful swimmers. One afternoon, the sun was very warm and we were out on the open beach without any shelter to shade us. By the time we got back home from swimming, both Virginia and Carole were so sunburnt that their faces and backs turned rapidly red. That ended our swimming activities. Walking downtown Tyre drew attention to our presence. We did it sparingly and with utmost discreetness.

To prevent things from becoming restlessly tiresome, we (Carole, Virginia, Qasim, Mother, and me) took a couple of days to go to Beirut and the nearby mountain resort towns for sightseeing and recreation. In that part of Lebanon, there was an abundance of outdoor nightclubs serving dinner, and offering live music and belly dancing performances. To go to one of these was a must to experience Lebanon and the affluent Arab way of life. One evening, we went to one of these popular nightclubs in the town of Bhamdoun, about a forty-minute drive up the eastern mountain slope from Beirut. From our table, we could see Beirut with its glittering lights magnificently lying in the plane below us, hugged by the Mediterranean beyond. It was a historical and fun-filled evening. My mother was reluctant to go with us, as these clubs did not meet her moral criteria of proper entertainment and conduct; but she did not want to spoil at least my fun. As the belly dancing part of the show began, I recall my mother, who sat beside me often looking the other way, murmuring prayers, "God have mercy on them and forgive their (the dancers) misdeeds!"

From time to time, Carole would yearn for a glass of cold pasteurized milk, with waffles or pancakes and the like, particularly at breakfast time. Usually, these were hard to come by. The closest to an American menu I could get to for breakfast was the nearby Uncle Sam Restaurant , which we ate at when we went to visit the AUB campus. Even then, it did not come close.

About a week after Carole's arrival in Beirut, it was time to carry on further with our itinerary. Recognizing that we were probably living once-in-a-lifetime days, we had preplanned to take my mother to Syria to see her two daughters, Haliema and Munawwar; Haliema and her family being in Damascus, and Munawwar and her family in Latakya. Haliema was by then widowed with five dependent daughters. Munawwar's family included at the time, a husband and five dependent children; three boys and two girls. It was a foregone conclusion that Qasim would accompany us. Because of the red tape involving travel in the Middle East, my mother had not seen the two daughters since before I left for the USA in 1957. This time, to avoid possible hassles entering Syria, I had gotten a visa to Syria from the Syrian embassy in Washington, D.C. before leaving the U.S. It was stamped on my USA Reentry Permit. Two years earlier, in 1961, I had changed my student visa to an immigrant visa, thus acquiring a permanent U.S. residency. The reentry permit had "the look" of a USA passport, although "Not a Passport" was specifically written on it. Yet, to many officials in the Arab States at the time, it seemed to carry almost the same prestige! Virginia and Carole, with USA passports, along with Americans and westerners in general, crossed borders with far less red tape. Qasim and Mother obtained permits to go into Syria stamped on their Palestinian Document of Travel, the latter issued by the Lebanese government.

On the appointed day (roughly around the first week of July), Mother, Qasim, Carole, Virginia and I got into a service cab, all of us headed from Tyre to Damascus. Qasim and I negotiated the fare beforehand with the driver. By American standards it was cheap, on the order of thirty dollars. Haliema had gotten advanced word and was expecting us. At the border crossing, things went smoothly.

At Haliema's place, we were met with a lot of emotion and tears of joy. It would have been at least nine years for me, and may be seven or eight for my mother and Qasim, since the last time we had seen each other. She had her apartment of two bedrooms conspicuously very clean, and had cooked a lot of old-fashioned Arabic food. Because I had not seen her place before (she had moved out from her first Damascus abode since my last stay with her) and did not know what to expect, I did not know how to plan for the overnight. For the lack of other plans, we decided that Virginia, Carole, and I would stay with Haliema for the night, along with, of course, Qasim and Mother. Carole, Virginia and I slept in the living room; the living room was small, and the sleep was crowded. Qasim and Mother slept in a small back bedroom, and Haliema and her five unwed daughters slept in the main bedroom. Despite Haliema's best efforts, the sleep was uncomfortable; never mind the lack of privacy. In fact, both Virginia and I saw bed bugs in the bed, and woke up with some bites. Carole did not intimate anything to me the following morning; she did not need to. I let it be known, that for the rest of our stay, we would find a hotel for the three of us. There was no argument. Haliema and Mother gave our well-being top priority. For me, it was no time to pinch pennies, especially because of my eagerness to make Carole and Virginia comfortable. I therefore went for one of the best hotels in the heart of Damascus, The Semiramis, and reserved two rooms.[156] I thought Carole needed the privacy for sure by then and should have a room of her own. It was disappointing, after settling in, that the hotel, in terms of cleanliness, privacy and plumbing, was not anywhere near as good as it was reputed to be. The air conditioning was malfunctioning, and we all sweltered in the Damascus heat.

---

156 We did not have phones to reserve, hence my physically going there in person.

Further in Damascus, we did some sightseeing and visited more relatives. Sightseeing-wise, we hit major places. It included the Ummayad Mosque, the shrine enclosing John the Baptist's head, and the tomb of Saladin. I enjoyed showing off my knowledge of Damascus to Virginia and Carole from the times spent there years before. Both Carole and Virginia confided sometime later that they got pinched in the rear, at different times, when we meandered in the Hamidiyya bazaar; this bazaar is often so crowded that mischievous men feel they can, and unfortunately do, get away with it. Carole also mentioned that she was also pinched in Beirut. As a consolation, their safety and possessions were at no time threatened.

Visiting relatives was mandatory, especially Uncle Mahmoud's family (brother of Mother). At one of these visits, we were served fresh Damascene fruits (grapes, pears, melons, among these), which were attractive to the eye, of enticing aroma; and we did eat! Alas, hours later, Carole manifested symptoms of diarrhea. The symptoms showed up with Virginia in a milder form a couple of days later. It was time to reassess what we could and should not eat; in particular, to avoid fresh fruits, their juices, salads, and generally, uncooked vegetables. Syrian fresh produce was particularly notorious in this regard, but somehow, I had not realized it.

After three or so days in Damascus, Virginia, Carole and I took a service cab to Amman, Jordan, a distance of about sixty miles. Being so close, it was an opportune thing that we go to Jordan, more importantly the West Bank, home of Jerusalem, Bethlehem, Jericho, and Hebron, among other important holy sites. In 1963, the West Bank was under Jordanian rule. I had previously secured a visa for myself; Americans did not need them to enter Jordan. For Mother and Qasim, going to Jordan was low priority; they therefore stayed behind which gave them time to have a fuller visit with Haliema and other close relatives. After a week in Jordan, we would come back to Damascus, pick up Mother and Qasim, head to Latakya, and visit Munawwar and family for three or so days before returning to Lebanon.

At the border crossing into Jordan, a border patrol policeman came to our car. I sat in the front seat next to the driver, while Virginia and Carole sat alone together in the back seat. The patrol policeman asked for our passports. He briefly glanced at Carole's and Virginia's passports and welcomed them into

Jordan. He had nothing to question of the chauffeur, as he was a regular driver on the Damascus-Amman route. In my case, he took a close and hard look at my reentry permit, and could find nothing to object to. I proudly exchanged a few sentences with him in my beloved mother tongue, Arabic. I did not for a moment consider not using Arabic with him. He then asked to search my bags. They were in the trunk of the car. I got out to open the bags, only to find that they were locked, and as was customary, Virginia had the keys. So I walked to the back seat to ask Virginia for help in opening the bags. His demeanor suddenly changed, asking me if I was with the two American women. I, in a quick reflexive mode, pointed to Virginia and replied, "She is my wife." He looked startled and apologetic and said, "Never mind, she does not need to; sorry for the bother." I restrained myself from saying anything as I walked back to the front seat. He ushered the driver to proceed. It was one of many manifestations encountered over the years of an "Arab complex" summarized succinctly by an Arab saying, "*Kul shi franji brinji*," which simply means, "Everything Western is okay." One might call it, for brevity, the "*Franji Brinji* complex*," or in English, the "Western Okay complex." It has deep roots and reasons for being, which have been intertwined within the history of at least the past two hundred years of Arab decline, and twentieth century Western colonization.

In Jordan we hit the major landmarks in Amman, Jerash, Jerusalem, Bethlehem, Ramallah, Hebron, the Dead Sea and the Qumran Caves, home of the Qumran scrolls. In Amman, we called on my ENCP former teacher, Taher Faydhi, and spent an evening with him and his family at his home. By sheer accident, I ran into AUB student friend, Fallah Essaghir, and exchanged quick updates on each others' activities since AUB; he had become a high school physics teacher and author of physics textbooks widely used in the Jordan public schools system. Virginia, Carole and I finally called on my UMN friend and one-course classmate, Subhi El-Qasim, in Nablus, and stayed with him and his family two nights. He showed us some of his enterprising work in starting and developing chicken farms, which significantly helped the West Bank food economy. Last but not least, I decided to make extra effort to locate my (half) Aunt Nazmiyye in the West Bank, the only relative that I was aware of living there. We paid her a short visit. She is half sister of my father on his father's side. I had not seen her since the year of the Nakba, 1948. In the meantime, she had married and lived with her husband and several children in the town of el-Bireh, near the biblical town of Bitunia or Bethany. Aunt Nazmiyye was very happy with our stop over, and fussed like mad to make us feel welcome.

The visit to Jordan (West Bank included) proved a lot richer and far more interesting than I had anticipated. We retraced our way back to Damascus. Once in Damascus, we picked up Mother and Qasim, bade the Damascus relatives goodbye, and headed that same day to Latakya.

The trip to Latakya was the longest; about two hundred miles. None of us, Qasim, Mother, or me had been to Latakya before. The service car we hired was kind of ancient. I was told that importing cars into Syria was difficult and had a one-hundred percent import tax imposed on them. So, most cabbies could not afford to import anything but old, second hand cars, and then, stretch their lifetime to the hilt. On the trip, I felt that the car could fall apart any minute. I was concerned that one of the wheels might come off loose; a thing that I had experienced years ago during my student days' travel between Tyre and Beirut; though nobody was hurt. I recall Virginia pointing out to me that the headlamps' beams were out of adjustment, widely divergent away from the road ahead! I admired her noticing it. If it were left for me, it would have been a long time before I might have, and only *might* have! [157]

We made it safely and gratefully to Latakya by the early hours of the evening. We only had an approximate idea where Munawwar lived in the city. Addresses there were not numbered; specific and accurate descriptions were hard to come by. You had to kind of feel your way through the short and narrow alleys of the old city where Munawwar lived. We had planned that upon reaching Latakya, we would first go to the hotel recommended to us by Haliema and family, nearby Munawwar's neighborhood, for check-in. The check-in was for the three of us, Virginia, Carole, and me. We would leave

---

157 Adequate maintenance of modern machinery, including cars, did not come easily or naturally to the culture of the people of the Middle East, including weaponry, at least back then. Speaking for myself, I did not appreciate the minds and motivations that conceived modern technological devices, nor the socioeconomic settings in which they surged and flourished, i.e., the West. That is not to say education and modern industrialization can't take care of this; it is easier said than done, however; it takes a lot of time and diligent effort to change old ways.

Carole and Virginia in the hotel. The cabby readily found the hotel. Carole and Virginia were dropped off, while Mother, Qasim, and I headed to Munawwar's immediate neighborhood. After a few queries of passersby, we made it to Munawwar's home! It was only then that we let the service car go; the hotel turned out to be a walking distance to Munawwar's place. As in Haliema's case, we had a very emotional reunion. I stayed long enough for the tears to dry and for a quick cup of Turkish coffee; I then walked back to the hotel to join Virginia and Carole for the night, with the plan for all three of us to show up at Munawwar's home for breakfast the next morning.

At the hotel, the three of us had not had any supper. I went with Virginia to the dining area in the hotel and inquired of the manager for some food. He said that it is already well past the food service time and there was not much food to serve except for some uncooked fish that he was willing to have fixed for us, considering our special circumstances. Fish is one food that I had not been able to eat in any form, for taste and smell, as far back as I could remember. It is something I must have inherited from my father who, through all his life, did not care for fish to the extent that he used to even run away at the smell of fish when my mother would be preparing it. This time my hunger pangs prevailed. We, all three, had fish for supper.

Our trip to Latakya was mostly family visitation. Carole was still recuperating from her bout with diarrhea; we allowed her time to stay in the hotel to rest and take it easy. The hotel was a pleasant villa and had relaxing surroundings, a pretty garden facing the Mediterranean Sea. Virginia and I, and some relatives, took occasional "cab service" around the town just to acquaint ourselves with it, purely out of curiosity on my part rather than special interests. There was only one exception; my brother-in-law, Muhammad, sensing our interest in the ruins, did arrange a visit to the site of the ancient Phoenician city of Ugarit, nearby. He arranged for an official from the Department of Antiquities to conduct a private tour for us. Ugarit, we found out, was a major ancient site of the Ugarit Kingdom that dated back to the fifth millennium BC! It provided a wealth of information to modern archeologists and historians of the ancient Middle East. The tour lasted several hours and was very enlightening.

The three days allotted for Latakya passed quickly; it was time to return to Tyre. We took the coastal road, which would go by Tripoli, where we would stop for a night to say a last goodbye to brother Hamadi, his family, and Fouad's family. The coastal drive again was pleasurable and inspiring. At the Syrian border, crossing back into Lebanon, we were all asked to get out of the car so it could be searched. While out of the car, the Syrian officer who checked our papers was impressed by the U.S. passports and my U.S. document to the point that he ushered Carole, Virginia, and myself into a visitor's lobby and offered us coffee. As for Qasim and my mother, he left them indifferently standing in the hot sun outside. Mother, was clearly elderly looking and a bit hunched over! As soon as I realized what was happening, I went back out to my mother and Qasim and had them go in ahead of me. I could read in my mother's face the thought, "Lord, forgive them for they know not what they do." Thank God, the officer did not argue with me. We all declined his coffee. It was a short time before the officer came back to tell us everything was in order and we could get back into the car. As we drove off, he wished us a safe journey (*ma essalama*). A few miles into Lebanon, my mother asked me with a smile, "Is there a way you could get me a document of travel like yours?"

Once in Tyre, we had only a few days before departing Lebanon and bidding Mother and the rest of the family farewell. By then, the total time spent from landing in Lebanon to flying out of it added to about six weeks. A sense of gloom threatened to engulf me on that day. Mother, nevertheless, serenely wished us safe and harmonious further travel and return to the USA as I kissed her hand, and she, Virginia, and Carole embraced. It was the last farewell. Ever since, I ache at goodbyes!

Our next stop, as planned, was to Egypt again; this time exclusively to sightsee most notably, ancient Egypt; in particular, the Sphinx and the pyramids. The airline that was to take us there was United Arab Airlines. At the Beirut airport that very same morning, we found the flight had been cancelled without an explanation. The news was quite disconcerting.[158] It meant at least a twenty-

---

158 Amid this distress, I happily ran into my grade school pal, Illyas El-Jisr. Illyas had become an airport official. We had a very warm but very brief exchange. Many years later (almost twenty years), Illyas and I ran into each other one more time in a hotel in Detroit, Michigan. We had a more leisurely visit then. I found out that he found his way to the U.S. as well. He was by then, owner and manager of a travel agency, Calvary Travel, in New York City. Also at the airport, I also saw from a distance, Dr. Fouad Sarruf, AUB vice-president, and a mentor in my first newspaper publication. Oh, how I wished I could have updated him on myself then!

four hour delay. The emotions within us, and the farewell party, were so high that I was anxious not to prolong them. I therefore inquired into other options out of Beirut, in short order, going west instead. In so doing, we were skipping sightseeing in Egypt, a rather an unfortunate skip.[159] Our frame of mind was, "So be it." Fortunately, on the other hand, we found out there was a flight to Athens via Olympic Airlines in matters of hours, with three seats available. It was our next stop after Egypt anyhow. The time intended for Egypt was simply added to our allotted time in Greece.

The flight to Athens was somewhat less than two hours, and we landed in Athens in the early afternoon. We headed to the hotel (Omonia Hotel, in Omonia Square, downtown Athens) where we had made reservations before the start of the trip back in the States, but starting a few days later. At the hotel, they extended the reservation to accommodate us right away; we were relieved not to have to deal with any further hitches that same day.

In Athens, we visited major landmarks; most notable among them was the Acropolis. We also toured churches and the major national museum in downtown Athens. After Athens, we flew to Rome and then to Venice. From Venice, we flew to Munich. On all these stops, we took the usual sightseers' tours that tourists typically take. For example, in Rome, we toured the Coliseum, Saint Peter's Basilica, the Sistine Chapel, etc. From Rome, we flew to Venice, and from Venice, to Munich. After Munich, we flew to Zurich for a few days' visit with two cousins of Caroline, my mother-in-law. One cousin lived in the city and another in a town of about fifty miles away, called Chur. Those cousins had visited the Schultz and Yegen families in North Dakota a few years earlier. They received us very warmly; their hospitality and their showing us around exceeded all our expectations. Among many other things, we were treated to a visit of the Polytechnic Institute, where Einstein was a student, and walked into the office of Wolfgang Pauli, a major architect of quantum mechanics and the formulator of a key principle in understanding atomic structure: the Pauli Exclusion Principle, which is named after him. After Zurich we flew to Frankfurt. The plan there was to visit another cousin; this time of Enoch, my father-in-law. The relative lived in the town of Alsfeld, about forty miles

---

159 Alas, Virginia never made it back. I was fortunate to have made it back to Egypt in the summer of 1986, where I spent ten days touring.

away. We were to stay there one night. However, we hit a snag upon landing in Frankfurt; I was denied entrance into the country! It turned out that the visa I had obtained into West Germany on my U.S. reentry permit was a single entry. A few days earlier, I had used it up when I had entered at Munich. It was an unexpected snag, a result of faulty planning by the travel agent. Virginia and Carole, with U.S. passports, could enter without a visa. I tried to reason with the airport authorities to allow me in, explaining the *single entry* was a silly oversight. But they would not hear of it. Rules are rules, I could not change their mind; I was to leave as soon as practically possible. Our next stop was London, England. There was a flight that afternoon. We decided, as a result, to book on it. This left us with several hours. Virginia and Carole decided that they would go into the country, rent a car, drive to the cousin's place and visit to the extent permissible. I stayed in a transit passengers' section. They were successful in finding the cousin (Marie Lippert) and had a couple of hours with her. It was a significantly shortened visit; but a visit, nevertheless.[160]

As far back as I could remember, I had heard about London, capital of Great Britain, home of the people who defeated the Ottomans, the people who took my father as a war prisoner, and had a primary role in the Palestinian Nakba. It can only be, therefore, an underestimation to say that I looked forward to seeing it with eagerness. We arrived around sunset. It was cloudy and gloomy-looking as we rode the cab to the hotel. Our stay was spent taking the usual tours; Piccadilly Square, Buckingham Palace (watched the changing of the guards), London's Tower, Saint Paul's Cathedral, Westminster Abbey, The British Museum (we saw the Rosetta stone), among other attractions. We also went to see a live theater play one evening. At Westminster's Abbey, I was awed as I stood by the tomb marker of Isaac Newton. Suddenly, he became a real human being, not an abstract genius whose bust is sitting on a pedestal.[161]

---

160 Fifteen years later, in the summer of 1978, Virginia, her father, stepmother, and I did travel to West Germany, and realized a four-day visit with that cousin of my father-in-law, Enoch. We further met additional relatives. The visit was, under the circumstances, most gratifying and fulfilling to all concerned. By then I had become naturalized U.S. citizen.

161 Some years later, 1992, as I visited Westminster's Abbey once more, I stopped by Isaac Newton's tomb again. This time I recited the traditional Muslim prayer (Al-Fatiha), asking God's mercy upon his soul; it was spontaneous and natural and I was at peace! Ever since, I felt an almost personal kinship with the man Isaac.

Toward the end of the London stay, it was time for Carole to head back to the States, this time by air; we saw her off. We, on the other hand, had one more stop before our scheduled U.S. return; this one last stop was Paris, France.

In Paris, we had one personal connection and visit. In my latter years at the UMN, I met a chemistry graduate student who was from Damascus, Syria: Issam Jano. We quickly developed a friendship. Issam was dating a young Minnesotan coed, Becky. She had grown up on a farm about a hundred miles west of the Twin Cities. He was on a government scholarship, which afforded him only a year of study at the UMN. Becky's and Issam's dating became serious, and they got engaged before he went back to Syria. Virginia and I got to know them pretty well in the meantime, and had them over few times to our home. A year or so later, Becky followed Issam to get married in Damascus. Issam shortly thereafter managed to get another scholarship; this time to pursue his studies for the PhD in chemistry; but it stipulated France as the country of study. At the time of our travel, he and Becky were in Paris, he being a graduate student there. This made the Paris stopover more personal and meaningful. Again, in Paris, we took the typical tours, and there were many. Suffice to say, that among the many wonderful tours, were the Louvre and the Versailles Palace.

From Paris, we flew back to Minneapolis, as planned, in mid-August. Professor Yennie arranged for Virginia and me to stay at the Guest House on the UMN campus. With my PhD thesis in hand, and a paper and a pen in the other, I proceeded to draft the paper for the *Physical Review Journal* in accordance with the *Journal's* guidelines. Since all the material for the paper was in the thesis in detail, it was relatively easy to write up the draft. Professor Yennie and I conferred daily on the precise layout and wording of all the sections. After a few revisions, he was satisfied with it. There remained the task of typing and submitting it. Professor Yennie's secretary would do that. It would take some time and he would supervise the process. He said that once typed, he would send a copy to me in Ann Arbor for final editing and proofreading; which was eventually carried out and the paper published.[162] As I bade Professor Yennie farewell, he reminded me again to draft a paper

---

162 G. Q. Hassoun and D. R. Yennie, Phys. Rev. 134, B436 (1964)

based on my coupled resonance work for publication in the *Nuovo Cimento Journal*. He said that it was "good work, was publishable, and would help me professionally." He wished me well at the University of Michigan (UMI), and said, "Keep in touch."

We flew from Minneapolis to Detroit, Michigan; Detroit's airport serviced Ann Arbor as well. As I landed at the airport, I was engulfed by a sense of gratitude to the U.S., such as I had never felt before, for all the good that had been mine. I wanted to kneel down and kiss the ground. I did not do it, however, lest I be thought of as a crazy fanatic. I saw clearly the contrast between the spirit of the Old World and that of the New World. I was ready to settle down for a new phase of my life as a Postdoctoral Research Fellow in Theoretical Physics, my new status.

CHAPTER 22

A STATE OF FLUX

My postdoctoral fellowship was for one year, renewable once. It was an important professional opportunity that did not come by often. By any measure, to accept it and make the best of it were the right things to do. In the context of my plan to go back to the Middle East and work there, it simply meant that I would be better equipped and established in my field and hence, in a better position to serve.

My trip back, and travel in Syria and Jordan along with Lebanon, opened my eyes still wider and broadened my horizons beyond words; dictatorships, self-centralized-power monarchies, feudalisms, nepotism, disrespect for law, and above all, the individual, his freedom and dignity, were the order (more appropriately, disorder) of the day. The depressing state of affairs of the Palestinians, particularly those in refugee camps, and the unresolved Palestinian problem continued to gnaw at me. In the back of my mind, I kept asking myself, *What do the Palestinians or Arabs care about coupled resonances and angular momentum of radiation, or quantum mechanics?*[163] *Should I decide to return, where would I fit? Precisely, what will I do? How relevant is a quantum field high-energy theorist to the immediate social, economic and political problems there?* Six years in the U.S., and my marriage to Virginia, made the Middle East look like one hell of a place to live in. Virginia's devotion and support had been essential to my achievements in the U.S. heretofore. It made it all the more important that I guard and secure her welfare.

At UMI, I joined the theoretical high-energy physics group. Professor Marc Ross headed the group, an arrangement similar to the UMN group and

---

163 My brother Yousef in his eternal humor may have captured some of what was at work. He was so very proud of me, his baby brother, having become a doctor of physics; yet he did not see any immediate visible benefits of it to him, his family, or the community around him, given their daily struggles. Therefore, he would go around introducing me to his friends, during our Lebanese visit, as his Doctor Brother; then he would say with a grin: he is a doctor of physics, the kind that does not do anybody (in his immediate community, that is) any good! By implication he was also saying I was not an MD!

Professor Yennie. As a post-doc, I had considerable freedom to pursue research of my own choosing. I had no supervisor per se. The idea of being a research fellow was that you participated in weekly seminars to become familiar with the research of people around you, received stimulation and ideas to guide and benefit your pursuits; in turn, you give seminars on your pursuits and findings for others' benefit. You were judged by the problems you worked on, solutions you found out, and publications you put out. I was free as never before to do as I pleased. Yet, the expectations to publish were proportionally never as before.[164] For a few months, I wandered around among the theorists in the department at many levels; established faculty members, postdoctoral fellows, and graduate students. I did not settle down to any specific research project. I gave seminars on my Ph. D. thesis research. After several months, with not much to show for, I began to feel considerable pressure building up within me. I had to do something; otherwise, I stood to not have my fellowship renewed for the second year. I collaborated on a research project with a young PhD student of Professor Marc Ross, Kyunsik Kang. Kyunsik had just completed his PhD thesis in high-energy particle theory. He was on a temporary research support. Kyunsik hailed from South Korea. The project dealt with a method of calculating the mass of the sub-nuclear resonance (particle) named rho meson, alluded to in my thesis. The work was not far removed from my previous research. In a span of three months, we succeeded in producing a paper that we submitted for publication to the *Physical Review*. After some minor revisions, it was accepted.[165] Professor Ross helped us with the revisions. When the evaluation of fellowship renewability occurred, this publication, along with the timely appearing of my paper written with Professor Yennie in the *Physical Review*, validated me and resulted in renewal of my fellowship for a second year.

At work, the people I came in contact with were some of the nicest and most supportive people one could ask for. Professor Ross, in particular, was especially friendly. Yet, I was uncomfortable with my work situation. The discomfort I was feeling was internal to me. I did not seem to be able to put

---

164 Hence the adage, "Publish or perish!"
165 G. Q. Hassoun and K. Kang, Phys. Rev. 137, B955 (1965)

my past experiences in Palestine and Lebanon out of my mind. I was not able to convince myself that I should be doing high energy theoretical physics research. Emotionally, I wanted to be among the Palestinians, even at the refugee camps, teaching and preaching, sharing in their pain. Rationally, it did not seem the thing to do. Here, I was being given these rare opportunities to be on the frontier of human knowledge, to advance myself in physics and benefit society in a way that transcends religious and national boundaries; I ought to seize the moment. Yet, I could not free myself from these inner conflicts to pursue the work at hand with the passion and devotion it needed and deserved.

The research group, by renewing my fellowship, was giving me more time and a chance to perform. I accepted the chance to try further, to better understand my inner hold-ups and try to overcome them. I did not want to give up on myself without a real fight.

As for Virginia, she initially had a lot of work setting up a home in our new apartment by the campus, a walking distance from the physics department. After the bulk of that was done, she prospected for some work. This time, we felt that the work should be in line with her education; this meant, in the field of textiles and clothing. After some serious looking, nothing worthwhile turned up. Ann Arbor and surrounding areas were the wrong place for that field; it did not come to us as a surprise. We did not feel urgency for her to work outside the home. My annual salary of $8,000 was enough to support us at the level we had lived in Minneapolis, plus some. She had worked hard heretofore; there was merit in her taking it easy for a while, and for both of us to take stock of what might be next. Virginia attended the Christian Science Church in Ann Arbor, and we developed friends from the church, the neighbors around us, and some of the Arab community there. The Arab community at UMI was in fact, considerably larger than the one at UMN. When the subject of having children would come up, it would be set aside. We did not feel ready. I, in particular, was neither settled nor comfortable with what I was doing.

Towards the end of the first year, Virginia argued that since in one way or another it appeared that I was likely headed into some role in education, she would try to synchronize with that. So, she determined that a teaching certificate in home economics would be worthwhile; it would make her more marketable for work down the road. My stance was simple: I would back up her decisions fully, whatever she saw fit. UMI did not have home economics or home economics education departments. However, eight miles or so east of us, in a town called Ypsilanti, was Eastern Michigan University (EMU). EMU had a respectable home economics program and a well-developed program of teacher education.[166] We would need a car. By this time, we were in a good position to buy one. We bought a new Chevy Two car, stripped down to bare minimum features. It did not even have a radio.[167] Virginia argued that since I did not know much about cars and repairs, we should not settle for a second hand car.[168]

Upon visitation and consultation with the appropriate faculty at EMU, she found that she had other options, besides obtaining a home economics teaching certificate. With a couple more science courses, she could get certification to be a junior high school science teacher. Also, the Department of Home Economics offered an M.S. degree in home economics. She determined that by judicious planning and design of courses, she could draw up a program that would enable her, as a full-time student, to fulfill the requirements of all three objectives in a span of one academic year and two summers. Virginia had my wholehearted blessings. By the start of the summer school, 1964, she was enrolled at EMU. By the end of the summer term of 1965, she successfully completed all three requirements. I was impressed by, and proud of, her accomplishments beyond words. For her M.S. degree, she chose food and nutrition as the area of concentration; for the thesis, she wrote up a paper on Middle Eastern cookery. It was never published, but many family and friends shared parts of it over many years.[169]

After the paper with Kyungsik, I took a deep breath and indulged in more soul searching. In the meantime, Kyungsik got a postdoctoral fellowship in the physics department of Brown University, Providence, Rhode Island, and propitiously, moved there. My dissatisfaction with my own drive, initiative,

---

166 EMU, in fact, was originally founded as a teacher's college.

167 In hindsight, we were too drastically miserly!

168 Few months later, Virginia had me take an evening course, "Know Your Car", at the Ann Arbor High School nearby.

169 Her thesis tried to outline qualitatively, common features and strategies of Middle Eastern cookery, and quantified scientifically, through American standard measures, certain traditional qualitative recipes of common food ingredients e.g., tabbouli salad, hummus dip, yogurt, and baklava.

and inadequate productivity in high-energy research caused me to think in terms of exploring other areas. In fact, I could not get myself motivated enough to write up the article based on my coupled resonance thesis work and submit it for publication, in spite of Professor Yennie's urgings and to his chagrin. It appeared to me that the high-energy theoretical research front was changing at too breathtaking a speed for me to keep up with.[170] I thought in terms of a slower paced research area, where the approaches and methods might be less changing. It seemed thus that the statistical mechanics/plasma physics group could, perhaps, suit me more.[171]

Come fall 1964, I, therefore, began to attend the seminars of the statistical mechanics/plasma physics group. Professor George W. Ford, a well-regarded expert in the field, headed the group.[172] I was welcomed in. In a matter of weeks, I started researching plasma (charged particles) dynamics in a variable electromagnetic field. It quickly became apparent to me, far from being straightforward, that this area of research was quite involved and demanding too. Thoughts and doubts as to the correctness of my pursuits, just as the previous year, began to stir again in my mind, such as, *How pertinent or useful were these pursuits to my family and my people?* My internal conflict was real and severe. I struggled hard to find an acceptable way out. I even considered, for a time, going back to school to earn a PhD in international relations with emphasis on the Middle East. Somehow the idea of becoming a graduate student again, after all the recent past struggles, seemed unrealistic, even if it had a chance to resolve my inner conflicts. How all this would affect Virginia was never away from my concern. I could not submerge myself into the plasma physics research any more than I could submerge myself in the high-energy field; it was in fact, less! The fruits were hardly mentionable; no papers resulted from this specialization. Professor Ford left me to answer for myself. There was never an overt pressure, though there were expectations.

---

170 In the distant hindsight, this was a cover-up for my inner conflicts.

171 Plasma refers to the ionized state of matter, in contrast to a gas, like air, where the constituent atoms and molecules are neutral charge-wise. Plasma physics is important in understanding the internal physics of the sun and the stars, the process of fusion, among many other applications.

172 He was a student of George Uhlenbeck, internationally renown during the first half of the twentieth century.

In the absence of a clear and viable option, I wrestled with my conflicts, sometimes circuitously, hoping somehow in time things would clear up, and I would find my way constructively and passionately. Around this time I was also conscious of my mother's failing health. Even at the time of our visit, summer of 1963, her health was marginal. Nobody seemed to know what was causing it. She had tripped and fallen a few years before while carrying a bread dough tray (about three feet in diameter) over her head to the public oven. Ever since, she had complained of pain in her back and limbs. She also had signs of a hunching back and an overall body shrinking.[173] Doctors had examined her, yet there was no clear-cut diagnosis. The excitement of our visit had lifted up her spirit so much, she rose above her pains, moved fairly freely around and traveled joyously with us. About halfway into January 1965, I received a letter that my mother had passed away (January 5, 1965), in Tyre, in brother Yousef's household. There was about a week between my receiving the letter and the actual event. I received the news with profound sadness. My mother never gave up hope we would go back to our homes in Haifa. She clung to the houses' keys until her last breath!

The sadness had a special pain to it, primarily due to the fact that I was not around and with her during her last days on earth. I was many thousand miles away. I was not around to walk in her funeral and see her body interned; somehow it hurt deeply. It was not fair that people who had such an intimate bond should not be together at the moment of final earthly departure of one (or both). Her passing came at one of my darkest and most confused moments in my professional career!

In the spring of 1965, Virginia's mother decided to join a travel group touring several eastern Mediterranean countries, which included Lebanon. It was not unlike her to do so, as she had undertaken overseas tours before, especially in the Far East, to places such as Japan, Thailand, and Hong Kong, among others. She expressed interest in connecting with some of my relatives while there. Fortunately, brother Fouad, by then a successful civil engineer, was working in Beirut at the time; he was the ideal contact person. We worked out the logistics in advance, and she successfully made the connection. As she was tied to the

---

173 In retrospect, Mother probably had osteoporosis and arthritis.

travel group schedule, she only could break away from them for a day. Fouad drove her down the southern coast to Sidon and Tyre. She met several of the relatives in Tyre; most notable were my brother Yousef, his wife, sister Zahiyye, her husband, and several of the nephews and nieces. The family was still in a mournful state at the time of the visit, which undoubtedly dampened the excitement of the moment. She was taken to my mother's gravesite. Virginia and I regretted that the visit did not take place before Mother's passing. Before returning her to the hotel where she was to join the travel group, Fouad showed her some of the major landmarks in Beirut. I recall two impressions relayed back to me: one by Fouad, which indicated that she had a good time and was impressed by how modern Lebanon was; the other by my mother-in-law who remarked how troubled the Middle East region was, and that the threat of war hung heavily over it. In June 1967, sure enough, a war did break out between Israel on the one hand, and Egypt, Syria, and Jordan on the other.

CHAPTER 23

SETTLING DOWN?

In March 1965, I became a naturalized U.S. citizen. By then, it was certain that my research fellowship would end in August, and I would have to look for a regular academic job for the fall of 1965, teaching and research, at a college or a university. With my conflicted state of mind and modest research output, it seemed wisest to look for a position at a university that had a real need for teaching and did not emphasize research very much. Fortunately, at the time, there were many colleges and universities all over the U.S. that fell in this category. The American Physical Society (APS), of which I had by then become a member, had an excellent employment service and information exchange between potential employers and employees. Regarding teaching, I had by then a significant amount of experience. The experience went back all the way to my undergraduate years at AUB and into UMN. Furthermore, the teaching profession was not unfamiliar to me; I had two brothers that had extensive involvement in it, though at the grade and high school levels. I genuinely enjoyed teaching. I believed in its value, no matter where and to whom. It stimulated and challenged me. It gave me great satisfaction as a job well done, and I loved articulating concepts in understandable terms and communicating them to others.

I applied to a handful of places. Most of them required visitation to the campus and a presentation/interview. From among the offers made, I ended up accepting a position as an assistant professor in the physics department at Alfred University in Alfred, New York. It was a tenure track, nine-month academic year job, beginning in September, at $9,000. Alfred was a town of a couple of thousand in population (exclusive of the university), in upstate New York, in the Allegheny Mountains. The university was a well-regarded private undergraduate liberal arts college of about two thousand students. The department was made up of four full-time faculty members; it had a full undergraduate physics program leading to the B.S. degree. A major role, however, was that of servicing other majors and a well-established and developed pre-engineering program. Associated with the university, and on campus, was a College of Ceramics. The college was a public state college of several hundred students and of national reputation. It had a sizable faculty that included scientists in the fields of chemistry, material science and solid-state physics. It also had a full graduate program leading to the PhD degree. The university serviced the ceramics students with their general university course requirements.

The appeal of Alfred University was primarily four-fold:

1. The teaching load was reasonable, two to three courses a semester of reasonable enrollments, about nine contact hours a week. The courses, mostly undergraduate, were well within my ability and skills. A course typically had about thirty students, which meant that the amount of grading was not exorbitant.

2. Its geographic location was away from large population centers, yet not too far from important cities. It provided a peaceful setting for soul searching and reflection, which I seemed to need. It was within easy access to the two major universities of Rochester and Cornell.

3. We were provided with a one-bedroom apartment in a university-associated housing at a modest cost on the edge of town, on top of a somewhat wooded hill with a view of other (wooded) hills. It was a manageable walk to the office, but I took a ride whenever I could, either from Virginia or some of the neighbors.

4. The position was largely a teaching position. It had research expectation, but was gauged in general and mild terms of scholarly pursuits, which allowed room for interpretation. I was not sure what it all entailed, but took the attitude that I'd cross that bridge when I got to it.

The academic year 1965-1966 got off to a good start. It felt good to be in the classroom again. I had no problem justifying to myself what I was doing against nagging Middle East concerns. I have always felt full responsibility for my own care and self-support. My mother was a constant example and reminder. Rightly or wrongly, I saw teaching as a legitimate and honorable livelihood pursuit regardless of the place, in contrast to the research I had been attempting, which seemed to be a luxury that my past did not justify or even condone. Granted, emotionally, I might have gotten greater satisfaction from teaching in a Palestinian or Arab setting, but that seemed unrealistic and entailed diverse risks and sacrifices that I was too unsure to make. Before long, I had a student following who seemed to enjoy my teaching; a couple of second year students were even inspired to become physics majors. Every so often I would be asked to give a campus pop lecture of a general nature on current research in elementary particles and high-energy physics. These lectures were well-received and gave me surprising publicity.

A few months into the school year, I became aware to my great bafflement and disillusionment, that the department chairman was too parsimonious in applauding my work, while many others were heaping praise, including the dean of the college. For sometime, I could not fathom what was behind this. Eventually, I understood that the department chair was a chemist by training, that he had gotten the job in the department a few years earlier when PhD physicists were hard to come by, and that he saw me as a potential threat to his position. None of that was in my thinking or expectation; it was the first time I encountered such a situation. I kept Virginia aware of what I was experiencing. Interestingly, Virginia did not accept my reports on their face value. She challenged me to be sure that it was not somehow my imagination. Eventually, she verified them to her own satisfaction through personal contacts and social interactions. Since we had no great attachment to the place, we decided, come the end of the school year, it would be best to move on to greener pastures.

It did not help matters that Alfred did not offer worthwhile work opportunities for Virginia, considering all she had done the previous year to make herself marketable. Virginia, for the first couple of months, concentrated on homemaking and getting acquainted with the community. There was nothing available, job-wise, for her in home economics or general science teaching in Alfred. Virginia's teaching certification was transferable to the state of New York unqualifiedly. Having started prospecting only after we got somewhat settled was a drawback. Virginia, undaunted, cast her search outside Alfred in the surrounding areas. By the start of the second semester, she found a job as a science teacher in the middle school of the town of Hornell, about seven miles to the east. She accepted it even though it meant driving about fourteen miles a day on a narrow winding hilly country road. Virginia's spirit and devotion to our welfare was a bulwark for my morale and an inspiration; it never ceased to amaze me and spur me on.

The most memorable fun activity Virginia enjoyed at Alfred was a bell ringing musical group that gave recitals to the community every now and then, most often around the Christmas season. The week before Christmas, we flew to Bismarck to spend the holiday there. This time, there was the added pleasure of being part of (Virginia's sister) Carole's wedding. Carole had received her M.S. degree in home economics/food and nutrition from Michigan State University in East Lansing at the end of the 1963-1964 school year. She was working out west in California when she met her husband-to-be; he was a Christian Scientist. Carole honored us by having Virginia be her matron-of-honor and me, one of the groom's men. It was my first time to wear a black tuxedo.

My search for a job beyond the end of the school year1965-1966 began in earnest with the start of the new year, 1966. I had maintained an occasional social contact with my friend Subhi El-Qasim. When he found out about my unhappiness at Alfred, at which time he had become the Dean of the College of Agriculture at the University of Jordan (UJ) in Amman, he invited me to apply for a position in the physics department of UJ. He felt confident that I would be welcomed aboard with attractive terms. After considerable thought and discussions with Virginia, I did not feel it would be the right move under the circumstances. I was not ready, emotionally or professionally, to make such a major and potentially irreversible move. The sum total of days I had physically been in Jordan by that time did not exceed ten, and only as a tourist. Instead, I set out to confine my search for a position to the States. I applied to several universities, interviewed at three of them by the end of February and secured two offers out of the three interviews. Before the end of March, I accepted the offer from North Dakota State University (NDSU) Fargo, North Dakota. It was a tenured track position offer at the level of associate professor, with a seventeen percent increase in salary, effective September 1, 1966.

There were many conducing elements to the decision. NDSU, Fargo, and the state of North Dakota were quite familiar places to us, not that unlike

Minneapolis, and the neighboring state of Minnesota. NDSU was the alma mater of Virginia's brother, John, and sister, Carole. It was the Land Grant University of North Dakota and the second largest in the state, having a student population in excess of sixty-five hundred (6,500) at the time. The position was at higher rank and salary. Fargo was the largest city in North Dakota, together with the sister city of Moorhead, across the Red River into Minnesota, it had all the elements of a lively growing metropolitan area (FM, for Fargo/Moorhead) of about eighty-five thousand. The physics department was in an expanding mode and had seven full-time faculty members. The university and the department had, in terms of future goals, all the ingredients that fit my background and potential abilities. I felt confident that I could contribute significantly to their goals.

In so far as Virginia was concerned, NDSU had a College of Home Economics, and the FM metropolitan area had two other colleges, aside from several high and middle schools. The move offered her many opportunities. North Dakota was also Virginia's home state and within a few hours of driving from her parents in Bismarck. For me, I had become accustomed to the Midwest after six years living in the Twin Cities. The winter weather, harsh as it was (and is!), was not all that much of a shocker to us by then. We had many reasons to be optimistic and forward looking.

The school year at Alfred ended the first week of June. There were thus, about three months of summer of uncommitted time. Through the employment service and information exchange of the American Physical Society, I managed to get a civilian summer physics consulting job, at the Naval Weapons Laboratory in Dahlgren, Virginia, about fifty miles south of Washington, D.C., on the Potomac River.

My summer work started a week or so before the end of Virginia's school year at Hornel. I flew down to be on the job on the appointed day. Virginia followed me after her work was completed. We sold virtually everything, furniture-wise, which did not fit into our Chevy Two car. Virginia drove the Chevy Two, by herself, to Dahlgren. I was given temporary housing facilities on the Naval base and ate at the PX (Cafeteria) until joined by Virginia.[174] Civilian couples

---

174 PX (cafeteria or store) is a common reference term to such facilities on military bases run by the military and usually of prices that are at a great discount or bargain.

were not allowed living privileges on the base. The experience was a treat and very inexpensive. With Virginia joining me, I had to find housing off base. Housing was tight in Dahlgren and nearby areas; nevertheless, we managed to rent a house a few miles from the base. It was actually more of a shack than a house; however, we got by with it all right. The summer heat was quite trying, especially since the shack had no air-conditioning. Virginia drove me into the base in the morning and picked me at the end of the day. During weekends we often drove into Washington, D.C. for sightseeing, theater, concerts and savoring international cuisine.

The summer work at Dahlgren went better than I expected. I was put, as a theorist consultant, on a project related to radar radiation hazards and safety on the deck of aircraft carriers. The details of the work were classified and therefore, required clearance.[175] The classified nature of the work and its novelty made me wonder concerning its availability to a person with my background, being a Palestinian refugee. Like all applicants, I had to fill out forms for the clearance part, which I did. In a relatively short time, the forms were processed and the clearance granted. I gained greater appreciation of the term "America the Beautiful" and why so many sing "God Bless America." My admittance to the job was on the basis of qualifications and merit, without regard to national origin. Associated with the project was a small experimental group. I was attached to that group. As a theorist consultant, I performed calculations for physically informative quantities out of the raw experimental measurements to better evaluate and interpret the raw measurements. Happily, I enjoyed the work, and the experimentalists welcomed and appreciated my contributions. It made me feel useful in goal-oriented research; its benefits to human safety were tangible and easy to see. During that summer, I helped in scrutinizing the experimental strategy and techniques needed to enable the experimentalists to get a better grasp of radiation hazards and their causes. I led an effort for a more comprehensive evaluation of the work by Professor A. R. Von Hipple of the Applied Physics Department at MIT.[176] The lead experimentalist and I followed it by flying over to MIT to meet in person with Professor Von Hipple.

---

175 My comments here are thus within this constraint.
176 Father of Frank, my pal during the Summer Institute at Brandeis University, 1961.

The meeting's purpose was to go over some of the finer issues of the evaluation and consequent recommendations with him. Every now and then at Dahlgren, high-ranking naval officers in uniform stopped by to be briefed on the progress of the work.

By the end of my summer term, the Dahlgren group expressed interest in making my position full-time and year-round. Of course I loved the compliment, but I was not free to accept, nor was I really inclined to accept, given my previously-accepted position at NDSU, and that deep within me, I had already cast my lot in academe. At departure time, they encouraged me to stay in touch and consider coming back the following summer. On that happy note, Virginia and I headed to Fargo in our Chevy Two.

Somehow during that summer, the conflicts I had with research at UMI (and UMN) seemed to take a backseat. Looking back at this after years of maturation, I attribute it to several factors: 1) The research was applied and goal-oriented in terms of tangible societal benefits, features that I could readily appreciate. It was neither ad hoc (to my mind at the time) nor seemed self-aggrandizing luxury. 2) The physics tools for the work were within well-established theory and the general boundaries of my previous education. 3) I was hired and being paid expressly to help in solving a problem, which was causing well-documented harm and damage to people and property in the U.S. Navy. I felt morally and legally bound, therefore, to give it my best effort. 4) The job was short term; I knew it was only for the summer. It thus, did not have long-term implications upon other things I might wish to do.

Since we had not had time to find housing in Fargo in the intervening time, NDSU kindly provided us with housing on campus, in the Bison Court, for the first academic year. The apartment, with two bedrooms and a short walk to my office, was at a very modest cost and proved to be quite convenient and satisfactory.

The first year in Fargo and at NDSU went quite smoothly. I was happy with my course teaching assignment. I enjoyed my situation very much and was well accepted as a major member of the department. I was assigned to several committees within the department to help develop the undergraduate course offering and put the M.S. program on firmer foundation. I became the major advisor of one of the two M.S. graduate students in the program. The committee I enjoyed being on most, and where I found myself well-positioned to contribute the most, was the Curriculum Committee. When the contracts for the following year came out, mine had a ten percent raise, assessed at the time as a relatively healthy raise. The summer school had two sessions; there was no problem in my getting work in one of the two. Under the circumstances, there was no need to go back again to Dahlgren. I taught a course in the first session. I took off the remainder of the summer to refresh and be ready for the following school year. All in all, I seemed to fit the needs of the department and the department fit my needs.

Virginia and I quickly felt very much at home. On campus, I made many friends, mostly among faculty, but with some graduate students as well. We attended many campus events, such as public lectures, fine arts series, homecoming gatherings. We did not feel any urgency for Virginia to work right away. Virginia joined and became active in the Fargo Christian Science Church. Socially, the church community became our primary home base, and we got integrated into their extended family. I genuinely respected, admired, and liked these people. Supporting Virginia's religious pursuits became with me, par for the course. It did not present me with religious or intellectual conflicts or compromises, as long as I was not being asked or expected to think in a certain way, or accept certain notions or beliefs, or become a church member; no matter what outside onlookers may have wished to reason or think.

We typically spent major holidays, such as Christmas and Easter, with Virginia's parents and the extended family in Bismarck. Virginia's mother, alternately, enjoyed visiting us in Fargo. In particular, she enjoyed getting to know the Christian Science congregation of Fargo and attending and/or participating in some of the church-related activities, such as the Bible study and the Fargo church's sponsored Christian Science public lectures. [177] She also enjoyed accompanying us to Christian Science lectures sponsored by neighboring churches. I occasionally wondered to myself, in view of her early concerns about my being a Muslim and a foreigner, how she felt about me attending so many Christian Science lectures along with her, and seemingly settling in North Dakota; figuratively, in her backyard.

---

177 These lectures were part of the local churches service to the community, to enrich the spiritual life of members and to acquaint others with the faith.

It had been a curious thing to me for quite a while that at the time Virginia learned of my serious interest, coupled with happy expectations, in the open position at NDSU, she seemed to evince some "lukewarm-ness" at the prospect. I had taken it for granted that she would be very happy to be close to her family. I further had tended to reason that being close to her family was second best to my being close to my family. It turned out to be not that simple. She was not sure that it would be all that good to be within a driving distance to her family; perhaps for concern of us getting drawn into family politics. I was thinking like a good, emotional, and naïve Arab boy who saw his family as a security blanket in more ways than one; a sense of interdependency is common in Arab (tribal) ways. Virginia, on the other hand, was thinking in practical terms of whether this proximity would affect our life positively or negatively; vis-à-vis, privacy, freedom of conduct and independence, old American values of living. Given the fact that her mother had resisted our marriage, and her seeming reservation about my being her son-in-law, Virginia did not take it for granted that things would necessarily go all that smoothly between her mother and us as I tended to want to think. Virginia had another concern, which took me a good deal of time to appreciate, namely: Virginia had a sense of being somehow a sort of an underdog within her nuclear family. With Virginia being a middle child, it may have also been compounded by the so-called "middle child syndrome." Because of the kind of family I grew up in, where the notion of an underdog child was non-existent, I truly had a problem for quite sometime understanding Virginia's trepidations. Be this as it may, I continued in my Pollyannaish optimism about moving to Fargo.

At the end of the school year 1966-1967, we moved out of Bison Court. We relocated into a nearby apartment in a newly-completed apartment building, just as convenient and close to my office as the Bison Court one.

During our first year in Fargo, Virginia, as it had become customary, was primarily engaged in the process of getting settled. Since our marriage in September 1958, we had moved eight times in the span of nine years; she was due for a breather. She said to me once about that time, somewhat jokingly, that if I decided to change jobs again any time soon, she was going to let me do all the packing, the moving and unpacking!

At the start of our second year in Fargo, 1967-68, Virginia thought, work-wise, primarily in terms of teaching science at the middle school level or home economics at the high school level. This was largely occasioned by her recent experiences in Ann Arbor, Michigan and Hornel, New York. She did not feel ready to commit herself to full-time work; therefore, she signed up in the area school systems of FM for substitute teaching in either general science or home economics. This gave her the flexibility she desired. Also, she was not quite sure if long-term teaching was her forte, notwithstanding the successful, but limited, Hornel experience. The notion of trying work at NDSU in some capacity was not seriously entertained right away. As a substitute teacher, she discovered that there was considerable demand for her general science teaching. During that same year, as members of the NDSU faculty got to meet her and know of her background, she was called upon to teach as a part-time instructor in the Department of Food and Nutrition in the College of Home Economics, which she happily agreed to, and gave up substitute teaching. Her M.S. work in the field of food and nutrition at EMU qualified her for the job. It was "a foot in the door" of the college, and Virginia assured herself that college teaching and life was to her liking.

Virginia's part-time job at NDSU became a full-time at the start of the school year 1968-1969. Virginia's becoming a member of the NDSU academe harmonized well with mine. This evolution enhanced our optimism for a promising future at NDSU and in Fargo. She was able to carry her weight (figuratively!) well within the college, her credentials fared respectably vis-à-vis other faculty members. Nevertheless, to strengthen her standing further, she took, within the year of her appointment, a couple of graduate courses in the College of Home Economics at the University of Minnesota (UMN). To do that, she commuted by train to the UMN's campus twice a week.[178]

On our second year, the subject of having children certainly came up, but we chose to hold back a bit longer, until we had more concrete signals of job security.

Simultaneously, my job situation was proceeding well. My teaching, undergraduate and graduate, was well-received. I had graduated one M.S.

---

178 She would ride the train from Fargo in the evening before the class day to arrive in Minneapolis the following morning, attend the class on campus during the day, and come back to Fargo the following evening!

advisee by the end of my second year and had an M.S. advisee due for completion and graduation by the third year, spring of 1969. I was also active and effective in my committee work, both at the department and the College of Chemistry and Physics levels. I channeled most of my efforts towards where I thought the needs of the department were the greatest, particularly curriculum developments. My tenure status was due for review and action by the end of the school year 1968-69. I was granted tenure in the spring of 1969, effective with the start of the school year 1969-1970. By then, I had contributed significantly towards enriching the quality of the undergraduate physics major program and expanding and strengthening the nascent M.S. graduate program.

In the fall of 1969, Virginia and I felt secure enough to begin house shopping. We were ready to move out of the rented apartment and settle into a house of our own. This we did as the calendar year 1969 came to a close. The house we bought was also by the campus, less than a hundred yards away from the apartment, again an easy walk to work for both of us. We spent most of the Christmas recess preparing the house for the move; a family of five, including three young children, had previously lived in it. Its condition required some repair and a lot of cleaning and refurbishing. Virginia was masterful at leading and organizing the housework plan. Frankly, and in hindsight, I did not have a good grasp of what I was getting into by becoming a homeowner in North Dakota! I fully trusted Virginia's judgment and simply carried out tasks as she assigned them to me. The close proximity between the apartment and the house greatly facilitated the transfer of furniture to the house. Some of our friends lent a hand. Come January 1970, we were moved into our own house. For me, coming from being a refugee in February 1948, becoming a homeowner in America gave me a sigh of relief and a special thrill. As the school year 1969-70 was drawing to a close, we were becoming well-established members of the university and the Fargo community.

Virginia's mother seemed to like our new house and what we were doing to it. She visited us more often in the new house than previously at the apartment. We always welcomed her with open arms and found all kinds of fun activities to do together. Despite her reservations about our marriage, or perhaps because of them, I generally went out of my way to be hospitable. Deep inside of me, I wanted to win not merely her grudging acceptance, but a change of heart that Virginia and I were after all right for each other.

The summer and fall of the school year 1970-1971 proceeded pretty much uneventful, not unlike the preceding year in terms of schoolwork and community-church related activities.

As had become our custom, we went to Bismarck to celebrate the Christmas of 1970. That particular Christmas, however, we found ourselves committed to show up for a dental appointment in Minneapolis, a few days after Christmas Day. I had been having gum problems that the local dentist recommended I address without delay. He referred me to a periodontal surgeon in Minneapolis for the work. At the time, there, were no periodontal surgeons practicing in the Fargo/Moorhead area. My first visit to the Minneapolis surgeon, made weeks before Christmas, was a general examination and evaluation. At that visit was established the need for gum surgery to be performed in four sessions, the first of which was to begin shortly after Christmas.[179] This required us to head back to Fargo the afternoon of Christmas Day and to Minneapolis the day after. Normally we would have spent all of Christmas Day in Bismarck. Unlike usual times when we would have welcomed my mother-in-law along, Virginia and I became uncomfortable when she asked to accompany us to Fargo, and thereafter, to Minneapolis. My mother-in-law had been a student at the UMN, some years ago, in the 1920s and enjoyed visiting the campus and the Twin Cities. She was a restaurant connoisseur and knew of several restaurants and cafés in the area that she loved to go to. Because I was going to Minneapolis this time for surgery on one-fourth of my teeth, and did not expect to be in a condition to sightsee or be able to eat much, her coming along did not seem the right thing to be doing. Yet, neither Virginia nor I could bring ourselves to talk her out of it. We gently and politely tried to explain and dissuade her, but to no avail. Thus, on the afternoon of that Christmas Day, the three of us drove back to Fargo. Virginia did the driving, her mother sat next to her, and I rode in the backseat. This was often the formation in which we traveled.

The day after Christmas, after a few stops in Fargo calling on friends and minor shopping, we headed to the Twin Cities. This time I was driving. Virginia was next to me. My mother-in-law was in the backseat directly behind Virginia. The day was fairly sunny and not particularly cold. As we approached the town

179 I wanted to get as much as possible of the surgery done during the holiday to minimize interference with my schoolwork when the university will be in session.

of Fergus Falls, fifty miles out of Fargo, the sky became cloudy and mild fluffy snow began to fall. The snow got heavier as we drove around the town on Freeway I-94 and the visibility was diminishing significantly. Freeway I-94 gently rolls up and down and is mildly winding in that vicinity. As we were rolling along and chatting, I saw all of sudden about fifty yards ahead, and without any pre-warning, crashed cars sitting across and blocking the freeway. I quickly applied the brakes and discovered the road was slippery; the car began to swerve. I eased up on the brake just enough to come to a stop before reaching the crashed cars by about twenty feet. Our car came to a stop at an angle facing the right shoulder of the highway, but was still in the right driving lane. At that moment, I immediately turned my face towards my right shoulder to see what was coming from behind—only to discern a typical-size car coming at us like a rocket and at a speed that clearly showed no awareness of what laid ahead. There was no time to say anything to Virginia or my mother-in-law. The next thing I remember is finding myself gaining consciousness with people around our wrecked car with me inside the car. Both Virginia and my mother-in-law had been ejected out about thirty feet ahead of our car wreck, on the right shoulder of the freeway, and were lying unconscious. Virginia was on her back with her eyes wide open. Her mother was lying on her side with her eyes closed. Seat belts were not yet on the market and the car had none. It was obvious something terrible had happened. I began to cry uncontrollably and call on God for help! People standing by tried to calm me down.

Within minutes of my coming to, an ambulance arrived at the scene. Virginia, my mother-in-law and I were taken into it to a Fergus Falls Hospital. Within a half-hour or so after arrival and admission to the hospital, the doctor on duty informed me that my mother-in-law had passed away. He estimated that she passed away within twenty minutes from the time of the accident. The cause of death, he explained, was rupture of the aorta and collateral internal bleeding. Virginia, however, was in a stable and fair condition. As for me, I was treated for bruises and a minor cut on my right-hand index finger, and needed no admission as a patient. I was provided with a place near the hospital to stay and be close to Virginia.

The news of my mother-in-law's passing left me stunned and distraught beyond description; *how could it happen so fast and out of the blue?* My feelings, nevertheless, were somewhat assuaged by being told that Virginia was expected to recover; particularly since my first sight of her on the shoulder of the freeway was so ominous.

There remained the immediate and very painful task of having to call the family in Bismarck with the news, knowing of the centrality of my mother-in-law's position in the family. In more ways than one, she was the family's backbone. I wished there was a way around it. But I knew there wasn't, and I had to before word leaked out through other channels. The news media were already on the scene of the accident as well as police. I decided to call Virginia's brother John, instead of my father-in-law, feeling that he would be the most capable of handling the shock and making further contacts. Luckily, I got him right away. He remained quiet throughout, as I attempted to sketch to him what had happened. The accident turned out to be a car pile-up of historic proportions, over thirty cars!

To my great relief, Virginia made a rapid recovery with no serious injuries. She was checked out of the hospital and back home in Fargo in a matter of days. I felt it was a miracle. In time, I contacted the Minneapolis dentist and let him know what had happened, rescheduled the appointments, and went through the surgery at later times. Life at the Schultz family in Bismarck was never the same after the accident. My father-in-law grieved deeply for months to come. Virginia and I visited him often during that period. The car accident, months later, was tried in court and I was absolved of any wrongdoing. Although I was convinced of that, and maintained it all along; nevertheless, the court decision vindicated me to anyone who may have thought otherwise.

My father-in-law eventually remarried a neighbor widow lady. He was not a domestic person and the general condition of his house and quality of life were beginning to deteriorate. All his children, cognizant of his pain and need of company, joyously supported and celebrated the marriage. While his second marriage helped matters some, he was never the same after the death of his first wife, a wife of about fifty years.

The death of my mother-in-law in the manner she died was one more and forceful reminder of our mortality. You are here today, but who knows where will you be tomorrow? Our outlook on life and the daily pursuits acquired anew a transient temporal dimension and perspective. Virginia and I had a lot to work through and out of.

With the onset of the year 1971, we had to get back in our grooves at the university. The news of the accident and our part in it was public knowledge in the community and on campus. Friends and colleagues expressed sympathies, support and encouragement to carry on.

As the school year moved further along, and the events of the accident in the background, the thought kept coming to me that I must go to visit the family, see the brothers and sisters and their families. It had been eight years since the historical visit of 1963, much had happened, and a visit will do Virginia and me a lot of good. By mid-spring, I determined that I could take the trip right after the end of the school year. I made no professional commitments for the summer. One month seemed about the right duration. It would be the first visit with no mother to meet me. Virginia was tied up with a school-related conference right after the school year end. We settled on my going ahead of her for the first two weeks: she would join me for the rest of the month. During the time by myself, I would have intimate and old-fashioned Arabic style visits with the family, particularly the brothers; visits that might not be as feasible or convenient if Virginia were with me, or that she might not find of particular interest.[180]

My appearance in Tyre evoked a mixture of tears of pain and joy. Pain, for what Virginia and I had been through with her mother's passing, and the fact I was there among them without Mother to see me. Joy, for I was back alive amongst them, to breathe their air and experience their daily activities, to feel their struggles and learn of their hopes and aspirations!

After several days stay in Tyre, I headed to Beirut, strolling the streets of the city that were full of rich and stirring memories of days past, not the least of which were those around and on the AUB campus. Often I would be accompanied with one or two nephews.[181] My brother, Fouad, who would have been the most natural companion, was tied up at work in Muscat, on the Persian Gulf. His work demands would only allow him to join me (and

---

180 One aspect to such situations is the language. It is typically awkward in a group where one or more cannot manage Arabic well enough for all to be included in the conversation. Even if all or most of the other members do manage English (usually at different comfort levels), there is a strong tendency to want to speak Arabic; after all, it is the mother tongue. It is not an issue of rudeness. It is rather, a yearning to speak in the native tongue.

181 Often these were: Qasim, Yousef's oldest son; Mufid, Hamadi's oldest son, and Munier, Fouad's oldest son.

Virginia) in Lebanon for the latter two weeks and upon Virginia's arrival. The nephews provided me with companionship filled with joyous reminiscence and mutually informative chatter. These activities were quite cathartic and better than any medicine from a bottle.

After Beirut, I still had time enough to skip over to Tripoli to see brother Hamadi and family before Virginia's arrival. I was welcomed with the traditional embraces. However, I sensed an absence of the kind of excitement and cheer that were there in abundance when I visited in 1963. Hamadi and I did a lot of walking in his section of town, El-Mina (the city harbor area), as we had done often before when I visited him back during my AUB days. Somewhere along the walk, we took time out to sit at an outdoor corner side café. Without many preliminaries, he took a deep breath and looking me in the eyes asked outright, "Why did you come back?" Not expecting such a bold and seemingly cold question, I said I was hurting to see you, the family that I miss so much, and the life I left behind in the Arab World. He answered, "Forget the Arab World! You have been fortunate to get out of it. Don't look back; it is a miserable place, particularly for us Palestinians. Concentrate on taking care of your life in the United States. As for the family, as you see for yourself, is hardly managing!" I was initially flabbergasted, but very saddened above all else. I quickly knew that it was his painful living conditions causing the utterances. I was not offended. I knew he loved me very much, as I loved him. On further reflection, I realized that the Tyre family members, particularly brother Yousef's, were not much better; they merely were not as upfront about it.

On the way back to his home, Hamadi bought me a corncob roasted on an open fire from a sidewalk peddler, a customary treat in those surroundings. After I ate the corn, I held onto the bare cob. We were walking by a sea wall. The sea below was about ten feet down. He asked, "What for are you holding onto the cob? Why don't you toss it over into the sea?" I said, "It would pollute the sea." He said in wonderment, with his arms wide open, "But this is the sea!" inferring it was too big to be polluted by a cob. I said, "Notwithstanding, it will still pollute; what if others did the same?" His eyes got really bigger. For a while he could not fathom my answers. Eventually, we walked by a trash basket wherein I dropped the cob. Shortly before we got back home, he looked at me with a smile and said, "You have a point!"

Shortly before leaving Tripoli, I told Hamadi in reassurance, "Just as we have been a team before, we are still a team today, nothing has changed!"[182] It was the last time we were together.

When I was joined by Virginia and Fouad, we were all ready, after a couple of days of celebrations in Lebanon, to turn our attention to visiting the sisters Haliema and Munawwar in Damascus and Latakya respectively. I found out from Fouad that at the time, he had not seen Munawwar and her family for well over ten years. Fouad, his wife, Fay (nickname for Fakhriyye), Virginia and I, therefore, geared up expeditiously for the Syrian travel. We hired a car with a driver and headed for Damascus as our first stop. The visits of the two sisters went very well. We further had a chance to visit extended family relatives, with all the excitement and hospitality that traditionally went with them. The visits were filled with tears but fulfilling and gratifying for all.

On our return to the U.S., Virginia and I made one preplanned stop in Frankfurt for a couple of days. It was the town denied to me in 1963 for not having a multiple entry visa. This time I was welcomed in without a visa. I had a US passport, having gotten naturalized since! There we savored what we could of German ambience and cuisine.

We made it back to Fargo in the early part of August. There was sufficient time left in the summer vacation for us to shift gears and to face the new school year, 1971-1972, with vigor and uplifted spirit.

---

182 Brother Fouad, being an engineering manager in a large construction company with projects all over the Middle East, had already been helping in this regard, especially through finding employment to the qualified and worthy young men in the extended family. Specifically, at the time, he had found work within his company for Hamadi's second oldest son, Walid. Within a short time following my visit, and with my added desire for him to do the same for Yousef, Fouad found work likewise for Yousef's third oldest son, Sa'id.

CHAPTER 24

THERE SHALL BE AN ANSWER

For the next three years after our return from the Middle East, Virginia and I settled down to work diligently at our respective jobs, in order to build venerable professional standing and appreciable economic security. In the academic year 1973-74, we began, however, to think of other things. I felt overdue for a sabbatical leave and Virginia was thinking of higher professional attainments.

Our sense of security at our jobs, and within Fargo, allowed me to think in terms of reaching outside academe, in the form of community service. Through a friend who was an avid backer of the scouting program for young people, I agreed to serve a neighborhood Boy Scout troop as an assistant scoutmaster, and later, as a scoutmaster and fundraiser.

Shortly after we moved into our house, we decided it was time to stop our birth control regime and welcome new additions to the family. Before long, we found out that it was unlikely we could have our own children. The problem lay in my low sperm count caused by my having had measles while going through puberty. The doctor we consulted with just threw up his hands and said there wasn't much he could do about it; he said further he did not think there was anything that anybody could do about it! On Virginia's part, given her Christian Science faith, she felt that the issue was in God's purview. As such, she did not push me to go further in the medical direction. Instead, she recommended that we engage a Christian Science practitioner (a sort of a spiritual teacher or guide) to work on the problem. We did. After several months of seeing no results, we essentially dropped the matter altogether.[183]

---

183 As I reflect on this now, I am awed, even perplexed, that Virginia did not press the issue harder; because I am quite sure that she would have liked very much to have had children of her own. The best explanation I can come up with after all these years is that because the problem was due to me, she did not want me to feel failing in such a basic male role. On my part, I have grown up among many children, particularly those of my brothers and sisters. These children were not for the most part well provided for out of necessity, and presented major financial challenges to their parents. Thus not having my own, I saw (rightly or wrongly) as no big loss.

By 1974, at NDSU's College of Home Economics, the notion of having a PhD (or Ed.D.) was increasingly perceived as important for tenure and further advancement. Virginia was then at the rank of assistant professor. Reading the signs on the wall and not wanting to be disadvantaged for a lifetime, she decided to explore the feasibility of working for a PhD. On my part, while I was performing well at my job, I felt that I could use a year leave for enrichment and reflection. I was particularly and earnestly searching my soul for stimulations to become more productive in research. I had the ambition, but lacked the conviction. During the academic year 1973-1974, Virginia was invited by Professor Fern Hunt of Ohio State University (OSU) to consider pursuing the PhD degree at the OSU's College of Home Economics. OSU and its College of Home Economics were nationally recognized for excellence. Virginia had met Professor Hunt at one of the national conferences, and the two had hit it off well together. This development brought matters to a decision point. Virginia and I succeeded in getting leaves of absence from NDSU at the end of the school year 1973-1974 for a full year. Virginia enrolled right away as a full-time graduate student in home economics at OSU. Professor Hunt would be her major advisor. Virginia's (NDSU) college was very favorable to Virginia's plan and awarded her for the year leave about forty percent of her academic salary. My leave of absence was, however, without pay. It was explained to me in terms of lack of funds in my department and the absence of a specific research proposal on my part. My leave without pay did not bother me much. We had enough savings by then to be able to manage. I strongly felt the need to be free from any obligations to anybody to take stock of what I had been doing with my life up to that point, and to allow myself time for assessment as to what was next for me (and for us). The physics department at OSU was kind enough to grant me an adjunct professorship with a private office of my own. It meant no stipend, but carried the privileges of a faculty member on campus. This suited me fine! The physics department chairman explained to me, at the time, that if I wished to seek support, I could try to do so by associating myself in a mutually agreeable way with some of the "grants-supported" research groups in the department. Frankly, the suggestion and prospect, though very well-intended, did not appeal to me.

By the first week of June, having rented out our furnished house to an NDSU professor for a year, we packed just the gear we needed to survive for the year into our 1971 Buick Le Sabre and headed for Columbus, Ohio, a drive of about a thousand miles.

Our new abode in Columbus was an efficiency apartment significantly smaller than our first apartment after marrying. It was a bit off the southern edge of campus, an easy walk for Virginia to the College of Home Economics building. Upon arrival, Virginia did not waste any time. After drawing up her PhD program of study with Professor Hunt, she began the process of first fulfilling the course requirements. Accordingly, she enrolled full-time in appropriate courses that were being offered that first summer. Her aim was to complete all the course requirements for the PhD degree before having to return back to NDSU in the fall of the school year 1975-1976. What would remain thereafter would be the dissertation, a status often referred to as ABD, an acronym for "all but dissertation." It was essential therefore that she be allowed to concentrate on her studies with minimal external distractions. I gladly agreed to take care of most of, if not all of, house cares and chores. I cooked, washed dishes, did laundry, cleaned the apartment and bought groceries. She, however, played an important advisory role in virtually all of these tasks; for one thing, she was really the pro and I was the amateur. She involved herself most in grocery shopping.

I welcomed the domestic work. Since I had not committed myself to any professional duties, not gainfully employed, and feeling the need for breathing space, the domestic work gave me something worthwhile to contribute to the overall family enterprise. It gave me a sense of usefulness to Virginia, which I found very satisfying.

During that year I allowed my mind to wander freely. I even tried to write poetry, all of which was of a very personal, consoling and cathartic, nature. As an adjunct professor in the physics department, I had the freedom to attend any seminar or colloquium held there. I attended many of them as well as a couple of national physics meetings that happened to be held during that year on the campus of OSU, including a lecture by Subrahmanyan Chandrasekhar.[184] I was invited and went to social get-togethers at the homes of some faculty members,

---

[184] A giant of a physicist of the twentieth century; he was a master of the general theory of relativity and an originator of the notion of black holes. He shared the 1983 physics Noble prize with William A. Fowler.

and a departmental picnic. I could not seem to get excited or drawn into any meaningful research project or endeavor. Most of the emotions stirring within me were not unlike those that I experienced as a postdoctoral research fellow at the University of Michigan. Emotions that I can best characterize as inner conflicts, deeply felt, revolving around a sense of obligation and concern for Palestine, Arabism and Islam. I felt sorry for myself for being, metaphorically speaking, at one kind of a drinking fountain, but thirsty for an altogether different fountain.

Virginia school's work went quite well; she obtained mostly A's in her courses. Her relationship with her advisor was very harmonious. She even constructively participated in some research of her advisor during school breaks and holidays. By the end of the summer of 1975, she accomplished the ABD status, just as she had planned. What remained was to define a research project, carry it out, and write up the findings as a dissertation towards fulfilling all the requirements for the degree.

It was easy to see that Virginia was more at ease and freer in her situation as a graduate student than I had been. I saw clearly why this was so. Virginia seemed sold on her new undertakings. She did not seem to look back or sideways at other lines of pursuits. She was excited about the prospect of obtaining the PhD degree in home economics. In contrast, I had strong competing motives and goals for my life. I was not convinced, even rather discontented, with what I was into in the U.S. At a very raw emotional level, it was a recurrence of "wishing to be living closer to my people and their problems."

While on the OSU campus, I spontaneously associated with the Arab community there, which was sizable, and made up of both students and faculty. I learned more about Arab-American organizations, at the local and national levels, and what were they doing to promote Arab causes. I also associated with Islamic groups, especially at evening time during the holy month of Ramadan, but to a lesser extent. I derived emotional satisfaction from such associations. Meanwhile, Virginia found a Christian Science Church, which happened to be nearby, to attend services. She was very faithful in her attendance of Sunday and Wednesday services, and occasional Christian Science lectures in and around Columbus. As had become customary, I accompanied her to these functions. We made lifelong friends from among the members of that nearby congregation. We also found time to attend worthy cultural events on and off campus.

One association that drew me in and impacted me indelibly was the Arab-American University Graduates (AAUG). AAUG was a national association with informal groups affiliated within it in major Arab-American population centers, often by university campuses. Such groups got together and discussed "problems of the day," particularly vis-à-vis America and the Arab World. OSU had such a group.

AAUG was formed shortly after the June 1967 so-called, Six-Day War. It was, for the most part, launched by a group of Arab-American academics, at American universities, who had been stunned and stung by that war, its outcome, and profound implications; also, by the seemingly imbalanced euphoric news coverage of the events of the war, in terms of grand and glorious victories of Israel in battle over the inept, misled, and misguided Arab armies of Egypt, Syria, and Jordan. It seemed like the 1948 war all over again, if not worse. These founding members felt a heavy responsibility and realization that there was a great deal of work to be done to inform and educate the American people as to the other side of the story, and to the true realities of the Palestinian-Israeli and Arab-Israeli conflicts. I could not read some of the AAUG literature that had been put out by then, and in circulation, fast enough.[185] As an upshot, I found out that the next annual national convention was planned to take place in October 1974 in Cleveland, Ohio, a hundred and fifty miles or so northeast of Columbus. The convention days were largely over a weekend. I had no doubt that I should attend it. Virginia, upon finding out, wanted to attend too.

My first AAUG convention was a big eye opener. Some of the best Arab or Arab-American minds and friends of the Arabs, scholars and specialists, were present. They were either giving papers or participating in panels dealing with many aspects of Arab/American/Israeli-issues and relations. Among these issues were: Palestine and Israel; the Six-Day War of 1967; and the October war of 1973. The caliber of the presentations and discussions was of

---

185 More precisely, I had seen some rudiments of their literature while in Fargo, but it seemed distant, and inconsequential; just another pamphlet or a propaganda brochure to read! But it had an altogether different effect when it was studied in conjunction with live people who had been involved directly in the organization's meetings and proceedings.

the highest level that I had ever attended up to that point. I was particularly enamored by, and resonated with, two of the luminaries of that convention, namely: Ibrahim Abu Lughod and Edward Said (pronounced Sa'eed). They spoke to my heart. That convention was the start of over two decades of my association with AAUG.

Virginia and I returned back to Fargo at the end of the summer of 1975, in time to start the school year 1975-1976 at NDSU. We were quite heartened by the richness of the experiences of the past year. Virginia's progress towards the PhD was better than we had anticipated. We departed Columbus with the idea that Virginia could work out the research for her dissertation on the side during the school year, and that she would go back to OSU in the summer of 1976 to put the finishing touches on the dissertation for its final submission. The basic outline of her research project was drawn already. It dealt with the use of a list of household appliances by American homemakers, and how their use could bear on kitchen design and storage. It involved a survey of a selected representative group of homemakers, and the analysis of the survey-collected data.

As for me, the association with AAUG made me very aware that my homeland and ethnic pains were not exclusively mine, but shared in diverse ways and degrees by many; and that I had to come to terms with them more intellectually and less emotionally. Academics in the social sciences, particularly those in sociology and political science, found outlets that combined their professional pursuits with their concerns for their homeland's problems and their urge to serve. Those were, relatively speaking, perhaps the lucky ones. For me, a practicing physicist, it was difficult; as I saw it, it was like serving two masters! I just had to settle down, control my pain, and suppress it if necessary, in such a way as to enable me to perform satisfactorily and even competitively on the job. I could realistically see no other viable option.

In December 1975, I was among AAUG delegates to a three-day conference in Kuwait dealing with "Developing Human Resources in the Arab World." AAUG and the State of Kuwait planned it jointly. Kuwait was the host of the conference and as such, financed it to a large extent. My contribution would be in roundtable discussions of matters related to advancing science and technology education in Arab society. I was granted partial (mostly nominal) air transportation support, but free room and board for the duration of the conference. Virginia accompanied me; her expenses were largely our responsibility. However, her stay at the hotel turned out to be complimentary, and she was a welcome guest at social functions, often with meals served. Speaking of meals, they were mostly sumptuous feasts of a high order, reaffirming legendary Arab hospitality. They were reminiscent of wedding feasts I had known in earlier times, but done on a more massive and professional scale.

The conference was of high impact in so many ways. I would like to single out two encounters that were especially interesting, which took place at the Sheraton Kuwait Hotel, home of the conference.

The first occurred at one of the banquets where I found myself sitting at the same table with Abdel Salaam Al-Majali, Prime Minister of Jordan, at different times. The way it happened was that just before participants were to sit down at the different tables in the banquet hall, I was chatting with my AUB friend, Hanna Nasir, president of Beir Zeit University. Hanna was a friend of AAUG and occasional participant in their conventions in the U.S. As attendants began taking seats, Hanna took me by the arm to join him at a nearby table to continue our chat. Virginia was on my other side. Al-Majali came to the same table and sat on the other side of Hanna. Hanna introduced us to each other. I have a lasting impression of how forceful and opinionated Al-Majali was from that encounter. I did not think I would find it easy to work with him.

The second was having breakfast alone with Salah-Eddine Al-Bitar. Al-Bitar, with Michael Aflaq, was a founding father of the Al-Ba'th Party. Both Bitar and Aflaq are native Syrians. Al-Ba'th, more than any other party in the modern history of the Arab World, has influenced events in the Middle East for over a half a century. Specifically, Al-Bitar played a key role in uniting Syria and Egypt into the United Arab Republic (UAR: 1958-1961), and became a vice-president, next to Nasser. The encounter was almost unreal. On one of the days of the conference, I got up earlier than usual to have breakfast in order to make an early morning session. The dining room was empty except for one table with one person having breakfast. As is customary in such gatherings, you try to meet and interact with as many of the conferees as possible. Therefore, I walked to that table and asked if I could join him. I did not initially recognize who he was. Without hesitation, he offered me a seat.

After introducing ourselves to each other, we quickly jumped into the politics of the time. Once I knew who he was, I tried to learn as much as possible from him about the Lebanese civil war, which was in full swing. I recall trying to find out how he thought the civil conflict could be resolved, a topic that has been bedeviling Lebanese for generations.[186]

During the conference, a group of U.S. delegates decided to organize, in concert with the Beirut office of the PLO, a flight to Beirut, by way of the return to the U.S., for a stopover and a meeting with Yasser Arafat, and some top members of the PLO. Virginia and I, we were told, could join the group. After some deliberation, we chose not to. We wanted to stay behind in Kuwait a few days longer, primarily to visit with relatives and friends. There were quite a few of them living there at the time, some we had not seen in many years.

The Kuwaiti conference turned out to have a high impact on the extended Hassoun family as well, in terms of developing their human resources; particularly brother Fouad's nuclear family. The civil war in Lebanon made Fouad move his residual family (his wife, youngest daughter, Noha, and youngest son, Ismat) to his work home in Kuwait. They were living there at the time of the conference, whereas Fouad had been transferred to Nigeria, to manage urgent company projects; he had been in Nigeria only a few weeks. Nevertheless, Fouad's company allowed him to fly back to Kuwait to be with us for the duration of our stay.[187]

The Hassoun contingent in Kuwait (cousins, nieces, and their children) and friends put on a very festive New Year (1976) party. Over thirty people were in attendance at Fouad's (company-provided) home. It turned out to be a spontaneous mini-family reunion. Everybody at the party had a great and wonderfully memorable time.

The time with Fouad and his family in Kuwait brought us face-to-face with a problem in regard to the education of his children, Noha and Ismat.

---

186 I never actually found out whether he was a participant in the conference, or just happened to be having breakfast while on a different business. After the breakfast, I saw him no more; not in any of the proceedings. Bitar parted way from the Syrian regimes that followed the break-up of the UAR. Masked gunmen assassinated him in Paris, July 1980, while in exile.

187 An expression of gratitude is due to Fouad's company (the CAT company), which invariably was accommodating to Fouad in diverse family matters.

In Lebanon, Noha (eighteen-years-old) had just finished high school the preceding year, top in her class, and Ismat (seventeen-years-old) had finished tenth grade; both at the prestigious Choueifat National High School. However, they were idling around, education-wise, in Kuwait. Virginia and I, impelled altruistically, offered to do what we could to have them come to Fargo to further their education. The case was compelling though unexpected, and on a short notice. Fouad and Fay accepted the offer.

Thanks to the receptive and cooperative American Consulate in Kuwait, Noha and Ismat made it to Fargo before the end of January 1976. Ismat was immediately admitted into the 11th grade of Oak Grove High School in Fargo, a private Lutheran Church High School, while Noha was admitted as freshman at NDSU. Neither Ismat nor Noha had any documents to prove their academic standing at the time. The administrations in both cases accepted our word and assurances. It was impressive how readily and how well Ismat and Noha blended in at their respective schools. That is not to say that they did not present us (Virginia and me) with challenges of a disciplinary nature.

At the time, Fouad's other three sons were already in the U.S., in college in Fort Lauderdale, Florida. Other Hassouns followed in time; two sons of brother Hamadi, and the youngest son of brother Yousef.

While a lot had happened during the school year 1975-76, one important thing did not happen; namely, the projected progress we had anticipated in regard to Virginia's dissertation. It was clear that between the demands of Virginia's full-time work at NDSU and expanded family cares, resulting from Ismat and Noha living with us, the environment was anything but conducive for dissertation pursuit. By the spring of 1976, I began to encourage Virginia to think in terms of another year leave to spend on the OSU campus, and to be in close interaction with her advisor, Professor Hunt, for the sole purpose of completing her dissertation work. After initial hesitation, Virginia did apply for a year leave without pay from NDSU. It was granted. I stayed behind at my job; Noha moved into a coeds' dormitory on the NDSU campus, and Ismat was transferred to Shuttuck Military Boarding school near Faribault, Minnesota. Simultaneously, we continued to provide Noha and Ismat the supervision and guidance needed.

The year 1976-1977 saw Virginia and me going back and forth between Fargo and Columbus. Depending on the particulars of our work and study situations, we managed to get together every month to six weeks; either Virginia came to Fargo or I went to Columbus. Virginia had rented a room in a house owned and lived in by a single, retired home economics/extension service woman professor. She was very kind and accommodating to us, especially when I visited in Columbus. Virginia's work on the dissertation progressed quite well. By the summer of 1977, she had submitted her dissertation to the Graduate School. She took her final oral examination and passed it in short order. With school out for me by then, I was able to join Virginia in Columbus the last couple of weeks before her final examination.

We celebrated her accomplishment in a big way with her professor and many of our Columbus friends as we planned for the graduation and commencement ceremonies. Virginia's sister, Carole, flew from California to be with us on Virginia's commencement day. It was perhaps one of her happiest life occasions, with the possible exception of our wedding celebrations. On the flight back to Fargo from Columbus, shortly after graduation, Virginia wore her cap and gown on the plane all the way home, including during an airplane transfer in Chicago O'Hare airport. She wanted to tell the whole world that she is now a PhD! We took the cap and gown with us on the following trip to Bismarck, which we undertook within days from our arrival to Fargo. Virginia wanted to parade them in front of members of the Bismarck family, particularly her beloved father. With much merriment, she did. Her father smiled from ear to ear as he watched the newly-christened "Doctor daughter." At one point, when her father was watching his happy daughter in her cap and gown, he said to her, in his typical dry humor, "You still have to work for a living!"

The following year Virginia and I settled back down at our respective jobs. Virginia, in recognition of her attainment, was recommended for promotion to associate professor and tenured. Both honors were granted effective the start of the school year 1978-1979. Virginia and I donned our caps and gowns and marched together, for the first time ever, during the NDSU faculty march of the spring commencement of 1978. This became an annual ritual for both of us for the next four years. We derived special satisfaction in marching together in our academic regalia.

At the turn of 1978, Virginia began to think in earnest in terms of her father going to Germany to meet his relatives with whom he had kept in touch over a lifetime, particularly during the Second World War. He had entertained the hope, over many years, to make this trip "one of these days." By then, her father was aging fast and suffering from arthritis. His mobility was decreasing and he was increasingly requiring a wheelchair to move around for any distance. Virginia felt it was the summer of 1978 or never. I shared her sentiment and gave her my full blessing to pursue the matter earnestly. Virginia and I would lead the trip and her stepmother would accompany us. The stepmother, who at that time had not traveled much outside the U.S. and never to Europe, enthusiastically welcomed the prospect. Virginia got to work planning for the trip; therefore, by the summer of 1978, all the arrangements were in place including contacting the relatives. There were three families; a cousin, a grandnephew and a grandniece. They were all living in and around the town of Alsfeld, fifty miles away from Frankfurt. Virginia arranged for a five-day cruise on the Rhine River following a three-day visit with these relatives. The cruise began from Rotterdam, Netherlands, and concluded in Basel, Switzerland.

There was much excitement during the family reunions. The main relatives did not speak much English. My father-in-law, Enoch, spoke German at home as a child but had never studied it formally. It did not come back easily for him. Virginia and I had learned some German at the university; we had brought the books and a dictionary with us. One night I stayed up till 2:00 a.m. in our hotel room studying German words and sentences that I felt we would need the following day. On a few occasions, a young neighbor daughter who had studied English in school, was called upon to help. We all had a lot of fun. The generous hospitality we were afforded was so touching, and at times moved us to tears. I saw, beyond any reasonable doubt, the underlying oneness of human feelings and emotions that transcends culture, ethnicity and national boundaries.

At the time we planned the German trip, we found out that brother Fouad and nephew Walid (Hamadi's second son), with their respective wives, would be vacationing in Europe. We coordinated to meet them in Zurich for a few days. We also arranged to call on a Swiss cousin of Virginia's mother. The cousin lived in Klosters, a beautiful resort town on the slopes of the Alps, about fifty miles from Zurich. On the morning of the appointed day we were to meet with Fouad and company, we put my father-in-law and his wife on the plane back to the U.S.[188] Fouad and company checked into our hotel that afternoon. It had been two and a half years since we had last seen any of them in Kuwait. The following day, we called on the Swiss cousin. She invited all six of us to lunch at her house in Klosters. We took the train over; it was a beautiful sunny day, and the Swiss landscape was even more beautiful than it looks in the movies. The cousin served us an elegant lunch at her house (chateau) and engaged us in lively chats. We returned back to Zurich around mid-afternoon with hearts filled with gratitude.

After another day of sightseeing with Fouad and company in Zurich, Virginia and I parted from them. Virginia had arranged for us to ride the train from Zurich to Geneva to Paris. We wanted to spend a couple of days sightseeing in Geneva. I was very curious about the city because of its reputation as a meeting place for international conferences and meetings, especially those bearing on the question of Palestine. It was also the home place of the League of Nations, a predecessor of the United Nations. We flew from Paris back to the U.S.

In the spring of 1979, I came up for promotion to full professor, but was denied primarily because of insufficient refereed publications. I was told a couple of additional publications would have done it, as my accomplishments in teaching and university service were quite commendable. While I was disappointed by the denial, I understood it, and I did not let it overshadow the otherwise successful and happy progress in my life and Virginia's. By the spring of 1982, I had managed two publications. One of them was a letter to the editor.[189] It did not count for a full-fledged publication. I was again denied the promotion. This time it was quite a bit more upsetting to me. Nevertheless, I knew who I was within my very soul, and where I stood in the larger scheme of things. I made up my mind not to let a college dean, or a promotion committee, define me. In a short time, I put it out of mind and continued to be the best I could be at the job of teaching, service, and scholarship. It was the last time I

188 The German relatives visit was marred somewhat by Virginia and I noticing that my father-in-law, Enoch, would have memory lapses as to what we were doing. Thereafter, Enoch showed symptoms of Alzheimer disease. During most of that trip, I wheeled my father-in-law along in an old-fashioned wheel chair.

189 1. Op. cit. fn 138 [One- and Two-Dimensional Hydrogen Atoms, AJP 49, 143 (1981)] 2.Letter to the Editor, AJP 50, 105 (1982).

pursued the promotion, even though in 1989, I succeeded in accomplishing, with my friend and colleague, Professor Donald H. Kobe of North Texas State University, quite a significant paper on the correspondence between quantum and classical physics.[190]

Virginia continued to advance professionally on and off campus. During the energy crisis of the mid-seventies and the consequent interest in conservation, she put out important reports for the university extension service on how to conserve energy in the home. Some of these reports received wide regional circulation. Her work on home appliances, particularly the microwave oven, got her a position as an associate editor of *Microwave World* magazine. In recognition of her contribution to better quality of life for families of the Red River Valley, the Red River Valley Electric Women's Round Table nominated her, in 1981, for the "Woman of the Year" award given out annually by the YWCA of the Fargo/Moorhead area.[191] She came in second place.

The years between 1979 and 1982 were active and productive for both of us. Life seemed good. There were the usual university politics and committee work hassles, but that sort of thing goes with the territory. There was a change in the deanship in the College of Home Economics. The new dean did not seem to appreciate Virginia as much as the previous dean did. It caused Virginia some grief and tears. I often tried to lighten up such negative human interactions by falling back on some of my experiences with deans, department chairpersons, and colleagues, which involved all kinds of emotions ranging from love and admiration to jealousy, fear and resentment. I often would say to her, "Dismiss these things as immaterial; toss them behind your back!" Virginia seemed to have a much thinner skin than me.

In the summer of 1982, Eastern Airlines had a major travel promotion of twenty travel coupons for the price of $600 from anywhere to anywhere within continental USA. We felt that the promotion was a real bargain. We decided to take advantage of it. Virginia worked out an itinerary of travel around this

---

190 Op. Cit. fn 138 [Synthesis of Planck's and Bohr's Formulations of the Correspondence Principle, AJP 57,658, (1989)]; this publication and presentations related to it at national meetings led to my serving as a publication referee for the American Journal of Physics (AJP) for several years thereabout.

191 The Red River runs north, separating ND to the west from MN to the east and through Fargo/Moorhead, all the way into Canada.

promotion over the two months of July and August. The travel spanned west to California, south to Florida, northeast to Massachusetts, and back to Fargo. On the way, we looked up friends and relatives. In California, we visited with friends in San Francisco and sister Carole in Huntington. In Florida, we visited Fouad's sons and two of Hamadi's sons in the Fort Lauderdale area. Fouad joined us in travel to California and Florida. In the northeast, we spent most of the time in Boston, where we stayed a good deal of the time with friends. Also, Virginia attended the annual meeting of The Mother Church, a highly-desired and spiritually enriching activity and experience.

In Boston, in August, Virginia complained of discomfort in her tummy. It was not like her to be ill, much less to talk about it. I did not think much of it. I attributed it to something she had eaten that did not sit well with her or the heavy travel we were doing and the changes in climate, beds, or a combination of these factors. After a day or two, the pain subsided and we went on our merry way following our travel itinerary. We began the school year, 1982-1983, on an upbeat and positive note. Her coursework and style of teaching household equipment were featured in the Fargo paper, *The Forum* appearing in the November 29 issue, 1982, for their innovativeness and hands-on character. Innovations and style had won her an earlier certificate of merit from the *National College Educators in Home Economics*.

For my part, I planned to attend the annual joint meeting of the American Physical Society (APS) and the American Association of Physics Teachers (AAPT) in New York City, to be held in the latter part of January 1983. Typically, this meeting was four days in length. A day or two before my leaving for the New York meeting (about January 20), Virginia and I decided that we would go out for dinner. We did that every now and then to have quiet, unburdened time with each other and for diversion. It was at that dinner that Virginia told me that she had not been feeling well the last couple of days and complained again of pain in her tummy. I inquired as to its nature and seriousness, and whether or not I should skip the trip to New York and attend to the matter. Without any hesitation, she said, "No, I'll be all right." Again, I did not think much of the matter and ascribed it to some sort of transient indigestion. During my time in New York at the meeting and on the couple of phone calls I made to her, there was no mention of any pain or illness. When she met me at the airport on my return, however, I was quite disturbingly surprised to see her strained and ill. It was only then that I began to think beyond a mere indigestion problem. Virginia would not speculate as to what was wrong. Naively, I wondered if she might not be pregnant. I even voiced out loud to her that it would be a most happy development. She was quietly skeptical of my speculation. At that point, I did not connect her current feeling ill with what she had complained of in Boston, back in August. In order to find out for sure, we needed to go to the local clinic for a check-up. With Virginia's Christian Science devoutness, it dawned on me why Virginia might have had some hesitation to talk about her health problem before, and why she might hesitate to resort to a medical doctor for a diagnosis now. Yet, the need for a professional check-up was obvious, and the check-up would not commit us to anything more. The following morning, we went into the emergency clinic of Fargo's Saint Luke's Hospital for a check-up.

It was beyond my wildest expectation, when the doctor came back with test results finding, ovarian cancer! While standing listening to the doctor's report, I could feel my legs failing underneath me. I had to quickly sit down in a nearby chair. We talked with the doctor about a second opinion, and other related courses of action. The doctor said, "You are perfectly free to seek other opinions, to go to the Rochester Clinic in Minnesota, for example," as I had considered. However, he said the results of the tests were quite unmistakable and conclusive. "Whatever you decide to do," he pointed out, "you need to do it expeditiously, for time is of the essence." It was an active cancer with capacity to spread into the abdominal cavity and become harder to treat. The doctor seemed quite knowledgeable and competent. Before long, he gained my trust and respect. To seek another opinion would take quite a bit of time and effort, and involve travel under difficult conditions, physical pain and weather unpredictability. It was no longer warranted. Our responsibilities to our jobs also hung over our heads. We then inquired as to what the next step should be? He answered, "A surgical operation to remove the diseased ovaries and all, or as much as possible, of the surrounding cancerous tissues. The operation should be scheduled as soon as possible." The operation was doable in Fargo's Saint Luke's Hospital. The operation would likely have to be followed by radiation and chemo treatments. We could not respond at once for all that was unfolding before us. Both Virginia and I needed time and privacy to think it through.

Virginia seemed to wrestle with two major questions. The first was, how to reconcile her faith with accepting a medical course of treatment? The second question was, what was precisely entailed in the operation and its consequences? Specifically, she was concerned if the operation and follow-up treatments would handicap her in any significant way as to prevent her from living a normal healthy life afterwards, as an individual and as a spouse. I was amazed at her clear, calm, and considered assessments against a backdrop of threatening clouds of a serious illness. I was more emotionally engulfed and perplexed. We raised the second question right away with the doctor, and we got the answer forthwith. The operation would handicap her only to the extent of sterility, but nothing more. Since we had already been reconciled to a life without children, we did not see this as a hurdle. The first question, however, was particularly painful and only Virginia's to decide. Yet, the facts put before us seemed to require immediate decisions. Virginia was very mindful of how her decisions might bear on me as well, short and long term. On my part, I was more focused on the immediate issues and how best to deal with them right then, rather than longer term. At no point, however, was there any divergence in our views as to what should the next step be. After a lot of soul searching, we came to the conclusion that since she was clearly not demonstrating healing and the problem was evidently life threatening, Virginia would undergo the operation, and that we would cross the radiation and chemo treatment decisions when we got to them. It was a sort of a spiritual/philosophical compromise approach of, "Suffer it to be so now!" and pray and hope for a better day tomorrow.

As a general rule heretofore, Virginia would engage a Christian Science practitioner to work for her spiritually and metaphysically, to help her deal with problems or challenges of diverse kinds, be they physical, economic, human-relational, etc. She did this almost routinely and without consulting with me or even my knowledge; I demanded neither. It was a private matter between her and the practitioner, if she chose it to be. It was, after all, part of her full freedom to practice her faith. In any case, she had my full trust and blessings. In fact, as became clear to me later, she had a C.S. practitioner working for her to help her quietly with the specific problems at hand, previous to our going to the emergency clinic for a check up.

Past doctor's opinion, whatever it was, did not deter us from simultaneously seeking a practitioner's help. Furthermore, if in the recourse to a C.S. practitioner, we got no positive results either, it would not cause us to dismiss altogether the power, utility, and efficacy of the C.S. methods for healing. Over the years, I had become a beneficiary of this in many ways, including growth in grace that Christian Scientists speak of so often. In one important aspect, I became a more spiritual Muslim and less a ritualistic one. I appreciated Islam's spirituality, distinct from culture and rituals, better in the context of universal creation and humanity. I also saw the power of positive thinking and love in solving problems of all kinds. Very notably, I was healed of a chronic duodenal ulcer that had bothered me for over fifteen years. It involved getting rid of a sense of self-will, frustration, and failure in many of my daily activities and professional pursuits.[192] Virginia lovingly, and early on, would tell me that the ulcer was really in my head. I diligently listened, soul-searched, and conscientiously debugged myself from negative notions and ways of dealing with problems; notions such as self-pity, helplessness, or retaliatory anger.

Virginia underwent the operation a couple of days after the diagnosis. I spent the time during the operation in a waiting room in the hospital. Our colleagues, in our respective departments at work, rallied to support us emotionally and in terms of covering for our classes. Both Virginia and I had syllabi, lecture notes, homework assignments, etc. for our classes. We availed all that to our substitutes. We also kept in touch with them for ongoing consultation. Virginia would even call her colleague substitutes from the hospital to counsel and guide.

While Virginia was still under the effect of the anesthesia and just out of surgery, the chief surgeon came to me in the waiting room to give me his up-to-the-minute update. He said that the cancer had already spread considerably in the abdominal cavity. He did his best to remove as much as possible of the affected body tissues and parts. There were affected areas that he could not remove

---

192 Brother Hamadi suffered from a duodenal ulcer also, even over a longer period and in a more severe way. By family consensus, he and I, as youths, shared similar personality traits. Of note, and as an example, we both did not "suffer fools gladly!" Hamadi's ulcer literally dominated his life for over three decades. He eventually and in desperation surrendered to an operation that cost him the removal of over half his stomach. Yet, in contrast to me, he was not completely healed from digestive problems thereafter and was not free from a dietary protocol. There is no doubt in my mind that had Hamadi had the opportunities and benefits I had in terms of "spiritual growth and self-immolation," he would have been healed just as well.

because they were tied up with vital organs; such removal would have immediate danger to Virginia's life. He then said that he did not think that she would live beyond one year, and to put our affairs in order accordingly! At hearing the doctor's words, I nearly fainted again. I hurriedly sat down. He then continued with his update. He asked me to meet soon with the radiation and chemotherapy doctors, who would discuss with me what they could do for her. The surgeon was very professional and forthright. I, to myself, rejected his one-year forecast; *it just could not be*, I kept assuring myself. Just as in the Bible stories that I heard so often in church services, I wanted to believe instead that this "is not unto death, but for the glory of God," that His works may become manifest![193]

I met with the radiation and chemo doctors that same afternoon. They seemed to be on top of the state of art in their fields. I got the further impression that Fargo's Saint Luke's Hospital was well-equipped for the task, and that these doctors constantly consult and exchange ideas with their counterparts nationally as to the best programs and procedures of treatment on a case by case basis. They informed me that they would design an aggressive treatment program that would give Virginia the best chance to beat the cancer; but of course, they could not guarantee success.

Virginia's recuperative stay in the hospital was only a few days. It was already the first week of February when Virginia came back home. The radiation and chemo treatments would be administered while she was at home. It would be a week or so of further recuperation from the surgery before any of the treatment could or would begin. Beyond recuperation, there was much to weigh, consider, and decide upon. The local Fargo C.S. practitioner, previously on the case, stopped working for Virginia. The thought was that one must not mix *materia medica* with prayerful, spiritual, and metaphysical work. The notion of serving two masters seemed to be the basis: "No man can serve two masters: for either he will hate the one, and love the other; or else he will hold to the one, and despise the other."[194] As it further happened and was explained to me, this practitioner had been falling ill at that same time, and needed to take care of her own health situation. Nevertheless, it did not prevent or stop her from

---

193 Specifically, I was thinking of Jesus healing the blind man and raising Lazarus from the dead. Cf. John 11:4 and 9:3; King James Bible.

194 Mathew 6:24; King James Bible.

continuing her informal support of Virginia as a friend. Other members of the Fargo Christian Science Church Congregation and longtime friends rallied to support Virginia through visitation and by reading Christian Science literature to her. The big and presumably fateful question before us was whether or not we would follow up the surgery with radiation and chemotherapy. Virginia and I independently, yet concordantly, decided to take the Christian Science way. We believed in its power to bring about healing. We also felt that to bring about the healing, Virginia would benefit from a change in surroundings. We sought to find a supportive and inspiring Christian Science environment that would aid Virginia in working out her salvation in a healing demonstration. We were guided to Arden Wood's Christian Science Nursing Home in San Francisco, California. It was, and probably continues to be, a very fine place; one of the best for this purpose. Within a week or so, arrangements were made for both of us to live there for the duration needed. When we arrived at the San Francisco airport, we were met by a courtesy van provided by Arden Wood. I will never forget the pained and sad look on Virginia's face as I had wheeled her from the plane to the van.

Arden Wood was a beautiful castle-like estate surrounded with beautiful gardens and landscaping. We had a private room with many comfort amenities. There was also top of the line dining facilities and food service. There was a variety of ways and means to pray and receive inspiration, individually and collectively. We also engaged a highly thought of C.S. lady practitioner from the Twin Cities. Virginia communicated with her daily by phone. I will never forget a remark Virginia made the first day we were admitted, "I will either cart-wheel my way out of here or be carried away in a coffin!" For days, Virginia and I read Christian Science literature, listened to taped Christian Science testimonials on our room intercom and attended services on the premises. I had never before diligently and passionately studied religious literature and prayed for a healing. We befriended some of the nurses and staff there. One of them, Merrie Jane Waite, was a niece of a Fargo friend. She and her grandfather, who happened to be residing there at the time, became an extended family to us.[195] Merrie would

---

195 The grandfather, Mr. Roy Waite, was a long time friend of Virginia. At the time, he was already over a hundred years old, enjoying full health. Both Virginia and Mr. Waite were students of the same Christian Science teacher, Mr. Gordon V. Comer; they took class (part of learning the religion and its tenets) with Mr. Comer at the same time, with Virginia being the youngest, age seventeen, and Mr. Waite the oldest, over seventy!

take us every now and then for a drive by the ocean. It was about ten days after our arrival, with Virginia feeling reasonably settled down, that I thought I could get back to Fargo to attend to my NDSU job, while Virginia would continue working on her healing. I would, of course, be in daily touch with her by phone. We were already into March. Virginia supported the thought. We were buoyed by hope. I flew back to Fargo. It was the beginning of a new college quarter, and a couple of courses were assigned to me.

Back in Fargo, I tried to function as normally as possible at my job. It helped to have taught the assigned courses before, and have considerable course notes and related materials from previous times. For a couple of weeks or so, I would talk with Virginia every evening, hoping to hear of signs of progress. Unfortunately, I did not get significant encouragement; often she would be in tears. It was late in March when I asked if I should come to Arden Wood to be by her side, she said, "Yes, if you could." The next day I asked for another leave from my job. Our department chairman was very understanding. He essentially said, "Do what you have to do; we will manage." I flew to San Francisco the following day. I was appalled at what I saw. She had lost most of her weight. She could hardly sit up in her bed. Her C.S. practitioner asked that she be taken off the case and advised that we engage a local practitioner; none locally, however, would take the case. She was transferred to an intensive and full care unit. The staff was doing their utmost within the rules and guidelines of the institution to help her. Seeing Virginia again, notwithstanding the circumstance and physical condition she was in, gave both of us such sweet and good feelings of being together again. She told me how much she loved me, as I did her. She said it is important I take good care of myself and not do something rash, like getting married right away, when she was gone. We both cried. I was provided with a bed in the same room to be with her overnight. I could not sleep that night. I kept asking myself what could I do; what should I do? I could no longer leave the situation as it was. Clearly, there were no encouraging signs of improvement in her health to stay the course. In fact, the situation was desperate. Now, I just had to try *materia medica*. I kept hoping for a miracle. I told Virginia what I was thinking of doing. She said, "Whatever you see fit." Yet, I knew virtually nothing about health services in San Francisco that might help us. I resorted to the yellow pages in the San Francisco telephone directory. With my past positive association with

Presbyterians, I contacted the Presbyterian Hospital in the city and emotionally explained my predicament. The hospital agreed to take her in and guided my steps to expedite the process. I had to get an ambulance to transfer Virginia from Arden Wood to the hospital. I was shocked when I called for an ambulance, the first thing they asked me was, "Who will pay for this?" They did not ask me how urgently needed the ambulance was, or how soon! They mostly needed assurance they would get paid. I ended up guaranteeing it, very emotionally, by paying with a check. Once the Arden Wood people realized what I was about to do, they were very upset. They even tried to tell me I could not do it. Then I was told I had to sign this or that form. Unfortunately, some of the encounters took place in front of Virginia and I am sure they were painful for her to see. I essentially told Arden Wood that she was getting into the ambulance to go to the hospital even if I had to fight my way out, and that nobody was going to stop me. Eventually, they yielded; some of the nurses bade us goodbye with tears. Virginia was carried to the ambulance, wrapped in blankets, on a stretcher.

At the hospital, I had to fill out forms and give them as much information as I could about my employer, Virginia's employer and the insurance coverage we had. It was complicated by the fact that we were out of state. Once admitted, a couple of doctors attended to her. The hospital looked to me to be a major facility within the city and the doctors were professional. I felt I was guided to a good facility. Within hours, a doctor came and privately visited with me. She informed me that there was very little they could do for her at that point; at most, they would keep her comfortable. I told her how much Virginia meant to me and pleaded that they do whatever they could to save her life. It was very painful for me, and very probably to Virginia, after all our forbearance, to see doctors and nurses administer medicine to her, some by needle injection. I pleaded with them to administer no more medicine than absolutely necessary. I rented a motel room about a block from the hospital. Merrie came to the hospital to see us and let us know that we could still call on her for help. It meant so much! I contacted, an out-of-state, old time friend of Virginia's and mine, who had since become a C.S. practitioner and a teacher, to help us with the metaphysical work. I explained to him that we could not find a local practitioner to take on the case. He compassionately agreed to take the case. On the evening of March 29, after twenty-four hours in the hospital, I sat by her bedside. She asked me to read hymns from the Christian Science hymnal book to her. She specifically asked me to read a hymn by Mary Baker Eddy, titled, "Shepherd Show Me How to Go." Through tears, I managed to read it to her. She seemed to go to sleep. A little later, a doctor then came in and administered medicine to her by injection while I pleaded again, "No more than necessary!" She slept, and I went to my motel room. In the morning of March 30, 1983, at about 7:30 am, I made it back to Virginia's room to find that she, my angel, had just alighted into eternity. Her body was still warm; the morning sun was beginning to shine through a window into her room! I searched for thoughts and words to comfort myself. I found myself murmuring, "There was no god but Allah; of him we are, and unto him we shall return!"[196]

In my anguish and yearning to find words of solace, in days, months, and years that followed, I was led to these lines:

Oh my angel, my beloved Virginia!
For you, if I could, I would
build a Taj Mahal
on top of a high hill,
where all might see
a symbol of all that you have meant,
and always will mean to me!
For all the lovely things you have been and done,
rest assured, beloved Virginia,
there is already one built for you,
eternal in my heart!

Virginia's death threw me back into the wilderness. Yet there were many practical chores to do that needed immediate attention. Right at the hospital, there was the question of what to do with the body. I was told that it is nigh impossible to find a burial site within the city of San Francisco; also, the cost would be prohibitive. Transporting the body to Fargo would have been an option. There was a substantial cost to it. Bills from a multitude of sources

---

196 It is an Islamic view and common saying to comfort the bereaved.

had been accumulating since her illness diagnosis. On her side of the family, hardly anyone was aware of the seriousness of her illness. Christian Scientists generally attach little if any significance to the bodily remains of the deceased. Among a majority of them, I came to know, cremation is not objectionable. Early on in her life, Virginia tended to favor cremation. However, Muslims, according to tradition, disapprove of cremation. It was after years of marriage, and in deference to Islamic tradition, that she would express agreeableness to burial. I had to decide. I recalled once more to myself that in Islam, it is a cardinal tenet that God "wants for us ease and not dis-ease." With this taking precedence over all other possible traditional objections, I was comfortable, under the circumstances, with cremation. Her ashes were spread over the garden in the backyard of our Fargo home, where she had spent many happy hours gardening. With a beaming smiley face, she often would refer to the time in the garden as "horticultural therapy." Virginia had a green thumb, and the garden did yield abundant fruits and vegetables over the years of our living there.

To help me in dealing with the affairs of Virginia's death and my last days in San Francisco, I called, per her offer, on our friend Merrie. She was most obliging. In addition to knowing the logistics of getting around in the big city, she and her grandfather, Mr. Roy Waite, kept me in their company and provided me with much comfort. In fact, I was able to return to Arden Wood for the remainder of my stay in San Francisco. I needed to take care of Virginia's belongings, which had been left there during our hurried exit, and settle my account with them for all that I had owed. The last night in San Francisco, Merrie, Mr. Waite and I went out for dinner at a restaurant overlooking the ocean. I asked Mary to help me find such a place. With seagulls in view, it was an inspiring setting to reflect on the flight of an angel.

The following day, as Merrie drove me to the airport for my flight back to Fargo, Virginia's wristwatch, which I had placed in one of my pants' side pockets not knowing what else to do with it, kept annoyingly rubbing against my thigh during the trip. It was a quartz watch, a recent gift to Virginia from brother Fouad. Suddenly, it dawned on me. *The annoyance is an angel message*, "Gift this watch to Merrie." As I bade Merrie goodbye, I did precisely that. When Fouad gifted Virginia her watch, he also gifted me one of the same brand in a man's design. I wore that watch for many years afterward and I still have it.

The news of Virginia's death had a stunning impact on many who knew us. An appropriate memorial service was held for her in Fargo within the week following her death. Many came to my home to offer condolences; others sent cards. All through it, I was numb from the depth of the pain, the sorrow at her death, and of the fact that she would not be humanly by my side anymore. If I encountered her students, I would break down. If I met her colleagues, I would break down. If I went to shop at the neighborhood grocery store, I would break down. If I went to eat at our favorite restaurant, I would break down. If a customary waitress realized what had befallen, she would break down. Church friends and Mosque friends rallied to help. There were times when it was too painful to go to my empty home to eat or sleep. If it were convenient, I would stay at a friend's house overnight or at the mosque.[197] Every now and then a penniless Muslim student, who had been, for whatever reason, cutoff from channels or means of support, would be sleeping there as well. All through this, to my great surprise and gratefulness now, I clung onto my job and taught my courses to a successful conclusion as the spring term ended.[198] However, when it came to the end of the academic year commencement exercises, and for the faculty to march in their regalia, I would not and could not even consider marching without Virginia. In fact, ever since, I have yet to don my academic cap, gown, and hood to partake in any such ceremonies.

Once the spring term was over, and I had turned my classes' grades over to the university's Office of Admissions and Records, I collapsed exhausted and ill at my home for over a week. All my repressed and suppressed emotions for the past many weeks were let loose, gushed to the fore, and took their toll. At that point, Virginia's past local C.S. practitioner came to my help, at my calling, to metaphysically pray for my healing.[199] She lived at home with me until I was

---

197 People who slept in the mosque, back in the old country of my childhood, were usually people who had no where else to go; the sort of homeless and friendless people who had fallen down on their luck, in search of their last resort: the house of god; what better place?

198 The dean of our college did come to my office shortly after I got back from San Francisco and asked me if I would be interested in a leave to deal with my loss and grief. Providentially, I said no. Wanting to live up to my teaching obligations, coupled with the professional pride to carry them out at the highest level, turned out to be the best therapies for my grief.

199 Virginia's death in the manner it was did shake my faith in Christian Science, its methods, and its full validity, yet I continued to see some of its merits to my situation and continued to avail myself to them.

able to take care of all that needed taking care of. She was an elderly lady in her eighties; I referred to her as my "adopted mother." She welcomed that reference. The reference described how I really viewed and felt about her. It was the beginning of a lifetime friendship. For several months, we ate out often together and attended cultural events. She lived to be over one hundred years old.

Of all the comforting correspondence I got, none came closer to meeting my need and calling me to action than the letters I received from my brother Hamadi. He related most to my pain, empathized, and exhorted me to be strong and move on. "Life goes on and mine had to go on as well," Hamadi urged. In time, I began to reason that Virginia would not want me to fall apart either. In fact, to honor her, I gradually saw that I really do have to pick up the pieces and stay the course. The alternative must not be an option! I also found it very comforting to think of Virginia as not "dead dead," but alive at some different level in the bosom of God; even though I was increasingly realizing that I just don't have a good understanding of this God. He would have to be much more abstract a God and subtle than the one I had used to simplistically visualize or imagine Him to be before.

In June, Fouad and Fay came to Fargo to visit and to see what they could do to help. After a week, Fay flew to Florida to be with their sons, while Fouad stayed behind. Fouad and I planned about a month travel itinerary together, to visit interesting and notable places that at least one of us had not been to before and/or to look up relatives or friends that might bring us comfort and/or joy. The travel spanned parts of Canada as well as the east and south of the U.S. We stopped to sightsee at Niagara Falls, Toronto and Montreal, Washington, D.C. and New Orleans, before reaching our destination stop in Fort Lauderdale. In New Orleans, we savored in situ the culture of jazz music. It had been an interest of mine for a time, and Virginia had hoped to take me there to see it. She had been to New Orleans in her past travels, liked it, and spoke very enthusiastically of the place to the effect that I would delight in it. From New Orleans we took a quick bus trip to Lafayette, Louisiana to see Fouad's daughter Noha, her husband, Adnan, and their baby girl, Serena. Noha and Adnan were attending college there. In Fort Lauderdale, we spent the remaining few days with Fay and the sons at the end of which, Fouad and Fay flew back to Nigeria, his work place, while I flew back to Fargo, to prepare for the next school year.

The travel with Fouad was a big help and good soothing diversion. However, once back to Fargo and my empty home, there was a lot more healing work for me to do. Brother Hamadi, in turn, continued his weekly letters of exhortations, "Start a new life! Find a new life partner! Don't stay a widower too long."

It was my guided instinct, the small little voice within me, that told me not to break my relationship with the Fargo Christian Science Church despite failure to achieve Virginia's healing, and that I was never a member of the church. I highly valued the friendships developed over many years with many members of the congregation. In many respects, they had become an extended family. The help and companionship that my adopted mother practitioner, Margaret Fugle, was providing me reinforced this feeling. I continued to attend church services as I did when Virginia was alive. The congregation also continued to include me in their social activities and doings. In time, I began to talk with selected elder members of the church congregation, the motherly type that I had been close to before, including my "adopted mother," about the prospect of a new life-partner. I was sort of feeling my way, not knowing what feedback I might get. I got nothing but positive feedback and encouragement virtually from all of them. My focus slowly converged on a young widow member of the church, five years my junior, Linda Person Vennerstrom. Linda had lost her husband to a heart attack four years before and was left with three daughters to look after. The youngest was in college by then. I was well acquainted with Linda and her parents from before. They were all good people. Linda's ancestries were half Norwegian and half Swedish. Education-wise, she had B.S. with honors in mass communication from Moorhead State University (now Minnesota State University, Moorhead campus). Linda's social background was very different from mine. I, had Palestinian heritage and baggage, and a rather pure academic career background, while her late husband was in the insurance business and very active in amateur championship golf. She had three daughters, whereas, I had no children. Linda was primarily a homemaker who had put her college education to limited use, while Virginia was a rising university faculty star. I was not sure how all theses elements would fit together, and if she would even be interested in wanting to try. The wise women elders of the congregation, my confidantes, essentially told me not to sell myself or Linda short, to go ahead and ask her for a date and go from there. The rest is history!

Linda and I married on June 26, 1984. Linda's family, Fouad, Fay, their son Ismat, and the "wise women confidantes" from the C.S. church were present at the wedding. Fouad was the best man. It has been and continues to be, as of this writing, a very exciting and blissful new chapter in both of our lives. We had many occasions to travel together to Europe and the Middle East, to sightsee, visit relatives, and attend conferences. In the summer of 1994, we had a very memorable experience traveling back to my home in Palestine! Linda was able to see Jerusalem, Bethlehem, Nazareth, Haifa, among other important memorable places, and to learn for herself firsthand what the Palestinian Israeli conflict was all about. A lifetime highlight for me was being able to return and stand by my family house and birthplace at the Hadar, #7; Yona Street; and to walk through Wadi-Ennisnas. It was the first time a member of my family had returned to our home since we became refugees. Other notable and highly cherished occasions were visits to Beir Zeit and Nablus Universities, where I conferred with some of the faculties there, and the Gaza Islamic University where I gave a talk on some of my research in quantum theory.

Linda and I are still married and have disappointed the skeptics who thought we did not know what we were doing by getting married, especially on account of our vastly contrasting backgrounds. They thought it was a matter of time before things would unravel.

Linda's daughters, my stepdaughters, Cheryl, Jane, and Ann, are happily married and lead productive lives with their families. At the time of this writing: Cheryl (Vennerstrom Winger Zehoski) lives in Brooklyn Center (suburb of Minneapolis), Minnesota, with her husband Ken Zehoski. She has a son, Christopher Winger, who is a graduate of the UMN.[200] Jane (Vennerstrom Hulett) lives near Menomonie, Wisconsin, with her husband Michael Hulett, and their three children; Benjamin, Sara, and Megan. Ann (Vennerstrom Frost) lives near Saint Cloud, Minnesota, with her husband Don Frost, and their three children; Kelsey, Nicholas, and Brittany. We try to get together with them as often as possible. Celebrations of graduations, holidays (especially for the fourth of July at Pelican Lake) and various visits at other times and places

---

200 In the case of Cheryl, Ken is her second husband. Christopher is the son from her first marriage to Charles Winger, which ended in divorce. Charles has been deceased since then.

have brought our families together many times throughout the years. We are continually blessed by such gatherings.

While I retired from NDSU as an active member of the faculty in the spring of 1998, I am still associated with the university as a lifetime Professor Emeritus. My retirement has been and continues to be a very gratifying and busy one. Both Linda and I freely pursue our many hobbies. Our primary residence continues to be in Fargo. However, much of the summer months are spent at our lake cottage on Pelican Lake, Minnesota. We spend most of our winter months at our condo in Naples, Florida.

In Florida, we are within a driving distance from my brother Fouad and his wife, where they have settled since the summer of 1984, and are currently retired. This proximity and the feasibility of easy, convenient visits have given me a sense of continuity and connectedness with my childhood. Four of Fouad's children, as well as other relatives of the Hassoun extended family, live in Southern Florida. Being able to occasionally get together with them, individually, or in larger groups, has expanded and enriched this sense of connectedness, and provided a good soil for my roots to stay alive.

EPILOGUE

"I nurse my soul with hopes I yearn for;
how dim living would be, were it not for the sunshine of hope!"[201]

It was my lot, perhaps written by the stars, that I be born in Palestine at the time I was. It was a time of great fermentation carrying beneath its wings so much that is hard to characterize in a word, a sentence, or even a book! It was a time of Nazism, Fascism, Anti-Semitism, Arab Nationalism, Zionism, Western Liberalism, Communism, and Religious Fundamentalism. There was Palestine, in the thick of it. The world was about to unsheathe its most lethal weapons to drown itself in a sea of blood and grief; the Second World War erupted. Seventy-plus years later, I look back and wonder whether to thank or curse those probable stars for challenging my wits to survive, make sense of it all, and look for better days ahead.

My Arab/Islamic Palestinian birth, Arab Nationalism, and Zionism have been central to my life. Becoming a refugee out of the homeland with my family, with hundreds of thousands of fellow Palestinian Arabs, in the early months of 1948 during the Nakba, traumatized me to the core. I felt a profound sense of injustice perpetrated against us by the Zionists and their supporters, the Western powers. In the lead among them were Britain, the U.S., and France. It was further aggravated by the unpreparedness, inadequacies, and resulting inabilities of Arab societies and Arab regimes, notably, Transjordan, Syria, Lebanon, Iraq, and Egypt, to prevent the Nakba from befalling us. There followed a glaring and desperate need for self-examination. The Zionists, backed up by the advanced people of the West, seemed bent on forcing themselves and their will upon us: medieval Palestinians, Arabs and Muslims. Yet Jews and Westerners, politics aside, were just people that had lived and worked amongst us, and had times of positive cordial relations with us. My mother and Grandfather Issa were devout Muslims and at the

---

201 This is a liberal translation of an oft-recited verse of Arabic Poetry. It is a verse that I grew up hearing often and is attributed to the great Abbasid poet Al-Mutanabbi.

same time were great humanists. They had compassion for others *no matter*: Christians, Jews, and Muslims. I learned to love their ways. I carry this love with me to my dying day. I saw our recourse as dispossessed people had to be: Shake off medievalism with education and modernization to make our voice heard, be able to reclaim our rights, our homes, our heritage, and our honor!

As a refugee, with the help of family and many caring people, I completed my high school education, found my way to college, chose physics and mathematics as major disciplines, and pursued successfully graduate study in the U.S.

Once in the U.S., I continued to search my heart and soul for answers to the Nakba with deeper and broader examination and study. After much introspection and retrospection, and living in a culturally, ethnically, and religiously open and diverse society, exemplified and blessed to a high order by a loving wife and supportive families and friends, I saw the seeds of my childhood upbringing, of one big human family in this rich soil, grow further.

I saw the fragmentation of the world along racial, ethnic, religious, or national lines is an outcome of past history, full at times of misconceptions and misunderstandings, that will not stand for long against the accelerating influence of the information and transportation revolutions worldwide; the result of which is that diverse groups of peoples are getting to know each other more quickly and intimately in positive ways, and work better together.

I saw human *beliefs* about nationality, religion, and related identifications are useful practical models for good and righteous living, culturally intertwined, functions of time, history, and place. They are relative, subjective and evolving. That is not to say, however, they are not important and do not provide precious tranquility to their respective believers and practitioners. Nor is it to say that these models deny or do not stem from an underlying and universal spiritual source, and of faith and love. As a Muslim child growing up, I learned the adage: "Kul min ala dienu, Allah ya'eenu!" which is to say: "Each upon his religion, May God help him!" It is a remarkable statement of tolerance and positive coexistence. And the verse from the Quran (S.II, v.256), "Let there be no compulsion in religion: Truth stands out clear from error:" (English translation by A. Yusuf Ali, Amana Corp., Publishers, MD.) As such, I do expect that the evolution trajectory of the larger human family will be toward better mutual understanding among peoples, and toward less sharply drawn lines of separations and divisions.

It is instructive, in order to have a bigger picture of our human condition, to reflect on the progress of man's scientific knowledge of nature. It has been an *ongoing evolving process* from ancient times to the present, that is from a geocentric to a heliocentric planetary system, from Aristotelian to Newtonian physics to relativity and quantum physics, and from the Garden of Eden to the Big Bang. Yet, most natural and physical scientists continue to believe in an underlying universal truth, which motivates them to strive passionately and arduously for it.

In the words of Job 32:8; King James Bible: "There is a spirit in man: and the inspiration of the Almighty giveth them understanding."

It is in the context of celebrating diversity in humanity, combined with the underlying universality of man's spirituality, manifesting faith, love, and brotherhood, that I have been able to liberate myself from much of past burdensome inner conflicts and traumas. I have done so with considerable effort over a long time, and against great odds. Yet, I feel blessed to have been able to do so.

However, in the larger scheme of things, we certainly cannot and must not loose sight of current world problems and conflicts, rooted in nationalism or religion and related offshoots, such as ethnicity or race, some of which are severe and painful. The long-term human evolution toward a better-unified family of man should eventually repudiate and discredit hardheaded and fanatic self-righteous peoples, thinking of having privileged models. The unfolding in human consciousness of our underlying commonality and the trending closer together will open the way for more decent, equitable, humane approaches, and solutions.

It is most unfortunate that injustices in the world, in general, and the Holy Land and the Middle East in particular, are still grave. Animosities fester, and people continue to pay a heavy price in dashed aspirations, wasted lives, and social misery. This state of affairs disgraces our common humanity.

My plea and my prayer is:

"May we all
Cleanse our souls of the vestiges of the past,
Refuse to hate or hold grudges,
Work to heal the wounds of the mind and body,
Find common ground with good will,
Build mutual appreciation and trust,
And insist on justice and dignity,
As the sure way to peace!"

On this life-journey, I see in the distance, a clear and sunny horizon of a new promised land for all Mankind, of a "new heaven and a new earth." Might we, all the people of the world, have the wisdom and the passion to take the highway of hope, inspiration, and understanding? Might we walk out together toward that horizon, and into its sunshine?

ACKNOWLEDGEMENTS

To try to put into words my sense of gratitude to the many who have changed the course of my life in a major way would limit doing them justice. Nevertheless, I am most fortunate to have had a very devoted caring mother who spared nothing within her powers to facilitate my higher pursuits. She did this at great sacrifice to her own economic security and welfare, and eventually, at great pain as I boarded a ship heading away to a remote part of the world, on the other side of the globe, not knowing whether she would ever see her youngest son again.

Once in America, I met Virginia. The two of us became life partners for almost twenty-five years. Our union launched my life on a new and a higher path. She was a great anchor and a buttress. Her role in stabilizing my life emotionally, socially, and economically during some of my most challenging years of the American experience cannot be overestimated.

Then there is Linda, my dearly beloved second wife and companion through thick and thin. She has added to my blessings and provided multivariate support to stay the course. Her encouragement to do this work; editing, advising, serving as a sounding board, have been invaluable in seeing this labor of love through to the finish line. Her passion for photography made her the natural provider of the photos for the book, the author's photo as well as the book cover ones.

I am also fortunate to have had supportive brothers and sisters that cheered me on and took pride in my educational pursuits. Of these, I single out, in particular, my brother Fouad, for his care and love, and for the special closeness I have had with him throughout my entire life; he has enriched my life beyond what I can say.

In the process of writing this memoir, I have become starkly aware of my debt to so many outside my immediate family circle, people and institutions, to whom I am very thankful. I wish to single out the Jaffariyya College, the Evangelical National Protestant College, The American University of Beirut (AUB), and all those who made these institutions exist and survive.

It is with a deep sense of humility that I acknowledge from AUB the late Professor Harvey Beatty, dean of students at the time, for solving a major housing problem when I was an undergraduate; the late Professors Byron Youtz and Salwa Nassar of the physics department, for compassionate academic guidance; and the late Mr. Farid A. Fuleihan, AUB registrar, for identifying indispensable sources of financial aid. All of them spared no effort to help me while I was a student, when the clouds of possible failure hung thick over me.

I am also very grateful to the University of Minnesota (UMN) faculty, staff, administrators, and classmates. More specifically, I am very grateful for the physics department's accommodating me understandingly and lovingly over a period of six years. Among the faculty, I especially want to acknowledge by name the late Professors Clifford N. Wall, Edward L. Hill, and Donald R. Yennie, for their unflinching encouragement and faith in me as I stumbled along finding my eventual path to graduation.

Among classmates at AUB, I have been fortunate for years of friendship and camaraderie with Muhammad H. Saffouri and Said F. Mughabghab; and likewise at UMN, of Donald H. Kobe and Robert J. Oakes.

I am also very grateful to all the people of North Dakota State University (NDSU) and the people of the state of North Dakota. They provided my late wife, Virginia, and me with the environments and opportunities to do "our thing" in our respective fields over the greater portion of our professional lives. For me in particular, they provided a sense of home away from home.

Additionally, there have been teachers, friends, and philanthropic organizations that rallied to my aid throughout the course of my life and made a big difference. It would be impractical to try to list them all here by name. A deep sense of gratitude toward these individuals and organizations is never far away from my thoughts.

I have had an earlier draft of this book sitting on a shelf for several years, not knowing how best to go about publishing it. I had heard all kinds of stories about how the field of publishing can be full of pitfalls and heartaches. This discouraged me from wanting to jump in, until one day, while chatting with my tennis pal, Larry Hulce, who when finding out that I have a draft of a book in need of a publisher, gently let me know that he knew of one to check out, his daughter, Lise Marinelli, President of Windy City Publishers. I wasted no time to approach her.

Once introduced to Lise Marinelli, Linda and I knew that we had found the person and the company that we could trust to guide us caringly through the maze. We have not been disappointed. Thank you, Larry and Lise!

Lise met generously with us time after time, charting and guiding each phase. She set up a team of fine individuals to render the different services for the project. In particular, we are very grateful to Alice Refvik, the editorial reviewer. Alice's keen sensitivity led her to capture the theme of the manuscript and to see its inner workings like no other reader before. Her pointing out some of the strengths of the writing style of the manuscript brought tears to my eyes and to Linda's. We felt that at last here is somebody who gets it! We are also deeply grateful to Dawn McGarrahan Wiebe, who led meticulously all aspects of the design and preparation of the manuscript for its publication. She patiently heard our questions and concerns and addressed them positively and graciously. It is a pleasure as well to gratefully acknowledge the memoir's commendable editorial and proof reading work of Elizabeth Schwaiger, the fruitful book marketing and promotion exchanges with Kristyn Friske, and the valuable assistance of Laura Hardwicke in setting up a website. Finally, I wish to also thank the rest of the general staff of Windy City Publishers, who undoubtedly performed valuable services in a less direct way toward the successful completion of the project.

When I look back as the process nears its end, I am at peace that all has been every bit worth it, and the memories will everlastingly warm up my heart.

GHAZI Q. HASSOUN, PhD
is Professor Emeritus of Physics at North
Dakota State University. He was born in
Palestine during the British Mandate. He
became a refugee in Lebanon in 1948. He
holds a B.S. in Physics from the American
University of Beirut and M.S. and PhD
from the University of Minnesota.

While actively pursuing his profession as a physicist over four decades, his
experiences as a child in the politically torn country of Palestine and his
refugee days in Lebanon continued to haunt him and demand explanations
to fundamental questions and issues relating to national identity, religion,
ethnicity, East vs. West, war and peace, among others. Questions and issues,
which nagged him for years, were a cause of much travail and tribulation.
He promised himself, upon retirement, to confront them head on, to try to
understand them, and to explore how might they be turned around from
stumbling blocks to stepping-stones. This book details the quest in this
journey and invites the reader to come along.

TESTIMONIALS

Professor Elaine Hagopian

Elaine Hagopian is a Professor Emerita of Sociology at Simmons College in Boston, MA. She is one of this country's leading Arab-American spokespersons, a founding member of the Association of Arab-American University Graduates (AAUG), which included among its members such scholars as Edward Said and Rashid Khalidi, and served as its president for the year 1976.

- My immediate reaction is that you must send a copy to the Arab American National Museum. It has a Library and Research Section in which it collects such important items as your book.

- Your book was a real page-turner.

- Your life and experiences are so compellingly portrayed in your book. They demonstrate the victory of the human spirit over the multiple adversities you and your family faced.

- I congratulate you on writing these important reflections on your life experience. They are so humanly rich.

- Most fascinating memoir.

Professor Bilal Ayyub

Professor Bilal Ayyub is an accomplished Professor of Civil and Environmental Engineering, Director of the Center for Technology and Systems Management, Affiliate Professor of Engineering and Public Policy, University of Maryland College Park, MD. For many years, he has been active in international conferences concerning the Middle East, its future developments, and modernization.

- Ghazi Hassoun's remarkable memoir interestingly encompasses the history, culture, emotions, values, tragedy, disarray, hopes, spirit, resilience, and determination of the Palestinian people.

- This extraordinarily well-written book provides personal accounts of a tragedy in life starting from a violated land, moving to the welcoming land of Lebanon stressed by its generosity, and finally settling in the land of the free and home of the brave.

- Growing up as a child with Jewish and Christian neighbors and family associates made him at ease with diversity in his dealings throughout his life.

- This very timely book documents the life of a refugee. The Palestinian culture is deeply enriched by Hassoun's compassionate documentation of this tragedy, his personal triumph, and his relentless pursuit to achieve a matching, yet illusive, success for the Palestinians.